THE THEATER OF SPORT

The Theater of

SPORT

Edited by Karl B. Raitz

The Johns Hopkins University Press
Baltimore and London

© 1995
The Johns Hopkins University Press

All rights reserved
Published 1995

Printed in the United States of America
on acid-free paper

04 03 02 01 00 99 98 97 96 95
5 4 3 2 1

The Johns Hopkins University Press
2715 North Charles Street
Baltimore, Maryland 21218-4319
The Johns Hopkins Press Ltd., London

ISBN 0-8018-4908-X
ISBN 0-8018-4909-8 (pbk.)

Published in cooperation with the Center for American Places
Harrisonburg, Virginia

Library of Congress Cataloging-in-Publication Data
will be found at the end of this book.

A catalog record for this book is available from the British Library.

CONTENTS

PREFACE

Karl B. Raitz

A sporting event takes place in a distinctive setting that is a kind of theater. For sporting events, just as for plays, purposeful, directed, and structured activity is enhanced with props and performed with the end of providing a gratifying experience for participants and spectators alike (Kuntz 1973, 307). Each sport has appropriate places, and to remove activity from those places or to change or modify them is to alter performance and change the quality of experience for both performers and audience. Different social groups involve themselves in sports as participants or spectators, and their habits or requirements alter both the sport and the place where it is practiced. Further, the economic context within which sports are practiced changes through time and across space, dramatically affecting the character of sports places, which in turn alters the way sports are practiced and the way they are observed.

In the eyes of participants or spectators, there is an ideal or a perfect place for each sport—one that makes the sporting experience incomparable. Not everyone will agree on which place is perfect, but most will concur on a list of qualities that the ideal place should have. Many would argue, for example, that the grandstand, infield, and reddish brown sandy loam track make Churchill Downs in Louisville, Kentucky, the best place to hold an important Thoroughbred stakes race; that the steeply banked track at Daytona Speedway in Florida is the best place to watch NASCAR races; or that the pristine bosk of Augusta National Golf Course in Georgia makes this the best place to hold an important golf tournament.

The places where we play at sports have not always been grand stadiums, the multipurpose concrete and steel rooms with interchangeable floors for basketball, hockey, or rodeos. Nor have horses long raced along tracks of chemically treated sand which drain rapidly after a rain. And golf courses of thick green turf are newcomers to the rocky deserts of Arizona and southern California. Ballparks were once open fields at the edges of small towns; racetracks were narrow paths sliced into woodland; and golf courses were hardly more than paths among coastal sand dunes. This book is about such sports places. Each chapter is devoted to a single sport and illustrates the relationship between place and activity and how certain special places have become theaters of sport. The theater metaphor is apt, because while pure sport is first and foremost physical activity, it has become performance and, increasingly, entertainment. This unusual perspective requires some elaboration.

Ask people why they watch or take part in sports, and the answers all boil down to one thing: they want to obtain some type of satisfaction or gratification. Certainly part of that gratification comes from an appreciation of the skills employed or the strategies exhibited by participants. The narrow sports enthusiast might obtain sufficient satisfaction from merely watching the action and empathizing with the winners. Viewing unfamiliar competitors in an unfamiliar place may provide a sufficient amount of pleasure for some spectators. But the sports milieu is not a neutral, antiseptic, isotropic plane. Rather, the sports place offers substantial opportunity for perceptual stimulation and enhanced gratification.

But what is it that people are seeing when they attend a sporting event? People have different levels of perceptual acuity, so that no two individuals will witness the same event and obtain the same level of gratification from the experience, or find the same things stimulating or exciting. For one person, a sporting event might involve simply enjoying the action and outcome. For another, it might be an introspective philosophical consideration of metaphor, meaning, and symbolism. What this means is that the sporting experience does not begin with the onset of play, nor is it confined to the actual space of competition, say the soccer field or the bowling lane.

Geographer Fred Lukermann has written that places can be differentiated by their environment and the types and relationships of the cultural artifacts they contain (1964, 169–70). A particular grouping or arrangement of artifacts will distinguish one place from another. The theater of sport is housed within a larger environment, an integration of place and artifacts that French geographers call an *ensemble*. A central theme in this book is that sports places are really complex landscape ensembles, and the sporting experience, therefore, is not simply the playing or viewing of an athletic event but an interaction with the sports landscape so that both the game and the place contribute to the experience.

To appreciate the nature of the sporting experience, one has to consider the role that the sports place or ensemble plays in that experience. A Saturday afternoon college football game, for example, takes place within an ensemble of familiar buildings on the college campus where the football stadium stands, including the restaurants and bars along the campus business strip where postgame social activity centers (Raitz 1987b, 56–58). The sporting experience may even include the past environments retained in nostalgic memory, upon which expectations for future experiences are built. Conversely, the simple sports place may be augmented by mental images of more complex arenas, as it is for the youngster practicing basketball on an inner-city court who imagines himself to be playing in the finals of an NCAA game where to sink the winning shot is to become a hero.

The sports landscape has become an integral part of a gratifying sporting experience, for spectators and participants alike. On one hand the sports place, like the theater, shapes the play. On the other, for the spectator, the sports place provides a context for experience. How different are two baseball games, both played by the same professional teams, if one game is on an artificial turf field, surrounded by forty thousand plastic seats, under an inflatable dome, inside a concrete doughnut that squats in the middle of a forty-acre asphalt parking lot, and the other is on a grassy field that lies at the edge of a small midwestern town? Certainly the players' skills do not change from one venue to the other. The outcome of a three-game series played in both places should theoretically be the same. The games as experienced by the players and the fans gathered to watch, however, will be dramatically different.

This elementary observation has implication upon implication. If the character of the sports place is integral to the sporting experience, then changes in the place will result in changes in the experience. Sports places are not static but have been altered and modified as the sport has moved from one region or environment to another. It is common for places to be deliberately modified, to accommodate larger crowds, for example. If simple sports places become more complex through accretion of additional artifacts, then the sporting experience may become more complex as fan and player have more with which to interact. Increasing complexity, though, can detract from the pure sporting activity. Adding banners, cheerleaders who yell encouragement, bands and songs, or any number of structural changes in the field, stands, or other parts of the ensemble may alter the fan's concentration on player movement and coaching strategy. For many fans, especially those with little understanding of a game's nuance and complexity, such additions may supplement their perception of play and increase their enjoyment.

Sports landscapes, and therefore the experience of sport, change in several fundamental ways. The requirements for appropriate sports places or landscapes may change when a sport is carried from one physical environment to another, requiring some alteration in rules, modification of traditional equipment, or adaptation of game structure. Purists argue that true cricket can be played only in the south of England, where old elm trees bound a village green, and a church clock tower, barns, and haystacks provide a proper backdrop. For them, proper cricket cannot be played in Australia or Canada, where these landscape elements are not to be found. Some horse-racing fans express displeasure with the new synthetic tracks and glass-enclosed grandstands in Oklahoma or Alabama because they cannot replicate the experience at established eastern courses such as Saratoga, Churchill Downs, or Keeneland with their classic architecture, mature vegetation, and the medley of sounds that comes from creaking leather, riders' chatter, and the soft thunder of forty hoofs striking the ground the instant the starting gate springs open.

Sports landscapes have also been altered to accommodate changes in the social milieu. Golf, baseball, tennis, and fox hunting, among others, have historically been practiced by social elites. English squires adopted tennis as a garden party diversion. New York's elite formed the Knickerbockers baseball team. Later, as the middle classes began to play these games, the elite departed to other activities, such as yachting and polo, where the expense of participation would guarantee exclusiveness (Hugill 1984, 23). As baseball became a popular public sport, fences soon enclosed open fields and stands provided seating. Similar changes occurred when horse racing was no longer the exclusive domain of wealthy men match-racing their horses on private tracks, and racecourses became public profit-seeking venues. Such modifications gradually altered traditional sports landscape elements.

As sporting events have become more popularized and accepted as entertainment, the sports landscape has been increasingly subject to economic influences. Many sports have been commodified, a process that has had a major impact upon the various structures built to house sports activity, be they stadiums or golf courses. Cricket began to assume the character of a commodity in the eighteenth century when admission was first charged. Gradually cricket, racing, tennis, and many other sports became entertainment businesses, and business principles began to rationalize and direct the form the sports landscape should take to try to guarantee profits. One product of this conversion has been standardization. The baseball field evolved from an open field at the edge of an Ivy League college town, to an enclosed wooden stadium placed on cheap, marginal urban land near a rail or trolley line, to a patch of artificial turf contained within a huge concrete stadium that looks exactly like the stadiums in a dozen other cities. In such places economic considerations, not the game, direct location, design, and construction.

In their frenzy to host professional sports teams, cities now employ public funds to erect huge, multipurpose generic stadiums. Of course, the field requirements for each sport are considerably different so that no fans are well served. Spectators in the new baseball stadiums often sit in tiny, cramped seats in steeply pitched stands so far from the field that they can see little more than the players' shapes. Distances are far too great to see facial details or even names on uniforms. Huge electronic scoreboards must bridge the gap between fan and player, and one is left to conclude that the game is far better seen on television, the final stage in the complete commodification of sports landscapes (Immen 1990). Professional baseball, ensconced in its look-alike concrete doughnuts, has largely lost all semblance of unique character (as has professional football). Most stadiums are now placeless, removing from player and spectator alike the detailed elements of the sports place ensemble that made sites like Wrigley Field unique venues in which to enjoy the game (Lancaster 1987, 33). The new stadium at Baltimore is a welcome retreat from the trend toward placeless stadiums.

Commodification may result in other extensive landscape changes.

Golf courses have long since moved from the sandy coastal dune environment where the game originated and are now often used as central attractions in new subdivisions, with the result that houses or condominiums line the fairways and influence the way one plays the game. Ski areas in northern Michigan, Wisconsin, and Minnesota are now served by elaborate chair lifts rather than simple rope tows. Skiers schuss hills that are covered by carefully groomed artificial snow, and the warming house has become a condo resort that centers on a large, alpine-style "lodge" where "after ski" activities increase profit margins.

One finds few signs that sports landscape manipulation, and the concomitant modification of the sporting experience, is abating. Rather, change will probably continue and will be increasingly influenced by the needs of television or the ancillary goals of a wide range of business considerations, from real estate development to the sales of fast food and souvenirs to the donations or financial support of fans. Many college football stadiums are now attended by special reserved parking places with direct access to select seating. On one campus, old railroad cabooses have been moved onto the football stadium grounds and outfitted with furniture and kitchens for pre- and postgame entertainment.

For some sports places, manipulation has taken a new direction as television has come to compete with and then replace the live experience. (Until radio and television, one had no need to characterize a sporting experience as "live.") How is a fan sitting at home in front of a twenty-one-inch color television set going to enjoy a game if only the players and the play are shown? Television producers add to the pure play by employing zoom lenses on cameras perched around the field which produce detail on the screen greater than one can see sitting in the stands. Technicians attach microphones to the baskets so viewers can hear the basketball hitting the net, and mikes placed in the bottoms of the cups at golf tournaments produce the same effect. In auto racing, cameras mounted inside cars give the television viewer a sense of the track which no grandstand fan can share. Television producers realized some time ago that if they were to compete with the live event they would have to do more than simply reproduce the play or the action; they had to reproduce the place in as much detail as possible. They have succeeded to such a degree that a sports fan who has never seen a live game may come away from the first experience disappointed. A variation of television's influence on the form of sports places is occurring in golf, where new championship courses are designed with earthen amphitheaters around the greens for seating spectators and placing television cameras during tournament play.

During the 1980s, many communities across the United States found themselves competing with other places for professional athletic teams, in part for the increased revenues such teams were expected to bring to city business, but also because of the belief that hosting a professional team meant that a community had "arrived." The corollary, losing an established team to some upstart city elsewhere, produced the horrible prospect of loss of face and loss of revenue. Across Florida, this competition has focused on the spring training sites for professional baseball teams. To hold a team or attract one, some cities went to extraordinary lengths, including building new stadiums.

Consider Fort Myers, Florida. In 1987, the Kansas City Royals left there for a new location near Haines City. To attract the Minnesota Twins, local boosters built the Lee County Sports Complex, which opened on March 7, 1991. Standing in a cow pasture, the new stadium does not resemble the new look-alike concrete doughnuts that deface so many cities. Instead, architects gave the fan's ballpark experience full consideration. The stadium strongly resembles the small, classic city parks of the 1920s. The outfield fence is painted with billboard advertisements for local businesses, just like small town parks across the country. The seats are painted "a warm, traditional green, the same color as seats in old ball parks, instead of the cold blue common in many newer stadiums" (Miller 1991). The highway median leading to the stadium and parking lot walkways are landscaped with palms and tropical plants. The Twins wanted a park that was fan-friendly, so few fences separate players from the spectators, and even the bull pen has a three-foot fence so that children can see the pitchers warming up. The day after the Twins opened the Lee County facility, George Vecsey's article "More Odd Ball Parks Needed in Baseball" appeared in the *New York Times*. "There oughta be a law," he argued, "that all ball parks be individual, with at least one folly like the sloping left-center field at Cincinnati's old Crosley Field, where even Willie Mays would occasionally stumble" (Vecsey 1991).

If the trend toward commodifying sports places is to be stanched or reversed, then some considered thought must be given to the design of future sports places. Architect Philip Bess, for example, has called for an end to the construction of the sports megabuilding because it is "a blight upon our cities and upon our games. The time has come," he continues, "to abolish these monsters, and to restore the aesthetic, urban, and athletic sanity of the single-purpose sports facility" (1987, 97). The forty-thousand-seat urban stadium that Bess has designed for south Chicago is intended to fit within the confines of the existing street grid as did the parks of the 1920s and 1930s—without "blowing out" the neighborhood for the parking acreage required by a concrete multipurpose megastructure. Such insight should prompt optimism about the future of sports landscapes and the quality of the sporting experience. Yet sports seem destined for more control by entertainment business interests, not less, so that one might anticipate that the sports places of the next century will more resemble artificial amusement park caricatures than organic places that were the product of local customs and conditions.

Here, restated through the writings of Vecsey, Bess, and others, is this book's central theme. The sports places that make games interesting and gratifying are not the placeless cookie-cutter concrete stadiums with plastic seats set along standardized fields covered with plastic turf. The place that offers a unique artifact and landscape ensemble is the one that offers spectator and player alike the richest experience, the one most likely to be regarded as the perfect place for a sport by local fans.

This book is not intended to cover all sports in all countries; rather, it focuses on a few of the more popular sports and on sports such as cricket that illustrate the link between sport and place particularly well. The Introduction elaborates upon this premise and presents an argument for considering the role of place and landscape in sport. Often the context, shape, design, or other attributes of sports landscapes can be attributed to larger social processes so that a historical consideration of how games have been played and how they have diffused from one place to others is relevant to understanding present sports ensembles. Ball and field sports treated here include cricket, tennis, golf, soccer, football, basketball, and baseball. Fox hunting represents the hunting sports; it is a sport with two very different variations, both of which are dramatically linked to a common heritage. Though each chapter differs in focus, the themes of making a place for a sport and the role of that place in the sports experience are central. Chapters on horse racing, rodeo, and auto racing illustrate additional landscape themes such as the effect that seasonal change brings to horse racing or the role of myth in fostering a nostalgic image of traditional stock car racing—an image that is now threatened by the sport's televisionization and a severing of the link between sport and place. The concluding chapter on climbing brings the theater metaphor full circle. Climbing is a "risk" sport in which the participant is also the spectator, and the theater is a natural place, little modified to accommodate commercial interests.

THE THEATER OF SPORT

CHAPTER ONE

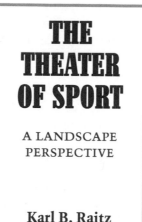

THE THEATER OF SPORT

A LANDSCAPE
PERSPECTIVE

Karl B. Raitz

Sport, Leisure, and Landscape

Over the past two centuries, automation has dramatically increased productivity in industry and agriculture. As a result, both urban and rural workers have gained more free time. People commonly refer to their free time as leisure time, in part because they often fill it with recreational activity. A list of recreational activities would be a long one. Many items could be further identified as sports—activities that require some physical effort, are competitive, and have traditional rules or conventions.

We should be clear in understanding the terms *sport* and *leisure* as I use them here. People participate in sport and people watch sport. Participants may be well paid and practice sport for a living (professional sports). For others, sport is leisure time activity: some pursue it as a hobby; others may simply take part for exercise. Whatever their level of interest, their perspective as participants is different from that of the people watching, who may be actively supporting one team or individual or simply spending free time observing. Most spectators (except scouts, recruiters, gamblers, and selected other professions) watch sports during their leisure time.

A sport's character may restrict it to specific locales or environments. Skiing and skating sports require cold temperatures or special topography, and so are usually found in northern latitudes in wintertime. Other winter sports such as basketball and volleyball require large indoor arenas, level floors, court boundary markings, and certain support equipment. Those places where sport is practiced, played, and watched, whether they are courts, fields, stadiums, lakes, pools, or dozens of other special places, all have a physical presence on the landscape. The term *landscape* refers to the common land surface that people live in complete with its office buildings and stadiums, roads and racetracks, lawns and baseball fields, harbors and yachting basins. The term can be further refined by adding the adjective *cultural*, recognizing that cultural landscapes are built and lived in by people with a common cultural heritage. It then follows that individual elements in the ordinary cultural landscape reflect that heritage. So, to understand how people structure landscape and how its parts relate to the broader community is to understand a good deal about the culture, values, concerns, and lifeways of the people who created and maintain it.

Ancient Greeks and Romans built sports stadiums, and ball courts were central structures in the Mayan cities of Central America. Europeans have carried their sports around the world; today, in countries dominated by European culture, people spend billions of dollars supporting professional and amateur sports. Modern sport is an important part of American culture. To help us understand sport's breadth of impact within society, I focus in this chapter upon the landscapes where sport is practiced. I outline how sports places evolved, how they use space, their relationship to the physical environment, and their role in the sporting experience.

How Sport and Leisure Places Are Created and Used

Why do sports facilities and leisure landscapes look like they do? Does the appearance of a facility have any relationship to how a sport is played or how it is experienced by spectators? Why are sports places located where they are? The functional design of baseball parks, tennis courts, and the like must be based on two different yet related concerns for how they are to be used. The first affects the players or participants. Rules or conventions under which a game is played will guide basic construction. These rules are comparatively constant from one decade to the next and from one place to another. It is the continuity provided by rules that permits games to evolve increasingly complex strategies for winning, but in addition rules allow fans and participants alike to measure performance against past accomplishments or records set in other places. Football rules require a football field to be 100 yards long and 160 feet wide. The goalposts on either end must be 10 yards behind the goal line. Space on both sidelines is reserved for players and the coaching staff. The field itself must be well drained because football is played in a wide range of weather conditions. Thus, the surface may be graded so that the center is as much as one foot higher than the sidelines. The slope across the field to each sideline will drain rainwater away relatively quickly, and drainage pipe laid below the surface will provide for rapid groundwater removal.

The second concern is to accommodate spectators. Although sports such as baseball and football were played by members of elite athletic clubs or students in private colleges in the nineteenth century with little or no concern for an audience, today these are spectator sports, operated as businesses, and some provision must be made to seat onlookers. A small town on the west Oklahoma prairie may have a high school football team but only enough students to field an eight-person team, and very few spectators. Small wooden bleachers seating thirty people may be sufficient to hold all the fans. A university football team, on the other hand, may have thousands of loyal fans, and it is not unusual for large stadiums seating seventy-five thousand to one hundred thousand people to dominate a campus. Providing a field, seating, services, parking or transport access, and electric lighting for night games is part of fulfilling the basic requirements for successfully putting on a game.

There are several additional concerns that affect what sports facilities will look like and where they will be located. Cultural traditions, taste, and social differentiation all interrelate to mold the form, design, and location of sports facilities. Consider two sports that involve riding horses in front of spectators—rodeo and Thoroughbred racing. Rodeo grew out of western cattle ranching with influences from Mexico. Horse racing became popular in England and was brought to America in the eighteenth century. Rodeo grounds can be found in many small western towns. The oval dirt arena is surrounded by a modest board or rail fence. Open bleachers align one side and spectators sit or stand wherever they please. To one side of the bleachers, next to the arena, are rough plank corrals and holding pens. Nearby is a dusty open field that serves as a parking lot. In some larger cities—Cheyenne, Wyoming, for example, where the annual Frontier Days celebration features one of the largest rodeos in the West—the same elements are present, although a substantial concrete and steel grandstand augments the bleachers.

Thoroughbred horse racing takes place in a very different environment. The racetrack is carefully constructed for comfort and landscaped for beauty. Large grandstands may line one side of the track. The infield is often landscaped with flowering shrubs or ponds. Dozens of horse barns cluster behind the track, and large grass or asphalt parking lots cover several acres. The paddock area where trainers saddle their horses before each race may be landscaped to resemble a formal English garden. Track patrons impose a kind of social segregation on themselves through grandstand seating preferences. Space for viewing the race may have at least three sections that tend to be favored by different social groups. Box seats, which are very expensive and seat six to twelve people, usually line the grandstand's second level at trackside. Cheaper reserved seats crouch behind the boxes. Standing room, the third viewing space, may be in aisles or at trackside. Box seat holders also may be members of an exclusive track club that has a restricted bar, dining room, and betting window.

The cultural traditions of these two horse-centered sports are different. Aesthetic appeal is important to many who attend Thoroughbred races—an interest that is rooted in the habits of eighteenth-century English gentry. By comparison, the rodeo grounds closely mirror the typical western ranch: unpretentious, practical, rough-hewn, and homemade from local materials. It seems clear, then, that the design, building, and placement of sports structures draw from our cultural reservoir. The result, be it a golf course, tennis court, or gymnasium, reflects differences in cultural tradition and in contemporary regional values and priorities.

Qualities of Presence

Some sports require formidable structures; others leave no trace when the game is over and the players leave. The sports structure, because of its size, color, design, or placement, has a presence that becomes part of a person's image of sports places—and if they know it well enough and experience it long enough, it creates an emotional tie to that place. This quality of presence has at least three aspects. The first is visibility. Stadiums seating tens of thousands are huge structures. When placed on a college campus in a small community, the stadium may be the largest building in town—or, for that matter, the county. Even in a large city, the distinctive size and shape of a stadium makes it a landmark. It is not only the site of periodic athletic competitions but often a source of civic pride and a symbol of victory and accomplishment. Therefore, it represents success. In the off-season it serves as a navigational marker and, like Three Rivers Stadium in Pittsburgh, or Yankee Stadium in the Bronx, may also symbolize the city itself. This is the kind of symbol that can be successfully exploited in advertising photography.

The second aspect of presence is permanence. Large, expensive sports structures tend to be used for decades. The qualities associated with visibility, when carried from one generation to another, reinforce the images and symbolism associated with sports places. Scale is the third important aspect of presence. A large structure simply has a greater visual impact than a small one, even if both are used for the same activity. In inner-city neighborhoods in many of America's eastern cities, children play ball games in streets or on church or school playgrounds. A stickball game played on a narrow south Philadelphia street might use cars and manhole covers for bases and sidewalks for foul lines. The schoolyard where a baseball or softball game may be played is only slightly more formal, with a fence bounding the edge of the outfield and base paths worn in the grass. Children often play basketball in equally modest places. A basketball hoop attached to a garage roof may suffice in town or city. In rural areas, the Appalachian Mountains of eastern Kentucky, for example, basketball goals are fashioned from available materials and may occupy the only flat space on a yard or driveway. The small-scale ball field or basketball court is utilitarian and serves as a place to learn the game's conventions. Children may find these qualities appealing. As a sport becomes commercialized, beginning in high school and college and culminating in professional games, the structures built to accommodate spectators increase in size and distinctiveness. Consequently, the increasing scale of the structure may have an increasing impact on the images and emotional bonds we have with these places.

The ball field, track, or stadium is a center of activity, a focal point where people in their roles as players or spectators experience meaningful events. The sporting event itself may be influenced by the place's character. We develop strong associations between past, present, and even expected events and the place where they occur. This process leads to the development of a sense of place. We tend to have strong associations with places where we grow up, live, and have moving experiences. A sense of place is a central part of our individual identity and cultural tradition (Relph 1976, 42–43).

Cultural and Social Contexts of Sports Landscapes

Culture is the learned behavior, habits, and beliefs of a community of persons who live in a certain place. The term *community* is not necessarily dependent upon scale. Culture groups may be small enough to occupy little more than a city neighborhood or large enough to extend over considerable territory. While occupying a place and making a living from it, a group brings its ideas, values, technology—in short, its culture—to bear on the land. People lay out roads and bridge streams. They plow prairies and harvest crops. They build houses for shelter and shops for business. These structures are part of the group's cultural landscape and we regard them as material culture. A culture group also may speak a distinctive language, hold certain religious beliefs, practice particular foodways, and play games. Such practices are termed *nonmaterial culture*. Nonmaterial culture may leave a signature on the landscape in the form of churches and synagogues, libraries and school buildings, and country clubs and stadiums.

The social dimension of human culture involves human relationships and interaction. Long-practiced attitudes and values prescribe appropriate behavior for a variety of situations in which people come together to raise families, make a living, and pursue life. Our social habits may designate subgroups within the larger society that are differentiated by some real or imagined characteristic: class, race, sex, age, occupation, wealth, or talent. Such imposed differences may be reflected in the material landscape of sport. For example, the country clubs found today in most American communities of five thousand or more all trace their heritage back to the first American country club opened in 1882 at Brookline, Massachusetts, as a place for Boston's upper class to play polo and golf and to race horses (Mruzek 1983, 109). The idea of an exclusive club, which defined its recreational space as separate from public space, spread across the country. Membership was by invitation only, and criteria for acceptance included social acceptability, profession, and wealth.

Today, such clubs may control several hundred acres of sequestered land with beautifully landscaped grounds and golf courses. Members also enjoy large club buildings with dining rooms and elaborate locker and bathing facilities. Access is restricted to members and guests. Sport is practiced here in rigidly defined and enclosed space, not in public view.[1] The landscape dimensions of the country club have definite cultural and social meaning. The club is enclosed, segregated, and exclusionary, but inside its fences and gates it is spacious, open, and attractive.

A second example is the hunting of water and shore birds and upland game. America has two dramatically different hunting traditions. The first derives from the medieval European tradition in which all hunting was reserved for aristocratic landowners, the so-called lords of the manor. Elite landowners in France and England reserved vast acreages of forest land for their hunting pleasure. Eventually an English hunting tradition evolved in which gentlemen who sought an Arcadian experience would hunt "game birds" for pleasure. By the 1850s, a sports literature chronicled their interests and vividly described their sporting experiences. This tradition was brought to America and was readily accepted by wealthy patrons (one suspects they were the same people who frequented country clubs), who leased huge acreages of coastal marshland around the Chesapeake Bay and elsewhere on the eastern seaboard for their exclusive hunting use.

Meantime, a second hunting tradition was maturing among pioneers who moved westward into the continent's interior. A meager frontier diet might include wild game at almost any time of the year. Gentleman hunters frowned upon the taking of game out of necessity and generally dissociated themselves from the person who "pot shot" game—a term originally referring to game killed for the cooking pot but eventually associated with killing wildlife through cowardice (Schmitt 1969, 10). The Old World hunting tradition, though diminished, has ample landscape manifestations in the quail-hunting plantations of the Georgia coastal plain (fig. 1.1; Prunty 1963, 16–21).

The frontier tradition, while pervasive across America and evident each fall when hunters await the time when they may legally stalk migrating birds and rutting deer, has a less obvious impact on the landscape. One must look to high traffic volume on highways, no trespassing signs around cornfields and rice paddies, and clusters of vans and pickup trucks at restaurants and bars to appreciate the hunting season's magnitude. The major exception is the specialty site. Stuttgart, Arkansas (pop. 11,000) sits amid rice farms and Arkansas River backswamps on the state's eastern flood plain. It is also underneath the Mississippi Valley flyway for migrating ducks. Each fall, Stuttgart becomes the Duck Hunting Capital of America—its restaurants, hotels, and equipment shops cater to hunters' needs.

Bowling provides a third example of how sport's social and cultural aspects become part of the landscape. The country club and the bowling

FIG. I.I. Quail-hunting courses on the Greenwood Plantation near Thomasville, Georgia.

alley, if assessed in terms of prestigious social images, are at opposite ends of the scale. Many believe that bowling is a blue-collar sport. It is open to everyone, including the handicapped, and bowling alley managers spend much of their time recruiting people to form teams which then participate in league play. The landscape impact of a democratic sport is manifest on two scales. On the macroscale, one finds bowling alleys in highly accessible places: next to shopping centers, near high-volume intersections and well-traveled inner-city streets. Exclusive residential subdivisions rarely have bowling alleys. On a microscale, the internal design of the typical bowling alley is one of openness and access. People can stand in groups, sit and watch favored bowlers, or frequent the lounge and bar areas. Design encourages interaction and collegiality. The only restrictions on personal access pertain to the men's and women's locker rooms.

In a tangible way, sport is an autobiographical slice of the larger world we occupy. The same behaviors and conventions found in our culture as a whole are also manifest in sport and are carried over into the landscapes that sport creates. Sport is much more than individual competition or a recreational experience. It is not confined to watching athletes perform or to the making and breaking of records. Like work, family, education, and the arts, sport is integral to our social and cultural structure. Understanding sport's full dimension—how the values, attitudes, and symbols we associate with sport are manifest on the land—will help us to understand our cultural makeup and breadth.

Historical Roots

The practice of setting aside a special place to conduct a game, as well as of erecting special buildings or other structures for play or seating spectators, goes back thousands of years. Ancient Greeks raced horses on hippodromes—large, flat areas dedicated especially to that purpose and laid out near a city. Greek stadiums were often simply grassy fields, and spectators sat on earth banks to view the games (Mandell 1984, 45–77). The Romans approached sport more systematically. They turned the rude Greek stadiums into marble piles with gates, seats, and colonnades. They built hippodromes from stone and wood at their cities' centers. By A.D. 70, the Romans were constructing colosseums not only in Rome but throughout their empire north of the Mediterranean (77).

Form and Environment

Medieval Europe originated many sports that eventually were brought to America. Often the form a sport was to take—that is, the type of surface it was played on, basic use of space, rules for play, and elementary structures for playing and viewing—began in early European villages and adjacent farmlands. Many villages focused on a common or green where residents held fairs and markets, grazed livestock, and played games. The churchyard may also have served as a playground. Other games that required more space, such as football, were played on church land controlled by wealthy landlords (Baker 1982, 71).

Eventually, Europeans brought games to America that were initially played in the same types of places until commercialism began to enter sport in the late eighteenth and early nineteenth centuries. Entre-

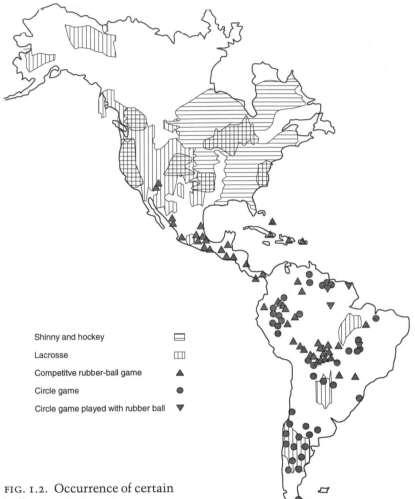

FIG. 1.2. Occurrence of certain
ball games in America.

preneurs laid out grounds specifically for horse racing, for example, or
football so they could build facilities for spectators and control entry
into the grounds.

Winter sports had their roots in higher latitudes. Some archaeologi-
cal evidence suggests that the ancient Norse may have used skis as
early as 2500 B.C. But skiing was probably pragmatic winter transportation, not a sport. Building ski jumps and clearing hills for ski runs were
not common until the 1860s in south Norway (Flower 1976, 22–24). In

medieval Holland, ice sports were popular during the winter season when marshes and canals froze over. When the Dutch established a colony at New Amsterdam on Manhattan, the island's ponds and marshes provided a similar environment. Enthusiasts practiced winter sports such as skating, hockey, iceboating, and distance skating on the Hudson River from the settlement's earliest days (Lucas and Smith 1978, 21).

New World Contests

Perhaps a thousand years before Cortez arrived in the New World, Native Americans throughout the Western Hemisphere played ball games on fields and courts (fig. 1.2). In Canada and the United States, Indians played a stick and ball game on broad open fields using long sticks that had small nets on one end. Teams would pass and run with the ball held in the stick's net and attempt to throw it between two poles at the opponent's goal. The game could be found across wide areas in the north, south, and west. Europeans who saw the game in the west called it rackets. In Canada, a French Jesuit missionary coined the term "la cross" for the game, because the shape of the stick with its small net reminded him of a bishop's staff topped by a cross (Baker 1982, 71).

Sport as a Distinctive Use of Space

Rules and the Stability of Play Space

People play games according to rules. As Paul Weiss has noted (1969, 57), to engage in a sport is to be rule-bound by it. Many rules that control how games are played are intended to create an artificial space within which those rules apply. Outside that space, the rules have very little meaning other than as symbols. On the football field, a rule prohibits defensive players from tackling a quarterback after he has thrown a pass. Off the field that rule lacks meaning, but symbolically it may represent fair play or "good sportsmanship." The spaces or volumes created by rules are usually clearly demarcated in field and track sports and other games played both inside and out-of-doors. In track events, the length of each type of race is measured within centimeters. Tennis court dimensions have been standardized for decades, and though painted on the playing surface also extend vertically—and invisibly—to form an imaginary cube that contains play. The tennis referee's primary purpose is to interpret and enforce the hit ball's encroachment on this invisible vertical line.

Some game dimensions are rooted in cultural history. A cricket pitch, for example, is 66 feet, one of the dimensions of the old English acre. The acre was four rods or 66 feet wide by forty rods or 660 feet long. Sixty-six times 660 equals 43,560 square feet, or one acre (Raitz 1985, 3). Replication of basic rules from one site to another in some sports has the effect of creating rigid play space that is essentially unvaried and wholly replicated at each site where played. The participant can rely on this consistency to improve performance, and the stability of space and rules allows comparison of one performance with another (Weiss 1969, 82).

Other sports places are not consistent from one game site to another but count environmental uniqueness as a major dimension of participation and enjoyment. Golf, both downhill and cross-country skiing, bicycling, yachting, and hydroplane racing are all examples. In golf, the length of each game is measured in holes. Participants usually play nine, eighteen, or twenty-seven holes. Yet each hole on each course around the world is unique. Slope, vegetation, and prevailing wind direction all vary, as does trap placement and green size, shape, and pitch. Physical environment becomes part of the game. Play strategy and technique depend upon how the course designer configured each fairway in consideration of these elements. Each hole presents the player with different obstacles to overcome and distances to traverse. Even playing the same hole on different days can alter the experience, because wind direction or speed may change and the hole's placement in the green will be different.

Symbolism and Historical Ideals

The meaning that each participant and spectator gleans from a sporting experience is necessarily different. On the surface, some people enjoy a sport because it pays well or because they are skilled athletes and enjoy testing themselves against other athletes. Some people may be fans and watch games merely because they provide entertainment, a way to relax, an excuse to gamble. But sport also contains deeper meanings and symbols that people readily acknowledge as important to their enjoyment and as supporting their rationale for watching or participating. Some appreciate games because the rules create an order, both social and spatial, that is not found outside the playing site (Huizinga 1970). For others, a sport's environmental context, be it land or water, may appeal to their sense of idealism or nostalgia for the rural, the frontier, the wilderness.

Hunting and fishing may be more obviously associated with symbolism than most other sports. Few enjoy these sports because they are game hogs, interested only in getting their limit each time they go out or catching the biggest fish. Their interest lies in the experience. Enjoying the fresh air, being out-of-doors, renewing a communion with nature. Narrow is the duck hunter who, while crouched in an Arkansas duck blind, does not reflect on the beauty of life when watching a dawning sky shade from black to pink to magenta. Unimaginative, too, is the mule deer hunter in Wyoming's Black Hills who does not think about the meaning of "wilderness" while walking along a sharp ridge crest, seeing little but ponderosa pine for miles in every direction. Symbolism in sport is not new. A century ago, hunters viewed New York's Adirondack Mountains as paradise because of the "beauty of scenery, [their] health-giving qualities, [and the] easy and romantic manner of [their] sporting" (Schmitt 1969, 7).

"Ruralness" or "wilderness" are relative ideas that humans assign to places. They have a great range of personal meaning that depends on one's expectations or situation. It is hard to avoid contemplating ruralness, for example, at a baseball game. *Home* plate is the center of activity. Pitchers warm up in a *bull pen*. Players called *fielders* defend an *infield* and an *outfield*. The stadiums where the game is played are called *fields* or *parks* (Raitz 1985, 2). Michael Oriard (1976, 33) believes that baseball is the most pastoral game and that its relation to open space is fundamental in its importance to city people. The ballpark is open, grassy, spacious, and (in many parks) sunlit. It is a vestigial remnant of rural America within the crowded concrete and asphalt city. The field is an oasis where jaded urbanites can renew their relationship with earth and sun and can share vicariously in the ritualistic defense of the home turf against invaders.

Boating, especially yachting on the open ocean or large lake, presents an encounter with sea and wind that is part of the age-old symbolism of the sailor's struggle against open water. To the mariner, images of epic journeys or even naval war may reside within an innocent afternoon's outing.[2] Consider this description of a brief sailing adventure:

> The god called AEOLUS, that blows from the north-east of the world (you may see him on old maps; it is a pity they don't put him on the modern), said to his friends: "I see a little boat. It is long since I sank one"; and altogether they gave chase, like Imperialists to destroy what was infinitely weak. I looked to windward and saw the sea tumbling, and a great number of white waves. My heart was still so high that I gave them the

names of the waves in the eighteen *Iliad*. . . . But they were in no mood for poetry. They began to be great, angry, roaring waves, like the chiefs of charging clans. . . . I hung on like a stout gentleman, and prayed to the seven gods of the land. (Belloc 1921, 198–99)

The Architecture of Sport

While many sports combine symbolic behavior with a symbolic place—practicing good sportsmanship in a pastoral setting—sports structures do not necessarily carry the same symbolism. The grandstands at small town baseball fields across the country are functional and utilitarian. But other than being a place to socialize during the game, they probably do not have a deeper significance.

Some sports buildings are unique to sport; not found, say, on farms or in industrial areas. No one required a stadium to play football until the activity passed from being a folk game, played by college students and witnessed by a few fans who simply stood along the sidelines, to a spectator sport. About 1869, Ivy League colleges organized sports clubs, established consistent rules, hired officials to monitor the games, and formed a national regulatory association. The transition to commercialized spectator football was well under way by the 1890s (Rader 1983, 70). By the turn of the century, Harvard and Yale had built huge new stadiums (seating many more people than the total enrollment at those institutions), and within a few years, land-grant universities in the Midwest had also built stadiums that would provide models for similar structures for decades thereafter (Mandell 1984, 294).

Building baseball parks paralleled football stadium construction but with a significant difference. All football fields have the same dimensions; Baseball fields do not. Each baseball field conforms to its stadium. Fenway Park in Boston and the Polo Grounds in New York were different in size and shape, each posing different conditions for play (Oriard 1976, 39; fig. 1.3). Many older baseball stadiums are or were not particularly attractive. Owners painted the poured concrete walls and exposed steel girders but did little else to improve their appearance. Yet each stadium had an ambience that provided the persistent visitor and nearby resident alike with a distinctive sense of place.

Since World War II, as organized baseball expanded franchises to more cities, cities have built new stadiums that provide essentially symmetrical playing fields. Some new stadiums are round—RFK in Washington, D.C., Riverfront in Cincinnati, and Atlanta–Fulton County in Atlanta—identifiable on aerial photographs as great white concrete

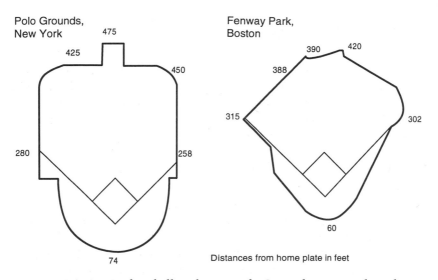

FIG. 1.3. Distinctive baseball stadiums: Polo Grounds, New York, and Fenway Park, Boston.

doughnuts. Seeing one such place is little different from seeing another; only their surroundings differentiate them. Many new stadiums have been built in suburban locations. Because a stadium and its attendant parking lots consume space best measured in acres, the preferred location for new structures is on cheaper suburban land. The Truman Sports Complex at Kansas City, home of the Kansas City Royals, for example, stands several miles east of the city at a freeway interchange. Such complexes cover a dozen acres or more and may attract suburban residential and commercial developments that rival the central city.

Other alterations in stadium design, lighting, and playing surface have changed the way participants play baseball and football and how spectators experience the games. To extend their playing schedule and increase attendance, professional baseball parks began to install lighting by the 1950s. In 1965, a revolutionary new stadium emerged in Houston, Texas—air conditioned and fully enclosed under a roof that blocked out the hot southern sun. Backers called the colossus the Astrodome, and it provided a radical departure in sports environments. Grass would not grow inside the dome; so the following year an artificial playing surface, Astroturf, replaced the grass. By 1984, ten of twenty-six major league baseball teams played on artificial grass, three in domed stadiums (Raitz 1985, 17).

Associating Sport with Environment

Most people experience a well-developed sense of attachment to certain places or material environments. Yi-Fu Tuan (1974, 93) called this feeling *topophilia*, which literally means love of place. This attachment may occur for several reasons. One person may appreciate a special environment because it is beautiful. Another may find a certain place meaningful because it is associated with pleasant experiences. People can also be expected to develop strong attachments to their home environments, and farmers may love the land from which they gain a living.

The association of pleasant emotions and certain environments also applies to sport. In a general sense, the change of season from winter to spring may be associated with the sports of spring and summer. Schoolchildren in the northern states begin practicing baseball when the last of winter's snows are melting in March, and the radio or television brings spring training ball games from southern states. Tennis and golf are outdoor games, associated with mild weather. Sport's environmental association also extends to topography. Driving through central Colorado in any season may evoke in the avid skier the desire for deep powder snow and a season lift ticket at Aspen, Vail, or Telluride.

Some sports can be appropriately experienced only in certain environments because the association with topography or climate is very strong and steeped in tradition. The steeplechase—named for an Old World cross-country horse race in which riders used church steeples as landmarks—can be held in a wide range of environments wherever sufficient acreage can be found to lay out a high-quality course with jumps and obstacles. The appropriate environment, though, is rolling open parkland with creeks, low hills, and great old trees scattered across a lush greensward. Western horsemen may feel a flush of emotion when they drive by a vacant rodeo ground as memories of good times flood the mind. More generally, the same person may follow the professional rodeo circuit, which today schedules events in large athletic arenas and stadiums in eastern states. But this is not the real environment for rodeo; for the long-time rodeo fan, it is only a disappointing imitation.

Automobile racing has regional and seasonal associations for both fans and participants. Hot rod drag racing has its roots and strongest environmental association with southern California. Grand National Stock Car racing originated in the southeastern states. The mere mention of Darlington (South Carolina) or Talladega (Alabama) to a NASCAR fan brings forth images of high-banked asphalt tracks set amid pine forests under a hot summer sun.

In at least two instances, racing of a special type is so strongly associated with a specific environment that many fans cannot conceive of this kind of race being held anywhere else with a similar level of enjoyment. From the late 1940s through the 1960s, auto racers held world land speed and endurance record trials on dry alkali lake beds in Nevada and southern California, and on northwestern Utah's Bonneville Salt Flats. Such places are remote, imposing special logistical difficulties to overcome. Once there, the piercing sun and stark, wind-whipped salt surface is an almost otherworldly environment, and to coax a race car past 300 miles per hour in such places imbues racing crews and fans alike with an incomparable feeling of accomplishment. Another distinctive type of racing is run by the kind of cars used at the Indianapolis 500. The premier track on this race circuit is the "brick yard" at Indianapolis, a two-and-one-half-mile motor speedway oval built in 1911. The mention of "Indy" among race fans evokes strong images of Memorial Day races, brightly painted cars, and stands and infield teeming with fans.

A final link between sport and associated environments is the special case of boundary restrictions placed on the hunting sports. Hunting upland game, quail, pheasants, rabbits, foxes, and the like often takes place on private farmland. The South has a tradition of game hunting that has its roots in English practice. Raccoon hunting, for example, is a "good old boy" folk sport in which a pack of especially bred and trained dogs or hounds hunts at night and attempts to chase the animal up a tree so that it can be killed or captured. Should the dogs follow an animal across a property boundary, the question of trespass and illegal entry onto property is immediately posed.[3]

Medieval English law provided strict limitations on movement by peasants onto the gentry's hunting lands. In America, that legal tradition has been modified in an interesting way. In the South, where English settlers introduced the aristocratic tradition, the basic trespass law is still intact. The Code of Virginia states that trespass by hunters pertains to "any person who goes on the lands, waters, ponds, boats, or blinds of another to hunt, fish, or trap without the consent of the landowner or his agent."[4] Alabama law is similar. The law does provide an exception in both states when hunting fox, coon, deer, and opossum. If a chase using dogs begins on one property and crosses a boundary to another's land, the chase may continue and the hunter may enter to retrieve the dogs. In Alabama, the law is even more liberal, with no spatial restrictions on hunting with dogs.[5] This liberal attitude toward trespass may be rooted in the commoner's dissatisfaction with English game and land control traditions. In many northern states, hunting game animals with dogs is considered unsportsmanlike; and in Minnesota, trespass law forbids hunting of any kind on agricultural land during hunting season.[6]

Sport and Place

The geography of sport incorporates questions about sports places, about how those places come to look and function as they do. We can make an initial distinction between sports places based upon whether they are created by and intended for use by local people (vernacular places) or if they are created by entrepreneurs as commercial places intended for mass consumption. This distinction is important because vernacular and mass consumption sports places are organized and built in very different ways. To refine the distinction we can employ the concepts of site and situation. *Site* refers to those place characteristics that provide context. For example, a site will have certain physical characteristics, perhaps a flat surface with sandy, well-drained soil. Site character also has a human dimension: an open churchyard with a street on one side, a burial ground on another, and the church itself on a third. This elementary list of site characteristics describes a vernacular place where neighborhood children play games after school and on weekends.

Situation helps relate this playground to other places. What is near? What is farther away? By what routes do you get there, and how must you travel? The church playground may be within an Irish-American inner-city neighborhood bordered by a street grid that extends across town in every direction. Some children who use the playground live across the street; others live six blocks away. The kids across the street use the playground every day. Those who live farther away usually come only on Saturdays. Industrial smokestacks loom over the trees on the playground's west side; during the week when the mill is running, smoke obscures the sun, and the diffused light turns the air a yellow-orange color. A river flows to the east and north, large enough to entertain barge traffic. On a quiet day, children on the playground can hear the diesel-powered tugs laboring behind their loads. Occasionally the river floods, covering the churchyard, filling neighborhood basements with water, and stopping traffic for a few days.

Some sports places rarely change (although the way people use them may change), and the vernacular playground is such a place. Other places—especially commercial sports places—change and evolve, altering the relationship between player and game; player and spectator; player, spectator, and place. Change may reflect broader changes in society: improved communication, advances in technology, new modes of transportation, a new sense of taste or social priority. Some sports might be purposely changed by their players. A great many more—and, I believe, the most important changes—have come because players, spectators, and those who promote and profit from sports have used social or technological change to alter sports sites or situations. Such alterations will in turn change the sport. Consider two examples.

Horse racing began as a vernacular sport in colonial America. By the 1680s, New York horses were running races on sandy Long Island paths. In the 1650s, English loyalist Cavaliers fleeing Cromwell's England embarked for the Virginia Tidewater country, where they engaged the fledgling plantation economy and indulged their passion for horse racing on local race paths (Lucas and Smith 1978, 17–18). Their Virginia racecourse was a one-fourth mile straight track laid out at a convenient place, a crossroad or abandoned field. Large crowds attended, but colonial law proscribed racing for all but the gentry.

New York horse owners gave considered attention to selective breeding in hope of improving their horses' running ability. They imported Arabian and Turkish breeding stock, and their Thoroughbred offspring proved capable of distance racing over much longer courses (ibid., 118). The informal race path was too short to challenge the Thoroughbred, and communities often built circular one-mile tracks as replacements. The new track required a permanent site and as much as forty to fifty acres of land. Open land might be found at town's edge, but roads (often named Race Street) had to be built to the track, and the grounds required leveling and maintenance. People attended the mile-long races in increasing numbers, and soon entrepreneurs enclosed the courses with fencing and charged admission (Holliman 1931, 113). The entrance fee provided money for winning purses and funds for building a grandstand for spectators. Track owners built stables for racehorses and made arrangements with local liveries to provide hay and oats during the races. Eventually the racecourse grounds included betting offices and restaurants for spectators.

Circular track racing was expensive. Breeding stock cost thousands of dollars, and maintaining a breeding herd or simply campaigning a racehorse from track to track cost more than any but the wealthy could afford. Meanwhile, the one fourth mile, or quarter mile, horse race did not disappear. It moved south and west with the pioneers, eventually reaching the Southwest, where it is still found. Today, "quarter horses" run quarter-mile races across the west on tracks such as Ruidoso Downs, in New Mexico.

Vernacular colonial racing has evolved into the nation's leading consumer sport. The sport is no longer local or seasonal. In the winter, horses race at tracks in Florida, California, Louisiana, or Arkansas. In late spring, the move north brings horses first to the Kentucky Derby, and to Baltimore's Preakness and New York's Belmont a few weeks later. Large jet aircraft shuttle American horses across the Atlantic to England, Ireland, or France, for breeding or racing, or bring European stock to the states. The contemporary racetrack is a very large business machine built and maintained to make money for its investors and provide tax revenues to state governments. Only in purpose does the commercial track resemble the crossroads race path of two centuries ago.

Baseball's origins are more obscure than horse racing, but here too one can trace the change from vernacular to commercial. The game probably evolved from stick-and-ball games played in northern Europe and the northeastern United States during the early 1800s. Children played these games on empty lots, in churchyards and schoolyards, and on lightly traveled streets. A team of wealthy New Yorkers called the Knickerbockers played a game recognizable as baseball, and the size and shape of their diamond followed formal rules that were probably written about 1845 (Mandell 1984, 180). Informal teams soon organized in other northeastern cities. By 1860, the game remained a hobby for athletic men, although some ball fields were enclosed and spectators paid a fee to watch (Furnas 1969, 656). Baseball spread across the eastern states after the Civil War as soldiers returned home, having learned the game in military camps.

The Cincinnati Red Stockings, the first professional baseball team, toured the country by rail playing local teams in 1869. The railroad permitted teams to travel long distances easily, and fans could use city trolley cars or interurban lines to attend games. One could make the case that the railroad allowed baseball to become a national commercial game (Betts 1953, 235). Investors built large new stadiums with access to trolley car lines. By World War II, professional baseball had expanded to two leagues with sixteen teams. Colleges built fields and stadiums, and their teams played league competitors. High school teams became common throughout the nation. Over time, the game's basic rules changed in minor ways and equipment was refined. The most significant alterations were to the field's site and situation. Those changes have been further elaborated with the construction of the Houston Astrodome and the invention of artificial turf. Baseball, at least the professional game, is often played in a huge stadium that is part of a larger sports or entertainment complex. Adjacent buildings may house conventions, concerts, or other sports. A web of streets, freeways, and interchanges usually entangles the site. One can still find neighborhood youngsters playing the vacant lot game, but its offspring has become the essence of commercial urbanity.

Sports Landscapes as Ensembles

Why do people participate in sports, and why do people attend sporting events as spectators? The answer to both questions is complex and has several dimensions. I will consider only one aspect of the answer here. A major reason people play or watch sports is for gratification. The sports fan is seeking a pleasurable experience. The young, the inexperienced, or the naive may experience satisfaction by simply watching the motion of play and rooting for a winning team. Yet one could experience this kind of emotion by watching a schoolyard game. To understand sport as entertainment, we should consider the more sophisticated participant and spectator and try to understand their interests. People who know a game's basic rules, who perhaps have played a game themselves, are likely to require a more elaborate or complex experience to achieve a satisfactory level of gratification. An important part of that experience is the landscape on which a sporting event takes place, and the attendant site elements one finds at a sports place, whether it is a ballpark, golf course, or racetrack.

Many sporting activities involve interacting with several individual yet related site elements. When combined, these elements make up a distinctive sports place morphology. If elements are eliminated, the experience would be modified; it might be simpler or even superficial, and therefore less gratifying. Downhill skiing, for example, should be viewed as an ensemble of site elements that, if perceived by the skier, should together add up to a satisfactory experience. If they did not, skiing would stop for that individual, or he or she would try skiing elsewhere. The ski area ensemble may include the resort hotel where one stays, complete with restaurant, bar, pool, sauna, and perhaps other features. Also included are practice slopes and advanced slopes, all with their individual characteristics. The ski lifts, including their type, speed, and destination—even the parking lots—add elements to the ski landscape ensemble.

Skiing, then, involves much more than simply tracking downhill on expensive metal or fiberglass skis. The ski experience would be incomplete, as well as less gratifying, without this wealth of landscape elements. Of course, some ski areas do not offer their customers a full range of ensemble elements. One has only to ask skiers what resorts they prefer to realize that the vertical drop and the length of slope are not the only criteria they use to assess their skiing experience. They rate the area according to site complexity because that is what adds up to a more desirable level of gratification. Ski resort owners have understood this principle for some time; this is why they compete actively with other resorts to offer the most complete experience. They know that American skiing cannot match the experience found in Austria or Switzerland, where authentic Alpine villages cluster along mountain valley roads near ski runs. So Americans build ersatz Alpine buildings to warm skiers and house the compressors that make artificial snow. Yet resort owners recognize the shortcomings of the ensemble they offer. "What we really lack is those old Alpine chalets," said an American resort owner in the midst of his concrete jungle. "We'd make a fortune if we had some weather-beaten stones" (quoted in Flower 1976, 131).

Ensemble as a Sporting Experience

People have different levels of perceptual acuity. We recognize such differences when we say that "people see things differently." But people's perceptions and tastes rarely remain static throughout their lives. They learn; they experience new places and ideas and come to appreciate things that may have previously escaped their attention. One can see how this expansion of personal perception is related to the sporting experience by looking at how people perceive a sports place's ensemble. We might argue that the most elementary level of interaction between people, be they players or spectators, and a sports place is in sporting experience.

Most spectators attending a game are somewhat familiar with the game's rules and the expected nature of play. They may know the players' names and the kind of performance each player can contribute. Yet, for most events, the place the game is held is not distinctive. It may be a small high school gym that, except for the color of the brick walls and a few minor architectural details, looks very much like thousands of other high school gyms. Nor is the gym's location likely to be particularly distinctive. It may be the largest building on the school grounds. Residential streets lined by look-alike houses may surround the school area. The spectator's trip to the game is probably visually uneventful, simply requiring traversing well-known ground.

Many sporting experiences are like this one. In games that are played indoors or at night under floodlights, the potential ensemble of site elements that could stimulate attention, interest, and add to one's experience is not present. If this is true, then gratification depends almost entirely upon the athletic event itself. Such events may not be well attended unless the level of athletic skill is high or the ensemble can somehow be expanded. (Adding cheerleaders, mascots, concessions, midgame performances, etc., all help. To appreciate the effectiveness of such additions, try to imagine an indoor high school basketball game between equally untalented teams without them.)

Ensemble as a Distinctive Sports Place

A second level of participant and spectator gratification can be reached if the sporting experience is in an interesting and stimulating place. Perhaps the event's site is different from others in layout, design, or the amount of detail contained in its ensemble and so produces a significant level of satisfaction. One example is the auto racing track. Stock car racing has been a familiar event at county fairground tracks in the Midwest since the late 1930s and early 1940s. Like the high school gym, these tracks are much alike. A quarter- or half-mile oval dirt track is attended by a small grandstand, and together they demarcate the fairgrounds from the surrounding farmland. As one moves up the auto racing scale into nationally organized events that require investment of tens of thousands of dollars in cars, crew members, and equipment, the tracks that entertain such races are very much larger and more complex places. Super speedways like Darlington in South Carolina may have steeply banked circular asphalt tracks two miles or more in length. Properly prepared cars can exceed 180 miles per hour on such tracks. Attendance may reach fifty thousand or more, and the management caters to fan interest by providing huge parking lots where fans may camp and tailgate, concession stands, and other services. At stock car races, and major sport car races as well, fans group themselves into "neighborhoods" that share interests. Serious followers of individual drivers may gather as close to the finish line as possible and record laps on clipboards and speeds on stopwatches. Another group may prefer to watch from the infield area beside the pits. The rowdy drunks may be in still another place (Wilkinson 1973, 25). The fans, to the perceptive spectator, become part of the ensemble of site elements. To maximize one's gratification, one would seek out the group whose interests and activities most closely match one's own.

Each year, the Indianapolis 500 is the best-attended single racing event in the nation, with a quarter million or more spectators. The race promoters' longstanding theme is that the 500 is "the greatest spectacle in racing." *Spectacle* is an excellent word choice because it addresses precisely the values embedded in the idea of landscape ensemble as a source of attraction and gratification in sporting events.

On a different, much more intimate scale, the ensemble may also play an important role in a lone individual's appreciation of a racing event. Stand beside an empty California sportscar track with Sylvia Wilkinson and experience, through her eyes, a time trial.

> Laguna has an unsettled climate, the wind blows in strong from the ocean, the trees are permanently shaped to the sweep of the wind on the dunes, twisted trees, almost oriental. When the sun is out, each leaf stands out as an individual form in the clear air, from a hillside almost a half mile away, objects are still clear. The orange Union 76 ball rolls like a Cyclops' eye-ball. A flock of blackbirds comes through, turns in formation, catching a flash of light on their backs before the sun disappears again. One of the McLaren Can-Am cars is practicing on an empty track, its bright orange body glowing under the darkened sky as if lit from within. There is the very special sound of hearing one car on the track, the fraction of silence between each shift, the rising of the engine muffled only when the wind comes through the trees. (61)

The Laguna track is a special place. Its ensemble has unique elements that add much to the perceptive individual's experience.

Ensemble as an Aesthetic Experience

Wilkinson's experience at Laguna illustrates that there is yet more refinement possible in one's perceptions of a sports place or event. A practiced mind stimulated by an appropriate ensemble can begin to appreciate the aesthetic dimension of certain sporting experiences. In fox hunting, beauty may be found in the physical environment or in the animation of dogs, horses, and scarlet-clad riders. An English hunt's sterling moment is recorded by Willoughby DeBroke.

Would he [the fox] but cross the turnpike road to the southeast, he would lead the hunt over the finest grass country in
the world. . . . the ground was hard and dry, and there seemed
no reason why the lean, long-legged customer should ever tire.
Away on the right, two miles to the south, was the hill country. Three miles ahead was a blackthorn covert, which seemed
to be his point, entrenched behind a railway and a formidable
brook. The whole [hound] pack swung to the right, except one
couple who could not leave the left-hand corner of the field,
and wormed their way through the black bullfinch as if they
knew something. And they were right. In another fifty yards
they spoke to their fox, and the body [the rest of the pack]
came eagerly and generously to the cry, well in front of all the
horses—one of the prettiest sights that fox-hunting can produce. (1921, 164–65)

The golf course may be the quintessential aesthetic sports place
because of its complex outdoor landscape ensemble and its potential for
rich perceptual experience. Course designers and country club developers know that they must create beautiful links to maximize appeal
(Muirhead 1970, 23). The best courses not only provide a challenging
game but are placed in especially attractive surroundings. The modern
golf course is designed by someone trained in landscape architecture or
experienced in play or both. The links are tastefully laid out to jux-
tapose topographic and vegetative variation. The transition of plant
cover from fairway to rough to out-of-bounds not only functions to
limit the play corridor but also provides an opportunity for purposefully
placing plants of different color, texture, or shape so that they combine
for a pleasing prospect. Whether this planned and manicured landscape
is as beautiful to all who see it as, say, a primeval redwood forest is not
really important. What is important is that the player considers the
appearance of the course to be part of the playing experience (Raitz
1985, 8–9).

An aesthetically effective golf course design cannot be achieved
through a standard plan or formula but must be shaped by local circumstances and tastes (fig. 1.4). The first American golf courses to be laid
out away from a coastal location with bare sand dunes (the Scottish
tradition) were inland courses across farm fields studded with large
trees, grassy knolls, stone walls, and farm buildings. The British ridiculed these early park courses, as they were called, as inferior and
inappropriate. A proper game, they argued, required proper ensemble

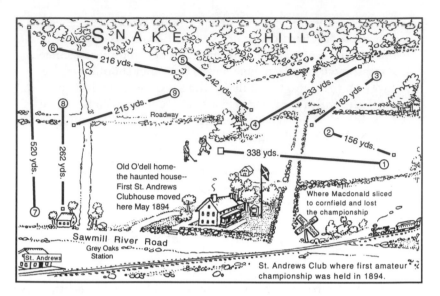

FIG. 1.4. The landscape ensemble of the St. Andrews Golf Course at Yonkers, New York, where the first amateur championship was held in 1894.

aesthetics (Martin 1936, 64–65). But a proper ensemble is also a matter of preference and habit. Before new or exotic ensembles can be fully enjoyed, spectators may have to adjust their attitudes.

Ensemble as Symbol

For some individuals or groups, a sporting experience may include an additional level of appreciation and gratification; that of the sport and its ensemble as a symbol with a larger meaning. This is probably the most abstract level of sports appreciation and may be limited to a few individuals and circumstances. Two distinct types of symbolism can be found at sports places: the environmental and the social or cultural. Environmental symbolism may be appreciated by the trout fisher casting flies in a western Wyoming stream. He or she may reflect on how that valley may represent wilderness, although a dozen other people are fishing less than a mile away. Ideas such as "wilderness" and "pastoral" are different for each individual, who assigns them meaning and importance based on personal experience (Mruzek 1983, 171).

Baseball has a pastoral image (Oriard 1976, 33). Its current imprisonment behind fulsome steel and concrete stadium walls belies its heritage of open sandlots in small towns and city neighborhoods. But even on the stadium field, baseball can be pastoral if one wants it to be. In *The Natural*, Bernard Malamud places his character, Roy Hobbs, on a common city ball field. Yet as the game progresses, the field seems less mundane, almost transformed into a rural dimension:

> The long rain had turned the grass green and Roy romped in it like a happy calf in its pasture. He seemed to know the soft, hard, and bumpy places in the field and just how high a ball would bounce on them. From the flags on the stadium roof he noted the way the wind would blow the ball, and he was quick fishing it out of the tricky undercurrents on the ground. Not sun, shadow, nor smoke or haze bothered him, and when a ball was knocked against the wall he estimated the angle of rebound and speared it as if its course had been plotted on a chart (1952, 83).

The sports ensemble may also hold social or cultural symbolism. The golf course at an exclusive country club provides an example. Membership in many clubs that feature golf, polo, or tennis is exclusionary. Those who cannot afford membership fees or those who are socially unacceptable are excluded. Country clubs—note that they are not called city or urban clubs—are guarded by gates, fences, and hedges, and strict controls on outsiders are otherwise maintained. Outsiders cannot see in, and they are physically beyond the view of those within the compound. In this way, a class distinction is created and enforced. Symbolically, the club golf course may become an edenic refuge—a secure, private, isolated place where one need not be concerned with the outside world's strident crudity.

Conclusion

Sports landscapes are multifaceted parts of the cultural environment. At one level, they reflect an obsession with leisure activity. At another, they represent the conversion of a traditional form of leisure into a capital-based entertainment form in which entrepreneurs spend or invest huge sums of money on sports structures and related ensemble elements. Such behavior, of course, reflects cultural values; but a sports landscape is more than this. On a personal level, material and nonmaterial landscape elements play a significant role in the level of gratification a participant or spectator may experience at a sporting event. The greater the gratification, the more likely one is to return for additional experiences (fig. 1.5).

Sport Place Examples, A–F

		Distinctions between Sports Places **(Most Places Are Different)**		
Complex	Place			High
↑	↑	A B C D E F		↑
↑	↑			↑
				Level of
Landscape	Sense	AB CD EF		Gratification
Ensemble	of Place			Attained from
↓	↓	**Some Distinction**		a Sport
		(Some Places Are Alike)		Experience
↓	↓			↓
↓	↓	ABCDEF		↓
Simple	Placelessness			Low
		No Distinction		
		(All Places Are Alike)		

FIG. 1.5. Perceived distinctions between sports place ensembles, sense of place, and level of gratification. The examples apply to any type of sports place: golf courses, ballparks, racetracks, etc.

All things being equal—individual perceptual acuity, for example—complex landscape ensembles are more stimulating to the senses than simple ones. As complexity and detail increase, the ensemble provides greater levels of gratification. These relationships are summarized in figure 1.5. If one considers any given group of sports places (ball fields, racetracks, golf courses, or whatever), one can assess whether their ensembles are simple, complex, or somewhere in between. The simple sports landscapes have only the rudimentary features required to conduct an event. Consequently, there is little to help the spectator separate the experience at one place from that at another. The result is that most of these places seem alike, and they provide low levels of gratification. They may be placeless in the sense that they look alike, feel alike, and offer the same kind of experience. Such places also need not be small: one modern multipurpose concrete stadium is much like another, and games played in these places are essentially indistinguishable (Relph 1976, 90).

As more diverse elements are added to the sports landscape ensemble, however, the additional stimulus may help the spectator to differentiate that place from others in its class. For example, the Paris, Kentucky, high school football team plays its games in the figurative shadow of Blanton Collier, a local boy who went on to coach football at the University of Kentucky and then for the Cleveland Browns (fig. 1.6). The Street of Champions is simply a fifty-foot-long section of a circular drive behind Paris High School, but it becomes a key element in the stadium landscape ensemble, as do the orange greyhound mascot symbol and the historical account of championships, painted on two sides of the concession stand. On fall Friday nights, the townspeople turn out to support the team, and the stadium grounds take on the aspect of a festival. In such settings, the level of stimulus and gratification increases and placelessness dissolves, leaving one with sharp, clear impressions of the event *and* its surroundings, impressions that are associated with a specific site and no other.

FIG. 1.6. Blanton Collier Stadium, Paris, Kentucky.

CHAPTER TWO

BASEBALL

Brian J. Neilson

On a corner in Portland, Oregon, a plaque commemorates the old ballpark that once stood there and the man who, like a temple priest, tended its green fields. In Pittsburgh, all that remains of the old ballpark, its home plate, remains preserved like a holy relic in the heart of the building that replaced it.

Baseball, more than any other sport, has lent itself to the metaphorical exploration of American life. The harmonic resonance between the life and rhythms of the game on the field and the cadences and textures of the collective dream life of American culture has produced a rich literature and art. The iconography of baseball permeates our visual vocabulary (Lou Gehrig as secular saint, ennobled by suffering; Casey Stengel as gnomic wizard) as its idioms permeate our language (They're playing hardball; He hit it over the fence). Baseball is, among other things, an instrument of national self-consciousness. It compresses and externalizes the psychic history of the American people.

Baseball parks are thus charged with a special emotional energy. They are among the few sacred grounds of a secularized society with deep and atavistic spiritual impulses. They are a locus of our residual yearning for innocence; the Puritan drama of grace, redemption, and social communion is still enacted in their confined precincts. We demand such rituals, and we turn over in our minds the games our fathers watched, the games of our own childhood, until they have been burnished with the perfect golden aura of (imperfect) mythic memory. These assertions may seem a heavy freight with which to burden buildings dedicated to sport and born out of the normal forces of a market economy, but only thus can one understand the sentiment that Americans have invested in baseball parks.

Football, with its martial language, suggests darker metaphors, driven by continental appetites and imperial ambitions, which are the constant dialectical counterpoints to the American search for recaptured innocence. The simplified linear geometry of football fields and the stadiums—not "parks"—that contain them suggest the impatient pragmatism of the pioneer breaking a frontier. They are the locus of a more austere sentimentalism, that of hard duty, will, and sacrifice, performed under the tyranny of the clock. They objectify the instrumentalist view of nature necessary to a nation of continent-breakers. One does not linger amid such implacable linearity; empty, they are a reproach to idleness.

The Early Years

Professional baseball, like many arrangements of modern American life, was a byproduct of the Civil War. The war released new energies and technologies, new appetites and ambitions. It gave birth to a new kind of person, restless and urbanizing, both defining and defined by the values of emerging Big Capitalism. This person's moral and intellectual world was born out of the collapse of the Jeffersonian vision of a Greco-Roman republic, austere and patrician in its ideal state (if not in its Tocquevillean complexity). Such values were already compromised before the war by internal expansionist fervor and wars of conquest against Indians and Mexicans. The psychic residues of the bucolic tradition were swept away by the industrialization and general massification of society during the Civil War years.

Sport was also redefined by the changes in American life. The aristocratic notion of gentlemanly amateurism, the habit of which remained among the landowning classes of Tidewater Virginia and the Atlantic South, forbid professionalism. More importantly, prior to the Civil War there were no American cities whose population had sufficient free time and discretionary income to support professional sports.

Baseball, or some evolutionary predecessor of it, had been played in rural meadows by country men, on commons by townsmen, and on more formally organized sporting grounds by such famous gentlemen's clubs as the Knickerbockers of New York. During the Civil War, with men of all classes and regions thrown together, the game was germinated, codified, standardized, and then carried back to farms, towns, and cities from the Atlantic to the western frontier.

In the decade following the war, several forces were converging toward the formation of professional baseball: a large audience familiar with the game; a concentration of population gathered by industrialization across the victorious North, from New England out to the Great Lakes; a worldly, anti-Puritan commercial ethic; and an awakened appetite for mass entertainments. In 1869 the Cincinnati Red Stockings were constituted as the first professional baseball club. There followed a loose confederation of clubs in other cities, which was formalized as the National League in 1876. Professional baseball soon began to define a part of the national consciousness. The baseball park, a new and uniquely American architectural idiom, entered the urban visual vocabulary.

The cities in which baseball now appeared were marked by both a new splendor (unrestrainedly individualistic by pre–Civil War standards) and a spreading industrial squalor. Their growth was fueled by infusions of foreign investment capital and by the first of many successive waves of rural and foreign immigration. (They were in these respects not unlike the boom-bust Sunbelt towns of the 1980s.) Pushing rapidly outward at the edges, they were little hampered in their growth by concerns for planning, open space, recreation, or decent housing standards; a later generation of Progressives and reformers would have to address the problems thus created. But by the 1880s the first signs of the nascent mass industrial society had appeared: the nationwide expansion and homogenization of a consumer-oriented material culture; the birth of a recognizable factory labor (if not exactly "proletarian") class; the problems of transporting the newly assembled work force between home and factory or office. Finally (and psychologically crucial to the rise of professional sports), one sees the growing separation of urban life into mutually exclusive spheres of work and release from work, and the consequent need for organized diversions (amusement parks), spectacles (traveling circuses and popular stage shows), and spectator sports, the first of which was baseball.

Though baseball has never entirely lost its connection to a rural past, the sudden popularity and subsequent growth of the professional sport in the context of the industrial city made its pastoral aspects a largely lost phenomenon. Baseball, which remains for Americans a renewable source of imaginative innocence, was born into the most rapacious era of American history, with the country unmoored (or liberated) by war from the prewar restraints on ambition and size imposed by the antiurban, anticommercial biases of the old landowning classes. (It is no small part of the mythic resonance of baseball in American life that it can cross the abyss between that vanished world and our own to remind us of archetypal republican virtues.)

These postwar boom towns were, like all such growing clusters, raw around the edges. The first baseball parks, as revealed in contemporary prints, were utilitarian and unadorned structures, minimalist solutions for a given set of requirements, just like their surroundings on the expanding periphery of the new industrial cities. These parks were typically built outside the compact if jumbled center, on vacant land adjacent to the factories and the new tenements built to house workers. The parks were usually reached from the city center by horsecars, and later by electrified streetcars. Sometimes the transit companies themselves built ballparks along the trolley lines, as speculative ventures.

There was, of course, no precedent for their design, no canon of forms as might be applied to a courthouse or a church. They were shaped and limited by the space available, the materials and technologies at hand, and the still-evolving rules of the sport itself. They are, except for horse-racing courses, the first large structures set into the landscape and dedicated to commercial "recreation," a category of experience that had not existed before the Civil War and which would have been inconceivable to Americans of the Revolutionary period. They announce a new age.

For our purposes, we should understand baseball not only as a sport but also as a business, and furthermore as a business system of ever-increasing rationality operating in a new and (a century ago) unknown market. The prototypical baseball parks embodied perfectly the volatility and unpredictability of the early years of the professional game: they were expendable. They were made of wood, because wood is cheap and easily worked, and because clubs were frequently sold, moved from one part of town to another, or transferred to other cities—or they simply disappeared into bankruptcy. These parks burned with alarming frequency (though seldom with loss of life) and were hastily rebuilt within weeks, even within days. They were, as urban landmarks, as ephemeral as stables or saloons. But, as the patriotic and community symbols of the Jeffersonian and Federalist periods—the courthouse, the meeting hall, the church—receded in importance, the ballpark became a landmark of the new protocapitalist landscape, a locus of attention and movement.

Their form was simple, but it contained the genetic code, as it were, for future parks. A look at photographs of early parks shows a wing of bleachers extending along one foul line, wrapping tightly around home plate, then reaching along the other foul line. Perhaps a roof shields the "better people" in the seats adjacent to the diamond; the others "bleach" in the summer sun. Wooden board fences now enclose the outfield from one foul line to the other, excluding the nonpaying public and setting limits to the field. This innovation alone altered strategy and created a new type of player, one who might aspire to power the ball over the fence. Previously, the outfield might extend, theoretically, from—say—Marietta, Ohio, out to western Kansas; but all frontiers are eventually closed. Though primitive, these first ballparks launched an idiom, the first rule of which remains the same: a ballpark is a box to contain a drama. (Some of the existing ballparks of the low minor leagues most faithfully reproduce in form, size, and materials these earliest parks.)

These jerry-built parks, easily built and easily abandoned, were not yet "architecture" in any conscious sense. They had the unadorned pragmatic linearity—and also the utilitarian charm—of the sheds, stables, and factories by which they were often surrounded. The reformist zoning laws of the early twentieth century, mandating the separation of industry, commerce, residential zones, and recreational areas, had not yet been formulated. So all of these activities were just beyond the ballpark fences, as well as empty plots of land, waiting to be filled by the next speculative leap outward from the center. These marginal structures, built on marginal land, provided a home for what, in the 1880s, was still decidedly a precarious and marginal business venture. (As baseball prospered, clubs would move to higher-priced land closer to the center, or the expanding city would consolidate around the existing parks.)

Professional baseball created a new category of workers in American life, the paid athlete-specialist. In the early years of the sport, their status was certainly no higher than that of other performers such as those in traveling actors' troupes, that is, below the level of middle-class respectability. They were farm boys, town boys, the sons of urban immigrants, at first mostly Protestants of English or Scots-Irish stock. Thereafter, with the assimilation of each succeeding wave of immigrants, they were increasingly German or Swedish, then overwhelmingly Irish. In the new century, there were Italians, a few Poles, a scattering of Jews. Baseball, even in the '80s and '90s, had already begun to function as a mechanism to introduce the newly arrived into the rituals and promises of American life: the ethnic fans followed the ethnic players into the ballparks. (This is happening in my San Francisco neighborhood in the 1990s, but the players are Chinese, not Italian.) A scattering of players were college graduates, nominally "gentlemen." But the photos and prints from that era make it clear that the players were separated from the fans by talent rather than by social class.

Period pictures show that the fans were working-class men, neatly, soberly, and fully attired: the working man's off-hour badge of decent propriety. The stands were very close to the foul lines, and when the fans overflowed the seats they sprawled on the grass within feet of the baselines and the batter's box. (One marvels at an America, still unlawyered and unlitigious, in which such a willing acceptance of danger was possible.) Women were conspicuously absent from professional games, though "ladies" were escorted in carriages to amateur (i.e., upper social class) club matches. The absence of dugouts is revealing of the lack of social distance between players and fans; there was no sanctum of visual privacy denied to the profane eyes of the masses. Rather, the players sat on simple benches in front of the stands, exposed to the cheers and taunts of those who were, at least in provenance, their peers. The physical and psychological distance between those who played and those who watched was minimal.

In the early years, most of each team's players were the cream of local talent, not yet the product of a nationwide capillary network of player development. The idea of a contest between "our boys" and "their boys," then literally true, would soon be made obsolete by the increasing movement of players between teams. But these early clubs, and the ballparks they played in, were among the first emblems of an urban self-identity, based not on the shared ideal tension of republican principles but rather on the pluralistic choice of pleasures in a free market. And each city, as its team traveled to other cities and hosted them in turn, was reminded that it belonged to a rapidly consolidating national web of similar tastes, similar pleasures, similar pastimes. Here, accompanied and abetted always by the spread of the popular press, are the roots of mass culture. These modest early ballparks were a locus of attention in the process of psychological nation building.

In the quarter century between the founding of the National League and that of the rival American League in 1901, the social and physical matrix of the modern American city was created. Successive waves of European immigration created mutually exclusive ethnic enclaves (not impermeable, however, to the wider attractions of American life). The infusion of non-Anglo-Saxon political mores and the increased demand for services—primarily patronage jobs and a capillary dole system—led to the formation of ethnic-based political clubs and the rise of "bossism." Though condemned for its open cronyism (i.e., loyalty rather than meritocracy as a defining value), bossism proved to be an efficient political device to deal with complexities never imagined by pre–Civil War republican theorists. The patchwork of ethnic and political turfs thus created was mitigated by the growing popularity of neutral places of amusement. The ballpark is a nonideological free zone, open to all, where we focus on our commonalities of identity. In a social atmosphere increasingly heterogeneous and reflecting the pressures of mutual ethnic suspicion, baseball can provide an escape valve. (This was also true in Detroit, after the fires and the fears of the 1967 riots. Nobody tried to burn down Tiger Stadium.)

At the same time, the Trolley Age was exploding urban space outward along the lines of the tracks, creating the first ring of commuter suburbs and establishing the new pattern of separation between work and residence. "Massification" is the operative word to describe the rapid social and economic evolution of the period: massification of populations, of political participation, of the formation of public opinion and taste through the penny press, massification of mobility through the new rail technologies, massification of capital through new oligopolistic corporate structures and strategies, and massification of habits of consumption through homogenization of production and advertising. These were precisely the premises necessary for professional baseball to flourish. It was the success of the National League in stabilizing its structure and increasing its attendance—in spite of periodic recessions and player revolts, and challenges by upstart leagues—that convinced Ban Johnson to invade the previously monopolistic major league field with his American League in 1901. The immediate success of that league proved that his speculation was right. Like the social conditions of the cities described above, the stable bilateral structure at the apex of baseball's pyramid was to endure in its essential lineaments until World War II.

The baseball parks themselves changed little during the period before 1909. They continued to be built of wood and continued to burn with regularity. When they grew in capacity—as attendance and funds permitted—they did so incrementally, so that in aspect they seem an assemblage of disparate parts. At New York's Polo Grounds, in Baltimore, in Cincinnati, and in Chicago, the wooden stands were modestly double-decked and roofed, so that the number of seats around the infield was increased. Photographs show the swells in their boxes wearing top hats to the game, but even the working-class men in the cheap seats are soberly dressed for public life: "leisure" was a new concept in American life, and there was as yet no category of clothing to accompany it. Major league players—though not minor leaguers—were no longer local boys, but rather a semi-nomadic, quasi-professional class, drawn from a nationwide talent pool.

Professional baseball players are among the first examples of a new human type, the "celebrity," the object of constant curiosity, adoration, envy, and scorn. Though most, in the early years, drew modest salaries and had little security, they were, by virtue of such unremitting scrutiny, beginning to be set apart from, and above, other men. As befitted their new status, they were furnished with dugouts, in which they could shield themselves briefly from the gaze of the omnivorous public and from the press, whose role it was both to formulate and to satisfy the increasing interest in fame and in heroes. But these heroes were significantly devoid of the stern old values, be they martial, republican, or religious.

Here, then, is the beginning of a mass popular culture that raises its idols from its own self-defined middleness and defines superiority in the skill and talent which they employ to amuse or astonish us. The early republican model of hero-citizen as gentleman farmer/legislator/inventor/amateur soldier became decisively eclipsed in the popular imagination by a model corresponding more exactly to an atomized consensus about social purpose. Perhaps baseball has been made to bear the weight of such grand metaphorizing in precisely the degree to which enthusiasm for sports and spectacle in general has supplanted an earlier boisterous pride in republican institutions.

Notably lacking in these pre–World War I ballparks was a discrete section for the sporting press, whose members have had from the beginning a mutually beneficial relationship with the rising professional sports. The early sportswriter, like the ballplayer, belonged to an emerging entertainment class. But even while he was formulating an opinion-making and fame-producing process, he was as yet a servant of that process, still a humble and nearly anonymous figure. Later, with the professionalization of the craft and the obligatory creation of journalistic "stars" (Grantland Rice, Damon Runyon, Heywood Broun, et al.) and with the advent of radio and television, reporters would rise from informed spectators to protagonists, celebrities themselves. At the turn of the century, however, for all the growing power of the popular press (i.e., the Hearst papers' rabble-rousing support of the Spanish-American War), sportswriters were not yet recognized as a separate caste; they still sat among the other fans in the stands.

Noticeably absent, too, were women and children. These early ballparks were rough places of male refuge, scarcely more decorous than saloons. The signs on the outfield fences advertised whiskey, tobacco, and men's haberdashers. Contemporary accounts confirm that the crowds were boisterous, profane, and vicious in baiting opposing players; the players knew how to respond in kind. In accordance with prevailing masculine fashion, men were voluminous smokers of cigars and spitters of tobacco. Admission to the "Booze Cage," a fenced-in area of San Francisco's Recreation Park, included the choice of a shot of whiskey or two beers, and was denied to women. The players said the enclosing chicken wire protected them, not the fans. In the prevailing Victorian view of gender and family life, men and women operated in two mutually exclusive moral realms, and women and children were to be shielded, if possible, from the vulgarity of men's diversions and the rapacity of economic life. Gentlewomen of the middle and upper classes were not to be thrown into chance encounters with men of strange aspect and "low" comportment, although such an experience might not be unusual for a woman of foreign birth in the large cities of the East.

As the new century was born, baseball parks had already become landmarks of the consolidating industrial city. They were set in a landscape of voracious and pitiless commercial energy, liberated appetites, and growing social contradictions. If the ideal city landscape was composed of Beaux-Arts wedding cake palaces, as at the 1893 Columbus Exposition in Chicago, the real landscape was increasingly made up of trolley lines shooting out from the center toward the city's edge, endless rows of tenements, a hodgepodge of small commerce, domesticity, and belching factories. In the middle of this burgeoning, bristling urban texture, the new home of the democratic Everyman, was a baseball park.

The Golden Age

With the establishment of the American League and the beginning of World Series competition with the National League, the major leagues entered an era of stability—if not always of prosperity—that was to last half a century. In that period, which continued until about 1950, the greater part of America's talent, ambition, and population flowed from the farms and small towns into the metropolitan centers. Employing the new technologies of steel framing and concrete fireproofing developed in skyscraper and bridge construction, fourteen of the sixteen major league clubs built large, modern stadiums between 1902 and 1923.

While clearly within the idiom established by the early wooden ballparks—a box around a field—these new ballparks were ambitious, were "architectural" in ways not seen before. They were built of durable (and expensive) materials, and so represented a long-term capital investment. The strength of steel beams and reinforced concrete made it possible to raise spacious second and even third tiers of seats soaring above the diamond, a feat not structurally possible before. Although the seats and the grandstand roofs were of wood, the steel structural members were highly resistant to fire; indeed, none of these new ballparks was ever seriously damaged by fire. These relatively permanent parks (only five of them remain in use today), all privately financed, were above all expressions of their builders' confidence in the expanding and increasingly rationalized market for professional baseball.

Their appearance is also linked to the advent of a nationwide cultural shift, emanating outward from the cities to the small towns of America like a seismic movement. The values of redemptive work and purifying thrift, planted in the native soil by the first immigrants and nurtured by the austere values of the young republic, were giving way to a city-bred taste for worldly diversion and individual consumption. A native-born working class, newly urbanized, recently wrenched from the solidarity of town life and activities, began to find a new focus of identity and national connectedness in such surrogates for traditional figures of virtue and authority as baseball players and movie stars. For newly arrived immigrants, baseball and movies were mechanisms of acculturation, an entry into a benign cultural nationalism. Baseball parks, movie theaters, and amusement parks were all part of a new city landscape generated by an equally new category of experience called "leisure time" and the organization of that time for commercial ends. (Such places were generally deplored by high-minded reformers, who recommended the salutary environment of green spaces and gardens.) The imposing new ballparks were not only destinations in the new city but were themselves landmarks. Although from the present nostalgic perspective they may seem artifacts of a lost age of innocence, they are better understood as proto-structures of the mass culture which was to sweep away almost all previous or competing cultures.

With the rise of this mass entertainment industry and its subsidiary industries, there began a process of convergence between the lives of women and men. Unlike saloons and pool halls, cinemas and amusement parks were gender-neutral and courted the business of women, indeed of the entire family. The new ballparks—clean, well maintained, with superior amenities, and with more rigid segregation of economic classes in the different tiers of seats and bleachers—offered a more genteel environment for women. Social strictures against public drunkenness were growing stronger in the years leading up to Prohibition. Already in the period prior to World War I, women (though not children) are more evident in photographs of ballparks. The increasing gentility of public space, which might be called feminization, is a characteristic of a maturing society already in evidence in the new ballparks of that era.

In period photographs, crowds continue to be soberly and rather formally dressed; men of all classes are shown wearing suits, ties, and hats, even in the sweltering summer. Women appear to have had large salad bowls balanced on their heads. (Were they politely but firmly requested to remove them?) The essential paraphernalia of modern fans—team cap, jacket, T-shirt, pennant—is strikingly absent. One wonders if the bounds imposed by propriety forbid such extravagant assertiveness, or if instead these persons were so securely (albeit oppressively) rooted in a place and a culture as to make such expression superfluous. The ballpark may well have been a theater of collective dramatization and release, but one's public presentation was still mask-like. Public places, even a place as raucous as the ballpark, required the presentation of the public self, that is, the framing of the self within implicitly understood and shared limits of dress and behavior. The post-1960s canon of expressive individualism through the public assertion of private sensibility, opinion, and taste would probably have seemed a social and psychological impossibility to the fans at Shibe Park in 1909. Indeed, their social mores would seem equally inexplicable to the bare-chested young man in the bleachers of the 1990s. But in the pre–World War I years, there was little blurring of the boundary between private and public realms.

The economic precariousness of the first two decades of professional baseball dictated that the ballparks be built with the least investment, on cheap land at the edge of the town. With stability, prosperity, and the prospect of an expanding market, owners could justify an investment in land closer to the urban core—closer, that is, to the concentrated fan base and the intersecting transit web of subways, surface trolleys, and elevated lines. Thus, the ballparks built between 1902 and 1923 were set in a preexisting grid of streets, light and heavy rail lines, canals, factories, warehouses, commercial buildings, residential blocks, and waste land.

The striking memorability of these ballparks derives from the extraordinary variety of their particulars and their settings within a commonly known building idiom. Each one was the unique product of its circumstances and of the architectural dialogue between two opposed forces: the diamond, the outfield, and the stands pushing outward, and the surrounding streets and structures containing them. Each of these ballparks, rather than being conceived as a free-standing object in its own space, is part of a continuous web of facades of similar materials, forming blocks, linked by streets, woven into neighborhoods. These new parks were not only urban but urbane, acknowledging the premodernist principle that cities are (or should be) a continuous fabric of harmonies and resonances, not an assemblage of isolated monuments. The pragmatic exigencies of accommodating the needs of both the sport and the spectators on a cramped urban plot, rather than aesthetic or philosophical considerations, produced the best ballparks ever built. The simple but highly elaborated vocabulary of a compact, double-tiered box, wrapped closely around a field, perfectly expressed the purpose of the structure: a container for a drama.

The dimensions and contours of each park reflected the unique circumstances of the plot of land that contained and limited it. So, while all of the ballparks were built up of a common vocabulary of elements—playing field, grandstands, fences, bleachers, a scoreboard—each park varied the arrangement of those elements, making it was instantly recognizable to baseball fans across the country. That curving horseshoe of stands could only be the Polo Grounds; that sloping grass terrace in front of the wall had to be Crosley Field in Cincinnati; the overhanging lip of that near right-field upper deck, Tiger Stadium; those airy pavilions with the beer signs in the outfield, Sportsman's Park in Saint Louis; those ivied brick walls with the brownstone houses just beyond (almost in) the outfield, Wrigley Field; that angled notch cut into the bleachers, Boston's Braves Field; that reentrant wall intruding into center field, with the trees and the tenements behind it, Griffith Stadium in Washington; and so on. Glimpsing a detail in a photograph, the fan could imaginatively reconstruct the park in its entirety, the jumbled assemblage of slanting angles, curves, expanses, straits, hollows, solids, shadows, voids, corners, and backgrounds which composed the whole. Just as, for example, the Water Tower in Chicago and Pittsburgh's Golden Triangle are iconographic elements with which one can evoke in memory the cities they represent, so did the divided Gothic arches behind the stands at Comiskey Park or the looming stands bent around the foul pole at Forbes Field serve an evocative function.

Moreover, these ballparks were set deeply into the fabric of the cities they represented for millions of Americans. Most looked out over a landscape of quiet working-class domesticity and small commerce. Manhattan apartment blocks looked down into the field at the Polo Grounds from the adjacent Coogan's Bluff; freeloaders could take in the game while perched precariously in tree branches. The "elevated" rumbled behind the third base stands. Wood frame houses, with grassy yards and an air of midwestern quietude, lay just outside the fences of Cleveland's League Park. From the upper deck of Sportsman's Park one looked over the rivertown expanses of brick row houses; the onion domes and the spires of the churches built by the city's large German and Central European populations punctuated the skyline. From without, the ballparks were seen to rise from the familiar web of everyday domesticity, from the daily urban turf of street corners, saloons, shops, and schools; from the jumble of signs, trolley cars, overhead wires, and street vendors. From within, the team on the field, the fans in the stands, and the surrounding city landscape were joined in an indissoluble continuity of identity. In this view out over the field and the town, life, work, and pleasure were three intersecting circles of experience.

Four of these parks merit special attention, not because they are so different from the other parks but because they crystallize and augment the best qualities of all of them. Above all, each of the four parks elaborates, in a different way, an expression of the first criterion of the urban baseball park, that it be a frame for a drama in the living tissue of the city. Fenway Park is squeezed onto a rhomboid-shaped plot, wedged between railroad tracks, warehouses, garages, and factories, but only blocks from the Victorian gentility of Boston's Back Bay brownstones (fig. 2.1). The field is all odd reentrant angles, corners, and skewed asymmetries. Dominating all is the massive wall, the Green Monster, looming over the shallow meadow of left field. This inviting target, so tempting to right-handed hitters and so intimidating to left-handed pitchers, has for decades determined the team-building strategy of the

FIG. 2.1. Fenway Park, Boston.

Red Sox. The low, deep stands do not so much surround the field as wrap it in an embrace, so that the play on the field, rather than being a distant spectacle, seems more like the enactment of a Sophoclean tragedy in a Greek theater (at least to generations of Boston fans).

Approached from nearby Kenmore Square, Fenway is seen to belong to a baseball precinct, surrounded by saloons, shouting food vendors and hawkers of souvenirs, fans streaming from all directions. An anticipatory air animates the streets. The park, so tightly hemmed in by other buildings that it cannot, from without, be seen but in fragments, retreats almost demurely into the urban fabric. It presents itself as a low brick building of discreet Edwardian decoration, scarcely distinguishable (but for its light towers) from its industrial neighbors. One enters into the dark hollow under the stands and climbs the ramps toward a revelation. Then the preternaturally green field leaps at one like a diagram of the baseball Eden: the pre-Fall green of perfect harmony in a decidedly post-Edenic landscape. The space within is charged with the juxtaposed intensity of its angular enclosure, like an Italian piazza. Beyond the sloping triangular slab of bleachers in right field is a blocky insurance company skyline: hard Yankee calculation and the poetics of baseball are conjoined in a peculiarly American visual prose. Baseball was played here while the Habsburgs still waltzed in Vienna.

Shibe Park, scene of Connie Mack's early dynastic years (and later dismal ones) with the Philadelphia Athletics, was the first of its generation of parks to be built, in 1909 (fig. 2.2). It was, before Yankee Stadium opened, the most architecturally ambitious of them all. Occupying a square block, it was literally boxlike. Its main grandstand, which wrapped around the diamond in a right angle, had a dignified but lively facade derived from Georgian and French Renaissance models, with a rusticated ground floor, stringcourses, an arcaded upper floor supported on Corinthian columns, cornices, and dormers emerging from a mansard roof. At the corner behind home plate rose a turret surmounted by a cupola, in which Connie Mack had his offices.

No other ballpark expressed, with such respectful sophistication, its place in the architectural heritage of its city. The elaborate facade asserted that baseball was not only diversion but history and culture as well. Later extensions of the grandstands were architecturally undistinguished, but they increased the dramatic compression of the playing field by surrounding it on three sides with tall, double-decked banks of seats. On the fourth side, just over the right-field wall, lay the modest rowhouse cityscape of domestic Philadelphia, laundry drying on lines. (People in those houses could watch the games from their parlor windows or from the roofs, until Connie Mack, ever penurious, caused a taller fence to be erected in 1935, blocking their view.) Typical of these parks, built during the dead-ball era of speed, singles, and strategy, were the prairielike vastnesses of the outfields, which extended to the fences set at the limits of the plot. As increased attendance permitted the building of outfield stands (and the advent of the lively ball era dictated a power-hitting style of baseball), these plains shrank as the fences were moved inward.

In its latter years, Shibe Park (by then renamed Connie Mack Stadium) was marooned in an urban slum, a place from which all who could leave, had; and, like its neighborhood, was unloved and unkempt. The Athletics, and then the Phillies, could leave, however, and did. Weeds grew in its fields, as weeds had grown, in another time, in the streets of Rome. But Shibe Park, home of some of the best (and more often, worst) baseball teams of the century, belonged to the gritty texture of the city as a later stadium could not. It was once a superb frame for the drama of suffering without redemption endured by the fans of Philadelphia.

FIG. 2.2. Shibe Park, Philadelphia.

Brooklyn's Ebbets Field, built by Charley Ebbets in 1913, was not the largest, grandest, or most advanced of the new wave of steel and concrete ballparks. But it was the most nearly perfect stadium for baseball ever built (fig. 2.3). Like Shibe Park, it had a consciously "architectural" facade, with colonnades, arched fanlights, and pillars supporting Corinthian capitals. What distinguished Ebbets Field was not its formal design but the way it seemed to bring within its confines all the jumbled complexity and cacophonous vitality of domestic, parochial, immigrant Brooklyn. The double-decked stands, as tightly built as tenements, wrapped so closely around the foul lines that the visual and emotional distance between players and spectators was practically dissolved. The stands formed a perfectly realized three-sided box, containing and reflecting back to the field the intensity of the game, concentrating and magnifying the joy and anguish of the fans, binding those on the field and those in the stands in a mutually energizing ritual of hope, hope realized, and hope denied. The fourth side of the box opened onto the domestic landscape of walkup flats and modest brownstones, of brick shopfronts whose proprietors lived in the rooms above.

There was an unbroken continuum between the noisy domesticity

FIG. 2.3. Ebbets Field, Brooklyn.

FIG. 2.4. Ebbets Field, May 8, 1942. Flag-raising ceremony with sailors from the Brooklyn shipyards.

beyond the fence and the sport within. The famous Abe Stark haberdashery sign at the base of the scoreboard—"Hit Sign Win Suit"—was an
emblem both of Brooklyn's rising immigrant classes and of the common social matrix of fans and players. Such a sign in a major league park
is unimaginable today. The field itself, with its dozens of odd angles and
consequent unpredictable caroming of batted balls, presented the spectacle of benign idiosyncrasy and creative disorderliness which stood, in
the popular mind, for Brooklyn itself. (The Brooklyn club often played
as if inspired by such a metaphor.)

If the Manhattan skyline bristled with the icons of the imperial
capital, Brooklyn was its complement, the paradigm of home—the new
urban American home, which spoke many languages but found a common focus of identity in the democratic myths and loyalties of baseball.
To millions across the country, Ebbets Field seemed the distilled essence of Brooklyn: home as a passionately occupied urban turf (fig. 2.4).
It was home to its baseball club as no other park has ever been; its
slightly shabby gentility and cramped angularity offered a semiotic key
to the whole sprawled web of its neighborhoods. Then it ended. The
moment in American history that made a mythic "Brooklyn," poised in
stasis between parochial rootedness and cosmopolitan ambition, was
undone by the car, by the children's second-generation impatience, by
the house out on the Island: by success.

When the Dodgers left Brooklyn, it confirmed rather than presaged
the end of one social epoch in American life and the beginning of
another. Sentiment and the picaresque imagination could not alter the
hard streets of Flatbush, nor the equally hard imperatives of business.
When Ebbets Field fell to the wrecking ball, a wound was opened in the
body of the borough, and collective memory was weighted with rue. As
if struck from the earth by a natural catastrophe, Brooklyn vanished
from the national consciousness.

When Yankee Stadium opened in 1923, it offered a fitting culmination to the new generation of ballparks. In its size, in the ambitious
scope of its master plan (never fully realized), in the coherence of its
decorative scheme, in the sheer mass of its external walls, it was the
first of these structures to transcend the building idiom out of which it
had come. Anticipating the new era of sports which was arriving, it was
a "stadium," not a "ballpark" (fig. 2.5). Gone were all references to a
sentimentalized American past in the form of a simplified Georgian or
stripped Federalist style. Instead, the enormous concrete facades were
rendered in an austere neo-Roman imperial vocabulary, thus announcing the Augustan era of professional sports. (If this style had a supporting

FIG. 2.5. Yankee Stadium, 1964, before renovation.

ideology, it would be called proto-fascist.) Inside, the curving, triple-tiered grandstand rose as majestically as did the lower Manhattan skyline. It was surmounted by a broad roof that captured and compressed the rising drama of the game and the crowd. The famous rhythmic scrollwork on the roof facade became, like those same skyscrapers, an icon of the Big Time. Yankee Stadium exploded the previous parameters for ballparks, just as the concentration of wealth, talent, and ambition in Manhattan had defined the possibilities of the American city. The scene was set for baseball to be played in a new way, by a new kind of player. The players were watched by ever greater numbers of fans, who were themselves learning to become new men and women, prodded by the promise of more money, easier money, faster money, and by the first suggestions that fame was immortality. The figure of the modern super-star was born in Yankee Stadium.

Babe Ruth was not the first player to dominate the game on the field. Honus Wagner and Ty Cobb had been even more accomplished players, masters of every phase of the game. But Ruth's prodigious home runs, changing the course of a game in an instant, caught the imagination of a country looking for quick thrills and awakened to the pleasures of immediate gratification. Ruth's larger-than-life presence, his gargantuan appetites, and his manchild ingenuousness were seized upon avidly by a popular press formulating the lucrative mechanisms of star making and star worship. With Ruth the omnipresent force of herculean personality was introduced into American life. The building of Yankee Stadium, in what was then America's only capital of mass publicity and opinion formation, was, among other lines of force, a speculation on the value of celebrity. The short right-field foul line with the inviting, incurving stands was certainly an accommodation to the Ruthian power imperative, as well as a determinant of future Yankee team-building strategy. But it was also a fortuitous circumstance of ground plot which imposed a lozenge-shaped stadium, with a short right field and steppe-like left and center fields. (The field could hardly have been oriented otherwise without putting the afternoon sun in the batter's eyes.)

The Yankees' dynastic domination of baseball over the next forty years and their subsequent decline (the 1980s marked their first decade without a pennant) parallel the rise of New York to a position of hegemony over the image- and symbol-life of Americans and the noisy spectacle of its imperial decay. Yankee Stadium was, although not the most beloved baseball stadium in America (who can love Caesar?), certainly the most famous. Through the 1950s, the World Series was annually broadcast from there, as if dictated by some law of natural inevitability; its corners and great, sloping planes, the autumnal shadows creeping across the grass to announce the death of the year, were impressed on the national memory; they belonged to all of us. (The stadium was rebuilt in the 1970s. In its new form it works better as a "facility" but is inferior as a "place"; the new design lacks the haughty conviction of the old, its presumptuous boldness, its iconographic authority. It looks more like a corporate headquarters now, which, in a sense, it is.)

In the waning light of New York's golden age of baseball, in the middle of the century, Yankee Stadium and the Polo Grounds confronted each other like two baronial castles from their respective domains on either side of the East River. If the Polo Grounds was the preferred rendezvous of the swells, nabobs, and clubmen of New York's "old" (post–Civil War) monied classes, Yankee Stadium was the place to be seen for the aggressive, go-getter managerial class that rose in the wake of World War I. One could not, as a matter of social or aesthetic coherence, feel equally at home in both parks, nor root for both teams. With the departure of the Dodgers and the Giants for California, the

Yankees won the demographic battle for control of the New York market, just as their fans, most representative of the new corporate elite, won the struggle for the future of New York's economy from the old entrepreneurial-manufacturing class, which supported the Giants, and from the Dodgers' working-class fans (quickly being subsumed into an expanding and suburbanizing middle class).

Then, as always, baseball was a distinct cultural world that intersected with the other cultural worlds and forces of American life. Ballparks are not neutral places but are charged with all the dense sociological realities of the cities from which they grow. (The instant popularity of the picaresque-populist Mets may be understood as the social channeling of class conflict; they inherited both their colors and their fan base from the Giants and the Dodgers. The Mets' two raucous and tragicomic years at the Polo Grounds evoked the zany Brooklyn clubs—and fans—of the 1930s. But the day of picturesque and lovable ineptitude is probably as vanished as Ebbets Field; losing in the '80s became just plain ugly, as sports skated on an ever-deeper reservoir of angst.)

With the elevation of baseball players to the role of celebrities, the objects of attention, curiosity, and envy which transcend their performance on the field, a subtle psychological barrier began to distance fans from players. Ballplayers became increasingly remote as human figures even as their private lives and personalities were being probed and magnified by the mass press. The ritual of the pregame autograph signing, in which adoration is exchanged for the surrogate imprint of fame, replaces the easy banter possible between those who live on the same psychological plane of dailiness. There is no more easy mingling at the edge of the field, but rather a formal segregation between participants and spectators, enforced by ushers and guards (enforced by awe in the face of celebrity). The corollary of such exposure to the implacable glare of publicity is the need for privacy, the need to shield at least the person, if not the psyche. Thus the dugout withdrew down and under the stands, offering a respite from the intrusive gaze of a worshiping though abusive public; thus the clubhouse became a hidden inner sanctum, impenetrable to all save the priesthood of the sporting press. (Television, which relentlessly posits personality at the heart of all processes, now penetrates into the dugout, however, to show us the ruminations and chagrin of the ballplayers in their trials; nobody can say no to the imperatives of the omnivorous video eye.)

Inseparable from (and contemporary with) this phenomenon is the appearance of a distinct press section in the ballpark. As late as 1913

Charley Ebbets might simply forget to build one in his new park, but by the 1930s all major league parks had a press box, whose size and central location above the field reflect the mutual dependence of baseball and the mass press. The increasing segregation of the journalistic caste from the general public is revealing; it announced the rise of a reality-interpreting and opinion-forming elite, who filter the action on (and off) the field through the prisms of fame and personality. The professional sporting press formed a kind of secular priesthood, interceding between the profane public and players increasingly isolated from it by the aura of celebrity. The press box, then, is a separate, priestly precinct, entry into which is denied the uninitiated.

The evolution of advertising signs in ballparks also reveals the economic and material changes in American life. The first such signs appeared in ballparks (and on the walls of adjacent buildings) by the turn of the century. Their intended audience being mostly working-class men, they featured whiskey, beer, ready-made clothes, and tobacco: most men still rolled their own cigarettes. Significantly absent were razor blades. Men, if not bearded, were still shaved by a barber. Nor were banks advertised; the bank account remained a defining middle-class attainment. The new industries of mass-produced packaged food and cleaning products were not yet advertised in ballparks, since they belonged (and still belong) to a woman's realm of concern; and women were little in evidence. The products were all locally produced and so, although generically similar, differed in name from city to city.

By the 1940s, the signs would reflect both the dramatically increased presence of women in ballparks and the spread of a nationwide, homogeneous consumer culture. The whiskey and beer signs (and, now, those for razor blades) remained, but they promoted, increasingly, national brands. There now appeared signs for household products, bottled sodas, and packaged bread. A familiar process, the consolidation of productive mechanisms into fewer and larger units, was already evident. Even in the ballpark Americans were learning to be more disciplined and discerning consumers, to demand and purchase "brand names." Ballparks, even before World War II, were no longer a domain of rough male retreat. As sexual roles converged (both in the marketplace and at home), and the ideal of family "togetherness" was formulated, they moved toward becoming more genteel and gender-neutral places, suitable for the entire family. (Brooklyn's most celebratedly vociferous fan, armed with cowbell, was one Hilda Chester.)

The construction of Yankee Stadium in 1923 closed a fifteen-year cycle of new ballpark building. No ballparks were to be built, nor franchises moved, for the next thirty years. (Cleveland Stadium, a 1931 public works project, was a multipurpose park used irregularly for baseball until 1946.) Through the vicissitudes of the Depression and World War II, baseball endured a period of uneven prosperity but remarkable stability. The dynamic historical mechanisms of economic success, propelling an upward and outward dispersal of urban-core populations, were blocked first by the capital shortage of the thirties and then by the housing shortage of the war years. The effect, at least in the older industrial cities, was an atypical—in American experience—continuity of generations. For baseball, this meant a stable fan base. One might argue that this period, with its relative absence of horizontal movement of players between teams (but great vertical movement between major and minor leagues), and its continuous and deepening identities linking teams, ballparks, cities, and succeeding generations of fans, represented the fullest flowering of the culture of baseball.

Ballparks changed little in this period, although management continued the practice of moving outfield fences in or out to optimize the strengths (or ameliorate the weaknesses) of their own teams. Seating capacity was increased by increments, according to no master plan (except at Yankee Stadium) but rather as finances and attendance permitted. Some of the parks, most notably Shibe Park, Forbes Field in Pittsburgh, and Washington's Griffith Stadium, had the rambling quality of an old house with its mixed assemblage of rooms added over the years and the generations. This idiosyncratic ad hoc style, those who grew attached to them would argue, only increased their charm, their individualistic, homelike domesticity.

The only major technological change during this period was the installation of lights for night baseball. Between the first night game, in Cincinnati in 1935, and Detroit's first game under the arc lights, in 1948, all the major league parks except Wrigley Field were provided with lights. When the Cubs finally surrendered to night baseball in 1988, it was less a response to local demand than a capitulation to the imperatives of the television networks, which demand that playoff games be televised during the prime time evening hours. By the 1980s, the fat revenue tail of television increasingly wagged the cash-squeezed body of baseball. Night baseball began as an expedient, since it both attracted working fans who could not attend weekday games and spared the players the fatigue of playing daily under the midsummer sun. It arguably changed the nature of the game on the field, giving the pitcher a new advantage. (Some batters contradict this, insisting they see the ball better under the lights.) It also altered the sensual experience of watching the game, as the glowing green ballpark, charged with the dramatic spectacle of gleaming light, receded visually from the darkened city outside, presenting itself as a splendid green island in a dark urban sea. The tall light towers and the glare from within at night made the ballparks even more prominent urban landmarks, visible for miles around. Lights were the first, and most benign, technological change aimed at overcoming the limits imposed on baseball by nature itself.

Change

As had happened after both the Civil War and World War I, the end of World War II liberated powerful waves of social energy, ambition, and appetites which had been pent up for a generation. The demographic shifts produced by these waves were to sweep away the settled urban population patterns of the previous thirty years, unleash a movement from the center outward, and create a new social form in American life, the suburb. Baseball, always dependent on proximity to its fan base, could only follow the flow of the middle class out of the old neighborhoods and out of the old ballparks.

By the early 1950s, many of the classic ballparks were almost forty years old and aging fast. The once-respectable working-class neighborhoods in which they were built had begun to decay, both physically and socially. Their residents, riding the postwar wave of prosperity and hungry for space, quiet, and an identity less defined by ethnicity and social origin, abandoned them for the new rings of detached-home suburbs. (The lower-class black communities that filled these neighborhoods are best understood as a result rather than a cause of this centrifugal flight; inner-city housing stock passes from the latest successfully integrated group to the ones below it.)

These suburbs were organized, both socially and economically, around the mobility afforded by the private automobile. To a generation blocked in its ambitions by depression and war, and which found its freedom in such physical mobility, a house and a car were marks of one's entry into the psychological middle class. Having left the cramped inner city, such fans were reluctant to return to the rusting ballparks squeezed among streets that now seemed alien and hostile, especially since these late trolley-era parks offered little parking.

The Boston Braves, always a marginal franchise, were the first club to read the demographic handwriting on the wall. Faced with a declining inner-city fan base, a small, aging ballpark on a crowded site hemmed in on all sides, and the competition of the successful Red Sox, the Braves disturbed a half century of baseball stability by moving to Milwaukee before the 1953 season. There, in their first season, they drew almost seven times as many fans as they had the previous year. In the next five years, for analogous reasons, four other clubs were to abandon their crowded two- or three-team markets for other cities eager for major league baseball and willing to pay for it. Thus the Saint Louis Browns—a perennial poor sister to the Cardinals—moved to Baltimore, which had been a charter member of the American League. The next year, the Philadelphia Athletics moved to Kansas City, to a stadium built in only three months; for the next thirteen years, they functioned as a kind of vassal state during the years of the Yankees' imperial reign in the American League. Then, in 1957, the cataclysm (at least for New Yorkers): both the Giants and the Dodgers, two pillars of the National League, left for California. The Boeing 707 had made a coast-to-coast baseball league possible; the new markets made it inevitable.

Milwaukee County Stadium was the first of the ballparks built for the transferred franchises. It was the first publicly financed major league stadium designed expressly for baseball. It represented a transitional design, both traditional in its form and evolved in its context. It was a thoroughly modern steel and concrete structure that differed, however, in no essential elements from the ballparks built in the teens and twenties. But the relationship between the park and its surroundings was dramatically different. Where the parks of the classic period were set into a tight urban fabric and were served primarily by public transport or reached on foot, the new stadiums (in their size, regularity, and industrial finish—in their machine aesthetic—they can only be called stadiums) are set on, not in, an exploded suburban landscape of parking lots, expressways, commercial strips, and low-density sprawl. Milwaukee's stadium is an object removed from its familiar context and placed in a new setting, one defined by speed, mobility, an expansive horizontality, and a consequent air of dissociation from the old urban matrix.

If Americans tend increasingly to define themselves by where and how they go rather than by where they dwell, County Stadium acknowledges and ratifies this new locus of identity by its placement at the conjunction of expressways. The outside of the park is no longer experienced as a series of facades emerging from among other facades as one approaches along the urban network of streets. Instead, the new stadium is a plastic object seen in space and surrounded by space, revealed all at once in its entirety. While it is the locus of movement

from all sides, it bears only the most tenuous relationship to its surrounding environment, like a Gothic cathedral in a beanfield. If the
crowded inner city imposed a (sometimes stifling) organic unity geographically linking one's work life, family life, social life, and diversions, the new ballpark temples rising out on the blank edge of town
expressed the growing (and deliberately sought-after) separation of life's
parts into noncommunicating rooms. In the new model of social and
psychological freedom, one chooses pastimes according to personal
tastes rather than geographic, class, or ethnic affinities. (Such are the
people who move restlessly through John Cheever's and John Updike's
towns.) Baseball was finding a prosperous new audience, one with more
money and free time, though one whose loyalties were also more mobile. At the same time major league baseball was expanding its audience nationwide, it was beginning to present itself as but one choice
of pastime in a burgeoning industry devoted to creating and satisfying
the appetite for a new category of experience, freed from history, from
memory itself: for "entertainment," for "leisure," for prearranged "fun."

Like shopping malls, linear strip development, and freeways, the
new detached baseball stadiums contained the unresolved tensions of
postwar American urbanism: How could the centripetal and compres-
sive forces essential to true urbanity be reconciled with the centrifugal
forces unleashed by private, mass auto-mobility? (They could not.) The
seemingly irresistible imperatives of Corbusian exploded space, a re-
ductionist fascination with Bauhaus-inspired "pure" forms (purity is
always a resonant idea in the American psyche), and the seductive call
of convenience (defined as short-term utility) found a broad consensus,
or at least a passive assent, among many Americans. All older urban
forms and models that seemed to restrict or impede the flow toward a
more perfectly realized freedom were attacked by the forces of (cleans-
ing) progress. Dense, finely textured old neighborhoods were razed
because they were "blighted." Old ballparks were abandoned because
they were deemed obsolete, deficient in convenience.

Of the postwar stadiums, only those in San Diego (1968), Kansas
City (1973), and the monstrously scaled Olympique in Montreal (1977),
have realized in the design of their facades the sculptural possibilities
inherent in reinforced concrete. But all have been conceived as free-
standing objects which (like the newer high-rises) either disregard their
urban context or, if they are set on the low-density metropolitan periphery, are themselves the principal iconographic context.

Arlington Stadium (1965), first and most truly named Turnpike
Stadium, lay adjacent to the freeway connecting Dallas and Fort Worth,

FIG. 2.6. Arlington Stadium, between Fort Worth and Dallas, Texas.

midway between them. Its location thus reflected a reality more statistical than historical (fig. 2.6). Nearby, not coincidentally, was a large amusement park. From the upper ramps of Anaheim Stadium (1966), one looks out across a surreal late-American landscape of movement, redemption, and mass fun: parking lots, five linked freeways, and three icons of end-of-the-century belief—the 230-foot illuminated A outside the stadium, the concrete Matterhorn at Disneyland, and a televangelist's glass cathedral. Fans arrive at these parks having measured their trip not in subway stops, nor city blocks, nor even miles, but rather in freeway hours. The clubs acknowledge this new spatial reality (and the implausibility of naming a major league team "Arlington" or "Anaheim") by identifying themselves with their potential statewide fan matrix: the Texas Rangers, the California Angels.

Dodger Stadium (1962) was the last privately financed baseball stadium. Its builder, Walter O'Malley, who had led the flight to the West Coast, was among the last of those rulers who had built their empires from within baseball rather than from without. In that city which first and most fully reflected the social and spatial impact of the automobile, Dodger Stadium was the first park not only to acknowledge that fact but to embrace it in its design (fig. 2.7). Perched loftily on its hill above downtown Los Angeles, it is surrounded on three sides by freeways. Its plan brilliantly relates automobile access, circulation, and parking to the stadium, along concentric and radial roads. Approached from one of those roads, it has the cheerful utilitarian neutrality and car-bound familiarity of a shopping mall, an effect that, oddly, dedramatizes its impressive mass and flattens its iconographic impact and relates it ironically to the sprawl through which fans have just driven. It is in the city but detached visually and spatially from it; one might walk there from, say, the plaza in the old town below, but only with difficulty and some danger. Within, all is southern California pastels and bright, optimistic colors, and wide, spotless circulation promenades. It offers a domesticated and feminized environment, a place to bring a family. The fans are orderly, good-natured, and polite, a bit distracted rather than fully and passionately engaged (there is, after all, always the beach) and apt to leave early to beat the traffic. Beyond the bleachers and the parking lots are those improbable movieland palm trees and hills of scrubby chaparral. It is, in its own way, eloquently expressive of the cultural matrix from which it grew, deeply rooted in a landscape of rootlessness and movement.

Its six sweeping levels of cantilevered seats wrap closely around the field, which, like those in almost all new parks, is symmetrical in its dimensions. Freed from the vagaries of cramped urban plots, fields now conform to a kind of Platonic universality, uniform across the entire grid of a homogenizing America. The high wall of the grandstands (only Yankee Stadium seems as vertical) thrillingly fulfills the first criterion of good ballpark design, that it focus and contain the drama of the game. Like the stadiums in Milwaukee and San Francisco (1960), Dodger Stadium includes a mezzanine level of private boxes (and a glass-walled stadium club), now deemed essential in all stadiums. These boxes exist to display the rise of a corporate managerial class which claims among its privileges that of privacy in public, the prerogative of watching without being watched, in turn, by an undifferentiated mass. (A mobile form of this is the dark-windowed limousine.) These boxes are located on the same level as the press; the design of the stadium thus objectifies a new nexus of power and influence in American life. But Dodger Stadium made another contribution to the semiotics of ballparks, one that reflects a particularly southern California culture based on celebrity and its corollary, separation from the mundane. Its innovation was a section of seats level with, and between, the two dugouts. These seats are, of course, frequented mostly by "stars," upon whom, as upon ballplayers, is conferred the kind of transient transcendence due those whose images are magnified elec-

FIG. 2.7. Dodger Stadium, Los Angeles.

tronically beyond ours. The hardening of class lines evident in the seating segregation at Dodger Stadium is less one of pure economics than it is a hierarchical barrier separating those who make and manage images and those who can only consume them.

Dodger Stadium was among the last built in the traditional (albeit highly elaborated) form, designed for baseball only. Colt Stadium in Houston (1962), Parc Jarry in Montreal (1967), and Toronto's Exhibition Stadium (1977) were conventional in their forms, but they were built as temporary structures and were later replaced by domed stadiums. Royals Stadium in Kansas City, opened in 1973, was the last baseball-only stadium of its generation (the adjacent and contemporary Arrowhead Stadium is for football). It is notable both for the dramatic cantilevering of its crescent-shaped upper deck (a striking display of the structural possibilities of stressed concrete) and the computerized waterfall beyond the outfield walls, a visual non sequitur suggesting that its designers had in mind a theme park instead of a baseball park.

The American 1960s will be remembered for the last flowering of unquestioning confidence in a technocratic-bureaucratic vision of the future and for the erosion and collapse of many established social forms of authority. The American landscape was transformed by both of these forces, which paradoxically complement each other. The periphery of all American cities rolled ineluctably outward, laying down in its wake a uniform carpet of expressways, shopping malls, clustered pseudo-Miesian office blocks, and wide commercial corridors separating nostalgically named subdivisions with curving streets. Here was the concretization of dwellings based on speed, mobility, the substitution of bonds of interest and choice for those of ethnicity and family, and the discrete separation of activities and generations. In this context, it is not surprising that the stadiums built during this period departed so radically from the previous design idiom.

Between 1962 and 1971, ten new "superstadiums" were built.[1] All were publicly financed and were built to attract or to keep a major league franchise. All were built of concrete and steel; were (except for San Diego's) round instead of boxy; were capable of holding at least forty-five thousand spectators; were (but for three) bowls, closed to the outside; were intended to accommodate professional football as well as baseball; were regionally (rather than city-) oriented, built adjacent to expressways and parking lots. They were, together with the gleaming downtown towers of the techno-managerial elite, the new icons of the Big Time, indispensable symbols for any city that aspired to be, or to remain, big league.

These superstadiums were successful in realizing their purpose. Old franchises were revitalized, new franchises flourished, and a new generation of fans was attracted to the bright, clean, spacious ballparks. The game played in these new stadiums, however, was different in both its content and its context.

Plastic turf was developed as an expedient for the Astrodome, when it was discovered that natural grass could not survive in its sunless interior. The artificial turf was quickly adopted in five other stadiums (now it is used in nine of them—Kansas City, which had installed it, in 1995 became the first club to return to natural grass) for the putative advantages it offered. First, though it is initially more expensive to install, it is far cheaper to maintain, requiring neither watering nor cutting and not needing frequent replacement. Then, it is so durable that football can be played on it, even in the rain, without tearing it up (although this durability exacts a price in abraded skin, bruised muscles, and damaged knees). Also, it drains quickly and can be vacuumed of water, allowing games to be played which otherwise would be canceled. (This is no small advantage, given the enormous fixed costs of baseball clubs now, and the fact that weekend fans may come from within a two-hundred-mile radius.) Last, the plastic turf permits an industrially uniform, and thus more predictable, surface which, according to technocratic criteria, makes it inherently superior to grass. After the installation of lights, this was the next step along a line of increased technological interventions in the game on the field. Turf baseball has produced its own team-building and game strategies, as well as a type of ballplayer characterized by his slap-hitting ability and exceptional speed. (The Saint Louis Cardinals most successfully practiced this strategy in the 1980s, by developing players who could best exploit the characteristics of the turf.)

The round shape of these stadiums is a result of the need to accommodate both baseball and football, sports that have very different spatial requirements. (The multipurpose stadium is, in turn, a reflection of the enormous fiscal burden incurred in building them, and thus the need to maximize their use.) Unfortunately, the round shape is unsympathetic to both sports. In contrast to the old, boxy ballparks, the stands of which were bent tightly around the diamond and the foul lines, in the round superstadiums the bowed arc of the stands carries the fans far back from the field. Further, since a criterion of "modernity" in stadiums is the absence of internal supporting pillars, the upper decks must be cantilevered backward and supported on the outside of the stadium, rather than piled vertically one atop the other, as at Wrigley Field, Comiskey Park, or Tiger Stadium. Thus, from the uppermost seats of these new stadiums, the players' facial features cannot be discerned, without which contact the human link between fans and players can only be generic, not particular. In recognition of this, the players' images are now projected on huge television screens, that the fan might at least distinguish among them.

More than their size or surface textures, however, it is their round bowl form that alters the context in which we perceive them and the game they contain. Seven of the ten superstadiums were closed circles; two earlier stadiums (San Francisco and Anaheim) were expanded into closed ovals; and, of course, the four domed stadiums subsequently built are sealed from the outside. The circle is an inherently stable and absolutist form, admitting of few irregularities, quirks, idiosyncrasies, and circumstantial deviations. Having chosen the form of the container, the builders have little choice in the disposition of the elements within it. This is the source of the often-criticized blandness and indistinguishability of these stadiums, and of the difficulty in mentally reconstructing any one of them from its details. They are, in this respect, absolutely representative of the civic and corporate building ambitions of the 1960s and 1970s, in which "prestige" is identified with a universalizing abandonment of all local, particular, or historically resonant architectural references, in favor of the triumphantly neutral technocratic style.

If they are thus suggestive of other interchangeable, utilitarian places such as airport lounges, motels, and convention halls, that is indeed the intention. They are meant to be judged as "facilities," pragmatically conceived containers of entertainment functions. They are as iconographically neutral in their details as they are iconographically charged in their totality as urban status symbols. Their seamless smoothness, their emphasis on cleanliness and comfort, and the way they frame the sport in a familiar, middle-class ambience of escapist diversion have attracted an audience far wider than the traditional core of baseball fans. But something has been subtly changed in the relationship between the game and the people in the stands. Baseball, which flowered as a profoundly American but ethically and sentimentally distinct subworld, is gradually being subsumed into, and assuming the values of, a homogenized, nationwide entertainment culture. A game in Cincinnati's Riverfront Stadium, for example, simply cannot be experienced (or remembered) in the same way as a game in old Crosley Field, thirty years ago. Between the one and the other is a cultural discontinuity, which the apparent similarity of the game on the field cannot bridge.

In Cincinnati's old ballpark, as in Pittsburgh's or Philadelphia's or Saint Louis's, all of which looked out over the surrounding town landscape, the particularities of a geographical setting and a social-historical process were visually linked to the game on the field. In the new, closed stadiums, the game is separated from the social matrix that supports it, to the mutual impoverishment of both. The division of our American lives into discrete compartments is reinforced; work, shopping, recreation, and the life of the home are separated by space and time in the landscape, and the mind replicates the segregation of functions. The resonance that derives from their interplay is denied; experience is fragmented. In the perfect, closed bowl of the superstadium, baseball is cut off from its cultural context and made to bear the burden of an attention too narrow and too singular. As other ways of connecting to each other become more tenuous, Americans insist that sports bear ever more of the burden of a common identity. Deprived of a visual connective tissue that links it to a particular place and through that to our larger lives, baseball risks a self-referential reduction, risks absorption into a generic culture of electronic fame and envy, at once too large and too trivial.

Baseball is, in its fullest dimension, a garden in which grow memories and metaphors. The best baseball parks are those that help us frame these memories in the larger picture of our individual and collective lives. The American conceit is that we can escape history and its insistent child, memory, and so find a more perfect freedom. The Cartesian absolutism of the closed superstadium, its iconographic blankness, seems to place it in an eternally unfixed present, in a universalized geographical grid, as if any reference to our rootedness in a time and a place were an affront to our claims on immortality. This attraction toward the seductions of perfect abstraction is, of course, a central refrain of late-modern architecture (and of late-modern culture). These enormous, interchangeable sports machines are expressive of certain 1960s aspirations toward civic seriousness. Their suitability as frames for a baseball game is secondary to their status as emblems of ambition. The mental landscape to which they properly belong is not that of their respective cities but that of the nationwide television grid. They were built to be seen in the atomized fragments of reality that the screen presents to us.

The first domed stadium was built in 1965 in Houston, a city whose ferocious heat and voracious mosquitoes made even night baseball problematic for both players and fans. The Astrodome announced Houston's intention to shed its rough, cowtown image (its team had initially been called the Colt 45s) in favor of a high-technology future. In the contemporary process of city making, a domed stadium and a major league tenant are the quickest means of establishing a city's credentials as a player in the high-stakes competition for corporate headquarters buildings and the managerial elite to fill them. Four other teams have occupied domed stadiums, in Seattle, Montreal, Minneapolis, and Toronto, all cities with ambitions toward international recognition but marginal climates for baseball. Other domes have been built in New Orleans, Indianapolis, Vancouver, and Tampa, in hopes of eventually attracting a franchise.

The plastic turf devised to replace the withered grass under the opaque roof of the Astrodome has been placed in all subsequent domed stadiums. To the changes brought to the game by this innovation must be added two others peculiar to the domed stadiums. While before the vertical dimension of the playing field was infinite, now it is finite, and reachable. Batted balls have struck the roofs of these stadiums, or objects suspended therefrom, altering both the flight of the ball and the outcome of the game. Finally, the sophisticated air-conditioning equipment allows management to vary the air pressure inside the dome and thus manipulate the weather, so to speak, to its own advantage. At least in the microclimate of the domed stadium, the ancient dream of controlling the heavens and turning the winds has been realized.

Domed stadiums are the latest—though not necessarily the last—development along a line of increasing technological intervention in, and control over, the natural environment in sports. If arc lights have permitted baseball to overcome the limitations imposed by the solar day, and plastic turf has eliminated the irregularities and vulnerabilities of living grass, then covered stadiums have removed sports from the rhythms of the solar year, from the flow and flux of the seasons. One also senses an environmental dislocation, as when entering into the Kingdome from a crystalline evening, with Mount Rainier floating above Seattle; going inside to a ball game, under hundreds of tons of concrete roof; air and light and sound seem bent to a different rule, as though flattened into two-dimensionality.

The closed superstadiums removed the game from its social and historical frames of reference, removed play from its connection to the rest of our lives. Domes remove sport from every other context save its own, begging the question, To what end all this? The hermetically sealed sports capsule turns the game back only on itself, blocking the mind's reach through sun and shadow, wind and moonrise, toward memory and metaphor. Even when built in the heart of the city, it turns blank, inarticulate walls to the life around it. Seen from without, it resembles nothing so much as a bunker; it does not inspire joy or turn the mind toward idle thoughts of play, or inspire any idle thoughts at all.

Baseball, like all deliberate systems, tends toward ever-greater regularity, rationality, and predictability. In the business of major league baseball, competing for dollars in a highly articulated market for entertainment and burdened with ever-increasing (albeit self-imposed) fixed costs, there is little room for unpredictabilities like snow or rainouts. Domed stadiums are as much monuments to bottom-line corporate prudence as they are to modern technohubris. Given the doctrine of material progress shared implicitly—until recently—by most North Americans, when domed stadiums became possible they became inevitable. But domed stadiums are enormously expensive machines that depend for their operation on cheap, abundant energy; they are the products of a policy of cheap energy at any cost. If the world oil supply should begin to contract or be disrupted, domed stadiums could become economically unviable, empty cathedrals for a dying secular faith in unlimited petropower.

Toronto's Skydome, opened in midseason 1989, proved such an attraction that the club immediately established a new league attendance record. The Skydome resolved the dilemma posed by earlier domed stadiums: How to play outdoors when the weather permitted. The solution presents itself as a giant, articulated eggshell, whose segments fold back upon themselves along one side of the stadium. What results is more akin to a drum with a large hole in the top than to a truly open stadium, much less one that opens to the surrounding city landscape. Nevertheless, in a city with a long, harsh winter, the design admits the play of sun and shadow across the plastic field. Toronto's planners, correctly perceiving the iconographic importance of the massive white stadium in the city's skyline, have placed it near the lakeside and the city center. They effectively linked the stadium to Toronto's fine transit system, making the Skydome the first postwar stadium not oriented primarily toward the automobile. The dome and the CN Tower—the world's tallest—proudly resonate against each other, the secular capitalist equivalent of the cupolas and towers of the Italian city-state. Given both the aesthetic opposition of many fans to indoor baseball and the decreasing utility of car-oriented urban solutions, Toronto's successful project may indicate the direction of the next generation of stadiums, at least those in extreme climates.

The Skydome cost more than $350 million to build, and the expense imposed certain necessities on the design. Since sports alone could never generate enough revenue to amortize the debt, the building was from the beginning a multipurpose commercial center, containing many kinds of activities and open every day. It has restaurants and bars, private corporate suites for entertaining clients, cinemas, a video-game salon, and a first-class hotel, many rooms of which overlook the field. Ticket and concession prices are accordingly so high that one ballplayer imagined a father posing this question to his family: "Shall we go to the ball game or go to Europe?" One mistakenly thinks of this as a ballpark. In truth it is thematically akin to a shopping center, in which baseball is the "anchor" attraction. It belongs to an emerging genre of middle-class shopping and entertainment enclaves, in which a number of family-oriented consumer activities are organized under a common roof. The Skydome recognizes (and by investing in them, ratifies) certain realities of the late-century North American city: the anthropological disappearance of the old working class in the managerial-bureaucratic economy; the hardening of class lines and the resultant clustering of middle-class activities into protected, semipublic zones; and the feminization—or at least gender neutralization—of previously "male" spaces as women's and men's roles converge at work and at home.

Finally, the Skydome confirms the rise of the imperial and universalizing entertainment culture, which posits no hierarchy of cultural values but offers an unlimited horizontal choice of "leisure options." The corollary of such flattening is that all choices—a movie, a video game, a baseball game—are equal and neutral, attached to no history or values external to themselves, subject only to the criterion of diversion, of "fun." The massification of culture may be inherently democratic— we all have access to the same cultural products—but in a culture, as in architecture, the price of such universality is in the loss of particularity, in the loss of memory. Surrounded by the opulence of the Skydome, the player on the field is paradoxically reduced in stature. He is, after all, only a man; the real protagonist is the technological marvel in which he plays.

Scoreboards were originally a simple, linear space on the outfield walls, where the inning by inning progress of the game might be recorded. Now they are springs of electronic information, from which flows the sea of raw data on which baseball floats. Adjacent to the scoreboard is usually a computerized message board, which is used to inform ("Rocky is 24 for 49 this month"), to announce ("Happy Birthday, Janie Jones"), to sell ("Souvenirs available now!"), and to exhort ("CHEER: LOUDER"). A public trained to equate information and knowledge, and disciplined to grant authority to words that issue from a screen, must perforce regard these flashing lights as an enrichment of the game, rather as an intrusion into it.

The importance of this new information flow in framing and interpreting the game is most fully expressed in Kansas City's Royals Stadium. There the scoreboard rises beyond center field like an enormous kitsch totem, surmounted by a crown and surrounded by waterfalls; it is the dominant element in the ballpark. A poignant photograph from the Astrodome, taken in the mid-1960s, depicts a watershed moment in the cultural history of baseball: an Astros batter, having just hit a home run, is crossing home plate, but the backs of both players and fans are turned to him; all gaze instead at the animated cartoon images dancing on the center-field message board. In Oakland, the most unreserved partisan cheering is reserved for the dot racing, in which computer-generated dots chase each other around an oval course (prompting a variation on the old hockey joke: I went to an entertainment and a ball game broke out).

With almost poetic symmetry, the first giant television screens in baseball stadiums made their appearance in the two polar capitals of the image culture, Los Angeles and New York. (They have since been adopted in most other parks. When a technology becomes possible, it becomes inevitable.) Baseball executives realized that the best way to neutralize television as a competitor for the attention of the fans was to co-opt its virtues of intimacy and immediacy to their own uses. The immediate effect was to furnish the fans in the stadium with the same kinds of images available to viewers at home: close-ups, instant replays, slow-motion shots. This had the charm of restoring visual (and emotional) proximity and a human dimension to the fan's experience, and so mitigating, in part, the size and impersonality of the stadiums. Television also allowed fans to savor the startling balletic grace of a fine play and to understand the dynamics of the game from various perspectives.

As the sophistication of the television operators increased, and the demographic profile of the fans changed toward younger people raised on televised sports, the use of the screens was expanded in order to make the experience in the stadium more like that of watching a game on television. Since the idea persists among casual fans that baseball, with its pauses and intermittent rhythms, is "boring," management vied for the attention of this wider audience by filling in the empty spaces between the concentrated bursts of action with televised fillers. So, prepackaged baseball programs fill the long, slow hour of batting and infield practice. Important games in other cities are screened via satellite hookup. The interval between innings is filled with replayed highlights and—another breakthrough in the cultural history of baseball—commercials, all accompanied by rock music. Finally, as if in fulfillment of the Warholean prophecy, the camera is turned on the fans themselves, who obediently perform in their brief limelight. When the game resumes, it seems a respite from the acceleration of the televised images, but lumpy and amorphous by comparison.

Televised sports changed forever our perception of the game on the field, fragmenting it into the images that could be contained sequentially on a screen. Television changed, too, the relationship between fans and players, making the latter at once larger than life and, paradoxically, more ephemeral, more vulnerable in their person. Now it has altered our experience of the stadium, by eroding the unity of time and space by which we locate ourselves and determine "reality." If the effect of previous technological interventions upon the game of baseball has been to dislocate the game on the field from the rhythm of the days and the seasons, and from the crossed lines of our collective history, the effect of television is to dislocate us from the moment itself. I have often seen a crowd withhold its applause after an exceptional play until it has consulted the televised replay; this sequence surely describes a unique epistemological reversal in the history of human consciousness. But the way was prepared for it in the larger society, in which we now depend on television to confirm the existence or importance of events: it's not real until it happens on TV.

The temporal rhythm of baseball is looping, elliptical, nominally linear but nonuniform, always expanding and contracting. It doesn't follow secular time but is a kind of patterned meandering, impelled forward only by the internal logic of events on the field. But television brings into the ballpark the implacable urgency of its own logic, which is that of "entertainment," continuously discontinuous, all meaning fragmented, a relentlessly compressed linear juxtaposition of images. Television now pays the bills and underwrites the current opulence of the sport. Once introduced into the ballpark, however, it obeys a Mc-Luhanesque imperative, subsuming all that it encompasses into itself, making it *television*. The ballpark, instead of being an autonomous, extraterritorial free zone, with its own temporal laws—that is, the remembered ballpark of our youth—becomes, increasingly, a colonial outpost of the expanding, imperial tele-realm.

Some recent ballpark projects indicate a growing skepticism to ward the premises and promises about the postwar technocratic model of progress. New stadiums built in Chicago (to replace the oldest extant classic stadium, the 1910 Comiskey Park) and Baltimore reject the multipurpose bowl, domes, and plastic turf in favor of the traditional compact, baseball-only configuration, open to the sky, with natural grass. These are, not coincidentally, cities with a long and rooted baseball tradition. It seems probable, however, that some domed stadiums will continue to be built, particularly in places with extreme climates; Toronto's convertible-top dome may provide a model. But the number and the intractability of the social and infrastructural problems faced by all American cities may impose their own limitations on such big projects. Municipal governments, politically and fiscally squeezed, may have to devise regional financing schemes (which reflects a reality: teams are regional assets) or state support in order to build new stadiums. Or there may be a new form of collaborative funding between private, corporate, and public entities.

For those cities whose inner core has lost population and business

FIG. 2.8. Pilot Field, Buffalo.

to the centrifugal force of suburban expansion, a downtown stadium can be an anchor on which to hook redevelopment plans. Fans drawn downtown to a ball game, or workers induced to stay downtown after work will, it is argued, by their presence and the money they spend re-create the kind of lively, varied, and safe downtown life characteristic of pre-1950s America. The success of this strategy depends on the success planners have in weaving the ballpark into a continuous, inviting—and nonthreatening—urban fabric, not in merely creating a friendly destination in the middle of an otherwise hostile or barren environment. This, in turn, means rejecting an exclusively car-oriented plan, with its surrounding acres of sterile and dangerous parking lots, in favor of a compact, pedestrian-scaled scheme. And this, in turn, requires that public transit be close, convenient, and fast enough to offer fans an alternative to their cars.

Buffalo's Pilot Field (1988) demonstrates how a traditional urban ballpark can be made to work, both for its team and for its city (fig. 2.8). Built on a tight plot at the edge of the downtown core, it is only one block from the city's new light rail system and principal transit corridor. The minor league Bisons immediately outdrew some major league teams. Within, it resembles a smaller Wrigley Field and re-creates the scale and intimacy of the classic ballpark. Outside, it wears a postmodernist, neo-Palladian face, frankly "architectural" and unapologetically historicist, that resonates urbanely with its neighbors. It is in that respect a contributor to the consistency of form, texture, and mass essential to weaving the urban fabric of streets, in contrast to the absurdly discontinuous recent high-rises nearby.

Since Pilot Field is perceived first as a building set among other buildings, rather than as an isolated techno-temple dedicated to sports, it draws baseball back into its proper relationship to the rest of life. The outside addresses people as citizens rather than consumers, as citizens who live in a complex web of historical associations, who have a common cultural language and a common vocabulary of remembered architectural gestures. Inside, it speaks the language of baseball, which has its own unique requirements and resonances. That language is itself another form of American civic discourse, perhaps one of the few that can still speak across generations and class divisions. If baseball is, in the waking dreamlife of the nation, less a sport than a grand metaphor—or a series of metaphors within metaphors through which we explain ourselves to ourselves—then baseball parks are also theaters of nation making, wherein our ambitions and our thirst for grace take form, are imbued with light, and are transformed into memory.[2]

Epilogue

Just as the wider society, in the 1980s, had finally rejected the claims and goals of the international style in architecture and urbanism, with its unrooted universalism, so has the generation of ballparks built in the 1990s (in Baltimore, Cleveland, Denver, and Arlington, Texas) returned to an earlier construction idiom. Based on the postmodernist ethos of free eclecticism, the reappropriation of earlier forms and symbols, and a highly textured contextualism, they are decidedly *baseball parks*, not multipurpose stadiums; they are unabashedly architectural.

Their designers have sought to incorporate the best of the Golden Age ballparks, their intimacy, their quirky asymmetries, their boxy way of framing the particular drama of baseball. Above all, they have reopened that box with its emerald center to the surrounding city, which is the historical locus of the professional game. The dialogue between the life within the ballpark and the life without, that dialogue so rich in the metaphors of our national identity, has been rejoined.

CHAPTER THREE

CRICKET

John Bale

A cricket match is at all times a pleasant sight. These tall, lithe youths, with muscular arms, dressed in light attire, and surrounded by thousands of spectators keenly interested in their efforts; do they not remind us of the heroes of the Olympian games?   —Elisée Reclus, *The Universal Geography*

> *All fields we'll turn to sports grounds, lit at night*
> *From concrete standards by fluorescent light.*
>   —John Betjeman, *Collected Poems*

The cricket pitch, nestling among mature trees with the Norman church and half-timbered pub nearby is, to many, the quintessence of rural England. The sound of leather against willow is frequently regarded as an essential element of the auditory environment of British summertime. These rustic images are almost matched by one that implies that no other game is influenced as much by the natural environment. Rusticity and nature can be claimed as the dominant images communicated about the English cricketing scene by landscape painters, novelists, essayists, and poets. I do not dispute that such images are reflected in reality; indeed, the elements of many cricket landscapes have barely changed in over two hundred years. Like the broader entertainment landscapes of which they are a part, however, cricket landscapes are among the most artificial—and hence the most human—of environments (Salter and Lloyd 1979). As such, cricket landscapes (like all sporting landscapes) are part of our "unwitting biography, reflecting our values, our aspirations and even our fears in tangible, visible form" (Lewis 1979).

In this essay I explore the cricket landscape by utilizing concepts of territoriality, placelessness, and rational landscapes.[1] After briefly outlining the origin and spread of the game, I proceed to explore the elements and ensembles of the cricket landscape as projected by those who have sought to describe it in visual and literary terms. I then assess the accuracy of these images in view of the cricket landscape's tending to have become (despite the bucolic images) "increasingly ordered and confined in space and time" (Sack 1986), reflecting the territoriality, rationality, and scientific humanism of the broader society within which it is located.[2] Despite the increased artifice and territoriality in cricket, however, many cricket places are held in great affection, and the tendency toward efficiency may not necessarily produce absurdity and placelessness.

The Aims, Origins, and Diffusion of Cricket

It is difficult to describe the aims and rules of a complex game like cricket to those reared on other ball games. Basically, the game is played between two teams, each of eleven players. The team scoring the most "runs" (the unit of scoring) wins. The members of each team bat in turn, each batsman facing a bowler from the other side who attempts to get the batsman "out" by bowling a hard, leather-covered ball and hitting the wickets (or "stumps"), which the batsman seeks to defend by hitting the ball with his bat. One run is scored by the batsman running the twenty-two yards from his wicket to another set of wickets from which the bowler delivered the ball. Four runs can be scored if the ball is hit beyond the boundary of the field of play; six if the ball is hit beyond the boundary without touching the ground first. A bowler is allowed to bowl six times in each "over." Games are played for a prescribed number of overs or for a prescribed number of days (usually between one and three). A batsman can also be out if a ball hit by him is caught by a

Basic Features	Aim	Contestants	Examples	Modern Versions
Control or propulsion of a ball by hand, foot, or stick	To score goals or points	Teams	Football, Hurling, Handball	Soccer, Rugby, Hockey, Lacrosse, Handball, Volleyball
Striking a ball with a club or mallet	To project balls through rings or into holes, in smallest number of shots	Individuals	Golf, Pale-Maille	Golf, Croquet
Throwing and striking a ball, sides taking it in turns to bowl and bat	To score by running between two or more points	Teams	Stool ball, Trap ball, Tip Cat, Cat and Dog	Cricket, Rounders, Baseball

FIG. 3.1. Folk games of preindustrial England.

fielder without it touching the ground first or if a member of the opposing team fields a ball and by throwing the ball is able to hit the wicket when the batsman is outside his "crease" (a line drawn four feet from the wickets). An innings is completed when each a team's eleven batsmen are out or when the team's captain is satisfied with the score and decides to "declare." Games can be of one or two innings per team.

Unlike our knowledge of basketball, volleyball, and certain other sports, we have no convenient name, date, or place to associate with the genesis of cricket. The hitting of missiles with sticks or batlike objects was no doubt ubiquitous in preindustrial tribal and Western societies,[3] and variants of the present game are found in many forms throughout the world today. Baseball and cricket almost certainly have common roots.

Before their formalization as modern sports, competitive physical activities assumed a variety of folk-game forms. Although these differed greatly in character, it has been suggested that in England three broad types existed (fig. 3.1; from Brookes 1978). In addition to a wide variety of open-air games, which were enjoyed by the masses of the population, there also existed from the sixteenth century a number of courtly activities, which were undertaken in the spatial confines of the covered and enclosed hall. Such activities included ball games like tennis, gymnastics, fencing, and riding (Eichberg 1986, 99–121). Spatial confinement was not only incorporated into the rules of such activities (as with real tennis) but helped segregate the nobility from the masses.

Cricket did not evolve from such courtly activities but from the folk games of stool-ball, tip-cat, and cat and dog—games involving the striking of a ball or piece of wood away from the individual, who scored by running between two or more points on the field of play. Cricket in its folk-game form was played throughout Europe, but the game which from the sixteenth century became known as "cricket" appears to have been associated with England and specifically with the southeastern counties of Kent, Sussex, and Hampshire. It has been stressed that the game's etymology is associated with this region, "wicket" being part of Sussex dialect for the entrance to a downland sheep pen, with a crossbar across the pen being known as a "bail," while the word "stump" (used synonymously with the word "wicket") is Hampshire dialect meaning part of a fallen tree left in the ground (Brookes 1978).

Folk games were rough-and-ready affairs and because of their frequent association with violence were viewed by "respectable" people with considerable suspicion. The rough-and-tumble nature of play was reflected in the environment and landscape on which games were played. In the seventeenth century, cricket was played on terrain which happened to be available and where local conditions determined the style of play. Yet the eighteenth century saw cricket transformed from a folk game for ruffians to an activity enjoyed by, and increasingly dominated by, the English nobility. This process of gentrification has been explained in various ways, and it has been suggested that cricket, introduced by an emerging yeoman and merchant class with whom the nobility were increasingly coming into contact, provided a vehicle by which they could "escape temporarily at least from the claustrophobic predictability of court life"—an example of the quest for excitement in an unexciting milieu. In addition, and perhaps more importantly, cricket provided an opportunity for the nobility to act out personal rivalries "without resorting to duelling swords, but within another gambling medium" (Brookes 1978, 33). Cricket provided a stage for wagering, without danger but with excitement.

Out of the gradual organization imposed by members of the aristocracy in Kent, Sussex, Surrey, and Hampshire grew a form of cricket which deserved the term "sport" rather than "folk game." Although the written evidence from the early eighteenth century is hazy because of the relative rarity of newspapers, games were being played according to an increasingly standardized set of rules. The need for rules derived from cricket's "almost permanent association with gambling, [and] it was very much in the interests of patrons and protagonists to minimize the chances of disagreement." The first "attempt to impose a standard set of rules upon the numerous local variations" (ibid., 42) was in 1727, but many of the folk-game traditions remained, including the wickets, each composed of two stumps of varying size. Subsequent codifications occurred throughout the eighteenth century, the most significant being in 1774, when authority was derived from the president of the London Club—the Prince of Wales—and 1787, when the central authority became the Marylebone Cricket Club (MCC).

It has been suggested that "the spreading of the game in the southern counties may be attributed to the meeting of the hop-growers at the annual fairs" (Gale 1871, 14), but such a theory remains unsubstantiated. We certainly know that the committee framing the 1774 rules was dominated by "noblemen and gentlemen of Kent, Hampshire, Surrey, Sussex, Middlesex and London" (Brookes 1978, 44) and that the largest number of games appears to have been played in the southeastern part of the country. When newspaper accounts of matches played in pre–Victorian England are compared with county populations, we find that the counties of Surrey, Sussex, Kent, Hampshire, and Essex all had more than 4.3 times the national average per capita number of games. The frequency of early-nineteenth-century cricketing seems to have declined toward the north, while the metropolis too was an island of relative inactivity within cricket's "culture hearth" of the southeast (Bale 1981).[4]

Most cricket matches have been completed within the course of one day. Few people could, of course, afford to play a game taking more time. During the late nineteenth century, however, the county teams, or "sides," emerged to represent the highest order of English cricket. With them appeared the three-day game, which virtually required players to be either professional or of independent means. Professional cricket tended to be concentrated in the north of England, but the formation of county sides brought together professional and amateur in a unique alliance in British sport. By 1900 the county game had virtually bifurcated into major and minor county sides, a demarcation that has remained to the present day. Attempts to rationalize what amounts to a fossil of the early twentieth century have been conspicuously unsuccessful ever since (Walford 1983). Promotions to, or demotions from, the county cricket championship have been rare, and many of the counties in which cricket flourishes at the grass roots do not possess first-class county teams.

At the mass participatory level, however, the whole of England (but only pockets of Scotland and Wales) has been colonized by cricket, and it is in the north of England, notably in Yorkshire, that the game has taken particularly strong root since the Industrial Revolution (Bale

1982). At the present time, much of northern England has more than four times the national average per capita number of cricket clubs. A characteristic of northern club sides is that they became organized in a different form from those in the south. Specifically, northern and midland clubs organized their season's games on a league basis, reflecting the more professional attitudes alluded to earlier, in contrast to the more amateur ethos of the south of England where, until the 1980s at least, the fixture list, a more "gentlemanly" and less competitive arrangement, had been the traditional mode of organization.

The spread of cricket to the north of England has been interpreted in symbolic terms. It has been suggested that as the nineteenth-century English landscape became more industrialized and urbanized, cricket was regarded as having a civilizing effect on the new towns of the north; it was "a perfect vehicle for the myths of Merrie England" (Bailey 1978, 74). The slow pace of cricket may have conjured up images of a time before the acceptance of a rigid sense of time-consciousness, which accompanied the hectic pace of life in industrializing England. Cricket may have symbolically provided the perceived virtues of a bygone age for which Victorians nostalgically yearned (Lowenthal 1985), supplying the antidote of green islands amid the rows of terraced houses and factories. As in the case of baseball in the United States, such nostalgic pastoralism may have been one of the attractions of the game. Yet as Stephen Gelber (1983) has pointed out for baseball, the game's attraction may have been more related to its degree of similarity to the day-to-day work of the male business worker, with its division of labor, specialization of roles, and limited independence.

The spread of cricket in Britain was followed by (or, more accurately, overlapped with) the expansion of the game on a global scale. Cricket at the highest level is as good an index as any of the former membership of the British Empire. Apart from Canada (which in the nineteenth century did have a strong cricketing tradition), the major countries of the present (or recent) Commonwealth are all giants of world cricket. The Cricket World Cup is dominated by England, Australia, India, Pakistan, the West Indies, and New Zealand; and the English county teams frequently include "cricket mercenaries" from these and other countries.[5] The founding members of the International Cricket Conference (the global bureaucracy) were England, Australia, and South Africa. But it would be misleading to assume that no other countries play cricket. The Argentina Cricket Association was founded as early as 1913. The game is widely played in Denmark and the Netherlands, and even France has a club cricket championship. Today twenty-four countries are members of the ICC, the majority having joined since the mid-1960s.

The adoption of cricket in former colonies can be interpreted in a number of ways. In Australia, cricket was a natural vehicle for the expression of an emerging nationalism. In India, on the other hand, the game needed to have an interest created in it by the colonial government. Cricket could serve to further the process of Anglicization, players would develop "manly" qualities, and teamwork would build character. In the West Indies, cricket lay somewhere between the two; it served an ideological function but also provided the islands with the only activity that could give them any real international prestige (Tiffin 1980). But it has been argued that in the West Indies there appears to be a love-hate attitude toward cricket: on the one hand, they can beat the English at their own game; on the other, it is the game of the master (Patterson 1969).[6]

The Cricket Landscape as Cultural Image

If landscapes are regarded as cultural images, they can be studied "across a variety of media and surfaces: in paint on canvas, writing on paper, images on film as well as in earth, stone, water and vegetation on the ground" (Cosgrove and Daniels 1988, 1). By studying writings and paintings, we also acquire a sense of place and identity—and, it might be added, a sense of sport. In the context of the cricket landscape, to which I now turn, I will review the written and visual impressions of authors, poets, and artists in order to establish cricket's cultural image. The cricket landscape is invariably projected as a nostalgic, rustic idyll. The doyen of English cricket writers, John Arlott, noted that the sport is "as much a part of the pattern of the English country as the green itself or the parish church. Two hundred years ago, landscape painters who often and clearly had no knowledge of the game, would include a cricket match as inherent in the scene" (Arlott 1955, 7). It has been recognized that "by the early part of this century cricket had come to play an integral part of that strange, powerful formation of ideas about the English countryside and its history which swims through the national imagination" (Inglis 1977, 503). Today, coffeetable books containing glossy photographs projecting the "English countryside" often convey a similar image.

An interpretation of the landscape of cricket can be aided by an awareness of the various landscape elements that go to make up the overall cricket landscape ensemble. As Karl Raitz (1987a) has noted, the sports landscape ensemble may provide participants (players and spectators) with various experiences, including different degrees of gratification, an added aesthetic experience, or even the symbolization of higher values. Such experiences are obviously derived from more than the game itself; they result from the combination of various elements which contribute to the cricket landscape ensemble. Tim Heald, an observer of English cricket landscapes, implies that the ensemble contributes a major component to the overall cricket experience when he notes that "it is the ground as much as the game which makes cricket . . . [and] cricket needs an appropriate setting as much as worship needs a good church." Almost as an aside he adds that "if the game becomes exciting so much the better" (1986, 7). Neville Cardus adds that "cricket as a combat and as a display of skill could be fascinating in the Sahara, no doubt," but "you have never even wooed cricket, let alone won it, if you have looked on the game *merely* as a clever matter of bat and ball" (1929, 34).

It has been suggested that "in no other sport does winning so little affect the aesthetic, spectacular and entertainment values" (Arlott and Cardus 1969, 62), and it can be argued that in cricket the landscape elements are of greater significance to the potential level of overall participant gratification than in many other sports. This is because cricket's relatively slow and frequently interrupted pace allows (even encourages) the spectator's (and the player's) attention to wander from the physical activity itself and hence gain gratification from the milieu beyond the actual game. When waiting for players to take the field, during the run up to bowl, between overs, while recovering the ball from "fours" and "sixes," and while at lunch or tea, participants have time—which is an essential part of the game in which to absorb the elements and ensemble of which the play is but part.

The cricket landscape ensemble can be presented as a model, the elements of which can be elicited from those who have communicated remarkably consistent images of the game. For example, Brian Jones in "The Cricket Pitch 1944" refers to the field "ringed with elms" (cited in Ross 1981, 487); Neil Powell in "The Cricketers" watched the game "from the woodland's edge" (489); while Edmund Blunden's "The Season Opens" (405) starts with the following verse:

A tower we must have, and a clock in the tower,
Looking over the tombs, the tithebarn, the bower;
The inn and the mill, the forge and the hall,
And the loamy sweet level that loves bat and ball.

In *Linden Lea* Edward Bucknell sites the cricket field within "view of the Hall nestling among ancient trees, and an abundance of shade for the spectators from other trees along one hedge. An open pavilion commanded the ground from one corner, and another, sacred to the squire's wife and her friends, was ensconced under a huge elm hard by" (ibid., 60). Sir Norman Birkett, one of England's premier judges, composes the cricket ensemble thus:

> small white painted pavilion of the village ground, the tins for the scoreboard, the horse with its big leather shoes pulling the roller, the wooden benches at intervals around the ground, the great spreading trees at the boundary's edge, the flowering hedgerows . . . (1957, 9)

The classic view, as seen by Neville Cardus, is of "cricket set against a background of green trees, haystacks, barns, and a landscape of peace and plenty, remote from a world too busy getting and spending" (Arlott and Cardus 1969, 24). To A. G. MacDonnell in *England Their England* it was the cricket ground which was the very essence of *real* England, "unspoilt by factories and financiers and tourists and hustle" (1935, 107). The sun is shining; the sky is blue; the rhododendrons are in full bloom: Merrie England has been re-created. Indeed, to play in the shadows of an industrial landscape is considered by some observers of the cricketing scene to be "the fate" of the players so involved (Frith 1987, 43).

In England cricket has been projected as an essentially southern phenomenon. Cardus "heard folk from the south say of cricket at Sheffield that it is simply not cricket. Their preference has been for the game played with trees and country graciousness around" (1929, 27). This is a recurring theme in Cardus's writing; elsewhere he notes that "a Lancashire and Yorkshire match is inconceivable at Tonbridge . . . there is no nonsense about 'art for art's sake' in the Saturday afternoon matches in the hinterland of the northern counties" (1930, 173–74). Most cricket literature is set in the southeast. For example, Hugh de Selincourt's *The Cricket Match* and R. C. Sherriff's *Badgers Green* are both sited in the undulating chalk lowlands of Kent and Sussex. Much other cricket writing is sited south of the Trent; most, south of the Thames (Bale 1986).

The environment of English cricket has not been—and could not be—duplicated in the countries to which the game was exported. Australia could not adopt cricket in precisely its English form because "their meadows are not precisely as English meadows, they have no long summer evenings, their society has never known the agricultural background based on a village community" (Milburn 1966, 38). Instead of growing out of a landscape, facilities for cricket had to be created, in so doing creating a degree of perceived incongruity. Heald views the fact that cricket had been played at Moose Jaw, Saskatchewan, as quite incongruous. At such a location

> could there have been a pavilion and flags and a wrought iron weathervane incorporating stumps and a figure of Father Time . . . umpires in long white coats . . . a pub . . . a church with a tower and clock stuck not at ten to three but nearer four . . . and not Rupert Brooke's epideictic honey but cucumber or sandwich spread for tea and a tree, spreading or weeping about the long-on boundary . . . and the deck chairs . . . and old vicars sleeping therein? Surely not in Moose Jaw? (1986, 7)

In such writing we are urged to relate ensemble to location and to believe that particular ensembles in particular locations could not conceivably be authentic but would, if so located, be kitsch or ersatz versions—like the English pub at Disney World. Taken further, cricket played in "noncricketing" countries or locations is frequently projected in English cricket writing as a joke, which reflects a rabid form of Anglocentrism, verging on racism. Significantly, West Indian cricket is never projected in this way.

Representations of the English cricket landscape in painting and other forms of visual art also communicate the rural idyll alluded to above. Of seventy-five paintings from the seventeenth to the mid-nineteenth centuries reproduced in David Frith's monumental *Pageant of Cricket* (1987), 64 percent are unambiguously rural in their settings. Of cricket images depicted in Arlott and Cardus's *The Noblest Game* (1969), 72 percent have rural landscape settings. Among the best oil paintings of the game is "Village Cricket" by John Ritchie, depicting English rusticity in archetype.[7]

Cricket cartoons and the illustrated covers of modern cricket books provide the same image, summarizing in convenient and accessible form the landscape elements of the game and the resulting cultural image derived from so many artistic impressions of cricket's landscape. A cartoon summarizing the factors contributing to the value of real estate in the typical English village has the duckpond, half-timbered pub, Range Rover, church and, at its core, the village cricket pitch. A similar image is conveyed in many of the covers of the huge number of books on cricket (Bale 1994, 156).

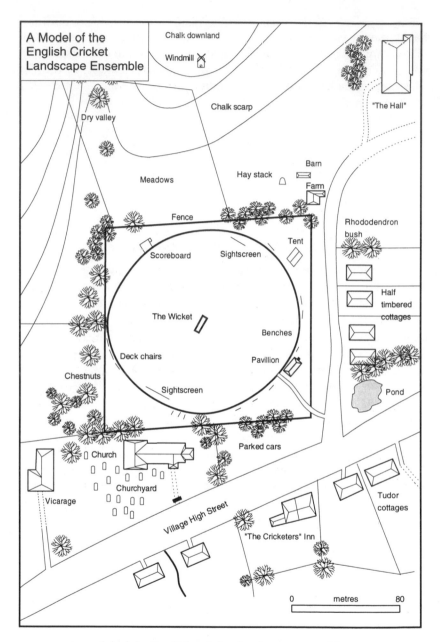

A Model of the
English Cricket
Landscape Ensemble

Chalk downland

Windmill

Chalk scarp

"The Hall"

Dry valley

Barn

Meadows

Hay stack

Farm

Fence

Rhododendron
bush

Tent

Scoreboard

Sightscreen

The Wicket

Half
timbered
cottages

Benches

Deck chairs

Pavillion

Chestnuts

Sightscreen

Pond

Parked cars

Church

Churchyard

Vicarage

Tudor
cottages

Village High Street

"The Cricketers" Inn

0   metres   80

FIG. 3.2. A model of the English cricket landscape ensemble.

A model of the English cricket ensemble can be constructed from the kinds of literary and artistic impressions typified above. Such an idealized representation contains a number of distinct elements (fig. 3.2). Trees, shrubs, church, barn, tent, woodland, spectators, and players themselves far from exhaust the total ensemble. Added to these will be different textures of the field itself, the immaculately maintained twenty-two-yard wicket contrasting with the greener outfield. Sight screens, scoreboards, parked cars, spectators' deck chairs, and children playing beyond the boundary all add to the overall picture.

Edmund Blunden, an observer of the character of cricket, was fully aware that the variety within the ensemble contributes to the level of gratification obtained from participating in cricket. While playing he noted that "the game itself grew dim, the action lost its precision and importance, and only the sweet-breathing, singing, shining, swaying, rejoicing universe of nature had any existence for me." He urges the young cricketer, waiting for the next batsman to come to the crease, to "glance from your post in the long field . . . away to those farms and woods, spires and hills around you; rest your high spirits for a moment on the composure of that young mother with her sleeping baby, on the old white horse as still as if he was carved in chalk on the down" (1985, 137).

While many elements are common to the hundreds of cricket grounds up and down the country, "how they are arranged and what their character is creates that quality we call individuality. Add the historical associations and the environs, and you have the *genius loci*— the spirit of the place" (Sampson 1981, 8; fig. 3.3).

So far I have focused primarily on "village cricket," the amateur, recreational version of the sport played by relatively modest standards. Although a German observer of English cricket, Rudolf Kircher, averred that in top-class cricket "the atmosphere of the village green is replaced by an audience of technical experts," at that level the game being "expert and artificial" (1928, 99), many of the principal grounds at which the county or professional clubs play do retain a distinctiveness derived from elements incidental to playing or watching the game itself. At Canterbury in Kent, for example, a mature lime tree stands inside the boundary; in the same county the ground at Tunbridge Wells connotes the smellscape of rhododendrons; at Taunton a soundscape may be evoked, "of the lowing of cows in the cattle market punctuating the applause of the crowd" (Allen 1984, 57); at Worcester—arguably the most beautiful cricket ground in the world—the backdrop is the majestic Gothic architecture of the cathedral.

FIG. 3.3. Sunday afternoon cricket in an ad for rural real estate. Note the various peripheral landscape elements, including the village church, trees, pub, and Land Rover.

It has been observed that Worcester has developed facilities for top-level sport while continuing to give the impression of cricket as a meadow-game (Kilburn 1980). Of London's major grounds, Lord's (the mecca of cricket) has "cosmopolitan amenities, opulence and spacious-ness," while the Oval at Kennington "is London, and to some extent genuine Cockney" (Cardus 1972, 45). Cardus, however, could not resist making somewhat environmentally deterministic assertions about cricket teams and their home fields, saying,

> does not the play of the side assume tone and colour from the scene? Yorkshire cricket has the aspect of Bramall Lane and Leeds—dour, and telling of stern competitive life with smoke and real industry about. . . . Does not there come through the cricket of Sussex the brown and the sunny flavour of East-bourne and Hove when the time of day is noon and the earth seems humming with heat? The plain homeliness of the Mid-lands is expressed by Leicestershire cricket: it has no airs and graces, no excessive refinements. (1929, 55)

The distinctiveness of the county grounds has been reviewed in detail elsewhere; it is widely accepted that no two grounds are alike.[8] At the professional level, English cricket grounds retain, in magnified form perhaps, the landscape elements of the village grounds. The parish churches are replaced by cathedrals, the village by the city, the farm by the factory. Yet in the city the places at which cricket is played are still called grounds—never stadiums. Many major county grounds have landscape elements—physical, olfactory, and auditory—which, according to Aylwin Sampson, "will not easily be destroyed. There will still be that sparkle of white wood, that sudden hush as the bowler delivers, the immemorial trees, the tents and flags, the smell of grass, the measured pace of the match" (1981, 9–10). The cultural image of English cricket is one of quaintness, rusticity, and nature. The cricket landscape as reflected in various media can be interpreted, like the English landscape itself, as an expression of English tastes and values. The cultural images of cricket glorify the bucolic, the picturesque, and the tidy (Lowenthal and Prince 1965). This image of cricket, as well as cricket itself, has a history—one that has been communicated by those writers and artists active in contributing to English landscape tastes.

This image is only partially accurate. Certainly, the model shown in figure 3.2 is in accord with much village cricket in the south of England; and many English county grounds continue to project an authentic, market town charm. But the modern heartland of English cricket is in Yorkshire—a northern county with over fifteen hundred cricket clubs (14 percent of the U.K. total) and with more than 4.5 times the national per capita number of clubs (Bale 1982). Here cricket is often played in the shadow of terraced houses and factories, with chimneys replacing chestnuts and moorlands replacing downlands in the ensemble. Though the grounds of Yorkshire are as authentic and idiosyncratic as those of the south of England, their landscape elements tend to be different and appear to have been almost systematically neglected in the myopia of the media, which have communicated only the most widely accepted images of the cricket landscape.

Authentic or Placeless Places?

Despite the individuality and the authenticity implied in my descriptions of the cricket milieu so far, it can nevertheless be argued that cricket has displayed tendencies toward placelessness, with some cricket places increasingly both looking and feeling alike. Both spatial confinement and artifice—territoriality and placelessness—have manifested themselves in at least three cricket contexts: first, the transformation of the *surface* upon which the game is played; second, spatial enclosure and landscape change at the *periphery* of the field of play; and third, a tendency toward a reduction in the number of elements making up the *overall ensemble*. These changes have combined to produce in cricket what Henning Eichberg has termed a "process of spatial separation and immurement" (Eichberg 1986, 100).

Yet it seems that in much of the cricket landscape the pressures for placelessness have not gone so far as to eliminate the affection that people characteristically feel for authentic places. Edward Relph (1976) sees placelessness manifested in a number of ways, each of which may be applied to the landscape of cricket. Placelessness, he argues, derives from (1) other-directedness in places, that is, places deliberately constructed for, and directed toward, outsiders; (2) uniformity and standardization of places; (3) formlessness and lack of human scale in places; (4) destruction of places; and (5) impermanence and instability in places. In the case of cricket, other-directedness and uniformity are most evident.

Placelessness has to be transmitted by various media and systems. Of the media identified by Relph, the most obvious in a sports landscape context are the sports equivalents of multinational corporations; namely, the governing bodies and global bureaucracies that enforce rules and regulations. These dictate standardized values of a spatial and environmental nature which are evident in the cricket landscape.

Folk cricket lacked a standardized setting and was wholly subject to the vagaries of the micro-geography of the field of play. No spatial limits were imposed, and no specialized sites existed at which games were played. It was the formalization of rules, which, as we have seen, occurred from the second decade of the eighteenth century, that for cricket (and other sports) included the specific details of the spatial demarcation of the field of play, or at least parts of the field of play. From 1787 it was the MCC that became *the* bureaucracy which administered the game at both national and global scales. With such a rule-enforcing bureaucracy, the standardization of the game could proceed, untrammeled by the vagaries of regional and local idiosyncrasy.

Other-Directedness in Cricket

Cricket typifies placelessness in several ways, each of which I shall illustrate in turn. Landscapes designed with "outsiders, spectators, passers-by, and above all consumers" in mind obviously characterize sports places in general, and cricket places are no exception (Relph 1976, 93). One of the features in the development of industrial capitalism was that various activities became territorially segmented (Sack 1986), with access to public space becoming increasingly restricted. Specialized spaces and places became allocated to particular users, sports increasingly taking place in clearly defined and on carefully prepared sites.

Once cricket became a spectator sport, it was necessary to provide appropriate accommodation. While Aylwin Sampson (1981) has suggested that admission charges were first levied with the intention of actually keeping spectators out, it is clear that by the mid–eighteenth century cricket was beginning to assume the character of a commodity. Only people unable to pay would now be excluded as the cricket ground became a territory—a specified space to be filled and emptied at prearranged times (Sack 1986). The first recorded admission charged to spectators was at London's Artillery Ground in 1744, this site being the principal metropolitan focus for the game and attracting crowds of about ten thousand (though even larger crowds have been recorded for eighteenth-century matches; and Hambledon, the famous Hampshire club, attracted crowds of over twenty thousand to its ground at Broad-halfpenny Down [Brookes 1978]). Clearly, at the highest level, but by no means totally absent at the local scale, cricket had moved from being an element of play to one of display (Stone 1971). In 1821 an artificial terrace seating eight thousand spectators was landscaped into Darnall cricket ground near Sheffield (Arlott and Cardus 1969). At the elite level, cricket had become theater: two teams and two umpires were not enough, and spectators became a *necessary* part of the activity. There is thus a tendency for the landscape in which cricket is played to reflect such other-directedness, usually manifested in a number of aspects of the ground's periphery. New structures to accommodate more spectators, in some parts of the world floodlights to ensure attendance at nonwork time, and an architectural dislocation between the game and the broader environment by means of a concrete bowl (from a ground to a stadium) are extreme cases resulting from cricket's commercial imperatives. Such rational, universal spaces "succeed only in defining a non-place . . . hostile to the bounds imposed by locale and history" (Neilson 1986, 46).

Some cricket places typify alternative forms of other-directedness. There is clear evidence of the "futurization" of cricket places in the evening games which take place in low latitudes, notably Australia. The aggressive marketing of cricket as a spectacle reached its apotheosis in the late 1970s following the successful television marketing of the sport by Kerry Packer, who brought a razzmatazz and glitziness to the sport which was alien to purists in both Australia and England. Such developments also exemplified the nurturing of nationalism by commercial interests through sport. Far from being a spontaneous response, the feeling of patriotism in Australia was stimulated by media magnates and their associated hype.

Floodlit cricket came into its own in such circumstances, Australian Rules Football stadiums being hired, given the initial reluctance of the establishment to allow Packer cricket to use their grounds. Such packaging sought to produce *"guaranteed* excitement, amusement or interest, while diminishing the effort and chance of imagination" (Relph 1976). The game, not the peripheral elements, becomes the focus—the only focus—for the spectators with the darkened backdrop of nighttime.

Uniformity and Standardization in Cricket Places

In the early days of modern cricket, without any specially prepared strip of grass on which to play, the teams agreed between themselves where the wickets should be pitched. Even after 1823 the pitch could be technically selected *anywhere* by the umpire, and not until 1947 did the laws of the game explicitly ascribe the selection of the pitch to the ground authorities. But the instant that the 1744 laws decreed that a cricket pitch should be twenty-two yards long (one chain, or four times one goad—a traditional English land measure), rudimentary aspects of placelessness became imposed on the cricket landscape. Throughout the eighteenth century, the general tendency was to "remove any local variations on the way the game was played" (Brailsford 1987) in order to provide a fairer basis than hitherto for betting and gambling. Yet in the early nineteenth century the surfaces of most pitches were uneven and unkempt. The roughness of these early grounds produced notoriously low scores in many nineteenth-century village games, and in some cases a rough pitch was actually encouraged in order to make the bounce of the ball unpredictable for opposing batsmen. At least one village in Hampshire "was reputed to spend the winter coaxing plantains or bents to grow about the length spot of their main fast bowler" (Arlott 1984, 69). Traditionally, therefore, the preparation of the cricket pitch "was managed by sheep" (Sampson 1981, 3), and cricket often had to wait for its field until after haymaking, hence leading to latitudinal variations in the start of the season (Brailsford 1987).

An improved surface was a "necessary condition for the development of cricket in its modern form," and although in 1849 it became permissible to sweep or roll the pitch between innings, the absence of fierce, overarm bowling meant that there was little incentive to tend the pitch further. "Without a good 'wicket'—a closely mowed and rolled playing surface—it was not possible to have either large scores or overarm bowling, both of which added immeasurably to the glamour and popularity of the game" (Allison 1980, 11). With the authorization of overarm bowling in 1864, it became necessary for the surface on which the game was played to be transformed and to be reclaimed totally from nature in order to reduce the chance of danger, inherent in an uneven pitch.

In 1864, the first groundsman was appointed at Lord's, and Sandiford noted that "the leading Victorian cricket scientists were . . . groundsmen [who] performed miracles on late Victorian cricket grounds" (1984, 279). The spirit of rationalization and technique, which was running through society at large, was becoming increasingly evident in cricket. The growing seriousness with which the affluent middle classes took cricket meant that the farmers' fields or squires' parks, loaned or rented for a day, were simply not good enough. For the village cricket clubs (which replaced the village teams, characteristic of the game in the late eighteenth and early nineteenth centuries), proper facilities were required; cheap labor was available to prepare the grounds, and even full-time groundsmen were sometimes employed (Cole 1982). The introduction of heavy rollers (first introduced to Lord's in 1870) further served to standardize the playing surface. The late nineteenth century witnessed the growth in production of specialized cricket equipment to aid the gradual leveling and equalizing of the cricket landscape in an age of rapidly changing technology. Cricket played its part in contributing to the expanding sporting goods industry, many implements being developed with the improvement of cricket grounds in mind.

By the first decade of the present century, the cricket groundsman had applied technology to the cricket pitch, freeing the sport from the "incalculable and unscientific misconduct caused by a rough and entirely unscientific pitch" (Arlott 1984, 78). Marl and liquid manure were regularly applied to the top-class pitches, and the MCC felt obliged to dispatch a memorandum to county club secretaries urging that the pitch be prepared by applying only water and roller. Nevertheless, in the interests of producing durable wickets, marling became a regular practice.

In addition to the changing surface, the nineteenth century was characterized by the marking of various spatial limits on the pitch. By midcentury, whitewash had been introduced to replace the shallow channels cut in the turf which had previously been used to define the crease (Broadribb 1985). Further spatial demarcation within the 360 degrees in which cricket is played has been resisted. A suggestion that a series of concentric zones, centered on the wicket, be marked on the field with a specified number of fielders in each zone in order to encourage more attacking bowling may be a sign of things to come (Lester 1980).

The twentieth century has witnessed the production of what Arlott (1984) has called "comfortable" wickets. By this he means pitches upon which fast bowling is difficult, thus encouraging high scoring. As a result, bowling styles have changed, but groundsmen have responded by making the wickets even slower. According to Cardus, "the groundsman, the producer or stage manager of cricket, made the mistake of producers in the theatre—he became engrossed in the setting at the expense of the play" (1972, 25). By "setting" Cardus meant the surface on which the action takes place.

Attempts to eliminate nature further included the covering of wickets in wet weather. The first experimental covering of wickets before matches at Lord's was as early as 1872 (Bowen 1970, 284). At Edgbaston in Birmingham, "a motorized cover was introduced in 1982 which protects virtually the whole playing area from rain, and can be rolled back to the edges of the ground, as soon as the weather relents, at the flick of a switch" (Martin-Jenkins 1984, 183). Beyond the wicket itself, fertilizers have made what had traditionally been, in dry weather, near-deserts, permanently green. At club level, artificial pitches, manufactured from tough green plastic, have proliferated. Artificial pitches are also found in many overseas countries, particularly in the tropics, where economy and nature preclude the construction of a good English wicket. At the highest level, however, the introduction of wholly artificial pitches has yet to emerge, though some believe that it is only a matter of time before such surfaces become accepted (184).

Newfound wealth and an idiosyncratic mania for cricket in parts of the Middle East led to the establishment of the incongruous cricket stadium at Sharjah in the United Arab Emirates. This stadium illustrates the ability of modern technology to produce a turf wicket and some of the most exquisitely cared-for grass in the Arab world in what is naturally a desert environment. Instant cricket places have also been created in Spain to cater to those on cricket-touring holidays.

Growing uniformity has also developed at the periphery at the field of play. Although enclosure of cricket pitches had proceeded from the late 1700s (Lord's had a fence erected around it in 1787), the specific inclusion of a boundary in the rules of the game dates from as late as 1884 as part of the MCC's revised code of laws. At that time, other sports were also establishing similar forms of spatial delimitation. The incorporation of boundaries into the rules can be regarded as the crucial act in its territorialization in that it finally separated the players from their audience. Boundaries were essentially a form of crowd control; traditionally, spectators had been somewhat arbitrarily demarcated from the play, crowds parting to let the ball and chasing fielder through—a lingering residual of the folk-game tradition (Bowen 1970, 169).

Once cricket became a serious business, attempts were made to reduce the significance of landscape elements at the periphery which might distract players' attention from the game itself. The forerunner of the present-day sightscreen—an attempt to neutralize landscape by providing a plain white backdrop to prevent bowlers' being distracted—were strips of white canvas, introduced in the early nineteenth century. Subsequently, large sheets of white canvas were erected, while today sightscreens have become substantial white metal or wooden structures. At the periphery of many cricket grounds, a number of elements have become standard features from the most modest village green to the headquarters of the MCC at Lord's. In addition to the now-ubiquitous sightscreen, advertisers' billboards have become increasingly common as commercial pressure has been felt at both top and bottom of the game's hierarchy. As greater care has been given to safety requirements at sports grounds, standardized architectural forms have assumed a more visible presence at the higher levels of the game. In Australia, India, and Pakistan, the concrete bowl has replaced the grandstand and pavilion; the metal structures supporting the floodlights have replaced the trees; action replays on giant television screens have replaced the 'inadequacy' of human vision. Cricket, like many other sports (and, indeed, like the urban landscape in general), provides visible evidence of new technological landscapes, the elements of which mimic those which preceded them. Such landscape elements represent a standardized cricket environment. According to Edmund Blunden, one thing in favor of such "austere cricket grounds, untouched with mysticism" is that the top class player cannot be "distracted from his function" by peripheral, distractive landscape elements. The gradual reduction in the number of elements moves the locality towards the placelessness end of the place-placelessness spectrum (fig. 3.4).

The most synthetic form of cricket is the indoor game. While cricketers have practiced indoors for centuries (using barns in nineteenth-century England), competitive indoor cricket in its modern guise was first developed in Australia in the 1970s. Indoor cricket is cricket for instant gratification. While the pitch is the traditional twenty-two yards, the entire "field" is only thirty yards by twelve yards. In Australia, such games are played in air-conditioned halls in suburban, subtopian,

		Distinctions between Sports Places **(Most Places Are Different)**	
Complex ↑	Place ↑	Village Cricket	High ↑
↑	↑	The English County Game	↑ Level of
Landscape Ensemble ↓	Sense of Place ↓	Australian Inter-State Game Floodlit Cricket	Gratification Attained from a Sport Experience
↓	↓	Indoor Cricket	↓
↓ Simple	↓ Placelessness	Video Cricket	↓ Low
		No Distinction **(All Places Are Alike)**	

FIG. 3.4. Perceived differences between cricket place ensembles, senses of place, and levels of potential gratification.

industrial parks possessing a placeless style of international architecture. In such situations, the "industrialization" of sport is both metaphorical and literal; it is part of the industrial suburban landscape. In Britain, where the indoor game is becoming increasingly popular, the number of purpose-built facilities is few, but growing. Although its advocates claim that the indoor game is meant to be fun, an Indoor Cricket Federation exists "to try to ensure that the game is played to standard rules with the best possible facilities" (Hamlyn 1985, 25). The immurement of cricket reaches its zenith with the commercial windowless cricket hall. As Eichberg (1986) noted, behind such ideas one can see the further step of video culture where computer cricket games are played in amusement arcades.

Lack of Human Scale

In modern sports, perhaps the most evident trend toward gigantism is in the massive stadiums that characterize top-level spectator sports. As stadiums have become bigger, a smaller proportion of the total number of spectators has been able to appreciate the detail of the action on the field of play. In the case of cricket, where the ball is small in comparison with, say, the soccer or rugby ball, it is difficult from some vantage points to actually see it at all. The largest cricket stadium in the world is at Melbourne, accommodating over 130,000 spectators.

Calcutta's Eden Park might well have a larger capacity, but it has been impossible to obtain an accurate attendance record. This gigantic stadium with concrete tiered stands contrasts starkly with the more homely English grounds.

Place Destruction and Impermanence

In the context of cricket, place destruction or impermanence can occur by expropriation and redevelopment or by the abandonment of grounds. Although part of the attraction of English cricket grounds is their longevity, their destruction and abandonment resulting from commercial pressures is common, reflecting a further manifestation of placelessness. Attempts to discontinue cricket at particular places can sometimes cause a reaction among those possessing an authentic sense of place; nevertheless, the imperatives of capital and profit usually triumph over sentiment in such situations. While affection for the Chesterfield ground succeeded in (at least) postponing Derbyshire County Cricket Club's decision to play all their games at Derby, Essex's former ground at Leyton was simply engulfed by the growth of London's eastern suburbs (Bale 1982). The destruction of the old Cardiff Arms Park cricket ground, to make way for the modernistic rugby complex, resulted in Glamorgan County Cricket Club's playing its Cardiff games at a new site at Sophia Gardens. It has been noted that while this new location is pleasant enough, it has failed to reproduce "the cosy atmosphere at Cardiff Arms Park" (Wooller 1984, 106). Such examples of affection for sports locations come close to the "intense identification between people and places" which Jackson and Smith suggest as modern world reactions to the loss of "authentic places"—those which generate feelings of identity and belonging (1984, 32).

Cricket has a long tradition of creating "instant places." In 1814, turf from Lord's second ground was transported and relaid at the present site at St. John's Wood, creating an instant pitch in a new location. Instant cricket places can be set up and the game played, with the land then reverting to its former use. In the 1970s, some downtown English soccer stadiums played host to floodlit cricket, with temporary twenty-two-yard strips being laid down. In Australia, the first years of Packer cricket witnessed temporary pitches being cultivated in local greenhouses and transported to Australian Rules football pitches after having been nurtured artificially in concrete troughs. Impermanence of this kind is likely to continue as the quest for instant cricket—the result of the demand for instant gratification—increases.

The Paradox of Rationalized Cricket Places

Many sports landscapes (like other modern landscapes) provoke ambivalent reactions because of the "development of powerful rationalistic techniques for manipulating environments and communities regardless of the values and qualities which might be displaced in the process. The benefits which derive from humanism are manifold, measurable and tangible. The losses, too, are manifold, but they are immeasurable and intangible" (Relph 1981, 15). In the case of cricket, changes to the surfaces on, and to the structures within, which it is played have been undertaken with the interests of players and spectators in mind. Indoor cricket means that the game can be played all year round; synthetic wickets mean that more cricket can be played; plastic tip-up seats instead of old wooden benches may be (marginally) more comfortable for spectators; concrete stands and floodlights mean that more people can watch cricket; electronic screens mean that the fine detail of the game can be replayed. There is almost nothing in these landscapes "that has not been conceived and planned so that it will serve those human needs which can be assessed in terms of efficiency or improved material conditions" (104). Paradoxically, however, the absence of spontaneity and expression of human feelings in these landscapes may serve to reduce the gratification obtained from the cricket experience. As Hargreaves has pointed out, "the rationalization of spectator sports has had counter productive effects in relation to audience satisfaction" resulting from the routinizing of performance and, one might add, the growing sameness in the sports landscape (1987, 157). In other words, as complexity and detail decrease, the ensemble provides reduced levels of gratification (Raitz 1987a).

As the size of the cricket grounds increases, one might expect reduced satisfaction. Commenting on modern Australian cricket grounds, J. M. Kilburn noted that

> cricket in huge arenas is cricket only distantly related to the game of the village green. It becomes cricket of wide separation between players and spectators, cricket of spectacle presented on a remote stage. . . . Players seen through field-glasses, if they are to be seen at all become objects rather than people of human endeavour and frailty . . . the too distant spectator fails to take part in the game's breathing and breeding. (1980, 258)

Henning Eichberg avers that "it makes a difference whether [cricket] is played in the open landscape between two communities, promoting adventure in the countryside, experience of the environment and social communication, or whether artificial and expensive facilities with plastic grass are laid out, manufactured and requiring environmentally costly automobile traffic and huge parking lots" (1986, 113). As cricket moves away from the place to the placelessness end of the landscape spectrum, therefore, it becomes increasingly "antinature." Although such views have been regarded as elitist, the popular response to landscape innovations in cricket *have* tended to be negative.

Let us consider some further examples from those who have themselves perceived such reduced gratification. In the 1920s, an article in the London *Times* admonished cricket groundsmen for their over-enthusiastic use of the heavy roller, such had become cricket's slowness, caution, and boredom (Bowen 1970). Since then, the negative feelings associated with "progress" have been numerous. For example, "until floodlighting was installed," Sydney's cricket ground was regarded as among the finest of grounds (Milburn 1966). The floodlights not only produced more cricket but in doing so had the effect of reducing the quality of the pitch through overuse. Witnessing the newly packaged cricket in late '70s Australia, an experienced cricket journalist noted how the game was at first played in Australian Rules football stadiums typified by "a huge soulless, concrete edifice with acres and acres of open concrete terracing." The first season of World Series Cricket was a revelation:

> The floodlights made the cricket seem unreal, to the extent that I found it difficult to believe that I was watching cricket . . . the atmosphere was gladiatorial . . . the crowd was very far from being the kind one would normally see at a cricket match; most would probably have gone to a drivein cinema had they not made the journey to VFL Park. (Blofeld 1978, 172)

The covering of wickets during periods of rain, while intended to reduce the period of waiting before the game can be restarted, is also viewed negatively by those who

> regret the total covering of the wicket as it rules out forever the magnificent sight of the master . . . coping with extreme difficulties of a rain-damaged wicket. The spin-bowler is likewise robbed of spectacular analyses. (Broadribb 1986, 85)

The gradual transformation of the cricket pitch from a meadow to a carpet, from tree-girt field to concrete bowl or air-conditioned hall, typifies what Johann Galtung has called the move toward "near laboratory settings in which the unidimensionality of competitive sports can unfold itself under controlled conditions. Pure nature has too much variation in it; too much 'noise' " (1984, 14). Likewise, Jacques Ellul notes that "in sport, as elsewhere, nothing gratuitous is allowed to exist; everything must be useful and come up to technical expecta-' tions" (1965, 384). Such viewpoints support the assertion that modern sport (including cricket) is basically antinature (Galtung 1984).

These interpretations can certainly be illustrated through an examination of the cricket landscape as it is typified by floodlit, indoor, and video cricket. However, the multifaceted nature of cricket makes the notion of placelessness and dehumanized landscapes inappropriate as a generalization about all cricket environments. Even the rules of cricket permit diversity. Like baseball, the ground can be any shape, and the playing area is contained within a boundary ideally (but note, not inevitably) at least seventy-five yards from a pitch set as centrally as possible. The ground should be even, but at Lord's the field slopes to this day. Furthermore, cricket can be located on a number of continua, from workform to playform, freedom to constraint, recreation to sport. Cricket's landscapes are not homogeneous; while in some cases the attitudes and outcomes of placelessness are obvious, in others authenticity of place clearly remains.

Conclusion

The cricket landscape emerged as a form of monoculture during the eighteenth and nineteenth centuries. Cricket's territoriality matched the growing territoriality in society as a whole. Artificiality, spatial confinement, and rule-boundedness increasingly came to characterize cricket as it was transformed from a form of play to one of display. Yet despite these unquestioned trends toward an increasingly scientifically humanized landscape, the cricket milieu has been overwhelmingly presented as picturesque and pastoral in art and literature. Such landscape "texts" reveal a continuing quest for pastoralism in sport, even though much cricket is played (or worked) in environments that are lacking in human scale, inauthentic, and highly standardized. Wherever cricket is played, and especially where it has become other-directed in character, its landscape has become more placeless.

Nevertheless, just as sport per se is changing at the present time (Eichberg 1986), so too is cricket. On the one hand, high-tech cricket is manifest at the highest level in its concrete bowls, floodlit stadiums with electronic playback facilities, and manicured pitches. This has been described as "a form of popularized, bastardized cricket full of instant appeal" (Blofeld 1978, 105), potentially suited to an American audience and, by definition, a sure indication of the nadir of the game from the perspective of the cricket purist. Technologized cricket has reached its zenith at the mass participatory level with the indoor version of the game with air conditioning and artificial lighting. Computer-video cricket takes the trend even further.

A second tendency is the continuing "greening" of cricket, played in England in its traditional surroundings and in authentic places with enduring landscape elements that contribute to a varied ensemble. Pressures exist to reduce or even eliminate this ensemble, but they are clearly resisted and sometimes restrained in the struggle between community and capital. To an extent, the traditional image of cricket is accurate, as visitors to much of England will testify. The social makeup of village cricket, however, in no way fits the traditional image, the village rustics having given way to upwardly mobile commuters in the composition of teams (Allison 1985). And such "green" cricket in no way rejects the basic ideology of sport, with its emphasis on quantification and competition. Indeed, traditional recreational cricket, while illustrating the continuing tradition of open-air and less serious sport, may be paradoxical because of the pressures to museumize it, to make it increasingly other-directed, inauthentic, or more serious. The development of the "national village cricket championship" (with the final played at Lord's) illustrates these tendencies.

A third form of cricket has not been touched on in this essay. This is because cricket as play does not require cricket landscapes. Folk cricket never totally disappeared. Most dramatically, perhaps, cricket has been returned to its folk traditions where the vernacular landscape has been reclaimed as an integral part of the game. The paradigm case is that of cricket in the Trobriand Islands off the southern tip of Papua New Guinea, where the islanders have appropriated a colonial game and integrated it into their own culture—and their own landscape. In Trobriand cricket, bushes, water, rain, and houses become part of the game's milieu, and the home team always has to win because this shows respect for the side that organized the game. "The score must not be too great, however, or else the visitors will feel offended" (Seward 1986, 37).

Elsewhere in the world folk cricket is found today on beaches, in the *bustees* of India, and in the few remaining traffic-free streets of Britain and elsewhere. While the tendency undoubtedly exists for planners to provide more formal environments for such play, it is doubtful if it will ever totally be contained. It is *not* inevitable, as history shows, that sport should progressively become more bland, more spatially confined, and more sanitized (Eichberg 1985).[9] The space for an alternative sport "is the space available in the complexity of everyday life" (Eichberg 1986, 112).

Cricket *does* possess placeless landscapes, and I have suggested in this essay that cricket has become increasingly placeless since the early eighteenth century. But many cricket places are still viewed with affection; as Relph stresses, "it is easy but erroneous to simplify placelessness, to see it everywhere in the post-industrial world" (1976, 80). The cricket landscape acts as a salutary exemplification of this cautionary statement.

CHAPTER FOUR

SOCCER

Martyn Bowden

Modern Football can only be played, theatrically presented, and joyously observed in societies that have been at least partly deracinated, partly tamed. . . . The nascent industrial classes of the twentieth century have become passionate consumers of a dynamically evolving new kind of theater.
—Richard Mandell, *Sport: A Cultural History*

A breath of the atmosphere of those lost afternoons, with their compound of compressed humanity, cigarette smoke on chill air, contagious excitement, tribal emotion, sense of shared ritual, and the hope, weekly renewed in spite of all experience that out of the ordinariness of life something startling and beautiful might be born.   —Paul Smith, *Saturday Afternoon Fever*

The speed with which association football came from behind to become the People's Game in Britain in the 1880s was matched by the rapidity of its diffusion as "football" throughout the world. As a consequence of the earliness of the game's introduction into the major ports of maritime Europe and Latin America in a era when Britannia still ruled the waves, there are some parallels with British development in both the history and the geography of early theaters or venues: they "just growed" cumulatively, like Topsy. Often the theaters became microcosms of popular culture, society, and region: cathedrals of the secular religion. I believe, with C.L.R. James, that "cricket and football were the greatest cultural influences in nineteenth-century Britain, leaving far behind Tennyson's poems, Beardsley's drawings, and concerts of the Philharmonic Society. *These filled space in print but not in minds*" (italics added).[1] The same is true today of soccer in Brazil, Argentina, Italy, and Cameroon.

Where the game arrived later, English influence in stadium building was less, and the shape and viewing area of the theater reflected much more each culture's sporting predilections. Both depended on whether the grounds were built and owned by private interests or designed by governments to reflect their political ideology. Grounds, seating, and standing capacities and quality relate to the country's stage of economic development, qualified by levels of interest demonstrated in the game by the upper social and economic classes, and recently by interest in hosting games controlled by soccer's international governing bodies. Provision of cover for spectators is similar, although climate and season of play are often critical here. Internal partitions and details—moats, perimeter fences, and rings of soldiers—are the governments' responses to the legacies of traditional mob football, to deracination and taming that is incomplete and in varying degrees free to express itself.

I therefore have two objectives: first, to recognize and explain the phases in the evolution of theaters of soccer; second, to characterize and explain the diversity in the major stadiums of the world's most popular game and differences in the quality of theater experienced therein, particularly in the theaters of soccer's superpowers.

The Stage of Traditional Football: The English Landscape

Poems written about the game and hung on goalposts nineteen hundred years ago tell us the Chinese were playing then. The ancient Greeks and Romans had their football games. But it is to England with its many recorded instances of the game, beginning in the ninth century A.D., that one must turn to learn of theaters. The richness of English written records may be the result of a deep cultural predilection to play in the open air on public grounds, as Danish writer Steen Rasmussen suggests. However this record keeping began, between 1885 and 1915 scholars and antiquarians displayed an intense interest in what so rapidly became the English national winter game, and they assiduously combed local records to discover and perhaps invent progenitors of the popular game.[2]

Deaths and riots in the theater of soccer, as well as the edicts of authorities who would ban "the exciting game," bring us tantalizing glimpses of "the fotebal" before the nineteenth century. Papal and other dispensations were needed for players who killed opponents, accidentally or otherwise. Litigation followed serious bodily injury to players and to innocent passers-by in city streets; failure to desist from playing the game on the Sabbath; and extensive property damage to windows and storefronts in towns and to fences of newly enclosed fields.[3]

There may have been well-ordered, peaceful variants of the game in England between 800 and 1800, but there are no records of them. Games were played on feast and saints' days and at weddings, the families of the newly married couple taking on all comers. The biggest games were played on Shrove Tuesday, on the eve of Lent. In the middle of chill February, spring crops were not sown, and winter wheat and grass had hardly begun to grow. In games sometimes lasting for days, with a cast sometimes of thousands battling in a theater often five miles long lying between neighboring towns, damage to fences and hedges was a problem. The three weeks after Shrove Tuesday, before sowing, gave time to repair broken fences and the bones of antagonists.[4]

Derby and "Local Derbies"

The thousands who played at Derby in the battle between the parishes of Saint Peter and All Saints took the whole town and its environs as the field of play (fig. 4.1, stage 1). They were watched by practically all the town's inhabitants at some point in the proceedings, which lasted a day or two or until a goal was scored.[5] So fierce was this rivalry between parishes that the town's name became synonymous with longstanding soccer feuds, called in Britain "local derbies." Other honors pale in comparison before the bragging rights attendant upon winning the "derby game." The most famous derbies in Britain are, or were until recently, still religious at base: Catholic Glasgow Celtic versus Protestant Glasgow Rangers, Catholic Everton versus Protestant Liverpool, Catholic Belfast Celtic versus Protestant Linfield, a battle so deadly for the former that the team was forced to disband.[6] In derbies,

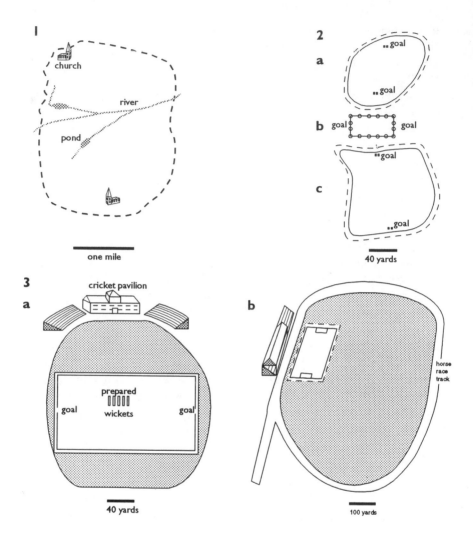

FIG. 4.1. Stages in the development of English theaters of soccer.
(1) Traditional mob football on vast, amorphous stage with no definite
boundaries, no separation of spectators and players; (2a,b,c) three different
English Public-School grounds, each with a unique shape and size, during
the era of transitional football; players and spectators were separated; the
rectangular field, b, is at Charterhouse's Carthusian Monastery; (3a,b) "big
field" Football Association (F.A.) games on cricket grounds, racecourses,
etc.: spectators stand on cricket ground or, later, sit on temporary
bleachers; (4a,b) "little field" Football League games on cricket grounds,
fairgrounds, and later on multipurpose (soccer primary) grounds: covered
stand with tier of seats above tier of standees in paddock on the west,

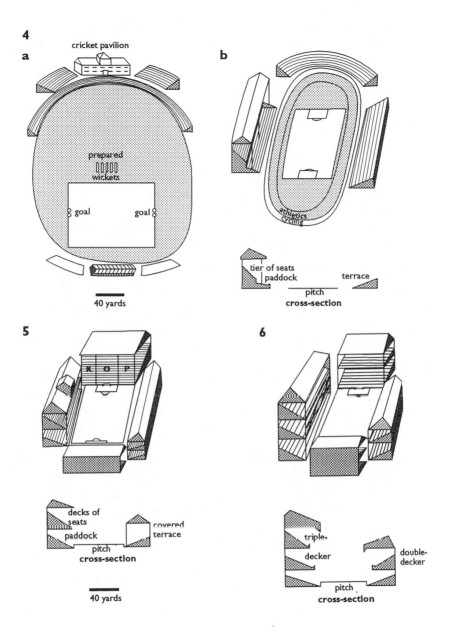

4

a

cricket pavilion

prepared
||||||
wickets

goal   goal

40 yards

b

tier of seats
paddock   terrace

pitch
cross-section

athletics
cycling

5

K O P

decks of
seats

paddock

pitch
cross-section

covered
terrace

40 yards

6

triple-
decker   double-
decker

pitch
cross-section

uncovered terraces elsewhere; (5) Golden Age of English soccer: west side double-decker, goal-end kop and terraces covered and increasingly overtopped by double-deckers on long sides; 6) modern era: west side cantilevered triple-decker, double-deckers over terrace/paddocks.

theaters are at capacity, the atmosphere is charged, and the actors play fiercely, often with such reckless abandon that "derby" is a byword for toughness and hard tackling.

In Ashbourne, next door to Derby, two teams picked themselves from among town members. Goalposts were set three miles apart, and teams charged through the streets, brawling through a stream, and fanning out into open country. The game had a water polo component in Hitchin, Middlesex, in 1772 when "the ball drowned for a time in the Priory pond." In larger places, streets were theaters. In seventeenth-century Manchester, edict after edict and two football constables tried to stop play in the streets. One can imagine the "grandstand" seats afforded by the vaulted second floor overhangs on the Elizabethan black-and-white houses of Deansgate as the seething teams of apprentices battled beneath, "breaking many men's windows and glasse."[7]

Suburban Fields of Fitz Stephen's London

In London, football was renowned and was played in fields in front of spectators at Shrovetide in the twelfth century. William Fitz Stephen's account of it seems quite modern: "To begin with the sports of the boys (for we have all been boys), annually on the day which is called Shrovetide. . . . After dinner, all the young men of the city go out into the fields to play at the well-known game of football. The scholars belonging to their several schools have each their ball; the city tradesmen according to their crafts have theirs."[8] The fields were clearly beyond the city wall, and many teams engaged in some sort of knockout championship.

What Fitz Stephen lauded at the time of Becket, English kings saw as a major problem in the fourteenth century. Londoners by this time were obviously playing football not just at Shrovetide, not quite as civilly as in Fitz Stephen's time, and apparently in the streets, for Edward II's proclamation of 1314 condemned the "great noise in the city caused by hustling over large balls . . . from which many evils might arise." He forbade "on pains of imprisonment, such a game to be used *in the city* in the future." This was the first of numerous attempts by monarchs to extirpate the game. Edward's proclamation also forbade playing "in the fields near the city."[9]

Apprentices and the Flying Game on London Streets

By the fourteenth century, the game now called "fotebal" had gained popularity among apprentices, who were playing it in the streets. Working long hours and often unable to get out in daylight to the fields beyond the wall, the apprentices were easily recruited for the wilder forms of the game, as at Shrovetide. Edward III blamed "fotebal" for diverting citizens from their military obligations as bowmen; his ban on play in the fields outside town and in the streets, on pain of imprisonment, forced the apprentices to play in churchyards, notably Saint Paul's, where they were joined by the clergy until the latter were banned from play. Play in a churchyard is not as strange as it may seem, for in the rural game the church spire was the distant goal for the players battling in the fields with either the church lych gate or porch the real "goal."[10]

Not only did the royal edicts go unheeded and the street games continue, but on one occasion the street game led to near insurrection, with so many killed that the game's ringleaders, including a knight, were executed.[11] As late as 1716, the poet John Gay describes the dilemmas of an unwilling spectator of a street game involving apprentices in London:

> Here oft my course I bend, when lo! from afar
> I spy the furies of the foot-ball war:
> The prentice quits his shop to join the crew,
> Increasing crowds the flying game pursue.
> Thus, as you roll the ball oer snowy ground,
> The gathering globe augments with evry round.
> But whither shall I run?[12]

Forbidden Games on Moorfields

In the fifteenth century, "early . . . professionalism" had crept into games: a proclamation of 1409 forbade money to be levied at weddings for "fotebal." In 1410 and again in 1414, Henry V banned football and ordered his people on the eve of the Battle of Agincourt to practice archery rather than football; in the year of Agincourt, the mayor of London put a postern called Moorgate in London Wall to enable citizens to get out to the moor quickly for archery practice. More significantly, however, he laced Moorfields with ditches that made it dry, thus dividing the land into rectilinear parcels that made it easier for the young to play the forbidden game of football![13]

For fifty years, there was a lull in antifootball statutes. But football was threatened in 1477 when Edward IV banned it, ordering the ablebodied to practice the bow. More inconveniencing were the actions of the mayor who, in repairing London Wall, searched Moorfields for brick clay, pitting the fields with holes "by which means this field was made the worse for a long time." The common fields beyond Moorfields then became the venue for London's sporting youth. But when the inhabitants of Shoreditch and Hoxton enclosed these common fields with hedges and ditches a decade later, this so incensed Londoners

> that suddenly . . . a great number of the city assembled themselves in a morning, and a turner in a fools coat, came crying through the city "Shovels and spades! shovels and spades!" so many of the people followed that . . . within a short space all the hedges about the city were cast down, and the ditches filled up, and every thing made plain. . . . The kings council . . . commanded the mayor to . . . forthwith call home the younger sort; who having speedily achieved their desire, returned home . . . after which time these fields were never hedged.[14]

In 1512 Moorfields was diked, bridged, leveled, and made "more commodious"; in 1527, the building of sluices and more ditches made the whole moor "main" and "hard." These civil engineering actions and the spontaneous actions of the "city assembled" occurred in the reign of Henry VIII, who outlawed the game in 1496 and repeatedly attempted to prevent its play, but to no avail. The game was deeply embedded in folk custom. This fact, together with the national penchant for outdoor sports, had as their corollary the demand for access to open space and playing fields, which monarchs found they could not deny without fear of a popular uprising. British monarchs learned, as Rasmussen shows, that to be popular among the people they must be seen as "good sports," and this meant to side with the people when it came to questions of fields of play.[15]

London's Parks for the People

The tradition of preserving and democratizing open space in London began with Henry VIII turning a blind eye to happenings at Moorfields and Shoreditch. It continued with a reluctant James II ruling against a developer and supporting apprentices who burnt the builders' supplies and obstructed construction on long-established playing fields: Lincoln's Inn Fields and Red Lion Square. The royal connection continued with the opening up of the ten royal parks, and it came to the present with the Duke of Edinburgh's advocacy of the National Playing Fields Association. The ubiquitous parks and open spaces in London and Westminster are the jewels in the capital's crown of democratic uniqueness compared to the absolutist capitals of continental Europe, according to Rasmussen. Proof is the Londoner's "unique involvement with the Royal Parks: he feels he owns them, even though the facts are otherwise," writes Hazel Thurston.[16]

Compared to the formal, geometric parks of Continental capitals, English parks look natural and unplanned. With their long views over flat to slightly rolling ground, they remain an open invitation to Londoners to play what they will, and the people's game of choice, under the oaks and in the mead, is soccer in its many forms. Here is the proud father with toddler and beach ball; there are schoolboys playing attack-on-defense or meet-the-corner, with coats for goalposts. In the royal parks there are goalposts without nets and full-sized fields without markings reserved for games between occasional teams, such as the annual contests between University College, London's geography and history departments, 1954–57, which I remember well. "Of greatest importance" in Battersea Park "are the considerable areas laid out as playing- and sporting-grounds . . . the large lawns typical of an English landscape garden . . . are always full of people. There are football fields, cricket pitches, bowling and putting greens. . . . Battersea Park is not an imposing stadion like those . . . laid out in many German towns since the war [World War I], *it is a garden for sport for the unambitious amateur*" (italics added), as is Hampstead Heath where "on the flat plain towards the south, boys play football while others run up and down hills kicking their balls about." Rasmussen argues that "the development of the modern London parks is . . . closely connected with the development of English sport," whose post-Arnoldian object is to keep fit. "In this spirit London has . . . developed an emancipated outdoor life, to which all classes have access. No one is nowadays too good to play with balls or to kick a football. . . . The number of public recreation grounds in the central parks of London has increased during the last century while it has diminished considerably in other great cities (especially Paris)."[17]

The Closing of Space and the Demise of Traditional Football

In the seventeenth century, a tide of words intended to drown "mob football" had no more effect in curbing the game than did royal edicts. But new theaters of play in the eighteenth century are symptoms of change that did much harm to the traditional game's popularity. Games of football were arranged for political ends at once-only theaters. Walvin cites four cases. In 1638 on the Isle of Ely, "a football match was organized deliberately to attract a crowd and to pull down the banks designed to drain local fens." In 1740, "a Mach of Futtball was Cried at

Kettering of five Hundred Men a side, but the design was to Pull Down Lady Betey Jesmaines Mills." At West Haddon, Northants, in 1764 those opposing an enclosure of two thousand acres instigated a "footbal match" that "degenerated into an overtly political mob which tore up and burned enclosure fences." Similarly, in Holland Fen, Lincolnshire, reaction to an enclosure in 1768 spawned three political football matches of about two hundred men in one month.[18]

All these examples are taken from areas that underwent massive landscape change in response to pressures of the Agricultural Revolution. The effect was to break up the large open fields and formerly common lands into small parcels bounded by fences and hedges, and to lace fens with embankments and drainage channels. The newfound barriers to the "flying game" everywhere, and the willingness of the new property-owning "improvers" to prosecute for damage led to widespread abandonment of the lengthy and spatially extensive games played in the countryside and small towns, particularly in areas affected by draining of marsh, reclaiming of heath, and enclosure. The heightened Sabbatarianism of the Methodists and Evangelicals in industrial areas prevented play on the workers' one free day.

In the new industrial towns housing conditions were so crowded, open space so scarce, and working hours so long that memory of the rural game was erased for lack of both energy and a place to play. Even in the older towns, pressures to abandon "mob football" increased as towns developed police forces that enforced the law considered necessary for the industrial economy. There was neither time nor a place for a game that needed a day or so to complete it in a vast theater. Joseph Strutt, early historian of English sports, wrote of football in 1801 that "it was formerly much in vogue among the common people of England, though of late years, it seems to have fallen into disrepute, and is little practised." William Howitt in 1848 wrote that "football . . . seems to have almost gone out of use with the inclosure of wastes and commons, requiring a wide space for its exercise."[19]

Transitional Football

The urban counterpart of the extensive country game was the freewheeling street game. While both forms of the game suffered between 1760 and 1840, one response in the old towns and the new industrial areas was to adapt the game to small spaces available for play and to the limited daylight time available for recreation in the new industrial society. In effect, the game that survived was similar to the games played at London's Moorfields from the fourteenth century. Small fields, tighter rules, balanced teams, specified balls ("blown bladder, and cased with leather"), and measured goals ("two sticks driven into the ground, about two or three feet apart") became the rule in the mid–nineteenth century. This new football carried through the period of transition between traditional and modern football (1820–55), particularly in towns on the southern flanks of the Pennine Chain—Sheffield, Nottingham, Derby, Manchester—where early representative soccer took off between 1857 and 1878.[20]

Thomas Arnold and the Playing Fields of Public Schools

The disciplinary problems in England's exclusive schools ("public schools") in the nineteenth century were great; they were often associated with the public schoolboys' playing of the local "mob football" game.[21] It was Thomas Arnold's genius, as headmaster of Rugby School in the 1830s, to introduce discipline and rules into games as a means of social control. Cricket had long been the summer game; he made football the winter game, and both became central to his message of "godliness and good learning" and to the "new public school virtues" of his followers: courage, selflessness, teamwork, and toughness. What Arnold did at Rugby the other public schools followed in the 1840s. In the 1850s, his ideas spread to the grammar schools of the upper middle classes, as did the versions of the game carried by the old boys of the Big Seven schools who went out as teachers, after a few years of education and football at Oxford and Cambridge.[22]

The games and rules at the public schools reflected the size and shape of the theaters of play (fig. 4.1, stage 2). The large fields were at Rugby and Harrow. The big "Close" at Rugby allowed a game of 20-a-side with the younger and smaller boys defending the goal against older boys (it was ever so). Because the field was large, perhaps, more handling of the ball was allowed there than elsewhere.[23] This eventually ensured that Rugby would give its name to the "handling game" later in the century, and led alumni even later to insist that rugby football was invented at the school when William Webb-Ellis "picked up the ball and ran" in 1823. Who can argue with a bronze tablet that says so?[24]

Quagmire and Monastery: The Dribbling Schools

The largeness of Harrow's field did not promote handling, apparently because it was poorly drained, sticky land that became a quagmire in winter. Consequently the rules at Harrow emphasized "dribbling" and de-emphasized handling. The other five major public schools, all with smaller fields and large numbers involved, favored the dribbling game, often with specific prohibitions. At Charterhouse, football was played in the cloisters of an old Carthusian monastery (fig. 4.1, stage 2b). Space was limited and, because of centuries-old windows, the ball could not be kicked high or long. When the ball got into the right angle of a monastery buttress, a melée of fifty hackers formed. At Westminster School, restricted space ensured that dribbling was paramount, along with a strong emphasis on heavy charging and tackling. Winchester's medium-sized field (eighty by twenty-five yards) encouraged a more open game based on "accurate kicking and dashing play" and skill in scrimmaging, while at Eton, with its pitch longer and narrower than Winchester's and bounded by walls, there was long and high kicking as well as dribbling and scrimmaging.

In all the London-area schools handling was allowed, but it was forbidden to catch the ball and run with it as was done in Rugby. It was in the most northerly school, Shrewsbury, with its large field, that the game most like modern association football was fashioned. A strictly dribbling game, known as "douling," was developed and its rules regularized. It had firmly enforced rules about "offside." It was this game that was taken to Cambridge University in the 1840s, where a Shrewsbury man, J. C. Thring, convened a group of public schoolmen who regularized rules for play at Cambridge that emphasized dribbling and discouraged handling. Rules regularization was a response to games between public schools and the universities made possible by the coming of scheduled passenger trains.[25]

Modern Football

Perhaps the critical event of the 1850s was the meeting of the two streams of football in Sheffield in 1855 when Harrow School alumni (also Cambridge men) met and organized a team of "local village footballers" (Sheffield F.C.) whom, legend has it, the Old Harrovians persuaded "not to handle the ball, allegedly by providing players with white gloves and florins to clutch during the game." A number of teams, more heterogeneous in membership, are known to have organized soon after in the Sheffield area. This suggests that there were plenty still playing a variant of the "old game" in the towns near the Pennine Chain. Further proof is afforded by the response of five hundred men to an advertisement in the *Leeds Mercury* in 1864 asking for people who wanted to play football on Woodhouse Moor a few days a week "from 7 to 8 o'clock A.M."[26]

Things began to move quickly in the 1860s, led once again by Thring, who in 1862 issued a set of rules entitled "The Simplest Game," which were used immediately for a game at Cambridge. One year later, a number of London-area clubs met at Lincoln's Inn Fields to codify the rules of football on lines set out by Thring and to found the Football Association (F.A.).[27]

By the end of 1863 the F.A. had adopted rules against hacking, tripping, pushing, and handling (other than the "fair catch"); this sent the Blackheath group of proto-Rugby players on their separate way. Interestingly, the maximum size of the new theater was to be two hundred yards by one hundred yards, and the goals were to be eight yards wide with no specific height and no tape or bar across. The number of players was not specified, although fifteen-a-side was common in the London area at the time.[28]

Muscular Christian Missionaries to the Docks and the Satanic Mills

The missionary zeal of the public schoolmen, directed to the grammar schools in the 1850s, turned in the 1860s to the working class. They organized first where the game had survived in an unorganized fashion, as on the Pennine flanks; later, as "muscular Christians" and champions of the new cult of physical fitness ("mens sana in corpore sano"), they took the game to the dock areas of East London and Liverpool and to the coal fields of the northwest, where the old game, if not dead, had largely slipped from memory. The casual nature of labor on the docks and in the coal fields, compared to that in the more regulated and regimented textile mills, ensured that the new game would get a head start there—an initial advantage never lost by Liverpool, Manchester, and Thames-side London.[29]

The nationwide gains of the "muscular Christian crusade" of the 1860s were consolidated by two events—the representative games of 1866 and 1871 between the two early poles of soccer, London and Sheffield, and the establishment of the F.A. Cup in 1871, a knockout tournament for which all English teams, amateur and professional, are eligible and still the most exciting part of the English soccer season. In 1877, one set of rules was finally achieved with the incorporation of some Sheffield ideas, notably on the corner kick.

For a decade, the "muscular Christian" amateurs from the public schools and Oxbridge dominated the F.A. Cup played in London. But in 1882, twenty years after the earliest forays of the soccer missionaries into the industrial northwest, the working-class converts (Blackburn Rovers) came south to play the alumni of Eton School. They lost.

But next year, another working-class team, Blackburn Olympic, won against the Old Etonian amateurs. This game proved the end of the era of the upper-class amateur and the new domination by working-class professionals. Seven of the first ten F.A. Cup winners of the professional era, 1882–91, were from Lancashire, and when the Football League (of professionals) was formed in 1888, six of twelve teams were from Lancashire, and the other six were from the horseshoe-shaped area flanking the southern Pennines.[30]

The first three Football League championships were also won by Lancashire teams. The question is, why did Lancashire so dominate this era? Lincoln Allison argues that Lancashire had its own capital, Manchester, and its own industrial culture and philosophy (Manchester School), one in which alliances with the liberal bourgeoisie and with Tory reformers produced more respect between Disraeli's "two nations" than in London and the other industrial regions. The Lancashire working class simply identified itself with English society in the 1880s, and this led to incorporation, apparent or real, into that society. There was a special receptivity to the public-school missionaries in the 1860–80 period in the Northwest.[31]

Professionalism, the Spectator, and the Necessity for Ground Sharing

Within a decade of the introduction of "football" in the urban-industrial areas of Britain in the 1860s, some teams had sufficiently large followings that a need arose for enclosed and gated grounds where crowds could be controlled and admission charged. Building in the towns during the Industrial Revolution left little open space, and no stadiums had existed anywhere in Europe since Greek and Roman times, except for the bullrings of southern Europe and the Milan Arena. The only large and often partially enclosed areas available in English cities were undeveloped fair- and showgrounds for the three sports that preceded soccer in attracting spectators: horse racing, track and field, and cricket. It was to these venues that soccer teams turned in the early years.[32]

Nottingham Forest, the third oldest club in England (1865) and early English First Division team (1892–93), took its name from Forest Racecourse, where it first played. Derby County (1884), founding member of the Football League in 1888, played at the Racecourse in the early years. Wrexham, Wales's oldest club, plays at the Racecourse, which hosted Wales's home internationals. The teams that played at racecourses presented their spectators with a distant view of the field of play, across two sets of barriers and a wide track (fig. 4.1, stage 3b).[33]

Early Venues

Fairgrounds were used by two of the twelve founding members of the Football League—the Wolverhampton Wanderers and Aston Villa. Here the problem was the playing surface, which suffered abuse from the array of other activities that took place.

The area encircled by Powderhall athletics track, site of the famous sprint, was used in the early years by the two major Edinburgh teams, Hibernian and Heart of Midlothian, and in the 1930s by the now-defunct Edinburgh City. And the F.A. Cup Final of 1894 was played at Fallowfield Athletic and Cycling Track, Manchester.

Teams also played in the 1890s on the national baseball league's grounds—for example, Derby County, which still plays at the Baseball Ground, and Leyton Orient. Similarly, in the rugby strongholds of the north, English league teams—Bradford City, Huddersfield, Leeds, Hull, and Stockport County—grew out of rugby teams or used rugby grounds between 1900 and 1910.[34]

It was, however, the cricket connection that nurtured soccer in the 1863–92 period and that furnished places where soccer and its mass following fused to produce the prototypes of modern football theaters. Cricket was long established at the club level in the English south, and the muscular Christian missionaries introduced the summer game to the north before they encouraged the "new" winter game, soccer. Consequently, when the interest in football exploded, cricket fields were the only large areas available in grass and with a true bouncing surface in urban areas. Furthermore, the cricket fields often had pavilions for changing (otherwise soccer players changed in the nearest pub) and they were usually enclosed and gated for admission of paying spectators (fig. 4.1, stage 3a). Members of cricket clubs, interested in engaging in a winter sport, chose soccer, sometimes using the cricket grounds of, for example, Everton, Preston North End, and Kilmarnock, founding members of the English and Scottish football leagues. Other cricket club members played soccer on rough ground near their cricket grounds—for example, Manchester City and Tottenham Hotspur.[35]

Even more fortunate were towns that had county cricket grounds used during summer in the county cricket competition, which was well established in fourteen counties between 1875 and 1895. These were particularly important for soccer in the industrial north and the midlands. The Yorkshire County Cricket Ground at Bramall Lane, Sheffield, nurtured three famous teams: Sheffield F.C., the oldest team in the world; Sheffield Wednesday, which began as a cricket club that played on Wednesdays, and then played some soccer games at Bramall Lane before 1895; and Sheffield United, formed in 1895 by the Bramall Lane cricket authorities to play there permanently as their own club. After playing for decades with a twenty-yard overlap on the cricket field, and having spectators on only three sides of the playing field, Sheffield United ejected the cricketers in the 1960s and finally provided for spectators on the four sides of the playing field.[36]

Trent Bridge, Nottinghamshire's county cricket ground and one of the six grounds where the England test (international) team plays, early hosted two Football League teams: Nottingham Forest and Notts County, the English League's oldest club, there for twenty-seven years. Notts County, in fact, played during its first forty-eight years on five different cricket grounds! Nearby Derby County played on the Derby-shire ground and Leicester City (Fosse) on the Leicestershire ground. Other county grounds used by soccer teams were Sussex by Brighton, Hampshire by Southampton Town, Glamorgan by Cardiff City, and Wiltshire by Swindon.[37]

Kennington Oval, the Surrey County ground (and England venue) hosted twenty of the first twenty-one F.A. Cup finals. Here F.A. Cup crowds went from a modest 2,000 in the early phase to 32,800 in 1892. It was simply a matter of time before the cricket authorities decided to protect their hallowed turf from the wear and tear of soccer spectators sitting and standing on it. Soccer was ejected in 1893. Only one English League team today still shares a county cricket ground: Northampton Town with Northants, 1897 to the present.[38]

An advantage of cricket grounds for soccer teams between 1871 and 1887 was that the maximum size of soccer fields was 200 by 100 yards,[39] or almost two and one-half times the size of the average English League ground today, which is 113 by 74 yards (8,362 sq. yds.). As most cricket grounds are about three times the size of modern soccer fields, this means that, in the years before the playing field was cut down in size in 1887 (and before the number of players was reduced from twenty to fifteen to eleven), the disposition of spectators was similar for both games (with soccer spectators also on the grass cordoned off by rope barriers). In this early period, the sizes and shapes of the two playing fields generally ensured that the "wicket" would be in the middle of the "big" soccer field—an area torn up much less than the approaches to the goalmouths (see fig. 4.1, stage 3a). Today in Barbados, for example, soccer and cricket fields are commonly one and the same. On the small

FIG. 4.2. Theaters of soccer in Barbados, 1992. (a) Bank Hall, Bridgetown. Flags indicate the boundary of the soccer field. The base of the far uprights (white goalposts, white net) is just detectable below the cricket sight-screen; the small cricket stand, Sir Frank Worrell gate, and cricket pavilion are in the background. The lighter-colored rise in the middle ground is the raised area of the cricket wickets on the edge of soccer's center circle. Such fields were commonly used for English Football League games, 1887–1917. (b) National Stadium, Barbados. Multipurpose stadium similar to those used by English Football League teams, 1900–1925. Eight-lane athletics track with long jump/pole vault runway on west side surrounded by cycling track; covered stands with high rake on west side, but only those in the first fifteen rows of the main stand are in the optimum viewing area for watching soccer games, most of which are played here (common practice in third world countries).

fields, the wicket area is laid close to the soccer field's center circle (fig. 4.2). On bigger fields the wicket is laid just off the soccer field and parallel to it. Interestingly, in Barbados it is raised a foot or more above the level of the rest of the field and often roped off so that soccer scrimmages play around it. During soccer games, when ropes are removed, soccer players kick off to one side or the other of the raised wicket and try to avoid playing across it.

In the muddy British winter, of course, there was serious danger that the wicket would be torn up. Cricket clubs in this early period of ground sharing had to weigh the advantages of revenue from a soccer club against the disadvantage of the costs of repairs to the true-bouncing surface of the central area that would provide the summer's three to five wickets. The explosion in soccer playing and in spectator interest in industrial-urban areas with few, if any, enclosed green playing surfaces made cricket the obvious stopgap: an early but temporary venue. The first upswing in the cricket connection came in the 1877–85 years, with a downturn in the late 1880s (fig. 4.3). The potential and actual damage to cricket field and wicket ensured that the stay of soccer teams at cricket grounds would not be a long one. The average length of use is just over four years, but both mode and median of the stay is two years in the "big field" era.

After 1892, the new, shortened soccer field could be accommodated at one end of the cricket ground; consequently, the wicket was beyond the soccer field's playing surface (fig. 4.1, stage 4a). This gave a second lease on life to the cricket connection, particularly among teams getting under way in the South between 1890 and 1910. The second upswing peaks in 1899 (see fig. 4.3), when there were ten present-day English League teams with active cricket connections. Only one team, York City, developed a cricket connection after 1905. They took over a cricket ground, Bootham Crescent, in 1932 and still play there.[40]

Cricket clubs were interested in renting to soccer clubs when the wicket was far from the "small soccer field." The disadvantage for the soccer club was that the ground could have spectators on only three of the four sides of the playing surface (the fourth was one of the long sides, and therefore half of the optimum viewing area was lost). This became a serious economic problem as English League soccer moved into its great era of the spectator, 1920–55, in which grounds were often filled to capacity. The problem caused the soccer teams to take over the field and evict the cricketers (e.g., Coventry City) or move to a different ground (e.g., Leicester City).[41]

There is something unsatisfactory about being a soccer spectator in

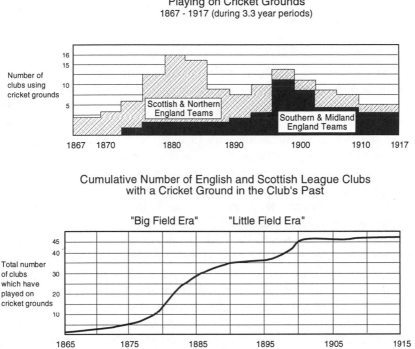

Number of English and Scottish League Clubs
Playing on Cricket Grounds
1867 - 1917 (during 3.3 year periods)

Number of clubs using cricket grounds

Scottish & Northern England Teams

Southern & Midland England Teams

Cumulative Number of English and Scottish League Clubs
with a Cricket Ground in the Club's Past

"Big Field Era"   "Little Field Era"

Total number of clubs which have played on cricket grounds

FIG. 4.3. The cricket connection in English and Scottish league soccer.

a ground completely open on one of its long sides. The pitch passes into open prairie, which disconcerts the eye (the high ball gets lost in a sea of green, and there are optical illusions that stem from the increased depth of vision and the distant background), and the acoustical bowl and the intimate cocoon are both lost. Thus, although the stay at cricket grounds was longer in this second, small field phase just over seven years on average, with the median and mode both five years— most of these cricket connections did not survive the coming of what Hobsbawm calls "the all-English football culture" and the "ground records" between the wars.[42]

Stadiums Built Primarily for Soccer

In the second phase of venues, owners laid out grounds and built stadiums mainly for soccer, although many still had doubts that soccer revenue alone could support the facility. As a result, many of the new grounds were laid out for multipurpose use. Cycling, speedway cinder tracks, athletics tracks, and, later, greyhound tracks ringed many fields (fig. 4.1, stage 4b).

Kops, Paddocks, and Terraces

In many towns, the only available spaces were dumps for the city's refuse and for industrial wastes. Aberdeen's famous Pittodrie means "place of dung," and Bolton Wanderers' Burnden Park was a "stagnant mess of dumped refuse and chemicals from nearby works" when the field was laid in 1895. Cardiff City in Wales, Birmingham City, Manchester City, Southend United, Hartlepools United, Halifax Town in England, and Arbroath in Scotland all play on the town's former rubbish dumps. London's Charlton Athletic plays at the Valley, a derelict chalkpit; Leyton Orient, on "waste ground"; and Fulham and Tottenham, on overgrown urban wildernesses.[43]

More widespread in this era was the use of waste products to build up the spectator areas. The biggest and steepest of these engineered hills was invariably behind one of the goals. Here the working-class home team supporters congregated, roared, and later sang in their serried thousands (fig. 4.1, stage 5). The main period of dumping to make these hills has been perpetuated in the common name for them: "kop," for the Boer War battle of Spion Kop (January 1900). In that battle British officers ordered a futile assault, unsupported by artillery, up a bare and steep hill held at the top by entrenched Boers. Hundreds of Lancashire men of the Second Royal Lancaster Regiment and of the Second Royal Lancashire Fusiliers were killed or wounded, producing what war correspondent Winston Churchill described as that "acre of massacre, that complete shambles." The name "kop" was adopted as a working-class memory of a working-class tragedy, particularly at the football grounds of Lancashire and nearby northern counties, where most of the named kops are to be found. The most famous and largest kop is Liverpool's, at Anfield, which stood thirty thousand in soccer's heyday.[44]

In the embankments of the north and the Black Country, cinders from steam engines, clinkers and slag from steelworks, and gangue from ironworkings were the main materials. Further south, where there were no coal fields and steelworks, cinders and other types of refuse, including street sweepings, were used. Once the embankment or kop was pressed and consolidated, steps were cut in and edged, usually with old railroad ties to produce terraces. Throughout the country, "kop" became the popular name for the standing-only areas of British grounds, except for the highest-priced standing area between grandstand and pitch, often called "enclosure" or "paddock" (named for the enclosed area that pens the thoroughbreds at the racetrack). In this second phase of ground development, waste was used as the base for the lower-rise terraces behind both goals at most grounds and often on one of the long sides (fig. 4.1, stage 4b). The fourth side was the site of the paddock backed by the grandstand ("stands") erected by the club's directors for those who wished to pay more to sit and watch the game.

Inevitably there was self-segregation by socioeconomic class, with the middle class in the stands, lower middle class in the paddock, skilled artisans on the long-side terraces, and unskilled and casual workers on the kop. There was also a rough differentiation by age, with the youngest behind the second goal, young to middle-aged adults on the kop, and the middle to older adults on the long-side terraces.[45]

Ground development in this second phase was aesthetically haphazard and rarely part of an organic plan. While the club raised the grandstand, it was often the supporters themselves who raised the money to erect rudimentary cover over terraces, usually beginning on the long side. Local names for these covers indicate the original intent of the structure and what people thought of it: "The Shed" (Chelsea); "Cowshed" (Exeter City); "Flowerpot Stand" (Plymouth Argyle); "Pigeon Loft" (Wrexham); and "Rabbit Hutch" (Fulham).

Archibald Leitch, the Big Clubs, and Double-Deckers

The partial exceptions to the rule of accidental growth and discordant texture are the twenty-five grounds designed by the Scottish mechanical engineer Archibald Leitch, whose football association began in 1902. Leitch's stamp was one full-length two-tier grandstand with seats at the back and a standing enclosure in front of it, and three open sides of terracing (fig. 4.1, stage 5). Between 1904 and 1914, at least nineteen major stands like this were completed. In the early decades of this century, only the wealthiest clubs provided grandstands of this type on both sides: Rangers and Celtic in Glasgow; Arsenal and Tottenham in London; Everton, Manchester United, and Sheffield Wednesday in northern England. Everton, always in the forefront of innovation, had stands on three sides early (1892) at the opening of Goodison Park, "the first major football stadium in England." It was also the first British ground to have cover on all four sides (1909).[46] In these things Everton was the exception to the grounds of the early twentieth century, but in two ways the club represented the successful clubs in the third phase of theater development. They decided to retain their center city grounds and, in their quest for more space for spectators, they built upward and pinched inward and often downward.

There were good historical and conservative reasons for staying at the center city grounds. By the 1920s many of them were amortized. Construction costs went up by more than 50 percent in the 1920s, while sources for capital became increasingly scarce in the interwar period. Furthermore, the grounds were well served by public transportation, important in a society in which the working and lower middle classes, which increasingly filled football grounds in the 1920–55 period, did not have cars. In addition, center city grounds were close to the central railway stations and accessible to the thousands of fans who came to support the visitors.[47] Once the decision to stay in the center had been made, generally in the decade after World War I, the clubs looked upward. In 1909 Leitch designed for Everton the country's first double-decker, "in which the seating tier was actually above part of the terrace. This was a major advance because it enabled more spectators to be accommodated in less space." Leitch's prewar design for Everton's Main Stand at Goodison Road became the norm for the wealthier clubs after the war, and as spectator interest soared, the leading clubs put in more and more double-deckers (fig. 4.1, stage 5). Everton had three Leitch double-deckers by 1926 and was the first club in the land to have all four sides in double-deckers (1939). Continuing the traditions of innovation and intensification, Everton was the first British club to go to the triple-decker (fig. 4.1, stage 6), which in 1971 replaced what had been the earliest English double-decker. Leitch's stamp on all these interwar double-deckers was a pedimented center gable on the pitch roof of the main grandstand and a white front for the balcony, crisscrossed with steel framing (fig. 4.1, stage 6).[48]

While the grounds expanded upward in the third phase of development, they also expanded inward, removing the tracks that had seemed necessary for survival twenty years earlier. Notable examples were Goodison Park (Everton), Burnden Park (Bolton), and Villa Park (Aston Villa). Terracing was extended shallowly downward across the former track right to the edge of the pitch, or depressed below the level of the playing surface (fig. 4.1, stage 5), as at Everton, where one of my delights was to get a front spot on the terraces with my eyes at pitch level, looking up at the players who appeared literally as giants on the hallowed Goodison turf. This pinching inward to extend the terracing also cut into the early pitches, which accounts in part for the small size of

English and Scottish grounds compared to grounds early in this century and to grounds on the Continent and Latin America. In extreme cases, the level of the pitch was actually depressed. In effect, in England in the third phase, even the grounds that had been ellipsoidal early in the century were converted to the familiar sharp-sided rectangle, with fans at the front of the terraces intimately close to the players on the field.[49]

Pitch-in-the-Round: The Enveloping Crowd as Actors

Crowd involvement with the players is widely recognized as characteristically British. Harold Hobson writes of Britain that "soccer is theater where the audience consists of actors."[50] This is so because of the early commitment to center city grounds, the need thereafter to build upward and to push the edge of the terracing to the rectangular edge of the pitch. All this happened as the fans, the majority of them *standing* on the terraces, increased in number to the high peak of involvement in 1949 when most grounds were stretched beyond safe capacity and fans packed in like sardines in a can. The British fans like it that way. They want to see the grimaces, the jubilation, the grace of their heroes, hear them call for the ball, curse, and feel the tackle and thud of the ball on head and foot. This you do if you are within what Harry Faulkner-Brown calls the "optimum viewing area" for football: less than 90 meters from the center spot and less than 150 meters from the farthest corner flag (fig. 4.4).

Without any coordinated plans and design, and evolving as a series of historical accidents and piecemeal reactions to changed circumstances, the traditional British football ground, with four rectangular stands and/or covered terraces parallel to the touchlines (fig. 4.4a), put most fans within the optimum viewing area (although columns and barriers necessitated plenty of leaning of bodies and craning of necks that set the massive crowd a-swaying). By contrast, elliptical grounds, which are the rule on the Continent and at England's Wembley Stadium (fig. 4.4d), and Scotland's Hampden Park (fig. 4.4b), place the majority of spectators outside the optimum viewing area and another 20 percent at least outside the maximum viewing area of 190 meters.[51] It is difficult to feel an intimacy and involvement with players who appear no bigger than ants, particularly if the spectator is sitting down. "This is because the stadium is so vast that a seat at the top of one of the stands inevitably provides a distant bird's-eye view, and not all of us are as long-sighted as hawks. I have watched a Cup Final," writes Ivor Brown, "from one of these perches and I felt that the performers were tiny articles not human beings."[52]

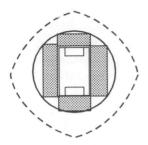

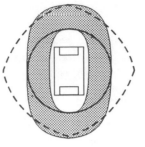

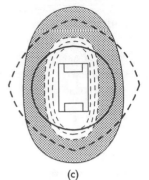

(a)	(b)	(c)
Typical English (Everton) Small Pitch	Scottish 'Service Area' (Hampden)	Multipurpose (Velodrome, Athletics with West-side Long Jump)

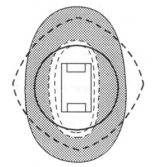

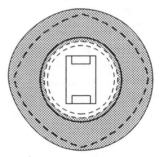

(d)
Olympic Style Athletics/Soccer
(with West-side
Long Jump and Pole Vault)

(e)
Brazilian Style,
with moat (Maracana),
Large Pitch

Edge of Maximum Viewing Area
Maximum viewing area = 190 meters from farthest corner flag
(after Faulkner - Brown, 1979)

Edge of Optimum Viewing Area
Optimal viewing area = 90 meters from center circle and about
150 meters from farthest corner flag

Spectators

FIG. 4.4. Spectators' views of action in five soccer theaters.

In the tight rectangle of terraces and grandstands in the golden age, the magic of British soccer was the feeling of partisanship and community. Payment of a shilling "turned you into a member of a new community, all brothers together for an hour and a half . . . cheering together, thumping one another on the shoulders, swopping judgements like lords of the earth, having pushed your way through a turnstile into another and altogether more splendid kind of life, hurtling with Conflict and yet passionate and beautiful in its Art. Moreover it offered you more than a shilling's worth of material for talk during the rest of the week."[53] Professional football helped create a sense of community and identification with place and "the terraced stadium . . . among terraced houses, and football generated a sense of belonging."[54]

The feeling in Britain's soccer theaters is that of Shakespeare's audience in the Globe Theatre. Soccer is staged intimately "in the round, in the center of the stadium, so the spectator confronts the emotion apparent on the faces of other spectators and is made even more aware of the mass of humanity sharing the event."[55] The ground as meeting place becomes a thunderous echoing bowl. Spectator participation is palpable, and the proof of its influence on the game is the fact that on essentially standard-sized fields with no significant idiosyncrasies the home team tends to win far more often than the visitors.[56] As the home team builds wave after wave of attacks on the visitors' goal, backed by a mounting crescendo of baying fans, it seems inevitable that the collective will prevail and the unrestrained animal roar be released.

Terrace Culture: Choirs in Their Cathedrals

Since World War II, other theater behaviors have found the headlines.[57] The standing crowd, seemingly more disciplined as a chorus, chants as mantra and uncannily bursts into song in unison. Just how do twenty thousand know which song to sing, in which key? For they close as powerfully as they begin. There must be cues known to the community; collective vibrations among the multitude; the same experience in soccer as in religion. Liverpool is the only English provincial city with two cathedrals: Roman Catholic and Anglican. But the city's real cathedrals are Liverpool's Anfield and Everton's Goodison Park, where the singing choirs stand for two hours and assert their affinity and devotion.[58] Recall the multitudes with honor guards, arms raised high and waving team scarves after the Hillsborough disaster, the sacred turf, for decades the repository for ashes of departed fans, totally covered with wreaths of flowers. From the ends of the earth pilgrims come to tread the hallowed pitch and visit the ground as temple, taking back ritual memorabilia to adorn personal shrines.[59]

To stand packed on a terrace is to become part of terrace culture, to feel the shapes and edges of at least four bodies. There is nothing quite so out-of-body and helpless as being part of a crowd craning to see action in a corner and feeling oneself part of an involuntary human wave of massive energy. More frightening is to feel the energy and weight in that wave breaking one's ribs on a crush barrier, squeezing the air from one's lungs; even more frightening is the thought that if that crush barrier goes, you will be a corpse mourned by that great crowd. My father was in the over-capacity crowd that watched the Bolton Wanderers play Manchester City in 1925 (he was 19). He paid to get in, saw the ball once, and got out of the ground twenty-five minutes after the kickoff with his trousers and shirt but without coat, jacket, and cap and glad to be alive. My own frightening memory was, as a student, being carried along from the Chelsea terraces down endless steps without my feet ever touching the ground.

Everyone who has felt the great crowd's surge knows at least the fleeting thought that one may pay the ultimate price for football fanaticism, for being an actor in the theater. There is risk on the terraces as there is on the pitch and as there is not for those sitting in the stands. That bond of risk makes the standing crowd feel superior to the sitters, developing in the actors a lifetime aversion to the thought of joining the passive seated crowd they have so long disparaged as sissified inferiors.

Ends, Cages, and Pens: The Second Game

Risk and disparagement on the terraces, of course, increased markedly in the late 1950s with the emergence of "football hooliganism." Invasions of the pitch, fighting on the terraces, generally between rival fans, became part of the aggressive behavior of what Dunning calls "the rough working-class" elements at the core of this elaboration of the action inside the theater. The response of authorities was to cage and segregate home fans and visiting fans on the terraces by giving them "ends" or "turf," frequently creating a no-man's land between the rival groups manned by police to prevent "invasion" and pitched battles.[60]

Segregated on the terraces, hooligans turned to bombarding opposing goalkeepers with toilet rolls and bottles, and the "other end" with stones, movable debris, and crumbling concrete from the terraces. Later, bombardments included ball bearings, darts, Molotov cocktails, and metal objects including sharpened coins. Verbal bombardment turned to chants and songs directed at the opposing team and its fans at the other end, using words and gestures that denied their manhood and their team's honor, using in the lyrics words such as "kill," "hate," "surrender," and "fight."[61]

The practice of "penning," widespread after 1969 in British grounds, "by allocating young rival fans to separate sections of terracing" probably "played a part in enhancing their solidarity and in giving them a sense of proprietorship over the goal-end areas of grounds." To beat the police in the second game inside the theater, hard-core hooligans removed insignia of allegiance in order to infiltrate the opposition and "take somebody else's end." They moved the scene of battle to the unsegregated seated sections of grounds and, before the match, to town-center pubs.[62]

Further crackdowns sent the "second game" to venues more difficult to police—to railway stations where rival fans disembarked and to streets along which fans marched, guarded by police on motorcycles and horses, and on foot. My frightening experience of the 1980s was after a Tottenham–Manchester United evening game, being caught in a "run" in which more than a hundred young males/skinheads in hobnailed boots came hurtling in phalanx looking either to flatten opposing fans or to breach the police defenses and hit their rivals. The compact mob missed me by two feet but left five others less fortunate gashed and bleeding in the gutter of Commercial Road.

The Deadly Game: Heysel and Hillsborough

The third venue for the "second game" was the Continental soccer ground and its approaches. Less police surveillance; grounds without cages and "no-man's lands"; grounds such as Belgium's Heysel, with its crumbling concrete terraces, loose metal, and stones, gave British hooligans, with twenty years of experience, a field day when Liverpool played Juventus in the European Cup Final in 1985. The chanting, bombardment, invasion, and run, followed by death, were all part of the "second game" and there for the world to see on its television sets, while the "first game" dragged on to its unwatched and irrelevant finale. Europe's major game of the year was played in deadly fashion on the terraces.[63]

The sequel at Hillsborough (Sheffield) in 1989 saw the cages and penwalls, which were built so strongly to contain hard-core hooligans and stop pitch invasion, instead claim the lives of ninety-five ordinary and innocent Liverpool fans, including young women and children, whose death agonies were also beamed on the world's TV.[64]

The next move by soccer authorities, after banning English clubs from competing in Europe, was to turn to the theaters. FIFA, soccer's governing body, decided in 1989 that at stadiums hosting World Cup qualifiers, all seats would be numbered and that "standing areas remaining in such stadiums after 1992 be unoccupied." This edict affected one national stadium in each country. But when UEFA, the European football authority, created a committee "to oversee the gradual phasing-in of all-seater stadiums for club grounds" that wish to host competitions under UEFA's jurisdiction, the die was cast for all the leading British clubs to convert the kops and terraces to "all-seating." Even Liverpool's kop is now a thing of memory. FIFA and UEFA proceed on the behavioral certainty that the standing crowd is active and difficult to control and that the seated are passive, accountable, and controllable. One hundred four years of British soccer theater dominated by the standing crowd of the working class has passed to the seated crowd, increasingly middle class.[65]

The separation of rugby and soccer in the 1870s and the emergence of the working-class "professors of soccer science" in the 1880s relegated to the terraces the maulers who had not gone over to rugby. On occasion they invaded pitches, attacking players and referees.[66] But between 1905 and 1949 they were vastly outnumbered and literally "lost in the crowd" of the cloth-capped cognoscenti of J. B. Priestley's Bruddersford United and of Ivor Brown's peaceful partisan, the "constant devotee of sport . . . eager spectator of . . . football on county and town grounds."[67] Amid this Greek chorus the unruly element was literally too tightly packed in and massively outnumbered in the great period of spectatorship. But after 1955 attendance plummeted as the car, TV, and do-it-yourself pursuits took the maturer men from the terraces. Groups of like mind and similar age and background could more easily find each other inside the ground. There was increasing room for maneuver, and the very act of maneuvering in the open spaces further hastened the exodus of the older family men to their homes or to the stands, there to join the passive audience.[68]

For twenty-five years, the second game within the ground brought maulers into the limelight, and for a while they recapitulated the "flying game" of mob football in their "runs." But they had no ball, and in the post-Heysel era, the authorities hope and expect that this violent element always around the ball in the mob football era will have no place, and certainly have no place to stand. The tragedy will be that, to rid the great game of the maulers, the authorities will alienate the devotees of the terraces and put many of them in seats. No one will mourn the passing of the maulers, but many will miss the magic of the theater—the symbiotic relationship, the heightened interaction between the principals on the pitch and the standing chorus on the terraces.

Theaters of Continental Europe

In soccer's diffusion to maritime Europe, Latin America, and the Caribbean, the general pattern of development in the early years in England was recapitulated. Many now-famous teams grew with cricket. Holland's oldest professional club, Sparta Rotterdam, was formed in 1888 as a cricket and football club; A.C. Milan and Internazionale split from a club formed as the Milan Cricket and Football Club in 1899; Italy's oldest team, proudly bearing its English name today (Genoa, not Genova—as does A.C. Milan, not Milano), began as the Genoa Cricket and Athletic Club in 1893 (winning six of Italy's first seven championships between 1898 and 1904). In Sicily, it was the Palermo Football and Cricket Club.[69]

On the Continent, with the exceptions of the Atlantic Coast and the Iberian Peninsula, association football teams tended to share grounds with sports that were already well established or contemporaneous in entry with soccer in the early twentieth century. The revival of the Olympic Games in 1896 occurred just as soccer was entering the Continent, and the six major Olympic stadiums built in northern and western Europe between 1912 and 1928 proved to be the models for the great number of joint athletics and soccer "stadions" built mainly by governments during the great western European era of stadium building in the 1920s.[70] The resultant tracks around soccer pitches, as well as government/public ownership in the 1912–70 period, inhibited the spread of the early British practice of extending the terraces inward to the edge of the pitch to produce rectangular stadiums. Consequently, English-style grounds (see fig. 4.4a) are found only in a broken and generally narrow band in the coastal zones of England's neighbors, particularly the Netherlands, Belgium, northern France, northern Spain, and Portugal; and in other places where English-derived soccer was firmly entrenched before the Olympic movement took hold, for example, in Switzerland, northwest Italy, and some coal fields and textile areas of Germany, Sweden, and Poland (fig. 4.5A).[71]

Iberia's Large Rectangles

In most of Spain and Portugal a tradition of rectangular grounds also developed, although it can be explained primarily by the absence of a strong Olympic movement and athletics in the 1900–1960 period

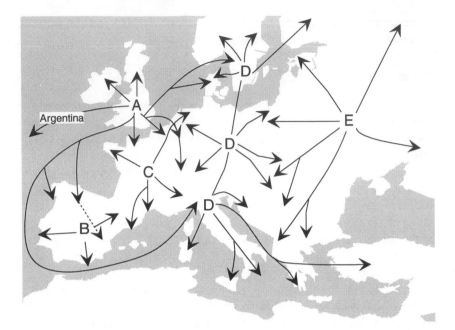

FIG. 4.5. The five European cultures of soccer. *A*, Typical English: private, soccer only, covered terraces and double-decker stands in a rectangle, moderate to high rake, high socioeconomic segregation; *B*, South and Central Iberian: private (owned by members), soccer only, covered west-side seats and uncovered tiers at ends and eastern *anfiteatro* in a rectangle; high to moderate rake, high socioeconomic segregation; *C*, multipurpose bowls of Western Europe: private, cycling and/or athletics tracks (and rugby union/league in France), tiers of terraces backed by seats covered on long sides and increasingly on all sides, moderate to high socioeconomic segregation; *D*, sports complex stadions: government-owned, Olympic-style athletics bowls with soccer in center, tiers of terraces largely uncovered except in part over the west-side seats, moderate rake, large pitch, moderate socioeconomic segregation; *E*, socialist super bowls: government-owned, all-seated, uncovered, concrete athletics/soccer bowls with low rake, large pitch, no partitions, and little or no socioeconomic segregation.

rather than by English influence. The north (San Sebastian, Bilbao) was an exception: there the early English introduction of the game produced rectangular stadiums with four straight-sided units. Of the seventeen World Cup venues, only the municipally owned ground in La Coruna in the northwest has a track. Most grounds have a unified design, either the complete rectangle with all four corners smoothed (Barcelona, Real Madrid) or three sides integrated and a separate main stand (Gijon, Atletico Madrid). Cover ranges from complete in the English-influenced and wet north to absent or limited on the dry Mediterranean. The most common form in the middle of this gradient is a west side stand, either cantilevered over the upper of two tiers or a double- or triple-decker, together with a very steep *anfiteatro* on the east side, generally of two tiers, but of three tiers in Spain's greatest grounds: Barcelona's Noucamp and Real Madrid's Bernabeu (see fig. 4.5*B*). In Spain and Portugal, as in Brazil, the patronage and early involvement of the economic and political elite ensured the development of exclusive clubs, each of which now has thousands of members (Barcelona, 110,000; Sporting Lisbon, 100,000; Benfica, 70,000), who own a vast sports complex focused on one or more soccer stadiums.[72]

Soccer in Other European Countries

Inland from English-influenced maritime Europe, three broadly defined zones of football culture reflected in stadiums could be clearly recognized before 1970: (1) France and the Benelux countries; (2) the Scandinavian countries, Germany, Italy, and their eastern neighbors before World War II; and (3) the Soviet Union and its western neighbors after World War II.

In the early growth of soccer in France and its northern neighbors velodromes were critical, hence the large number of French teams, particularly in the north and in Francophone Belgium, that took the surprisingly English name "Racing Club": de Paris, de France, de Lens, de Strasbourg, de Brussels. But the wholehearted embrace of Baron Coubertin's Olympic movement saw entrepreneurs build stadiums that combined cycling and athletics tracks with a soccer pitch in the center (see fig. 4.4*c*). In regions where rugby became France's third craze, the field had to be extended by two rectangles behind the goals, making the view for soccer fans even worse (see fig. 4.5*C*). Fortunately for soccer fans, the French people's recently discovered obsession with soccer and the French F.A.'s aspiration to host the World Cup in 1998 have led many French grounds to remove the athletics and/or cycling tracks in the last two decades and go *à l'Anglais* (rectangular), and there are examples of the same process in Belgium and the Netherlands.[73]

On the axis of Europe it was governments, ranging from municipalities to nations, that constructed sports complexes with joint athletics and soccer stadiums that took on the shape of the track (see fig. 4.4*d*). Only in the northwest of each country were there English tendencies to rectilinearity (Genoa, Italy; Munchen Gladbach, Germany; Norrkoping, Sweden).

ITALY

In Italy, in the great wave of fascist stadium building in the 1920s and 1930s, the showpieces were open ellipsoidal (straight-sided) bowls with one tier of seats around a running track, a half-cantilevered cover over much of one side, usually the west, and a marathon tower in the east. With two prominent modernist exceptions, they were built of brick, and occasionally of stone in the classical Roman model with the overall design of the Colosseum and with Romanesque external decoration. To the fascist dogma (seat the spectators) FIFA in World Cup 1990 added, for the Rome final, an edict (and for most other stadiums, a strong recommendation) that was new for Italian stadiums—cover the seating.[74]

GERMANY AND SWEDEN

In Germany, the typical soccer stadium began as a pre–World War I plan executed after the war. From Frankfort, where the model originated, it spread to many German municipalities during the progressive period of German liberalism (the Weimar Republic) of the 1920s. Developed in the wake of Continental enthusiasm for the Olympics, which became something of an obsession in Germany, the German theater was a combined athletics track and soccer stadion at the center of a municipally financed *Volkspark*/sports complex. The grounds were universally open and elongated concrete ovals with straight sides and curved ends, with one main stand, a small seated section, usually on the west side. The vast majority of spectators stood on three completely open terraces without cover. Grounds like these were the norm in the Scandinavian countries and Finland as well as in Poland, Czechoslovakia, and Hungary in the prewar years (see fig. 4.5D).

Sweden did much to launch the Olympic movement and the idea of the Olympic stadium with the remarkable Stockholms Stadion of 1912—and that stadium, home of Djurgardens FC, has just laid another athletics track. The two major stadiums constructed for Sweden's World Cup of 1958—Malmo's and Gothenburg's—both incorporated tracks and have retained them. The occasion of West Germany's World Cup 1974 prompted substantial increases in seating (more than half of ground capacity) and sizable increases in cover (about one-third of capacity) in the "main event" stadiums of Germany's Bundesliga, and trends in these directions have continued. But, with the exception of Dortmund, the multipurpose character of the soccer stadiums remains.[75]

THE FORMER SOVIET BLOC

Soccer and track and field were first and second in popularity in the Soviet Union in the 1930s when the government embarked on its policy of building multisport centers in the fast-growing towns. Consequently, all of the vast, open, single-tier, concrete bowls for soccer also had surrounding tracks (see fig. 4.5E). They were built in the dour, monotonous national style, often called Stalinist Gothic. Citizens of the USSR all paid the same for the universal bench seats in the vast stadium, even though 80 percent of them were outside the optimum viewing area and most were beyond the maximum viewing area, due both to the low rake and to the insistence on seating all spectators. In the former Soviet Union, seating was either without any cover (the vast majority) or all covered (the indoor domes of Moscow and Leningrad—now Saint Petersburg). This was because it would have been an ostentatious rejection of social egalitarianism if one group sat under cover while others braved the elements and if one group stood while others sat down. In complete contrast to the English case, there were no internal partitions in soccer grounds in the former Soviet Union—no pens, pitch perimeter fences, crush barriers, or no-man's lands. At every major soccer match there was simply a "wall" of soldiers ringing the ground between the fans and the pitch and sitting in the front-row seats![76]

In Eastern Europe, socialist superbowl building came as a post-1940s Soviet bloc "main-event" overlay on the German-style sports complex/stadions of most league teams built in the interwar years (see fig. 4.5E). The exceptions are the southern Balkan countries, where the structural legacies of prewar soccer were completely overshadowed by post–World War II stadium building in the Soviet mode, and Czechoslovakia, which resisted the Soviet superbowl and continued to offer three choices in its distinctive variants of the stadion tradition: terraces with crush barriers, uncovered bench seating, and seats covered in grandstands.[77]

Theaters of the Third World

The English and cricket connections in the early years existed throughout South America and the Caribbean. Peru's early exclusive soccer clubs were the Lima Cricket and Football Club and Union Cricket. Penarol, Uruguay's greatest team, began as the Central Uruguay Railway Cricket Club.[78] Nevertheless, two distinctly different poles of soccer culture developed in South America: in Argentina and in Brazil. Both countries, along with Uruguay, which lies between them geographically and culturally, have won the World Cup two or more times, which makes them the Western Hemisphere's superpowers of soccer. The contrast in styles and cultures is the result of two very different trajectories of development, which are reflected in different theaters of soccer.

Passion and Violence in Argentina's Melting Pots

Argentina adopted soccer from English sailors and railway workers in the early 1860s before the English game reached continental Europe. Passion and violence on and off the field are the distinctive characteristics of Argentinian soccer. They are endemic in the grounds of Argentina's Big Five clubs and epitomized in Boca Juniors' Estadio Barbonera ("The Chocolate Box"), with its sharp verticality of three "popular sides," each with three tiers, and no athletics track. It is the home of eighty thousand passionate, heavily involved fans. It has seen more violence off the field than most soccer stadiums in the world (more, perhaps, than any other); in Richard Henshaw's words, "no club has escaped the stadium's highly charged atmosphere."[79]

Four factors lie behind the passion and violence on and off the field in Argentina's melting-pot stadiums: first, the early introduction of the British dribbling game before the "hacking" elements were exorcized by the English F.A. Second is the early importance of English-style public schools, which favored charging and mauling rather than dribbling and passing. The third factor is the Italian immigration of the twentieth century, which brought with it Italian artistry but also physicality and violence. Fourth is the fierce, century-long, ethnically based, intrametropolitan (Buenos Aires) rivalry of the Big Five teams. Team followings, which grew rapidly in the early twentieth century, saw each team's stadium building follow the English model of spontaneous and piecemeal accretion in response to each leap in spectator demand. The result, as in England after World War I, was rectilinear and vertical stadiums that could hold sixty-five thousand to eighty thousand, including many standees, particularly at the ends but also on the long sides in front of the grandstands. Different from England is the moat and sometimes a track between players and spectators.[80] The other major difference between England's and Argentina's spontaneous stadiums is the cover, either absent or limited to a narrow span over part of the upper tier. As a consequence, Argentinian stadiums find their closest counterparts in the more regular, yet trackless, rectilinear, and two- and three-tiered stadiums of southeastern Spain, which has a similar soccer season climate (a warm winter with less than two inches of rain each month of the soccer season).[81]

Brazil: From Playgrounds of the Elite to Maracanás for the Millions

In contrast to the violence that is distinctive of the club and national teams of the Rio de la Plata, where soccer rivalries developed early in a relatively homogeneous society, Brazilian soccer piggy-backed on cricket in São Paolo and on sailing and cricket in Rio in the 1880s, and was a foreign (mainly English) gentleman's game.[82] In the early twentieth century, soccer was handed on exclusively to the local elites, who later admitted the white middle class to their large, comprehensive, and exclusive social clubs that offered far more than soccer. Rio's Fluminense (with its maximum number of rigorously screened members) "is considered the most elaborate soccer social center in the world. Its stark white walls, roofed with red tile form a compound" of soccer stadium, vast gymnasium, tennis courts, swimming pools, club buildings, and much more. It epitomized resistance to the admission of blacks and the lower class as players, and to blacks as social members. As a result of such entrenched elitism and racism, the onset of professionalism was delayed until 1933.[83]

With the black players, beginning in the 1930s, came a distinctive Brazilian soccer—a jubilant, creative artistry that incorporated the fluidity of the samba and the joy of carnival. "In soccer, as in politics," writes sociologist Gilberto Freyre, "Brazilian 'mulattoness' is characterized by the pleasure of elasticity, surprise, and rhetoric, bringing to mind capoeira moves, or the steps of a dance."[84]

Stadiums constructed in the "exclusive" years in Rio and Sao Paolo were small (capacity ca. 22,000) and were designed in the colonial manner; they exist now as the training grounds of the big clubs. When soccer as the "religião Brasiliera" became the outstanding passion of all the Brazilian people in the 1930s and 1940s following the signing of the great black players, the early home grounds were phased out as too small for big games. Flamengo, the first club to welcome blacks as players and members, became the focus of devotion of Brazil's black population, its name having a near-mystical quality among the sorcederos (voodoo charmers). So large was their following by the 1940s, particularly in the great Fla-Flu (lower- versus upper-class) rivalry that pitted the team of the blacks against the most exclusive (white) team, that construction of a vast stadium in Rio seemed inevitable.[85]

MARACANÁ: CARNIVAL AND CHARANGAS IN THE NATIONAL SHRINE

Built just in time for Brazil's hosting of World Cup 1950 in an era of great national optimism, which also saw the building of the new capital, Brasilia, Maracaná Stadium immediately became the largest and most famous stadium in the world, holding 220,000 when fully completed in 1952 (see fig. 4.4e). All the national, interregional, São Paolo–Rio, and intrametropolitan Rio matches are played here, in what quickly became the national shrine, the symbol of the New Brazil. The vast, spheroid, concrete bowl encircles the playing surface and a ten-foot-deep moat with ten-foot-high wire fencing; a magnificent roof covers the two tiers and some of the flats between moat and stands. In a country with a tropical climate characterized by afternoon and evening downpours, the vast, encircling roof is a necessity, particularly to the tens of thousands of spectators who come early to Maracaná to get decent viewing and spend at least four hours there. As part of the government's attempt to open Maracaná to the many, through the 1980s, low and fixed prices were maintained for standing room in the low flat between the moat and the first seating tier of reserved seats, as well as in the end bleachers in the high tier. Reserved seats for the middle and upper classes in the first tier and on the long sides of the high tier were high-priced and not controlled by the government.

In the great "derbies" among the Rio Big Four, the fans of the home team, whichever it is, occupy the home team side of the ground and the away team fans occupy the other. Few (particularly the lower classes in the end bleachers) are close enough to see the artistry of the individual players, and many see practically nothing of the game (see fig. 4.4e). But that hardly seems to matter to the believer caught up in the voodoo and prayer of the *sorcederos* before the game and enveloped in the festive, carnival atmosphere of the singing, flag- and banner-waving crowd, dancing and moving to the samba rhythm of the many charanga bands distributed throughout Maracaná.[86]

The pattern of big intrametropolitan, intraprovincial rivalries, with the big games played in one stadium having a capacity of at least 100,000, extended first to São Paolo (Estadio Morumbí, 150,000) and Belo Horizonte (Minerão). Riding on the instant popularity of the sports lottery in 1969 and the success of the Brazilian national team in winning its third World Cup in 1970, the government created a national championship in 1970. This was facilitated by the new air travel connections, with air travel for the teams financed from the lottery—as were most costs for the new futuristic Maracaná-like clones with capacities of 100,000–180,000, which had been built in seven more provincial capitals. The result, in 1980, was that Brazil had eight of the nine largest stadiums in the world (measured by crowd capacity) and ten of the largest twenty-two.[87]

Brazil is the only major soccer power that is a tropical country; there is neither seasonal nor diurnal escape from tropical downpours. Some provincial capitals have an average annual rainfall of more than eighty inches, so cover is important. Also, with such vast crowds, the referee (as well as the coaches and players) must be protected—consequently, Maracaná's protective moat design "has been copied by every major stadium constructed in Brazil, and in some other countries as well."[88]

The Third World: Intra-Primate City Rivalries and the National Stadium

The distinctive contrast between the structure of soccer in Europe and in South America, between the first and third worlds, is that in Europe leagues are intercity, while South American leagues are intracity/metropolitan, based on the million city (i.e., a city of over one million population) in each major province (Brazil) or on the country's largest city (as in Uruguay, where all teams are from Montevideo: there teams train in old, cozy, colonial-style home grounds and play their games in the huge Estadio Centenario, an open, concrete, multi-tiered bowl). The Uruguayan model is common throughout Latin America and the Caribbean (except Argentina). It is becoming common in the third world as each country builds its version of Maracaná, covered or uncovered depending on seasonal and diurnal rainfall patterns, to host the big crowds that come to intra-primate city club rivalries and international matches, as in the multipurpose National Stadium, Barbados (see fig. 4.2b). The result is that of the twenty largest stadiums in the world (based on capacity), nineteen are third world and one is first world.[89]

North America: First World Countries without Great Soccer Theaters

In North America, the football theater of the leading indigenous exponents was the "broad sandy shore, free from stones" of the Eastern Seaboard "or . . . some soft heathie plot, because of their naked feet." The goals, "two sticks placed slantingly across each other like the poles of the traditional wigwam" in Micmac country, were a mile apart in Massachusetts country, and "placed on the sands, which are even as a board; their ball is no bigger than a handball, which sometimes they mount in the air with their naked feet." As with the traditional mob football games in England, the ball was "swayed by the multitude, [and] sometimes . . . it is two days before they get a goal." These "great meetings of football playing" occur "only in summer" and pit "town against town." William Strachey, in the first years of the Virginia colony, described the "exercise of football, in which they only forcibly encounter with the foot to carry the ball the one from the other, and spurned it [OED: 'to strike against something with the foot'], to the goal with a kind of dexterity and swift footmanship, which is the honor of it." In all the seaboard territory except Nova Scotia, "where scalping was anciently employed as a means of disposing of an opponent," the Algonquians made every effort to keep the meeting festive. Strachey, contrasting English mob football with the Algonquian game, commented that "they never strike up one anothers heels, as we do, not accompting that praiseworthy to purchase a goal by such an advantage."[90]

From Roughhouse Football to the Ethnic Game

English mob football passed to U.S. colleges as roughhouse football in the nineteenth century, and this evolved into the proto-dribbling and passing game that dominated in America until the mid-1870s, particularly in the prep schools of New England and in the Ivy League colleges. In 1862 the first dribbling club known outside England, the Oneida Football Club of Boston, beat all comers in scratch games with a round ball on Boston Common, as commemorated in a plaque dedicated in 1925. The Ivy League adopted English rules of association football after the Civil War and played twenty-five-a-side on fields 120 by 75 yards; by 1873, Yale had restricted the number of players to eleven after adopting a field 133 by 84 yards. But the tide of U.S. nationalism took its own peculiar turn after the Civil War, summarily rejecting the three major British sports: soccer, cricket, and rugby. Soccer was relegated to an "ethnic game" played by "furriners" (new immigrants) who had embraced the game in their countries of origin just as American chauvinists used the game as a recognizable differentiator between "them" and "us."[91]

The theaters of the ethnic game were often within the factory complex (e.g., Saylesville, Rhode Island), overlooked by multistory mills and smokestacks in the immigrant industrial towns of Megalopolis and the Manufacturing Belt, including Saint Louis. Mill owners (e.g., Matthew Whittall in Worcester, Massachusetts) hired British professionals well into their playing careers and built semiprofessional teams around them.[92] Occasionally owners and clubs pooled resources and built a soccer-only stadium (e.g., an impressive one in the wooded country inland from New Bedford, Massachusetts, in Acushnet). It was a frequent venue for the semipro teams of New Bedford and Fall River (e.g., Fall River F.C., Saint Michaels A.C., and Ponta Delgada F.C., the U.S. team in four internationals, 1947–49), when this area dominated U.S. soccer and contributed many players to U.S. soccer's greatest achievement before 1994: knocking England out of the World Cup in Belo Horizonte, Brazil, in 1950.[93]

North American Suburbs: From
Stonedust Diamonds to Furrowed Flatlands

The arrival of Pele in 1975 saw Giants Stadium featured as a significant NASL stadium with sizable crowds, and the Tampa Bay Rowdies made the local stadium famous for soccer for a brief interlude. But the real theaters of soccer in America in the last twenty years are the thousands of municipal and private fields designated for youth soccer leagues. Having seen more than five hundred of these fields, I have some impressions as to how American theaters of soccer differ from the soccer fields of my playing experience in England. Initially, because many fields were multipurpose in America, there were sizable plots in which grass gave way to the stonedust of the baseball diamond's base paths (producing the inevitable strawberries on the thighs of slide-tacklers). But soccer fields with baseball mounds and home plates with their primal paw marks are now rarely seen. American football fields, often with surrounding tracks, were found to be too short and always too narrow for the good of the game, for the game is dominated by throw-ins and is at the mercy of the long-thrower who dominates action in the six yard box.

Nowadays, the newly emerging, no longer multipurpose soccer fields at North American schools and parks are notable for their flatness. This is a consequence of the demands of taxpayers in suburban communities for the best, and this means the use of fine-graders to level the land perfectly. Such fields are a far cry from the rolling cow pastures and sloping hillsides normal in my childhood soccer pitches. All have a grassless, ever-widening furrow that runs from one goal to the other on pitches used every waking moment of daylight from March to December in the eastern United States. Increasingly, portable bleachers appear alongside the fields to take pressure off the other two furrows of bareness that develop just beyond the sidelines, for in America when children play soccer there are at least as many spectators (relatives and substitutes) as players on the field. In all the games I played in England, I was never watched by anybody's parents. This may be changing, but it is very different from the choral presence of the community of supportive white-collar parents roaring their encouragement from the sidelines in North America.[94]

Until the tidal wave of soccer-playing children of the 1980s become parents with soccer-playing children, there will be no memorable soccer theaters north of the Rio Grande. Some venues for World Cup 1994 may stick in the memory of soccer fans the world over, particularly the Detroit Silverdome, the first dome ever to be used in World Cup play. The verticality and cocoonlike atmosphere in domes appear to have aided NFL dome teams and probably helped the U.S. team qualify unexpectedly for the second round of the World Cup 1994. Unfortunately, most of the World Cup venues in 1994 were NFL or college stadiums of one, two, or three tiers, all-seated, mostly uncovered, and set back far enough from the action that many spectators were well outside the optimum viewing area for soccer. Only when the tidal wave of soccer-playing youth becomes the great American and Canadian middle class in the twenty-first century will North America get its made-for-soccer, rectangular theaters, but get them it will.

Conclusion: The Quality of Theater in the Theaters of Soccer

To many writers, soccer in this century is a new kind of theater of the new urban-industrial society. What made it new in Britain was the level of involvement and participation of the vast audience which joined the players as actors. The Saturday afternoon drama was art played before cognoscenti who had played on lesser stages. The quality of theater in soccer was long measured against the British standard established during the Golden Age of the spectator, 1920–50. The special atmosphere of this era, the mystical relationship between players, ground, and fans, produced for some a special expression of working-class society: the terrace culture and community. That special relationship and feeling within the grounds on chill Saturday afternoons is called by many commentators the "traditional" atmosphere of soccer, a term still applied by Continentals to what they see as the palpable presence (fever pitch) of the British crowd in big games played in tight, intimate, enveloping rectangular stadiums, with an ambience that is worth a goal to the home team. These indefinables are seen somewhat enviously as major contributing factors to the success of British teams in the three international cups contested by clubs. As a consequence, stadium designers have tried to extract the essence of the British theater of popular culture and embody it in the designs of new stadiums, many of which have been so successful that they are the talk of soccer aficionados the world over.

What are the factors that make for greater theater in soccer? The quality of play and the game on the pitch, obviously responsive to crowd and ground, must conform closely to the crowd's culturally based demands for style and excellence in both performance and result. (English crowds would stay away in droves if they were served up an Italian slow-build-up-from-the-back, possession game that an Italian crowd at Fiorentina would rave about.) Beyond this culturally based taste factor, the British experience between 1920 and 1960 can tell us much about the more general factors that, *ceteris paribus*, make for good theater. First, crowd size is important. In the Golden Age of goal scoring in England (1926–39), crowds were often between thirty thousand and fifty thousand, enveloping the pitch in an audio-visual bowl, packed together but not dangerously so—that is, below the ground capacities of that era but well above the capacities mandated by the government in our safety-conscious era. Second, very important in the big crowd is the proportion of standees on the terraces. As every choirmaster knows, the noise that comes from within a seated body is much less than if that body is standing. In the British Golden Age in a crowd of fifty-five thousand, there would be forty-two thousand standing on the terraces. What the terrace denizens know in their bones, the legislators of FIFA and UEFA have built into their new specifications for grounds that host games under their jurisdiction: passion, involvement, crowd noise, antisocial behavior, and sometimes outright violence are all far greater in the working-class terraces than in the seated sections of the middle and upper classes. Soccer's governing institutions, like the owners of American football franchises, are most interested in revenue from TV, and to this end strive to produce passive seated crowds, often too far from the long-distance spectacle on the pitch to be any more expressive and involved than to stand up momentarily as the wave passes through each seated section.

Third, also critical is the optimum viewing area. In England, the small pitch and the intimate proximity of the high-angle terracing perimeter to the playing surface give all the actors on the terraces high angles of rake and a fine view of the whole pitch, even in the big end-kops. Fourth, the English tradition of constructing double-decker stands that project over terraces, and triple-deckers that overtop the double-deck, gives everyone proximity and high angle of rake, all within 150 meters of the farthest corner flag and 90 meters of the center spot (the optimum viewing area). This sharp verticality, along with the final factor, the provision of extensive cover, not only satisfies the English fans' demand to be protected from the raw elements and to see well, it also contributes to holding sound in the echoing thunderbowl.

Although in England there have been since 1950 more stands (decks and tiers) and more cover that should increase the thunder and spectator comfort, these improvements are more than counterbalanced by the decline in both crowd size and the proportions and absolute numbers of the audience standing on the terraces. A big game in the 1930s would have a crowd of fifty thousand, of whom forty thousand were on the terraces. The same game today would have thirty thousand, of whom twelve thousand would be terrace people. All are in the optimum viewing area, safer (in terms of ground conditions) and more comfortable. But there are breaks now in the enveloping bowl of sound: in no-man's land and at the ghetto end of the opposing fans, often very thinly populated. Such things have changed the character of theater, which now stages organized singing, chanting, and jeering between two deeply antagonistic crowds. Few would disagree that the quality of theater is not as high as that in the Golden Age.

On the Continent, major improvements in stadium building, far more comprehensive than in England and clearly related to upturns in spectator interest and numbers, have seen major increases in cover and verticality (tiers and occasionally decks) and crowds much larger than in England. This is true of Italy and particularly of the grounds of the big clubs in Spain. Real Madrid's Bernabeu has standing room in its ninety thousand capacity for sixty thousand standees (more than the new safe capacity of any English league ground), while Barcelona's Noucamp has thirty thousand standees in its stadium for one hundred fifteen thousand. Granted, many standees and some of the seated spectators are outside the optimum viewing area, particularly in the major stadiums of Germany and Italy, where crowds are still separated from the pitch by tracks and service areas. But in big games there are more within the optimal viewing section of these big stadiums than constitute the entire crowd in English stadiums. The theater today at big games in Spain and Italy may be different than in England, but it is compelling enough to attract vast crowds and bring them back week after week.

There was always a significant difference between soccer theater in

Scotland and England. The three great Scottish stadiums, all in Glasgow, were in 1903 the three largest in the world. They were relatively shallowly banked ovals with service areas behind the goals (see fig. 4.4b) and, at Celtic Park, an encircling track. This meant that at the largest of the three, Hampden Park with its recorded capacity of one hundred fifty thousand, all but ten thousand of them standing, a very different kind of "tribal theater" developed. Most of the crowd was outside the optimum viewing area, and there were tens of thousands beyond the maximum viewing area (190 meters from the farthest corner flag), presumably happy to be part of tribal ritual, for they could see little on the pitch. There were in effect at each end of the oval three staggered zones of sight, in each of which the great crowd saw and sensed events on the field split seconds apart. This zoning produced the "Hampden Roar," in which the noise from the different sections reaches the players' ears in a series of seismic waves that reverberate with aftershocks, an effect heightened, some feel, by swirling winds so common in a stadium without notable verticality. This is theater and sound unaided by favorable shape, verticality, close proximity, or cover of the stadium, none of which it has. It is, rather, the ultimate theater of the standing mass, deafening, stunning, and overpowering in its nationalism directed at the "Auld Enemy." It has its counterpart today in the national encounters played in the concrete bowls of the third world with their large standing capacities, and occasionally, as a faint echo, in the all-seated concrete bowls of the former Soviet Union and its bloc: the second world.

Perhaps the ultimate theater of soccer is provided when the grand scale and vast crowds of Hampden in the Golden Age of the 1930s are combined with the cover, verticality (tiers and decks), and closer proximity of Brazil's Maracaná, and of other major stadiums in Latin America. The wasted space (including the moat) of the common circular plan ensures that many, including a great number of the standees at the high ends, are outside both optimal and maximum viewing areas in the great stadiums of Latin America, so far away that many of the standees cannot see the game clearly. But as in Hampden when England was being beaten, and in the concrete bowls of third world national stadiums, this hardly seems to matter to the tribe, for whom the great thing is being there, and to be able to say that one was there. Literally tens of thousands at Maracaná hardly bother to look at the field they can hardly see, so involved are they with the bands, flag waving, dancing, and the action all around them on the terraces which in the Iberian

Peninsula and Latin America are often end tiers. This is a far cry from the high theater of the English clubs of the Golden Age, where the crowd on the terraces could touch the players and the ball.

The English ground has served for a century as the model of traditional theater in the first world. Brazil's Maracaná is the model of a new kind of theater for the third world, one in which the old importance of the standing crowd in the optimum viewing area is overpowered by the crowd's vast size, and overshadowed by action on the terraces that is both a complement and alternative to the grand play on the moated stage.

CHAPTER FIVE

TENNIS

Bruce Ryan

The Tennis Landscape—Origins and Evolution

On the seventh day, God probably played tennis. It is an ancient game, and its origins are lost in legends, two of which inspire attention, if not credulity. One etymology fastens upon the place known to classicists as Tanis (or Tinnis, or Tamis), which began as Avaris. This was the City of Rameses, and later the biblical Zoan. It became an independent principality after the attempted assassination of Rameses III in 1166 B.C., and stood near the northeastern outflow of the Nile. Here the delta produced linen, with which tennis balls were once stuffed. The second etymology, though less geographical, is candidly less dubious. It is the French claim that the English word "tennis" derives from *tenez!* (hold, or attention), the server's warning to his opponent that he was about to serve.[1] That is as it should be. Tennis certainly requires an arena, but is first and foremost an occasion. Its name should reflect the event, not the place, although badminton did take its name in 1874 from the Duke of Beaufort's country seat near Bristol.

The earliest reference to "tenetz" in English occurred in 1399, in a

FIG. 5.1. The pit game. Lawn courts of the Castle Tennis Club, c. 1940–55, inside the courtyard of Beaumaris Castle, Wales. North Gatehouse in background, sheep grazing left.

poem by John Gower, although what he rhymed was really *le jeu de paume*, translatable as "game of the palm" (that is, of the hand), which had been played in France since the eleventh century A.D. (fig. 5.1; Clerici 1975, 335). Stick-and-ball games, broadly conceived, have an even more venerable pedigree. Bas-reliefs in the Athenian ring-wall built by Themistocles about 490–480 B.C. show two ballplayers "bullying off" and others feinting, as in hockey. A similar game, hapaste, was played during the first century B.C. by cultivated Romans, among whom Augustus, Maecenas, and Julius Caesar have been claimed as competitors (Olivová 1985, 109, 185). *Jeu de paume* is not yet extinct: 580 Frenchmen were still playing the game in 1984, and it was contested in the Olympiad of 1908.

A topography of this ancient game will be an account of the landscape created by tennis over the centuries, in both its physical and human aspects. It will have four interacting elements—the arena on which the game is played, including the surrounding, ancillary spaces and structures; the equipment added to that arena, including that borne by the players; the characteristics of the participants, whether players or spectators, since a distinctive pattern of human interaction is the crux of the game; and the game itself, the actual engagement on the tennis court. In a theater of sport, these four elements correspond to the stage, its props, the actors and actresses, and the performance. So de-

lineated, a topography of tennis will not be focused on the godlike players and memorable matches that attract most tennis journalism, and
might not even mention them (Evans 1983b). But topography is never
inert. Like Red Square or the beaches of Normandy, tennis is simultaneously and inseparably both a place and an occasion, both geography
and history.

Predictably, any attempt to trace the ancestry of tennis courts and
their surrounds—the conformation of "game in landscape"—will be
confounded by hair-splitting disagreements about the precise definition of tennis itself and the legitimacy of including certain other games
in the tennis family. The stickliest of sticklers are those obsessed with
games. My attempt to trace the ancestry of tennis must therefore follow
a contour above these definitional bogs by maintaining two fixed as-
sumptions: first, that there is no "one true tennis"—that tennis, like
every other game, has endured a constant modification of its rules,
equipment, and tactics; second, that there is no "one true history"—
that every rule, tactic, and piece of equipment now used in tennis has
had a separate though converging lineage, all of them germane, none
more valid than the others. Givens are givens and curry no favorites.

Lawn tennis became an established sport with its own bureaucracy
and laws between 1860 and 1880, as did rugby football and association
football (soccer). The nineteenth century witnessed an almost manic
diversification of games in Britain, a second resurgence after the pu-
ritanical, perhaps more enlightened, but certainly more quiescent interlude of the seventeenth and eighteenth centuries (Haley 1978). The first
eruption of games mania in Britain occurred during the fifteenth and
sixteenth centuries, when the basic nomenclature of golf, cricket,
lawn bowls, shuttlecock, and real tennis entered the English language.
"Sport" itself, for example, is a fifteenth-century word, whereas "sportsman" and "sportsmanship" are eighteenth-century refinements. Games
flowered in these two lushly inventive, romantic, expansive eras. The
first corresponded to the Renaissance, the second to the British colonial
empire and its industrial progeny. Both eras brought revolutionary
change, not only to technology and the artistic imagination, but also to
popular culture. Viewed in this context, tennis is not a closed chapter in
the history of games, with known dates of inception and demise like the
Titanic, but is simply today's most popular version of what history has
proved to be a perdurable human enthusiasm for "court games."

Arenas, Players, and Rules are the banners behind which a whole
regiment of games marches out of antiquity. Today's generic "tennis" is
one generation descended from "lawn tennis," for which Major Walter

Clopton Wingfield entered a patent registration in London on February 23, 1874 (Arlott 1975, 604). What he dubbed "Sphairistiké" ("sphere and stick," from the collective Greek term for ball games), but prudently and less forgettably subtitled "Lawn Tennis," involved only a "New and Improved Portable Court for Playing the Ancient Game of Tennis." But the immediate popularity of his outdoor tennis kits among the nobility of Europe and the Anglo-Irish squirearchy established Wingfield in the popular mind as the "inventor of tennis." Even the Lawn Tennis Association accepted that appellation, thus inscribed, on the major's bust, which stands in the foyer of its London offices. The catalytic effect of his attempt to codify the rules, though resisted by irate prior claimants and thrown out by the self-arbitrating Marylebone Cricket Club in 1875,[2] changed lawn tennis from a garden party diversion for rorty duffers ("flannelled fools," Kipling would have called them) into a bally-hooed international athletic contest.

The "Ancient Game of Tennis" from which the entrepreneurial Wingfield adapted Sphairistiké was "real tennis," a.k.a. "royal tennis," "court tennis," or, to purists and pedants, just plain "tennis." The few darkly sinister indoor courts that remain today were common in France by A.D. 1500, but the game began without walls about A.D. 1050, in open fields where handballers squared off on opposite sides of a mound. The walled version also dates back to the eleventh century, first in monastic cloisters, later inside the moats and courtyards of castles, later still in university quadrangles and on town streets or squares. Antonio Scaino's inaugural treatise on tennis, published in Venice in 1555, addressed without apology such contingencies as balls landing on private doorsteps or in passing carts (Scaino 1951). The unbounded version was known as *pallone* in Italy and *longue paume* in France, where it survived until the nineteenth century in the Champs Elysées and Luxembourg Gardens (Arlott 1975, 828).

By the fifteenth century, the kings of France and England had released tennis from the cloisters, clothing it in the "royal and aristocratic" livery that it retained until the guillotine reduced their patronage. The Oath of the Tennis Court was taken on June 20, 1789, at Versailles, not by Louis XVI but by the locked-out French National Assembly. By then, the nobility had long ceased to monopolize the game. Throughout France, Italy, England, Spain, and Germany, it had spread to all classes, despite royal edicts forbidding its indulgence by the common people. "Servants shall use only bows and arrows, and leave idle games," Richard II of England had decided with as much success as Canute (ibid., 827). In 1292, the Parisian tax rolls listed twelve tennis courts. Most medieval French towns boasted their *tripot*, a court-cum-gambling den. By 1500, there were forty courts in Orleans and twenty-two in Poitiers. By 1600, Paris had 1,100 courts, 250 of them "enclosed." Others were tucked into every French town and chateau. During the sixteenth century, *Ballhäuser* were recorded in forty-six German towns. By 1635, there were even fifteen "well-equipped" courts in remotest London, including that built behind Hampton Court Palace in 1530 by Henry VIII, and another in James Street (now Orange Street, off the Haymarket), which served as the English game's headquarters until its demolition in 1866.[3]

Real tennis lost ground in France after 1600, when the *paumiers* found greater profit in hiring out their courts as theaters. When Molière toured the provinces between 1645 and 1647, he acted in tennis courts, and their shape is still retained in many French theaters. By the time of the Revolution, only ten courts remained in Paris and forty elsewhere in France. Few European courts outside France and England survived the nineteenth century. They included those at Saint Petersburg (now the university gymnasium), Madrid, Geneva, Brussels, and Turin, where moneyed leisure survived (Arlott 1975, 830–32). Britain became the bastion of real tennis, its revival there contingent on the pedigreed pretensions of exclusive country houses, private clubs, and the inane or quirky faddists of Cambridge and Oxford. The game reverted to the propertied, the patrician, and the highborn, abetted by the more plebeian appeal of Major Wingfield's alternative.

That mongrel alternative appropriated or adapted very little except the essence of combat from real tennis for which, in any event, regional variations still persisted. In Spain, the fashion was for white courts against which a black ball was silhouetted. In France, the ball was white but the courts were dark-walled with red or black floors, an effect obtained traditionally by swabbing them down with lampblack diluted with ox galls and bullock's blood. The Guinness family's court in Dublin conveyed the same effect in black marble (ibid., 832). Eager to be granted an exclusive patent, Wingfield stressed the crucial originality of Sphairistiké, with its hourglass court (narrower at the net, like indoor badminton), its ball borrowed from Eton fives (a variant of handball dating from 1840), its white shirt and flannels from cricket. His untested rules merely complicated an already chaotic situation, where the games-mad Victorian English played everything with anything, and Rafferty's Rules prevailed. Even Charles L. Dodgson, probably reminded by the melee of *Alice's Adventures in Wonderland*, contributed a tract, *Lawn Tennis Tournaments* (Dodgson 1883). It was only when the pontifical Marylebone Cricket Club became apprehensive about the addition of tennis courts to cricket clubs, and only when the upstart All England Croquet and Lawn Tennis Club instigated a national championship on a rectangular lawn court at Wimbledon in 1877, that sufficiently devious and powerful compromisers sullenly sat down and drew up a common code.[4]

What needed restraining and retracking had burst loose with the "lawn set" of Victorian England, with fashionable weekend parties of young people who gathered at elegant country estates and spas such as Leamington, whose cult of games grabbed and elaborated whatever the British army brought back from any corner of the Empire. French Canada contributed lacrosse in 1718. Polo arrived from Kashmir in 1872. *Poona* became badminton in 1874. But the immediate predecessor of lawn tennis was croquet, for which slivers of Capability Brown's flowing "landskip" had been tamed and leveled into well-rolled terraces around the country mansions by 1858.[5] Croquet lawns had no moss, no moles, no glades, no shrubs, no gravel footpaths, no undulations: they made ideal courts for tennis. Moreover, unlike such all-male preserves as cricket, rackets, and real tennis, croquet had accustomed the young Victorian woman to competing, however vapidly, with men. Lawn tennis took her emancipation several steps beyond merely striking a stationary wooden ball—into running, into chasing a bounding rubber ball, into loosening and lightening her clothing, and, with mixed doubles, into a matrimonial arena of her own choosing (McCrone 1988).

Initially, that manicured lawn in its domestic garden setting was crucial to Wingfield's campaign for relocating real tennis outdoors. Well-rolled, it offered uncertain beginners a reliably "true bounce," and its surrounding hedges or trees screened out both the deflecting wind and the unsettling gaze of better players or intimates. Players could pause to recover their poise while a lost ball was retrieved from the shrubbery. But the *fin de siècle* was almost upon Europe, and the rector's lawn fêtes (even when strawberries and Devonshire cream were served after three sets of tennis) were becoming passé for serious competitors (Raverat 1953). Suburbanites who lacked the wealth, status, or connections ever to be invited to country house weekends banded together to form tennis clubs—players' collaboratives whose courts were tucked into the vacant corners of languishing cricket grounds or laid out alongside moribund croquet greens. At the Manor House Hotel in Leamington (Warwickshire), Major Harry Gem and his teammates established the world's first lawn tennis club in 1872, over a year before the other major's tennis kits were even offered for sale (Tingay 1983,

19). Experiments with court surfaces and playing equipment were all the rage.

The Tennis Court—Construction and Equipment

In 1881, the first floodlit game was played at Cheltenham, where asphalt and clay courts already existed, and the Renshaw twins (soon to be winners at Wimbledon for eight years) built their own hard sand court on the grounds of the Beausite Hotel in Cannes. By 1900, red clay had become the traditional court surface in continental Europe (as it remains today), ostensibly because the perennially moist climate that favors grass courts in Britain (and especially Ireland) dries out southward and sunward toward the Mediterranean. The French called the material *terre battue* (beaten earth), but it was originally rolled, often with some gravel binding. At its Parisian best, in the Stade Roland Garros, "red clay" now consists of six layers, with 20–30 cm of flint stone at the base, just 0.2 cm of red clay at the top, and, between them, another 17 cm of gravel, thicker slag, thin slag, and pounded limestone (August 1986, 39–41, 51). Caked mud was used for courts in India (as well as superlative lawns); antheaps, in South Africa; dirt littered with pebbles, in Kenya; oiled laterite, in northern Australia. Other "natural" surfaces included crushed stone, shale, asphalt, cement, and bare boards, often with tongued-and-grooved joints.[6]

Sophisticates, patriots, and sales agents extolled the virtues of certain surfaces, adapting their playing styles and sweet talk accordingly. French and Italian players, bent on frustrating their energetic Anglo-Saxon rivals, perfected top-spin and slice as the weapons appropriate for their deliberately slow clay courts (especially when wet), finding virtue (and victory) in patience, perseverance, accuracy, endurance, and the well-timed cross-court slither. Californians soon excelled at the cannonball service-and-volley game that suited their cement courts so well, placing a premium on strength, speed, sure-footedness, and snappy reflexes. Court construction firms typically checklisted such qualities as drying time, abrasiveness, hardness, maintenance, repairs, resurfacing, slideability, uniformity and height of ball bounce, ball spin, ball skid, glare, ball stains, and traction (Duncan 1979, 60), evidently unaware that most players lose regularly on any kind of surface.

Lawn courts have retained or enhanced their patrician prestige, like any rare antique, but are dwindling in numbers almost everywhere. By 1985, only thirty-five private tennis clubs in the United States had kept their grass courts, and only twenty-nine others were available for public use at six resorts, among them the fourteen courts at the International Tennis Hall of Fame in Newport, Rhode Island (*World Tennis* 1985, 56–57). With the introduction of fast-drying, low-maintenance, all-weather acrylic fibers during the 1950s, the resurfacing of grass courts accelerated, such sacrilege having been precipitated by the steady deterioration of grass from industrial pollution. Acid rain falls on turf as well as on trees. In the Capitulation of 1975, not unmindful that TV contracts would be more lucrative without the program interruptions caused by slow-draining grass, the West Side Tennis Club of Forest Hills, New York, abandoned the grass courts which had been used for the U.S. National and Open Championships continuously since 1881. They were held instead, for the first time in a major tournament anywhere in the world, on Har-Tru, one brand of the new, hard, synthetic, claylike surfaces. Purists and reactionaries were appalled. For Herbert Warren Wind, tennis essayist for the *New Yorker*, the court's "grim, gritty" gray-greenness delighted the eye "hardly more than Kipling's 'great, grey-green, greasy Limpopo River'" (Wind 1979, 149).

Court surfaces are merely one of the elements of the tennis landscape, although their green, skylit luminescence from afar (and from above) signals the approach of tennis places just as unmistakably as the roar of an auto racetrack or the aroma of a zoo signals other proximities. Regardless of their setting, tennis courts require a level surface of standardized dimensions (seventy-eight feet long by thirty-six feet wide for the doubles game), unimpaired by surface cracks, "alligatoring," or "birdbaths" (the trade name for depressions). They are built to retain "perfect slope and planarity" for a court life of some twenty-five years, apart from periodic resurfacing.[7] All require such standardized equipment as the winched-taut net slung from its iron posts, but few are found without such optional equipment as a rectangular enclosure of chain-link netting fences ten or twelve feet high (popularly called "cyclone fencing") and sail-like windscreens of polypropylene which permit the passage of air while spoiling the wind, enhancing privacy, and screening out the distracting background activity of a school playground or busy road (fig. 5.2).

Tennis courts are like stage sets. The mind's eye can hardly visualize one without its squeegee or rubber roller hanging from the back netting, its stiff-bristled push broom for clearing away the fallen leaves, its scatter of yellow balls after a coaching session, its insect-swarming overhead lights at the junctions of several courts, its weatherproof bench draped with sweat suits and racquet covers and water dispensers,

TOURNAMENT OFFICIALS
Ⓤ Umpire
▦ Net judge
▶F Foot fault judge
▶○ Service judge
▶ Linesman
⊙ Ball boy

Flood Lights

Back Court

Forecourt

Back Court

78 ft.

Net

Left Service Court

Right Service Court

Wind Sails

Gate

Doubles Sideline

Singles Sideline

Service Line

Alley

Base Line

27 ft.

36 ft.

FIG. 5.2. The tennis court today—dimensions, configuration, and tournament officials. Officials are rarely used in nontournament games (amateur social tennis), where the players themselves keep the score, retrieve the ball, and call each other's infractions of the rules.

its trash receptacle filling with Styrofoam cups and empty ball canisters, its clock on the clubhouse wall reminding players that another match is imminent. In the distance will be a practice board, a rebound net, an automatic serving machine (booming the nearby residents to distraction), a patio furnished with tables, chairs, and sun umbrellas, a cabana that doubles as a storage shed and refreshment room, and the stealthy manipulation of netting by ivy, bittersweet, jasmine, wisteria, clematis, trumpet vine, bougainvillea, hydrangeas, and climbing roses. In earlier times and other places, there might have been a high chair for the umpire, a lawn roller, some geometric striations left behind on a soft-surface court by the drag mat, drag mesh, or steel-tined garden rake, some wooden pegs and string for resurveying the white lines, and a Heath Robinson machine for marking them on the stubbly lawn with powdered chalk or (horrors!) with lime (Macindoe 1987).

   The conventional orientation of tennis courts is north-south, although the U.S. Tennis Association recommends a shift of up to 22

FIG. 5.3. The great tennis stadiums—Wimbledon. Church Road ground of the All England Lawn Tennis and Croquet Club, Wimbledon. Visible are Centre Court and its encircling stands (incorporating the Wimbledon Lawn Tennis Museum and the Royal Box), No. 1 Court, South Concourse, and the Aorangi Park picnic area (*upper left*) with hospitality marquees.

degrees west of north for courts in the lower latitudes of Florida (Duncan 1979, 85). For English courts, the planner Lewis Keeble recommended "optimum" orientations of from 325 to 45 degrees west of north for "grass court tennis" (the same as he suggested for cricket and baseball pitches) and from 325 to 20 degrees west of north for "hard court tennis" (Keeble 1959, 177). At Wimbledon and Forest Hills the courts "march like soldiers in rows side by side," whereas the French tend to effect a highly irregular layout (figs. 5.3, 5.4). Examples include their forty curiously angled courts at the Racing Club de France in the Bois de Boulogne (the most eminent of French sporting organizations) and three of the eight courts at the Stade Roland Garros in Paris which are so concealed by "growing things" that even regular spectators, according to one survey, could not recall them.[8]

Indoor courts represent another landscape altogether, where orientation matters much less than a thirty-five-foot ceiling clearance above the net. Although national indoor competitions have been held since the late nineteenth century, mainly in wood-floored exhibition halls and armory field houses, the boom in indoor play followed World War II, when Armco Steel expanded its sales of adaptable prefabricated sheds and hangars. Indoor carpet soon became a popular court surface. The Swedish Bolltex "portable" court proclaimed its comfort for feet and legs, its cozy atmosphere in cold climates (tennis champions no longer sprang only from the sunspots), and its quietness. Players could concentrate better indoors, undistracted by passing helicopters or thunderstorms, reassured by the plop of that predictably true bounce. Bolltex advertisements pictured a player sound asleep on the carpeted court, hugging a pillow, doubtless having forfeited his match. The green carpet surface at Southern Methodist University's Moody Coliseum (built in Dallas in 1956) proved highly conducive to long rallies—and these, in turn, to enthusiastic spectators (Scott 1973, 182–83).

Indoor tennis is also played under inflated bubbles, the whoosh of the air pump alternatively soothing or distracting to the players. There

FIG. 5.4. The Great Tennis Stadiums—the United States Tennis Association's National Tennis Center, Flushing Meadow, New York. With a seating capacity of 20,000, steeply inclined Stadium Court has patriotically striped backrests in red, silver, and blue. Grandstand Court (left) seats 6,000. Also visible are twenty practice courts, media skyboxes, and, beyond the sixteen-acre site, Flushing Meadow Park. Originally the Singer Bowl, built for the 1964–65 World's Fair.

were fifty indoor tennis clubs in the United States by 1960, and fourteen hundred of them with almost two million players by 1991. Whereas outdoor tennis clubs are permitted in or near residential neighborhoods, the typical indoor club tends to be zoned more stringently into commercial or even industrial areas of the American city. It typically contains not only several courts but its own pro shop, offices, nursery, dressing rooms (with lockers for preppy commuters returning home from work), a sauna (for overindulged muscles), a reception area or lobby, tennis terraces, a snack bar, and a viewing area (for singles parties and those hors de combat). One feasibility study claimed that to break even financially, an indoor tennis club needed thirty weeks of inclement weather per year and 220 players per week, of whom 73 percent would be doubles players (Keighley 1979, 15).

Contexture—Tennis Places, Tennis Locations

Tennis courts are rarely isolated stages upon which a lost traveler might stumble in an empty desert, although at many lonely crossroads in the Australian Outback there is nothing more than a signpost and a "regional" tennis court. Courts are social gathering grounds that adhere to virtually every imaginable social institution, from private households to monasteries, casinos, and floating hotels (Richards 1972). Along the entire spectrum of sporting arenas, tennis courts are among the smallest and most ecologically versatile. They wear many a different livery and adopt many a different guise. For stately homes, a tennis court at the bottom of the garden is as *de rigueur* as formal attire for dinner. Such a gentleman's country residence was Nantclwyd Hall, near Ruthin in North Wales, where Major Wingfield attended that unexpectedly seminal house party and pheasant shoot in December 1873 and convinced the other guests to join him on the lower lawn to inaugurate a new game (Smith 1975, 38, pls. 14, 68). Such a sandstone castle is the state governor's residence in Sydney, with its tree-screened tennis court providing glimpses of Port Jackson. Another such stately hideaway is Lady Astor's Cliveden, outside London, where a clay court is separated by high stone walls from the infamous swimming pool where Christine Keeler and Mandy Rice-Davies compromised John Profumo, M.P., in 1963 (Cameron and Cooke 1980, 148–49).

Lowlier, even antipodean suburbanites could also boast of their private tennis courts. Hugh Macindoe's grandfather surrounded his backyard court in suburban Sydney with chicken wire netting and—frugal, logical Scot that he was—enclosed it with an outer perimeter of chicken coops from which he collected garden manure and eggs to the mortification of his tennis-sociable daughters, who would rather their beaux should think a gardener took care of the court and the chickens. Their brother became a celebrated ophthalmologist, and the mansion he bought in the 1940s had its tennis court in the front, where his solid financial status could be envied by passers-by while his sporting activities were screened from the "vulgar gaze" by a succession of flowering shrubs and trees. Four other families, also in proud possession of their own grass courts and dashing white attire, made up a traveling Saturday circuit with the Macindoe clan, each playing host in turn to the others. Promptly at four o'clock, that week's hostess would serve afternoon tea on the grassy bank overlooking the court—asparagus rolls, individually iced cakes, and cut fruitcake, all freshly baked at home (with "real butter"), in that order. Tea was poured from a silver pot into English bone china cups, and loaf sugar handed round in a silver basket with silver tongs attached. Backyard lemon trees assured a constant supply of freshly squeezed lemon juice. The Macindoe children were responsible for rolling, weeding, surveying, and marking the court, and could invite their friends to play there on the intervening Saturdays (Macindoe 1987). Few such private courts remain, having been choked out by higher residential densities and property values and by the proliferation of more demotic suburban tennis clubs. Real estate developers have now made tennis courts the gimmicky hubs of whole residential subdivisions. Entire "tennis suburbs" have appeared in Florida, the Fisher Island Yacht and Racquet Club forming one such nucleus on what was previously the Vanderbilt winter home on Biscayne Bay (*World Tennis* 1985, 57, 60–61).

More common in residential areas are the public tennis courts in city parks or on school playgrounds, many with durable but daunting steel mesh nets and asphalt surfaces, athwart which basketball courts have been marked out in paint of a contrasting color. Some occupy the most challenging and enchanting niches in the urban fabric. Two pairs of municipal clay courts lie hidden in the dense geometric forest of the Palais du Luxembourg in Paris (Cameron and Salinger 1984, 66). In the very center of London, in Lincoln's Inn Fields, across from Sir John Soane's Museum, several asphalt courts with their own tea kiosk lurk behind funereal fig trees, providentially hiding from view some of the world's worst interoffice competition. In the golden light of Venice, behind the Accademia, the stone walls of a convent school all but camouflage two courts that fill the entire playground. Right below the thundering approach to Sydney Harbour Bridge, a solitary court pretends to pastoral repose beside a mural scene, a *trompe l'oeil* by Peter Day (Earley 1983, 77). Tennis courts upgrade any neighborhood except, perhaps, in Hazard, Kentucky, where benches beside the public courts are advertised as having been provided, presumably as a public service, by the Egle Funeral Home. Egle was anticipated in A.D. 1316, when King Louis the Quarrelsome (Louis X le Hutin), having executed his wife, died while playing tennis in the Bondy Forest (*Petit Larousse Illustré* 1978, 1490–91).

The world's first tennis club was founded at Royal Leamington Spa in Warwickshire in the summer of 1872, more than a year before Major Wingfield claimed to have founded the game. From that club descended a line of recreational landscapes that now extends latitudinally from Hammerfest, Norway (70° 35' N latitude), to Punta Arenas, Chile (53° 10' S latitude), and ranges in size and cultural context from the Santa Ana Tennis Club of California (with fifty-five courts) to the crimped courts of the Beogradsko LETO Sa Teniskoh Skolom inside the Kalemegdan Fortress, Yugoslavia.[9] Some are venerable clubs like the Longwood Cricket Club of Boston (where the U.S. Doubles Championship was played for ninety years) and the Fitzwilliam Club of Dublin (where the Irish pioneered lawn tennis for women), but there are myriad suburban clubs that casually combine tennis with swimming, or golf, or skeet shooting (the Cercle du Bois de Boulogne), or lawn bowls and cricket (Richmond-upon-Thames), or with many other wonders and equally wild desires. Teenagers often prefer the casual smaller clubs, which eschew the stiffness prevalent at many country clubs. Not uncommonly, a community swimming club will be established first, tucked away at the end of a cul de sac, with tennis courts added later as the property is enlarged, along with the sensibilities of members (Ryan 1984, 31–33).

Tennis has long been associated with schools and colleges, initially with those for the Tom Browns of Victorian England. Dr. Arnold put Juvenal's dictum, *mens sana in corpore sano* (a sound mind in a sound body), firmly into the curriculum at Rugby School. Old Harrovians and Oxonians were the earliest Wimbledon champions, and such precursors of tennis as Eton fives, Rugby fives, and Winchester fives, with their different indoor court configurations, sprang from ingenious schoolboy rivalries. Squash originated at Harrow School in 1850, when boys who were waiting impatiently by the corner of a building for their turn on the racquets court took to using a softer, slower ball that could be "squashed" in the palms of their hands (Arlott 1975, 985–86). More recently, throughout what used to be the British Empire, tennis and field hockey have become staple sports at the ritzier private schools for girls, where both games contribute to the curriculum in social graces and liberation theology (Stoddart 1986, 139–40). American universities have been bastions of the game since 1883, when the first National Intercollegiate Championship was played. Until 1920, that trophy remained in the hands of the "Eastern Establishment" (mainly Yale, Harvard, and Princeton), but since 1920 it has been won almost routinely by players of both sexes from California, Texas, Louisiana, and Florida—with remarkably consistent successes at the University of California at Los Angeles, Stanford University, and the University of Southern California (USTA 1979, 324–32).

A similar American pattern is found in the locations of well-rated tennis camps for serious players of all ages and abilities, and of five-star tennis resorts for grey panthers, young matrons with their entourages, and the well-heeled hit-and-giggle gang. Of 307 tennis camps classified by *World Tennis* magazine (1986, 49–53), one-third had locations northeast of the Potomac River (mainly in the Appalachian Mountains), one-fifth were spread south of the Potomac along the Atlantic Coast into the Caribbean (with notable concentrations in Florida and the Carolinas), and another fifth occupied the Southwest (broadly defined to include Colorado and Texas). Of ninety-one tennis resorts, fully two-thirds clung to the Atlantic Coast from Virginia to the Caribbean, the latter offshore islands accounting for almost 30 percent of the total. Another fifth were southwestern (although none were in Texas), and only 3 percent were in New England. Such patterns almost suggest that the social elites that sustained the stately old homes of tennis in Philadelphia, New York, and Boston have now retired to Florida and points south, leaving behind them a northeastern tradition of tennis camps for talented youngsters and their aspiring parents.

The first summer tennis camp is thought to have been Mrs. Jean Hoxie's at Hamtramck, Michigan. What Mrs. Hoxie began in the mid 1940s was essentially a day camp with a few of the children staying in her own house (Wind 1979, 195). In 1957, John Gardiner opened his "tennis ranch" at Carmel Valley, California, eventually offering package deals for "five-day slim-down and shape-up clinics" to 120 campers at a time (charging $800 for "tuition" over a three-week session). In 1967, Gardiner gambled even more deliriously by opening the John Gardiner Tennis Ranch on Camelback, at Scottsdale, Arizona—for "purposeful vacations." His first forty-one casitas sold promptly for $50,000 to $68,000. Even the names of these tennis resorts evoke their *genre de vie* and their claims to topophilia, however presumptuously. Consider a list that includes Caesar's Palace Hotel in Las Vegas, Villa d'Este on Lake Como, the Palace Hotel at Gstaad in Switzerland (which may boast, the Michelin guide declares, "the certain presence of crowned heads"), the Tennis Club de Mougins near Cannes, Kapalua Bay Hotel on Maui, the late Lew Hoad's Campo de Tenis in a converted Spanish farmhouse on the Costa del Sol, the Wickenburg Inn north of Phoenix (a "tennis ranch"), and John Newcombe's South Pacific Tennis Ranch in Fiji ("Write: Paradise, P.O. Box 9074").

Fine distinctions exist at times between tennis resorts (Cancun, Mexico, and Palm Springs, California, for example), "tennis centers" (Sanibel Island, Florida, and Hilton Head Island, South Carolina), and hotels—often "grand hotels"—with their own tennis courts (Boca Raton Hotel and Club, Florida, and the Mount Washington Hotel in Bretton Woods, New Hampshire, with its once-voguish marathon veranda) (fig. 5.5). The distinctions are complicated further by the historical association of tennis courts and tournaments with gambling casinos, of which

FIG. 5.5. Tennis resorts on the coast. Sea Pines Plantation Company, Hilton Head Island, South Carolina. The racquet club (with the Stan Smith Tennis Academy) and the adjacent golf course lie hidden among the trees, beyond the clustered villas and boutiques of Harbour Town (founded 1957). The marina imitates a "Mediterranean fishing village." Of the thirty tennis courts, twenty-five have Har-Tru composition surfaces and five are lighted for night play.

Las Vegas and Monte Carlo, Monaco, are perhaps the best known. Despite its name, Newport Casino in Rhode Island is of another ilk, a vanished world of placid grass courts, copper beeches, English elms, and patterned shingle cladding, an almost Gothic anachronism which has housed the International Tennis Hall of Fame since 1954.[10]

Just as unlikely is the association of tennis courts with reformatories, jails, and strongholds—opportunities for demented antisocialites and besieged seclusionists to dissipate their anger and frustration. Squash flourished in London's Fleet Prison (where Mr. Micawber was imprisoned for debt in Dickens's *David Copperfield*), and it was there that the now aristocratic game of racquets originated as a time-killer early in the nineteenth century. The tennis court also fitted ideally inside a castle's walls, as it still does at Beaumaris Castle in Anglesey and behind ravelins of the city walls of Orvieto and Perugia in Italy. Medieval jousting arenas and city defenses make very dramatic and highly evocative sites for modern tennis courts. The chivalrous term "tournaments" is still applied to tennis contests. Possibly the earliest outdoor court in England was tucked into the ditch surrounding Windsor Castle (Whitman 1932, facing p. 40). The ball was rarely lost, and there was nowhere to flee from a winning opponent.

Each year, tennis produces its world champions, whose names are engraved in the walls, memories, and archives of the great tennis stadiums, the Valhallas of the game. Of these, the oldest and proudest is unquestionably Wimbledon, a name that inspires greater reverence among the sporting public at large than even Saint Andrews, Churchill Downs, Lord's, Le Mans, or Yankee Stadium (McPhee 1972). Yet this modest suburban home of the original All England Croquet and Lawn Tennis Club lacks many of the features that dignify the other famous tennis stadiums. Compared with the towering, striped, shimmering bowl of Flushing Meadows, it is merely a drab green wooden tinderbox. Compared with the heroic marmoreal statuary and sentinel-like cypresses of the Foro Italico (Mussolini's restitution of Imperial Rome), or the leafy, parklike informality and gaiety of Stade Roland Garros in Paris, Wimbledon's hedges, ivy, hydrangeas, roses, and doll's-house kiosks resemble those of an overgrown country estate. It is neither the fashion extravaganza of Ascot nor the musical comedy setting of the French Open, but rather the village garden party or church fête where the local parson appears to be masquerading as the presiding referee. In this way, unprepossessing Wimbledon enshrines much that makes tennis a simple ceremonial occasion, as much a part of heathen ritual and the church calendar as the harvest festival (but with strawberries

and cream), a game accessible to the common people, while imposing
its own civilized decorum on all but the most recalcitrant players
and spectators (Todd 1979). A champion once complained of Flushing
Meadow that fans "can play a saxophone in the stands and nobody
cares." Not at Wimbledon. At the Italian Open, one journalist wrote,
"botchery is carried so far it is almost an art form." Never at Wimbledon.

The Tennis Crowd—Players and Spectators

But stadiums, clubs, and backyard courts form only the inert physical geography of tennis. The players and spectators who make the
occasion are its cultural geography. A tennis arena beckons players and
spectators, selectively to be sure, from a surrounding catchment. Who
goes there to play tennis, or to watch it, and who mingles with the
"tennis crowd?" At Wimbledon, that demography includes beaming
tennis officials decked out in club blazers and association ties, very
English schoolchildren in their uniforms, shop assistants who have
saved a vacation day each year just for "the fortnight," smug socialites
parading their millinery and tippling their Pimms, dewey-eyed tourists,
the doggy landed gentry in their Range Rovers, and "silvered and grizzled" devotees who have not missed a Wimbledon "since the Relief of
Mafeking" (Wind 1979, 37). Tennis creates its own demography, a slice
of social space no less distinctive or significant for geographers than the
ghetto or shopping mall.

When the players of one arena challenge those of another, or when
crusaders brandishing racquets go forth to plant new courts in the
unconverted suburbs, the connecting links in a tennis network are
forged. Before long, tennis professionals are traveling on circuits across
this network. Even before that, the International Tennis Federation will
have contrived to control the game from hubs within the network, and
tennis buffs will be flocking into its "vacation regions" (Evans 1983a,
44–54, 62–69, 100–102). In global context, lawn tennis spread rapidly
after 1873 from England and Wales to continental Europe, spawning the
Decimal Club at Neuilly-sur-Seine in 1877 and reaching Bordighera on
the Italian Riviera by 1878 (Clerici 1975, 335). It entered the United
States by way of Bermuda in February 1874, when the vacationing Miss
Mary Ewing Outerbridge acquired the racquets and balls from a fellow
vacationist, a military friend of Major Wingfield's, and helped to establish the first American public facility at the Staten Island Cricket and
Baseball Club in St. George. Rival claimants contend that the first
tennis game was played in North America at Nahant, Massachusetts,

in July of 1874.[11] Tennis accompanied the British army wherever it went, and followed the Cook's Tours contingent into the tropics. It followed emigrants to the colonies and dominions, reaching Australia in 1874 and taking root in 1886 at Hastings, where the New Zealand Lawn Tennis Association was formed. But it spread less rapidly from these sunny bastions of gamesmanship into the non-Western world, where sportsmanship was not so solemnly central to civilization, and almost as slowly into boreal latitudes and alpine regions where outdoor games required thermal insulation.

From a private, home-based amusement, tennis was quickly transformed into a national sport, with all the trappings of national policy, organization, exclusions, and rules. In recent years, tennis fans in Sweden, the Czech Republic, Romania, Spain, and Mexico have developed the most passionate identity with their home-grown players, even when these globe-trotting professionals have behaved more like multinational corporations anchored next to offshore bank vaults. At one Mittel Europa Cup game, partisan communist spectators were subdued only when guards fired machine guns over their heads (Tinling and Humphries 1979, 314). A caricature of Sir Norman Brookes (1877–1968) appeared on an Australian postage stamp in 1981, to commemmorate his "services to tennis" during the era before the pros dispensed with patriotism and began serving themselves. Last century, at the U.S. National Championships of 1881 and 1882, the isolationist "American residents only" rule had been applied quite zealously. Only in 1884 did that competition become officially international. International competition was expanded and fully formalized when the Davis Cup rounds began in 1900, having arisen out of the older British-American rivalries. From 1922, France's quest for the Davis Cup gradually assumed the emotional commitment of a national crusade to capture the Holy Grail, and the Stade Roland Garros had to be built in 1928 to contain the hysteria. By 1934, every European country except Luxembourg, Bulgaria, and the USSR had entered national teams in the Davis Cup competition, and during the 1970s even they were joined—from the outer space of global sport—by Hong Kong, Bolivia, Taiwan, Nigeria, Kenya, and Algeria (Tingay 1983, 152–54).

In the wealthier, industrialized countries, very substantial proportions of the active population play tennis. By the late 1970s, at the peak of the latest American tennis boom, there were 32.27 million players in the United States (14.34 percent of a total population of some 225 million). The boom in court construction continued into the mid-1980s, when 220,000 were available (U.S. Census Bureau 1986, 217–

18). By 1986, the boom had gone bang. The number of Americans playing tennis had dwindled to just under 17 million by 1991 and, for the first time in fifteen years, was exceeded by the number playing golf (U.S. Census Bureau 1993, 252–53). In 1991, an American survey of all outdoor recreation activities found that noncompetitive pursuits such as walking, swimming, picnicking, and attending sporting events were the most popular: 40 to 50 percent of the total national population had taken part in them at least once during the previous twelve months (U.S. Census Bureau 1993, 254). Among competitive games, however, tennis ranked sixth after bowling, basketball, golf, volleyball, and soft-ball. Of thirty-three sports covered by the Deutscher Sportband (West Germany), tennis ranked third in male participation (after football and gymnastics) and second in female participation (after gymnastics) (Sta-tistiches Bundesamt Wiesbaden 1987, 389). In France, among sixty-one sports, tennis ranked second for men (after football) and first for women (Institut National de la Statistique et des Etudes Economiques 1986, 267–68).

Comparative sports statistics are notoriously difficult to assemble, especially for a casual "pickup" game like tennis, which requires such minimal equipment and only two players. In 1985, an Australian sports profile produced credible estimates of the numbers who were "truly active" in thirty-eight sports. It counted 1.10 million players of football, 400,000 "regular participants" in golf, 127,000 additional "participants" in ladies' golf, 400,000 "registered club players" of "lawn tennis," and another 600,000 "regular social players" of tennis. That is, out of a total national population of 16 million, 6.25 percent regularly played tennis (Australian Sports Commission 1985, 169–80). These proportions and rankings, judiciously ascertained, are closely comparable with those of the other industrialized nations.

Despite the ubiquity of the game, the typical tennis player is scarcely an average, garden-variety citizen, although the game is ame-nable to all age groups, to both sexes singly or in combination, and to all income levels. It can be played in all seasons of the year, indoors or outdoors, and at all hours of the day. It was miniaturized and patented as "ping-pong" in 1891, when the celluloid ball was brought from Amer-ica to England. Of American tennis players, 6 percent are under twelve years of age, 24 percent are teenagers, 34 percent are grown women, and 35 percent are grown men (U.S. Census Bureau 1986, 218). It is widely supposed that golf and tennis appeal to the same potential players, but a statistical comparison reveals their incongruence. The proportions who play tennis and golf differ among males (T = 18 percent, G = 20 percent), females (T = 16 percent, G = 7 percent), whites (T = 17 percent, G = 14 percent), blacks (T = 13 percent, G = 3 percent), and those who have completed four years of college (T = 31 percent, G = 24 percent). Among Americans whose family incomes exceed $75,000 annually, 17.82 percent play tennis, compared with 16–18 percent for golf and 14.33 percent for racquetball—the top three rankings. Only 2 percent of the American population over sixty-five play tennis, compared with 11.30 percent who play golf (U.S. Census Bureau 1993, 254). "Middle age," it has been observed, "is when you're too young for golf and too old to rush the net."

For their very existence, the great tennis stadiums depend on spectators, either physically present or glued to their television screens. Yet relatively few people watch tennis matches in either mode. Like swimming, billiards, and marbles, tennis is a participant sport rather than a spectator sport. Of the time allotted to sports by network television in the United States, tennis accounted for a mere 2 percent in 1971 and peaked at only 13 percent during the height of its boom in 1976. More television viewers habitually watch professional football, baseball, college football, boxing, college basketball, professional basketball, professional wrestling, and ten pin bowling (Schlosberg 1987). Those who do watch tennis, however, are distinctly wealthier and better educated than those who watch any other sport. Calibrated against the national norm (100), tennis watchers tend to be college graduates (163), professionals or managers (157), members of families that amass over $50,000 annually (149), and single (140). No other American sport matches or exceeds these indices, although golfers are the most likely to vote in an election (Walley 1992). Like track and field athletics, tennis is also watched most assiduously by residents of the American West. All spectator sports attract more males than females, but for women their highest attendance index (90) is for tennis (Yergin 1986, 42–43). It is clearly a game of steady concentration for self-absorbed thinkers, either to play or to watch. As one trainer put it, "tennis is 80 percent head and 20 percent legs."

Whole families are often members of the "tennis crowd" that gathers at the neighborhood arena. Tennis is a family game where parents and children can often compete as equivalent powers—usually either past or still approaching their primes—on the same court. There is even a generational tradition among enthusiasts for the parents to offer personal instruction to their offspring at the earliest age possible, hoping to bless them with the social graces as well as an accurate eye and the will to win. Many new recruits to the game are middle-aged or beyond. Some are attracted to it by the evident retention of skills by their age-peers. They note even older players still competing in the veterans' doubles matches at Wimbledon or touring with the Tennis Grand Masters—their sports heroes of yesteryear. Other grey panthers, often in early retirement, have discovered that regular practice under superior coaches can expose hitherto hidden talents, and that "if you can return the ball three times in a row, you will probably win the point." With fishing, golf, and shuffleboard, tennis has become one of the lifetime sports, part of the "wellness movement" with jogging, walking, and the Nautilus Clubs. What began with Paul Dudley White, the Boston heart specialist who preached an end to the nonsense about harmful overexertion beyond the age of forty, has continued with "little old ladies in tennis shoes" feeling good about themselves, taking charge of the important social causes, and outliving the rest of humanity.

At Algiers in 1943, however, General Eisenhower refused to allow the Red Cross to sponsor a tennis exhibition match (Tinling and Humphries 1979, 304). "This is a man's war," he announced, "and tennis is a woman's game." The "Fauntleroy stigma," as this attitude has been called, long associated tennis with prissy, decorous, effeminate players who spoke in condescendingly refined accents, if they condescended to speak at all. The place of women players long remained ambiguous. Only in 1935 were the U.S. championship events for men and women played simultaneously at the same venue—and the Wimbledon women's championship limped behind earlier women's events at the Fitzwilliam Club in Dublin, at Bath, at the Northern Championships in Manchester and Liverpool, and at Cheltenham. Many years elapsed before a woman champion could be described as "a mixture of Sarah Bernhardt and Maria Callas playing Medea," and it took a combination of brawny Nordic males, foul-mouthed clashes with umpires, and the sheer athletic artistry of female players to erase the Fauntleroy stigma. It faded further when 28.5 million television viewers (the largest American tennis audience ever) saw a liberated woman named King whip a geriatric chauvinist named Riggs in the Houston Astrodome (*World Tennis* 1986, 60–61), but some still accepted an earlier champion's edict that "women partners are a lot of bitches." This psychopathology of gender relations on the same side of the net discomfited married partners in particular. Divorces have turned on as little as a double fault, and, since 1922, only two married couples have ever won the Australian mixed doubles championship (Castro and Foote 1976, 34–43). As recently as 1985, a male professional could still claim that "men's tennis and women's tennis are different sports. We are rock 'n' roll, they're classical."

Choreography, or Tennis Made Manifest

Thus have been assembled the actors and actresses who perform in the theaters of tennis. The drama itself, however, depends on one last crucial ingredient besides the arena, the equipment, and these players. Tennis is a ritualized contest. It depends also on the rule-bounded, well-mannered routines of the game itself—on what might be called its choreography. Media tennis commentators use the endemic jargon of a choreography when they call the plays, strokes, tactics, tricks, antics, gyrations, positions, postures, feints, acrobatics, and gambits of a match. Tennis historians have traced the origins of these moves, attributing the volley to Woodhouse, the tossed ball or lob to Hadow in defeating Gore, the American twist service to Ward in 1900, and the seven hundred-year-old sexagesimal method of scoring to the faces of antique French clocks (Arlott 1975, 605).

Changes in equipment and attire over the years have continually modified this choreography. When the long-handled racquet strung with sheep's intestines was invented about 1500, a far zestier game emerged than was possible using the earlier wooden "battoirs" and parchment-covered paddles. The speed of play also increased after 1875, when racquets strung in loosely looped diagonals were superseded by those with cross-strings threaded tautly through the main strings (ibid., 827). Another shift in tactics occurred after 1846, when vulcanized rubber balls replaced the existing cork balls, and again in 1874, when the flannel-covered ball introduced by J. M. Heathcote proved such a boon to the exponents of spin and slice (Clerici 1975, 335). With any bouncing ball a golden mean is obviously desirable, somewhere between the uncontrollably frisky, the soft Pirelli balls which slowed rallies to a standstill, and the pressureless Tretorns. At higher altitudes, balls of lower pressure are now used routinely. Human speed and agility responded again when "bentwood" entered the language in 1862, and "tennis shoes" in 1892. The height and rigidity of the net have also influenced play. By 1878, the center of the net had been lowered, in stages, from four feet eight inches to three feet (Tingay 1983, 17). As Robert Frost backhandedly observed, "Free verse is like playing tennis without a net."

"How can we know the dancer from the dance?" asked W. B. Yeats.

In tennis, it must matter if one dancer wears a voluminous, ankle-length dress, a fruit-basket hat, and a choker, while her opponent wears only a Minimal Bounce Bra, athletic panties, and just as much polyester wrapping as it takes to display the insignia of half a dozen fashion designers and corporate sponsors (Keating 1987, 33). They belong to different choreographies, and to different landscapes. So do the stream-lined male players of today, with their sweatbands and amulets, and their nineteenth-century prototypes, those Keystone Cops in Norfolk jackets, striped jerseys, miniature four-in-hand ties, porkpie hats, boat-ers, tight knickerbockers, long stockings, and leggings (Schickel 1975, 41–43). De rigueur for both sexes until the 1970s was dazzling white attire, either baggy or dashing. "Creams" were the tennis equivalents of anonymous school uniforms, the democratic levelers of amateur social "hackers." Colored dresses were first worn by the winners of an interna-tional title only in 1972, at Forest Hills, New York, and when the first tropically flowered tennis dress made its appearance at the same arena in 1975, one old fogey remarked dubiously, "So we're into shower-curtains now." At the more pretentious neighborhood clubs, preppy fashions and designer insignia served as cues to group inclusiveness. Social climbers and self-appointed trendsetters wore their sneakers and tennis skirts to the grocery store, and rejoiced in the long-sought fusion of what was casual and what was respectable.

The ostentatious sportsmanship, fair play, and rather stilted man-ners associated with tennis owe something to its long association with royalty, to class consciousness, and to its inception among amateurs and Victorian gentlemen. Only during the past thirty years have insid-ious forms of psychosexuality and business psychology been adduced as motivations for playing tennis, and then often satirically, as droll inter-preters of the game have sought to rationalize the wreckage done to its etiquette by the now-dominant money-grubbing professionals. Cases in point include J. P. Donleavy's facetious novel, *De Alfonce Tennis* (1984), Theodore Saretsky's putative edition of Freud's tennis writings (1985), and Timothy Gallwey's *The Inner Game of Tennis* (1974). "Royal tennis" (or "real tennis") is still commemorated in the Royal Tennis Club of Barcelona and the royal tennis court built by Henry VIII at Hampton Court Palace in 1530. Royalty took to lawn tennis as soon as Major Wingfield advertised his patented equipment. Sets were promptly bought by the Prince of Wales, the Crown Princess of Prussia, Prince Louis of Hesse, eight dukes, eight viscounts, fourteen marquises, and forty-nine earls (Wind 1979, 103). In the early sixteenth century, Francis I of France was so smitten by the game that he had an enclosed court

fitted into his battleship, *La Grande Françoise* (Arlott 1975, 828). Today's ungainly deck tennis ("aerial quoits") is at best a misconceived
hybrid. King Gustav of Sweden ("Mr. G.") and Baron Gottfried von
Cramm were doubles partners, and King George VI of England competed
(briefly) in the Wimbledon men's doubles. Members of the British royal
family still present the Wimbledon trophies, and even republican com-
moners have found it possible to curtsy on Centre Court, proud to have
kept intact that unbroken historical chain between the monarch's court
and the tennis court.

In class-riven societies such as Britain and Italy, tennis served
during the early twentieth century to perpetuate the fraternity of power
and wealth. During the entire decade of the 1920s, several members of
the Italian Davis Cup team were wealthy aristocrats whose captain was
Baron de Morpurgo (ibid., 615). Tennis was a social bond for the leisure
class. Disporting themselves on courtside hammocks and Windsor
chairs, its members kept in touch with one another, but from behind
masks of self-discipline and impeccably well-bred manners (Raverat
1953). Dynasties were perpetuated beside the tennis court, over after-

FIG. 5.6. The season at Wimbledon. The most celebrated event in world
tennis, where strawberries and cream for the sociable tennis set sometimes seem to eclipse the competition itself.

noon tea with strawberries and cream. Where better could parents arrange a marriage or appraise the beauty, prowess, and genetic prospects of their children's friends? Decorum, chivalry, and a languid grace were the hallmarks of these conventionally handsome young socialites, the "beautiful people" of their generation. They were early upholders of Paul Fussell's adage that "the balls used in top class games are generally smaller than those used in others."

The choreography of tennis was infused with their attitudes and style. In winter and early spring, they congregated on the Riviera, under the palm trees of the Côte d'Azur beside the "smoothly lecherous" Mediterranean (Lee 1957, 15–20), then followed the sun and competition northwards to the French Open in Paris, thence Wimbledon and the other venerable grass-court tourneys on either side of the English Channel. Their migrations set the pattern for the more grueling professional circuits of today, with up to forty rather than the original fifteen events each year. The American tennis establishment did the same thing, inching up the Atlantic Coast with the seasonal sun, pausing for club tournaments at the heritage homes of tennis in Florida, South Carolina, Philadelphia, New York, and Boston. In the competitors' tea room at Wimbledon, deals are still struck and contracts sealed by the legatees of that leisure class (fig. 5.6; Karpf 1988, 4–5). British tennis, however, became "so arthritic with class consciousness, so weighted down with extraneous Air Vice Marshals, [and] so blatantly exclusive" that local standards of play stagnated, and Wimbledon became a showcase for champions from almost any nation except Britain (Green 1987, 52–53). Today's professional playboys, with their German sports cars and Nordic playmates, are heirs to this tradition, except that theirs is new wealth won by gambling on their own exertions—not old, inherited wealth which is therefore irreproachable.

Arenas, equipment, participants, choreography: from these four ingredients the many recipes for tennis are devised. Much of the choreography, to be sure, is staged just outside the court itself, or between matches, but at the heart of all these well-tempered rituals is the actual game—the trifling, almost frivolous excuse for all the Wimbledons, all the royal occasions, all the yearbooks, all 325,000 subscribers to *World Tennis*. It is a game of dominance where two unprotected individuals direct and redirect a single missile toward each other, trying to control its velocity, height, and direction above an intervening net and within the boundaries of a strictly confined space. It can be a grudge match, or the classic contest between an aging champion and a younger challenger. It restores self-confidence, and sometimes self-righteousness.

At the change of ends, as opponents pass each other around the net, a tennis game can settle social rivalries, clinch business deals, or defuse parliamentary squabbles. Stripped to bare essentials, it is a war game with two gladiators hurling and clubbing at arm's length. Like bull-fighting and the Roman carnivals, it is a pit game in which both players are trapped until only one emerges as the victor. Its symbol on Michelin maps is exactly right: crossed racquets with a ball below and betwixt, resembling the crossed swords that symbolize a battle site. For all that, tennis is not a contact sport. Ladies and gentlemen can play it together without blushing, although it has done nothing to discourage the conquest of many a rose-lipt maiden by many a lightfoot lad. To small green rectangles strewn around the world, it has added images of swiftness, precision, and perfect rhythmic movement. In its wake has followed a distinctly civilized topography.

> Brookes beat Wilding, who cares where?
> Rapt spectators stand and stare.
> Love the game but not the place,
> Chaste our Gorgeous Gussy's lace,
> Must we quibble over space?

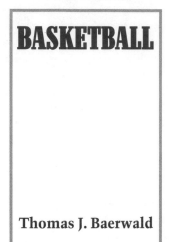

CHAPTER SIX

BASKETBALL

Thomas J. Baerwald

The player started dribbling the basketball about twenty feet directly out from the basket. Bouncing the ball steadily with the right hand, the player began to move slowly toward the right. A defensive player faced the dribbler, gliding to the left in order to remain directly between ball handler and basket. Suddenly, the dribbler's head jerked toward the left. The defender paused, frozen for an instant by the head fake and by recognition of another offensive player who had dashed up to block the defender's path to the left. Still dribbling, the first player burst to the right at the same moment the teammate pivoted and sprinted toward the basket. The defender hesitated for a mere instant before racing after the teammate, but the offensive player's half-step lead was too great. As another defender sped toward him, the dribbler stopped and arched a soft pass to the teammate, who in one fluid motion caught the ball over the left shoulder and lifted a gentle shot with the right hand off the backboard and through the rim. Before the net ceased rippling, both the dribbler and the shooter screamed with delight, and onlookers shouted their appreciation of the way that a classic play had been executed.

The "pick and roll" has been used by basketball players countless times, but for those who have performed it, for those who have tried to defend against it, and for those who have watched its execution, each attempt offers a new and exciting scenario. But in what settings have plays like this occurred? And how have those settings affected the ways in which confrontations like this and the game of basketball as a whole have been played and viewed? While reading my first paragraph, each reader imagined the action taking place in some familiar setting. Some day techniques may enable us to record the thoughts evoked by such passages, but for now, readers are asked not only to remember the context in which they mentally placed the action but also to envision the types of images that other readers may have conjured.

Who were the players? Were they world-renowned superstars challenging each other on a brightly painted wooden floor while more than twenty thousand fans cheered wildly through the final moments of a championship game? Were they members of a high school squad scrimmaging before a handful of coaches in an ancient gymnasium? Were they middle-aged athletes competing on a dewy weekend morning beneath a steel-plated backboard extending over a tennis court in a leafy suburban park? Were they nine-year-olds in baggy shorts and garish sneakers reveling in their imitations of older players, laughing their way into the twilight of an asphalt-covered block beneath hulking central-city residential towers? Were they male or female? Were their skins black, white, yellow, or brown?

And where were they playing? Somewhere in the United States—on a Philadelphia playground, beside a Tennessee barn, or in a California driveway? Were they competing in some other country—perhaps on an Argentine ranch, in a German village, in a Zambian gymnasium, or outdoors beneath snow-capped mountains in Japan? Readers contemplating a vignette describing action from a typical basketball game may well have formed a specific image of the imagined setting. When considering the range of images that likely formed in other reader's minds, however, the conceivable answer to each question about its setting was equivocal. Was it here or there? Was it one group of players or another? Basketball is played by these types of people in these types of settings, but it also is played by many other people in innumerable other locales.

Few other sports rival basketball with respect to the range of settings in which games are played, the types of people who play it, and the versions of the game that they play. Few sports also have enjoyed such rapid increases in popularity, both in terms of those who play and those who watch. Formal games have been viewed by a steadily increasing number of spectators. In 1936, *Literary Digest* estimated total basketball fans in the United States at 80 million. By the early 1970s, John Rooney calculated total attendance at nearly 150 million, more than the combined totals of crowds at baseball, football, ice hockey, and tennis competitions.[1] Similarly, the number of players throughout the world was estimated at 20 million in the 1930s; the comparable estimate now exceeds 200 million ("Favorite of 20,000,000" 1937, 32). In most parts of the world today, one simply would have to mount a goal and offer a ball in order to attract at least a few local residents who would start shooting. Within a few minutes, some type of game using regular rules or based on some intriguing improvisation probably would commence.

The Caged Court and Other Realms of Basketball: Roots

Leonard Koppett, who spent decades reporting on basketball for the *New York Times*, contended that basketball was "the only major sport that was consciously invented at a specific time and place" (1973, 3). Taken by itself, this statement is accurate, because all other major sports gradually evolved through countless variations over decades or centuries before they came to resemble the forms in which they are played today. Koppett overstated his argument, however, when he cited soccer for comparison as a sport that "derived from one of the oldest human recreational activities. . . . A game in which you try to kick a ball—or a rock or a skull—into a stipulated goal area, without the aid of your hands, has its roots in pre-history" (242). Games in which players tried to kick an object through a goal or tried to defend against such kicks have a long history, and they probably evolved in part because they gave expression to a basic human form of recreation, as is readily apparent whenever a small child who has never seen a soccer game persists in kicking a rock forward along a sidewalk. Koppett's implication that basketball's artificial conception has no such prehistoric roots ignores the possibility that throwing a ball or some other object through a goal has been just as common among our earliest ancestors. Furthermore, many other sports have had elements of that activity that were used in competition long before James Naismith arrived in Springfield, Massachusetts.

Native American tribes throughout North, Central, and South America played a variety of ball games. Some relied on sticks, clubs, or rackets to move a ball from player to player, although a few variations, such as the ball games played on courts excavated among Mayan ruins in Mexico and Guatemala, required players to move the ball with their upper arms, knees, or torsos. The largest of these courts was at Chichen Itza, with twenty-seven-foot-high (8 m) walls, ninety-nine feet (30 m) apart, on which stone rings were mounted vertically on a plane perpendicular to the walls. Although players generally were allowed to use only their knees, thighs, and hips to move a rubber ball, they scored points by propelling it through the hoop. Modern basketball players who have played in front of raucous crowds in cozy arenas might identify somewhat with another facet of that Mayan game, the periodic condemnation to death of members of the losing team. Victorious Mayan players frequently claimed the clothing of spectators, the ancestral form of fans "losing their shirts" over the outcomes of games.[2]

Jerald Smith (1974, 354) noted that the sequence for a typical scoring play in some of the Native American ball games played in the southeastern United States consisted of "(1) the toss-up; (2) the initial center scrimmage; (3) pass/carrying of the ball goal-ward; and (4) the scoring drive through the goals." Among the activities that frequently preceded games were formal presentation of starting lineups and heavy wagering among spectators, additional facets that also have strong parallels in modern basketball and other major sports.[3]

Much less evidence exists of ancestral games that used the most distinctive characteristic of modern basketball, the placement of the goal horizontally above the players so that the ball must be arched upward and then down through the ring. The prevalence of similar actions in everyday life leads one to question, however, the degree to which this means of scoring satisfies another fundamental form of human play. Chuck Wielgus and Alexander Wolff (1980, 17) noted a variety of ways in which people have integrated basketball into many facets of their daily lives, such as lofting wads of paper into a wastebasket placed in the farthest corner of the office rather than simply dropping those sheets into a container beside one's chair, or rolling through the correct-change lane at a roadway toll plaza in order to slam dunk some coins into a basket—a move that could never be attempted on a real court with a real basketball.

These actions may be common now because basketball has become so popular, but sports with much longer histories, such as marbles and golf, also have offered the same satisfaction of putting the ball into the hole. Such activity was even described in an epigram by the eleventh-century philosopher Omar Khayyám, translated as, "You are a ball, played with by fate; a ball which God throws since the dawn of time into the catch-basket" (cited in Arlott 1975, 62).

Development of Basketball As a Formal Sport

Regardless of its similarities to a variety of older sports, basketball's formal development was quite sudden and very explicit. To a great extent, it was the creation of an institution, the Young Men's Christian Association (YMCA), a confederation of local organizations sharing common interests that was in the forefront of late-nineteenth-century efforts to promote physical education and team sports "as methods for absorbing the idle time of poor city boys and instilling in them the habits of good hygiene, self-discipline and respect for officials."[4] Prospective leaders of local YMCAs came to study at the association's International Training School at Springfield, Massachusetts, where a former Presbyterian clergyman from Canada, James Naismith, was a physical education instructor. Physical education director Luther Gulick noted that students greatly enjoyed the popular outdoor sports, especially baseball and football, but when colder weather forced the classes inside, morale dropped quickly as students trudged through the standard indoor sequence of gymnastics, calisthenics, and marching drills.

Gulick challenged Naismith to develop a new game that would entertain the students as it helped them maintain their fitness. Naismith's major constraint was the area within which the competition would take place—an indoor gymnasium with an open wooden floor, walls on which were mounted different types of exercise equipment, and a running track elevated about ten feet (3 m) above the floor. After a few lamentable trials with versions of soccer, football, and different children's games, Naismith realized that a game played in such constrained space required rules that limited physical contact and the speed with which a ball was shot at a goal. He therefore decided to write rules for a game based on the following general principles:

—The game focused on a ball, preferably one that was easy to handle, that was difficult to conceal, and that had a predictable bounce.
—Players used their hands to pass the ball in order to advance it, thereby eliminating the need for defenders to tackle or use other forms of roughness in order to obtain it. Players running with the ball or using unnecessary physical contact during play were to be penalized.
—To encourage use of skill rather than strength, points were scored by throwing the ball in a curve through a small, horizontal goal, which was mounted above the heads of players, a location that discouraged the clustering of defenders around the goal.[5]

Naismith originally envisioned wooden boxes suspended from the running track as the goals toward which players would shoot, but when suitable boxes were not found, half-bushel peach baskets were substituted (Naismith 1941, 52–53). Dubbed "basketball" rather than "Naismithball" at the request of its inventor, the first game apparently was played on December 21, 1891, by two nine-man teams in Naismith's class, one captained by Naismith and the other by his faculty colleague, Amos Alonzo Stagg, who later achieved fame as football coach at the University of Chicago.[6] The closed-bottom baskets required use of a stepladder to retrieve the ball whenever a goal was scored, but that delay did not diminish enthusiasm for the new sport.[7]

The Diffusion of Basketball

So immediate was the fervor for basketball that Springfield students took handwritten copies of Naismith's rules home with them over the Christmas holidays. By mid-January 1892, the rules were published in the school's paper, further hastening basketball's spread through the national network of YMCAs, many of which had gymnasiums that could easily be adapted for the new game.[8] Although the first public demonstration of the game evidently did not take place until March 11, 1892, many spectators watched informal games in Springfield and at other locales where players improvised with the new rules. Before that first winter ended, women at Smith College were playing a version of the game, and female teachers from a school near the Springfield campus were learning the game directly from Naismith. Lessons must have gone well; Naismith subsequently married one of the teachers, Maude Sherman.[9]

Through the almost evangelical zeal of many early players, the game spread rapidly in the following years. Some movements were easily traced to key individuals. Stagg took the game to Chicago when he became athletic director at that university in the fall of 1892; H. F. Kallenberg inaugurated the sport at the University of Iowa at roughly the same time; and, in early 1893, Nicholas McKay introduced basketball to the state of Indiana when he added it to the physical education program of the Crawfordsville YMCA.[10] In addition to persons associated with YMCAs, members of the armed forces helped make basketball an international sport as the new century began. It was introduced into Paris in 1893, demonstrated in London in 1894, and taken by a missionary to Brazil in 1896 (Mokray 1963, 1:16). Sports historian John

Rickards Betts confirmed that the game was conveyed to the Philippines after the Spanish-American War and that it was played in China by 1898; J. A. Cuddon stated that it was demonstrated in Japan, Iran, and India by 1901.[11]

Although the bulk of the attention given to basketball throughout its history focused on play by males, girls and women also were active participants. Women's colleges in New England, including Vassar, Wellesley, and Bryn Mawr, rapidly joined Smith in playing the game in physical education classes and intramural competitions ("College Girls" 1902, 234–35). By 1895, it was played at Newcomb College in New Orleans, where Clara Baer interpreted correspondence from Naismith to mean that women should divide the court into three separate areas, where representatives of each team competed against each other in appropriate phases of the game, with only the ball passing from one area to another.[12] A version of these rules restricting three women from each team to one-half of the court while another half-dozen players competed against one another in the other half eventually became the

FIG. 6.1. Women at Smith College in Northampton, Massachusetts, prepare for a jump ball in a game played in March 1893. The backboard is wire mesh attached to the edge of a second-story running track. Gymnastics and exercise equipment surround the gym floor.

basis of the most popular athletic competition among high schools in the state of Iowa, where local pride mandated continuance of the older rules in 1971 when women's basketball elsewhere adopted full-court rules much like those used by men (fig. 6.1).[13]

The Evolution of the Basketball Court and Standard Rules

The language of the original thirteen rules written by Naismith in 1891 guided basketball as it spread, but distinctive conditions at different sites and the inevitable desire of people to tinker with new things resulted in a baffling array of local dialects in its early years. Within the United States, first the YMCA and subsequently the Amateur Athletic Union (AAU) and the National Collegiate Athletic Association (NCAA) published sets of rules in hopes of facilitating competition between different organizations. Not until 1915, however, did those three groups agree to form a joint committee to develop and maintain a standard set of rules within the nation (Menke 1963, 163). The Federation internationale de basketball amateur (FIBA) assumed the same responsibility for international play in 1932 (Arlott 1975, 69). Since that time, most national basketball federations have applied FIBA rules within their boundaries, although American governing bodies have made minor adjustments to suit their own tastes. These deviations have been relatively minor, however, and they have not altered the game's basic character.

Over the sport's century of development, average scores of basketball games have increased steadily. In January 1896, the University of Chicago beat the University of Iowa, 15-12. In 1905, Columbia University claimed to be the national champions because of victories over Minnesota and Wisconsin by 27-15 and 21-15 scores (Mokray 1963, 1:6-7). By 1941, collegiate scores averaged 45-34 on a representative night (Bracklen 1942, 12). During the 1947–48 season, major college basketball games averaged 106.5 points, but by the 1970–71 season, the average total had risen to 155.4 (World Almanac 1989, 855). A comparable increase took place among professional players. During the 1946–47 season, teams in the National Basketball League averaged 56 points per game. In contrast, the mean score per game for a National Basketball Association team during the 1974–75 season was nearly 103 points (Deutsch 1975, 58, 319). The Denver Nuggets set an NBA record by averaging 126.5 points per game in the 1981–82 season, and on December 13, 1983, the Nuggets and Detroit Pistons scorched the nets in a 186-184 Pistons triple-overtime victory (Information Please 1989, 879).

Professional basketball scoring reached such elevated levels that the 1988–89 Detroit Pistons were heralded for their excellent defense when they held opponents to only 94 points per game.

A major factor encouraging increases in scoring was the regular development of new scoring techniques. In almost every instance, certain individual players popularized new techniques that resulted in other players taking and making more shots. Hank Luisetti popularized one-handed shooting in the mid-1930s, and Joe Fulks did the same for jump shooting a decade later.[14] More effective offensive play by tall men playing close to the basket reached progressively more sophisticated levels from the 1950s into the 1980s because of new techniques displayed by George Mikan, Wilt Chamberlain, and Kareem Abdul-Jabbar. The development of inside moves by smaller men driving to the basket was glorified by players like Earl Monroe and Michael Jordan from the 1960s on. The recent enhancement of long-range jump shooting for three-point baskets has been typified most dramatically by Brazilian national star Oscar Schmidt.

Special players and improved skills contributed considerably to the growth in basketball scoring, but changes in basketball's rules also played a role. Naismith himself noted in 1937 that the fundamental principles on which the game were based had not been modified drastically, but rule changes gradually favored the offense at the expense of the defense (Menke 1963, 165). Were he alive today, Naismith would probably reaffirm that statement, although he would also note that refinement of individual defensive skills, as best demonstrated by Bill Russell in the 1950s and 1960s, and sophisticated new team defenses, such as those used by the University of California at Los Angeles teams coached by John Wooden in the 1960s and 1970s, prevented the game from becoming a purely offensive display.

As basketball rules were standardized and changed, so were the courts on which the games were played. For no other sport are the contemporary rules of play and so much of the game's evolution so clearly and tangibly represented as they are in the lines and objects that have become the essential parts of the basketball court.

The Number and Movement of Players

A few basketball rules resulted directly from the character of the court itself. One of the earliest rule adjustments was agreement that no more than five players from each team should appear on the court at any time. Naismith originally envisioned that the number of active players could vary in proportion with the size of the court, and some early games played outside on fields normally used for football or soccer had as many as fifty players competing simultaneously for the same team.[15] Basketball's most frequent and active competition came in the settings where it was born, however—small indoor gymnasiums where playing areas usually measured no more than 100 feet (30 m) by 50 feet (15 m). In such confined areas, games with more than a half-dozen players on a side became overly congested; and by 1895, teams had invariably agreed to limit the number of active players to five.[16]

Another series of adjustments evolved from Naismith's initial restriction on any player's running while in possession of the ball. He wanted to encourage teamwork by requiring that the ball be passed, but as the game evolved, it became clear that players handling the ball required a certain amount of mobility, because defenders were simply positioning themselves in the passing lanes. Rulemakers recognized, however, that ball handlers' mobility had to be restricted to prevent their taking unfair advantage of the fact that defenders could not physically stop them. Through trial and error, rules were modified to achieve the proper balance. As early as 1893, players were permitted to move one foot freely while they held the ball, provided that the other foot continued to "pivot" on the same spot.[17] By 1896, the concept of the dribble, which effectively allowed players to pass the ball to themselves, was widely used (Naismith 1941, 63–65). Over the next decade, dribblers were required to bounce the ball with only one hand at a time and to pass the ball once their continuous dribbling had stopped. An early constraint that prevented a player who had been dribbling from shooting the ball was removed soon after 1900.[18]

The Basket and the Backboard

One of the earliest adjustments in the court itself was modification of the basket. Naismith's peach baskets were too flimsy to endure steady pounding by a rubber ball that eventually was standardized at roughly 9.5 inches (24 cm) in diameter. Iron hoops with cloth or cord sacks were available by 1893 for mounting on gymnasium walls or for placement atop a pole driven into the ground. In many games, goals did not count unless the ball came to rest in the sack. Poles thrust into the bottom of the sack or pull chains ejected the ball (Naismith 1941, 91–93). Not until the early part of the second decade was the bottom of the net consistently left open, thereby speeding up the game.[19]

Early fans often intervened directly in the action, sitting behind baskets and using their hands and umbrellas to deflect shots. As a result, baskets soon were mounted on backboards. The first backboards consisted of wire mesh, but home teams often molded these surfaces to their own benefit, necessitating rules requiring smooth, hard wooden surfaces to be used. By 1895, a rectangular board measuring six feet (1.8 m) by four feet (1.2 m) had become the norm.[20] The backboard generally was mounted directly on the wall at the end of the court, but in 1920, it was moved out by two feet (0.6 m) in order to stop the practice of players literally running up the end walls to make baskets. In 1939, the backboards were moved out another two feet (0.6 m) to permit more movement under the basket (Mokray 1963, 1:8). Modifications of the physical characteristics of the backboards were made in the mid-1930s, when Ned Irish used glass to permit spectators behind the basket to watch the flight of the ball at collegiate doubleheaders he promoted in New York City's Madison Square Garden. In 1940, smaller fan-shaped backboards with a rounded top were adopted for use in high schools.[21]

The Out-of-Bounds Lines

The outer limits of the court underwent a comparable set of piecemeal changes. Naismith's original rules stipulated, "When the ball goes out of bounds, it shall be thrown into the field and played by the first person touching it."[22] Competition therefore continued even as the ball went out of play, with players scrambling to gain control, often at considerable risk to the spectators. Agreement was reached early in the 1900s to adopt the present rules whereby the team responsible for putting the ball out of bounds loses possession, with the other team throwing it back onto the court.[23] Before final implementation of this arrangement, however, a number of alternatives were tried, the most unusual of which reportedly followed a Trenton, New Jersey, sportswriter's comment that "the fellows play like monkeys and should be put in a cage." Inspired by this description, the Trenton manager enclosed the court with an eight-foot (2.4-m) wire fence, which kept the ball in play at all times. In some locales, rope nets were used, encouraging players to bounce off the ropes like boxers in a ring, but such strategies were dangerous if the net was made of wire (Mokray 1963, 1:9–10). Reminiscing about such courts, Moe Goldman stated, "You'd come out after the game with scratches and marks all over your body" (Salzberg 1987, 7). Another player from that period, Barney Ain, was paraphrased as saying that "a 'held ball' was called only when the player in possession was pinned so closely against the wire he couldn't move" ("Favorite of 20,000,000" 1937, 32–33). The cage experiment was short-lived, but the description of basketball players as "cagers" became an appellation by which they are still known today (fig. 6.2).

FIG. 6.2. The armory cage, Paterson, New Jersey. This was the site of American Basketball League games between 1919 and 1933.

The Foul Line and Restricted Lane

In basketball's early years, all rule violations, including running with the ball as well as excessively rough play, were treated as fouls. One of Naismith's original rules awarded a goal to the other side if a team committed three consecutive fouls (Naismith 1941, 54). Individual players guilty of rough play twice in the same game were removed from play, and if their actions were judged as intentionally injurious, their team was not permitted a replacement.[24] By 1894, however, players began to shoot free throws when they had been fouled, with a successful shot worth one point. Within a few years, the value of a goal made from the field during active play was established at two points.[25] Teams initially were able to designate their best shooter to take all free throws, but in 1923, rules were changed to require the person fouled to take the shots. Other rule changes at roughly the same time differentiated between "personal" fouls resulting from excessive physical contact and "violations" like running with the ball, for which offenders were punished through loss of possession (Mokray 1963, 1:8).

The line from which free throws would be attempted initially was twenty feet (6 m) from the backboard, but it soon was placed at fifteen feet (4.5 m), a distance that has remained constant ever since.[26] To permit the shooter a truly "free" throw, a circle twelve feet (3.6 m) in diameter was drawn around the line, and a six-foot-wide lane (1.8 m) was delimited along the axis toward the basket. The circle and lane were shaped like a keyhole, a term by which the area in front of the basket has been known ever since, even though the lines themselves have been adjusted on a number of occasions (Koppett 1973, 103).

The restricted lane between the free throw line and the basket took on added significance in 1932. A few taller players, the most famous of which was 6-foot, 5-inch (1.95-m) Joe Lapchick of a touring professional team, the Original Celtics of New York City, became so proficient at placing themselves close to the basket and turning for easy shots that American rulemakers decided to limit to three seconds the length of time that a person with the ball could spend in the restricted lane. In 1937, the rule was expanded to apply to any offensive player.[27] The rule worked well, but as more proficient giants emerged, the lane was widened. George Mikan, a 6-foot, 10-inch (2.08-m) center for the Minneapolis Lakers professional team, was largely responsible for the lane's widening to twelve feet (3.6 m) in 1952, a change replicated internationally in the same year and adopted by American colleges four years later.[28] In 1956, FIBA altered the lane used for international competition to be trapezoidal in shape, 19 feet, 6 inches (6 m) wide along the end line, while the NBA again widened its rectangular lane to sixteen feet (4.8 m) in the late 1960s (Arlott 1975, 69).

The Mid-Court Line and Center-Jump Circle

The lines through the middle of the basketball court have had a less complex history. The concept of starting a game by having players from opposite teams jump at a ball tossed between them in hopes of tapping it to a teammate was established early in the game's history, and for most of the sport's first half-century, players gathered after each basket around a twelve-foot (3.6-m) circle in the middle of the court while the best leapers on each team tried to control the tap. The persistent advantage under this regime went to the team with the tallest player, a situation as unappealing to many fans as were the regular interruptions of play to conduct the center jumps and the chronic difficulties officials had in tossing the ball fairly. American colleges responded in 1937 by restricting jump balls only to the starts of periods and to situations when players from opposing teams simultaneously gained control over the ball. Almost immediately, play became more fluid, and a more modern, faster-paced style of play ensued. Ironically, this new style led some observers to question whether the sport had become too strenuous and unhealthy.[29] In the 1980s, jump balls ceased to be used for any purpose other than starting the game (and overtime periods), as a system of alternating possession of the ball from out of bounds was instituted at all levels of play.

The line connecting the two sidelines midway between the end lines became an important part of the basketball court in 1932. American colleges enacted a new rule in that year requiring offensive teams to move the ball across the line marking midcourt within ten seconds after it took possession. Coupled with this rule was another restriction that prevented the offensive team from moving the ball back across the midcourt line after play had moved into the forecourt. Both rules were enacted after a series of games in which teams protecting large leads late in the game degenerated into exercises in simple keep-away, much to the dissatisfaction of spectators.[30] Despite adoption of these rules at other levels of play, stalling still remained a persistent problem. Following a numbing 19-18 victory by the Fort Wayne Pistons over a taller and more talented Minneapolis Laker team, the NBA instituted a rule in 1954 requiring teams to shoot the ball within twenty-four seconds after they had taken possession.[31] A thirty-second limit ultimately was instituted for international play, and the NCAA established a forty-five-second rule for men's play in the mid-1980s (Arlott 1975, 65).

The Three-Point Line

The most recent additions to the basketball court have been a pair of arcs radiating from between 19 feet, 6 inches (5.85 m) in college to 25 feet (7.6 m) from the basket in the NBA. These lines mark the area from which shots that pass through the hoop count three points, a scoring change enacted by the NBA in 1979 and the NCAA in 1986 (fig. 6.3).[32] The three-point field goal was initially tested by a pair of leagues that challenged the NBA, the American Basketball League from 1961 to 1963 and the American Basketball Association from 1967 to 1976 (Deutsch 1975, 163, 208).

Abortive Experiments

Although today's basketball court provides a graphic and tangible index of the evolution of the game's rules, a number of experiments would have had much more dramatic consequences had they taken hold. As early as 1906, the fast-paced style of the game encouraged entrepreneurs to hold tournaments for players on roller skates. Games with players astride horses or donkeys also have been held ("Favorite of 20,000,000" 1937, 32). A more practical experiment was tried at Acadia

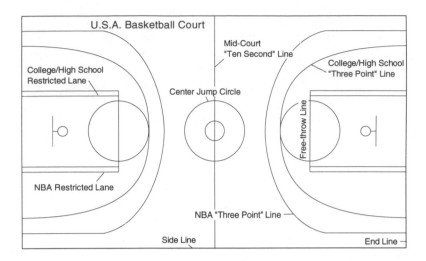

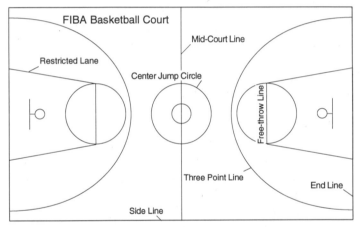

FIG. 6.3. The layout of basketball courts in the United States and for international play. U.S. courts are generally longer and wider than international courts meeting FIBA standards. Primary differences among U.S. collegiate, NBA, and international courts are evident in the size and shape of foul lanes and "three-point lines."

University in Nova Scotia in the mid-1930s, when a referee perched in a balcony overlooking the court used a compressed-air whistle to inform players and fans of violations ("Basketball Attracting 80,000,000" 1936, 38–39). In comparison with such mutations, the use of a red, white, and blue ball by the American Basketball Association seems but a mild aberration. Because of the ABA's role in popularizing three-point scoring for long shots, some basketball aficionados claim that tricolored balls are still best for practicing jump shots from the outer reaches of the court.

The Evolving Settings for Formal Basketball

In terms of its specific form as referenced in the game's rules, the basketball court has one of the most uniform playing sites of any major sport. The overall dimensions of the court may vary. American high schools generally have an 84-foot (25.6-m) by 50-foot (15.2-m) surface, colleges and pros usually play in a 94-foot (28.7-m) by 50-foot (15.2-m) rectangle, and FIBA rules call for a court measuring 85 feet (26 m) by 46 feet (14 m).[33] Those differences in distance effectively are accommodated along the sidelines and at midcourt, however, where relatively little play actually occurs. The overwhelmingly uniform character of basketball courts means that a game begun on one regulation court theoretically may be concluded on another without giving either team an advantage. On occasion, such a relocation has actually been necessary, as when strong winds tore off part of the roof of a building where a mid-1930s Washington state high school basketball tournament game was in progress. Players and spectators reportedly responded by simply walking to a nearby gymnasium, where they finished the game ("Million Witnesses" 1939, 33).

The ideal that basketball courts are uniform and unvarying has not, however, been realized in practice. Only if basketball games were played in settings where uniformity extended far beyond the out-of-bounds lines would true interchangeability be possible, but such an arrangement would essentially preclude the presence of any spectators, because the composition of crowds watching games varies so much among sites. Perhaps no topic in basketball has been as hotly debated as the relationship between the fans at basketball games and the action on the court, for as Koppett (1973, 135) observed, in no other sport are all participants—not only the players, coaches, other team employees, and officials, but also the spectators—all in such close proximity to one another. The separation between participants and fans has occasionally ceased to exist altogether. The Williams College varsity played its games in Lasell Gymnasium from 1900 to 1986, where front-row seats were so close, according to Robert Sullivan, that "referees have been tripped by fans who disagreed with their calls, and opponents have had hairs plucked from their legs while waiting to inbound the ball" (1987, 15, 18).

Many students of the game have analyzed the "advantages" that home teams traditionally have had in basketball. The statistical fact that home teams have won games with much greater frequency than would be expected through simple chance has been clearly documented. Social psychologist John Edwards noted that during the 1975–76 season, none of the NBA teams won more than 50 percent of their games on the road, and he quoted famed bookmaker Jimmy "The Greek" Snyder as stating, "Home teams have a 71 percent rate for success. . . . Figure the home court to be worth three to seven points depending on the team and the floor" (1979, 416–17). Sportswriter Koppett found that in the more than ten thousand games played by NBA and ABA teams between 1946 and 1972, the home team won 63.1 percent of the time. Koppett also discovered that good teams were just as prone to be better at home than they were on the road; the home-court winning percentage of the thirty-six NBA teams that won at least 60 percent of their games between 1962 and 1972 was 78.7 percent, while on the road, they won 58.3 percent of the time (1973, 87–88).

Although Edwards and Koppett agreed that a home-court advantage usually exists in organized basketball, they differed in their explanations of why such an advantage has endured. Edwards felt that a major factor favoring home-team players is the positive feedback provided by the cheering of local fans. Such active encouragement arouses home players to greater efforts and increases their stamina, and it possibly stimulates them to endure more pain. Because basketball is played in an enclosed arena that intensifies whatever noise the crowd makes, Edwards speculated that its intimacy heightens these tendencies. Visiting teams suffer by comparison, not so much because they are subjects of abuse, but because they are so clearly denied the same type of positive stimuli that benefit home players (1979, 420–34).

Koppett's analysis was not grounded in prevailing scientific theory, but he also systematically assessed possible factors that might lead basketball players to triumph more often at home than they do on the road. Because NBA teams have performed almost as well on neutral courts as in their home arenas, he decided that greater familiarity and comfort with the home court, the rigors of travel, and the direct influence of crowds on player performance do not adequately account for the variation. As these factors failed his analysis, Koppett concluded that the explanation must lie in the one factor for which no effective test is possible, the home crowd's impact on referees. The subtle, cumulative influence of crowd excitement for the home team and against visitors, he reasoned, makes referees subconsciously inclined to give the home team the benefit of the doubt on a few critical calls in each game, calls that often have direct bearing on the outcome of the contest (1973, 89–93). Regardless of whether one leans toward Edwards's or Koppett's explanation of the possible influence that a basketball game's setting has on the outcome of that game, the role of fans who closely surround the court and have close and constant visual and verbal contact with players, coaches, and officials seems especially crucial.

Basketball fans have always been close to the games they have watched. Early rule changes that resolved which team took possession of the ball after it had gone out of bounds demonstrated that spectators needed protection from the active play of the athletes, just as the development of the backboard confirmed that the game could be directly affected by a few zealous fans. Many YMCAs, colleges, and other institutions had gymnasiums around the turn of the century, but most of those spaces were small and designed for a variety of space-intensive, noncompetitive activities, such as tumbling and calisthenics. A large number of these gyms were rapidly adapted for use by basketball players through the simple addition of a few baskets mounted on walls and a few lines on the floor, but the popularity of the game often caused conflicts, because ten players could monopolize a gym that thirty or forty people otherwise might use for less tempestuous forms of exercise. Following repeated conflicts over gymnasium use and player behavior, many YMCAs banned the sport from their gyms within the first decade of the game's invention at its international training school.[34]

Whether because players were exiled from gymnasiums that had been their initial homes or because gyms had never been available for their use, many basketball games were played in a variety of other settings during the sport's first decades. Kansas coach Phog Allen recalled that his first game was in the loft above a livery stable, and future Big Ten conference commissioner Tug Wilson remembered games in his hometown's opera house, where one of the local players' favorite plays "was to disappear through one door under the stage and dart out the other, unguarded" (McCallum 1978, 37). Historians of Indiana high school basketball remember many unique settings for early games. The Atlanta team used an abandoned church; spectators in Carmel sat on piles of lumber while the local team played in the driveway of a lumberyard; and the Madison team used a roller-skating rink, inviting patrons to don skates in order to provide their own pregame, halftime, and postgame entertainment (Wind 1980, 56). The Benton, Illinois, high school team played games in a gym that had two pillars in the middle of the floor and a ceiling only about three feet above the basket, necessitat-

FIG. 6.4. A capacity crowd at the 1945 state high school basketball
tournament, played in the armory in Louisville, Kentucky.

ing a special rule that permitted banking the ball directly off the ceiling
(Furlong 1962, 18).

Such peculiar characteristics encouraged players to develop special
skills; 1940s professional basketball star Sonny Hertzberg later speculated that one reason New York City players tended to be good passers
and good dribblers was because they played in small, narrow gyms
where long, high-arced shots were not practical (Salzberg 1987, 15). In
addition to pillars, operating coal stoves and chimneys were dangerous
obstacles on many courts. Other contests were played in dance halls,
where the floor was ideal for the dancing that promoters offered before
and after games, but its slick surface made fast starts and stops futile
during the basketball games.[35]

As basketball's popularity increased from the 1920s into the 1940s,
the size and quality of the spaces in which it was played also grew (fig.
6.4). New, larger facilities became common in those parts of the United
States where the sport was followed most avidly. Many midwestern
universities erected new field houses, some of which seated ten thousand or more fans through the use of retractable bleachers, which

maximized the space available for seating during formal games and optimized the floor area available for use at other times by physical education classes and intramural recreational activities.[36] Many midwestern high schools constructed new, multipurpose gymnasiums, often equivalent in size to the rest of the high school. Many had seating capacities double or triple their town's entire population ("Kansas Town" 1958, 81–85). The classic arrangement in such gyms was for upper-level permanent seats and lower-level roll-back bleachers to face the court from the sides. A wall immediately behind one basket was bare except for a scoreboard and championship banners; the other wall was broken by a recessed stage from which a pep band played during games. At other times during the school year, folding chairs arrayed on the court provided seating for audiences while junior thespians performed on stage or orators droned during school assemblies.

Into the latter half of the twentieth century, the settings for basketball continued to become more spacious. Many new facilities were designed specifically for basketball and were used for few functions other than practices and games. Permanent seats descended on all four sides to within a few feet of the court in complexes like those of New Castle and Logansport high schools in Indiana. Starting in the 1970s, sumptuous basketball arenas seating twenty thousand or more fans were built at universities with rich basketball traditions like North Carolina, Kentucky, and Brigham Young.[37] The facilities in which professional teams played also tended to become larger and more modern as the twentieth century progressed, although most teams scheduled their games between hockey games, circuses, and trade shows in multipurpose facilities. The 1946 start of the Basketball Association of America (BAA), an immediate predecessor of the NBA, was the direct result of decisions by owners of a number of eastern arenas to start a league so they could schedule revenue-generating basketball games on days their arenas were not used for other events.[38]

Occupying multipurpose facilities did not always serve professional basketball teams well. Arena schedules could be arranged in advance to accommodate regular-season games, but playoff games were unpredictable, and teams often found themselves evicted from their home courts at the time of the year when the home-court advantage was considered essential. The seven-game NBA final playoff series in 1952 was played in four different arenas. A circus forced the New York Knicks out of Madison Square Garden and into the Sixty-ninth Regiment Armory for two games, while event conflicts mandated that two of the Minneapolis Lakers' home games be played in Saint Paul. The

Lakers were more experienced gypsies, having spent most of their history roaming between the auditorium and the armory in downtown Minneapolis, and they won the series in the seventh game (Deutsch 1975, 96). The Fort Wayne Pistons were compelled to play their "home" games in the 1955 NBA playoff finals in Indianapolis because the American Bowling Congress occupied the Fort Wayne Memorial Auditorium.[39] Perhaps the most embarrassing part of the ABA's history occurred at the end of its first season when the New Jersey Americans, unable to use the Teaneck Armory where they normally played, forfeited a playoff game because a substitute arena rented on Long Island was missing parts of the floors and had bolts protruding upward on other parts of the playing surface. Amazingly, the team chose to relocate to the latter arena for the next season, but their first game was delayed when ice seeped up through the floor, turning pregame drills into a demolition derby (Deutsch 1975, 208, 223).

The variety of facilities within which formal basketball games were played continued to proliferate in the latter decades of the twentieth century. New buildings that accommodated basketball, hockey, and other indoor sports were constructed in many cities. Arenas designed for concerts and other live arts performances in addition to basketball became more common. The desire to seat more spectators resulted in the placement of basketball courts on the floors of mammoth domed stadiums built primarily for the "outdoor" sports of baseball and football.

These varied facilities generally were more comfortable for players and spectators alike than were the roller rinks, fairground barns, and concrete floor armories where well-known teams competed into the 1960s, but they lent a different atmosphere to the basketball games played within them (Salzberg 1987, 67–141). In hockey rinks, improvements in machinery to make and remove ice and in the insulation under floorboards alleviated the chill that afflicted many cagers in older arenas where the court was laid directly over canvas-covered ice, but seating along the ends of the court usually was sparse or nonexistent because the hockey rink's greater length prevented installation of any permanent seats. When the University of Illinois opened its spacious Assembly Hall in 1961, attendance more than doubled, and fans enjoyed sightlines also designed for live arts performances, but the basketball crowds seemed more mute, leading one reporter to comment that the hall's designer must have placed the court in Urbana and all of the fans in Champaign.

Adjustment to domed stadiums was even more severe. When the University of California at Los Angeles tipped off against the University of Houston in the Astrodome in 1968, nearly fifty thousand fans watched—almost all from at least two hundred feet away, because the court was placed directly in the center of the stadium's vast floor.[40] As other domed stadiums developed seating configurations for basketball games, they tended to move the court toward one side or corner of the floor. This provided closer seating for fans in permanent seats and in portable bleachers constructed along the court's other sides, but it sacrificed more remote permanent seats that almost never are filled. The sightlines for spectators therefore were nearly as good as in more compact arenas, but the backdrops for players often were disconcerting, even when large curtains were dropped from the roof to make the space less cavernous (Conniff 1988, 122–23). The enormous capacities of domed stadiums have made them a favored locale for NCAA tournament games, but professional teams have slowly shied away from them because of their less than optimal playing conditions and the scheduling conflicts that have often resulted in such settings. In 1988, the Detroit Pistons left the Pontiac Silverdome, where they frequently attracted crowds in excess of forty thousand, for the twenty-one-thousand-plus seats of the Palace at Auburn Hills, where they were primary tenants. The entry of the Minnesota Timberwolves team into the NBA in 1989 was made conditional on the construction of a basketball only arena in downtown Minneapolis, which was to be the team's permanent home instead of the Humphrey Metrodome.

Although most formal basketball has been played in more traditional settings, the sport periodically has been found in far more exotic locales. Ezra Bowen recalled a tournament played late in 1945 on the flight deck of the U.S.S. *Midway*, an aircraft carrier patrolling the windswept waters of the Davis Strait. "Aboard the heaving bulk of a ship like the *Midway*," Bowen realized, "the best-aimed set shot in the world tends to come down not where the basket is but where the basket was—which usually turned out to be a yard or two from the original point of aim." In addition, "the shipboard player frequently finds himself passing off to a colleague whose path or elevation varies drastically after the ball has been thrown. On top of all this, when driving for a layup or leaping to block a shot, the mind must deal with such distractions as where the floor is going to be when one comes down, as opposed to where it was when one went up" (Bowen 1969, 62–67). Given the penchant of athletes for playing basketball in almost any setting, one wonders why Apollo astronauts never smuggled a basket and ball onto the moon, where reduced gravity would have created conditions for a stupendous slam-dunk competition.

The Diverse Domains of Informal Basketball

To an ever-increasing number of spectators throughout the United States and the rest of the world, much of basketball's appeal results from the facts that its formal games are fast-paced and exciting contests of skill and stamina and that its rules are easily understood. To the hundreds of millions who also play it, another facet of basketball's beauty is that the rules can easily be modified to fit the individual talents of the players and the distinctive settings where baskets are found. In a 1942 inventory of informal games played with baskets and basketballs on New York City playgrounds, Max Vogel noted four major shooting games and a number of other variations. The rules of these games bore little semblance to Naismith's original dictums, but all were still popular relatives of the basic game, and they were enjoyed by players ranging in age from youngsters barely able to heave a ball toward a basket to elderly athletes whose shooting touch long outlasted the spring in their legs (Vogel 1942, 622, 641). Almost four decades later, Wielgus and Wolff found all of these games still played on courts across the nation, and they noted another five shooting games and a half-dozen variations of more active competitions that comprised a basic list of ways in which Americans played "hoops" or "buckets" (Wielgus and Wolff 1980, 19–37).

Indoor Settings for Informal Basketball

Many informal basketball games are played in the same spaces where more formal competition is held, especially in the gymnasiums of schools, colleges, YMCAs, and other recreational centers. By installing accordion-like collapsible bleachers and cantilevered backboards that drop down from the ceiling, a gym that seats a few thousand fans around a single regulation court can easily be altered to accommodate two full-court games or four half-court games; alternately, its dozen or so baskets can each provide a setting for less active shooting games. If upper-level seating areas have the same flexibility, as they do in gyms of many larger high schools constructed in the last few decades, up to twenty baskets can be made available for informal play. Even in locales that never host formal games, the provision of space and equipment for informal basketball can be important. The renovation of a Fort Wayne church was delayed, for example, when parishioners discovered the church would not have a suitable basketball court (Biemiller 1951, 74).

Although informal basketball shares many of the same spaces as more formal contests, the atmosphere and protocol of pick-up and shoot-around competition is much different. Many gyms function on a totally ad hoc basis, relying heavily on the courtesy and good will of individual players. In locales where the number of players wanting to play often exceeds the number that can reasonably compete at any one time, house rules to order competition evolve through time-honored consensus or through formal postings by facility administrators. House rules usually cover matters like the length and form of games to be played and procedures for determining who plays in what order. In special settings, however, special rules apply. During their perambulations across America's basketball courts, Wielgus and Wolff discovered that Brigham Young University faculty and staff had the right to bump students off the courts during the lunch hour and that at the U.S. Naval Academy in Annapolis, Maryland, the "85-degree rule" applied between teams in which players distinguished themselves by wearing shirts or taking them off. If the temperature was above 85°F (29°C), bare skin was felt to be an advantage, so the team wearing shirts had first possession of the ball; when the temperature was colder, the reverse was true (Wielgus and Wolff 1986).

Outdoor Settings for Informal Basketball

Although basketball was invented as an indoor sport, from its earliest days players have found it equally rewarding to play outside. In as little as 200 square feet (18.5 sq m), one or more players can enjoy themselves with no more than a ball and a basket. The range of locales where these minimal requirements are met is enormous, but different types of sites predominate in urban, suburban, and rural settings.

The Playground and Other Urban Settings

For a major share of the basketball players in the world, especially in the United States, and also for a large number of observers, informal basketball reaches its most intense and most sophisticated forms on urban playgrounds. Borrowing a phrase from G. K. Chesterton, Rick Telander titled his evocative portrait of one summer's play in Brooklyn's Foster Park, *Heaven Is a Playground* (1976). In another publication, Telander described two outdoor courts, one sitting beside crashing waves beneath lush volcanic peaks on the north side of the Hawaiian island of Oahu, the other a broken glass-sprinkled cement slab with rusting backboards and sagging rims popularly known as "The Hole" in the Brownsville section of Brooklyn. Noting that hardly anyone ever played on the former court, while the latter usually was filled with players and spectators, Telander bluntly concluded that basketball is most at home when sets of asphalt and concrete courts are packed amid multistory buildings (1973, 51). Even more simply, Pete Axthelm began his eloquent look at basketball in New York City by bluntly stating, "Basketball is the city game" (1970, ix).

Because the number of residents and the range of their interests are so great in any major city, human endeavors emerge in seemingly endless variety. Walks through a city disclose a wide range of settings for basketball, with baskets sometimes bolted onto building facades, mounted on utility poles in alleys, and even perched temporarily on portable backboards, which can be placed on a parked car's roof to permit children to shoot at a hoop only five or six feet (1.5 or 2 m) above the sidewalk. The lion's share of a city's backboards are in parks and school playgrounds, however, and it is the courts in these locations that attract the most serious and skilled players. Wielgus and Wolff maintained that a distinctive subculture has evolved on city playgrounds (1980, 15). Telander observed that different playgrounds have different characteristics and different reputations. New York native Al McGuire, a former professional player and collegiate coach, recalled the pecking order that led players to schedule their appearances at the playground in accordance with their skills. Less proficient players had to arrive at less desirable hours in order to ensure themselves some time on the crowded courts. On Sundays in heavily Catholic neighborhoods like the one in which he grew up, McGuire remembered, one could gauge the talents of boys by the time of the mass they attended before they headed to the playground. The later the mass, the more gifted the player (Axthelm 1970, 23).

Playgrounds have long been the sites of a city's most diverse forms of informal basketball. Until relatively recently, contests matching an area's best players were "scheduled" through braggadocio and "promoted" literally overnight through a multitude of personal conversations (Telander 1976, xx). Casual tournaments were periodically organized by playground supervisors or by park regulars, but the formalization of "the city game" moved to new levels in the late 1940s, when Harlem teacher Holcombe Rucker organized a series of round-robin games to keep New York City kids off the streets and in schools. The tournament started at a playground at 7th Avenue near 130th Street with four teams and one referee. Despite Rucker's death a decade later, the tournament continued to grow, offering basketball games at a variety of levels from early morning until nightfall. Crowds of as many as five thousand people would assemble for games, ringing the court and sending more adventurous spectators perching high on fences or in trees for views of action in which local heroes competed with professional stars.[41]

As if to prove that the playground court can take only so much organization, however, the Rucker Tournament's continued growth in the 1970s altered its format. Outdoor courts could no longer accommodate the continuous crush of its games, forcing rental of indoor gyms, commercial sponsorship, and admission charges for fans. Changes in the Rucker and elsewhere led Axthelm to lament in 1975, "Playground basketball, once a private ghetto rite of manhood, has gone public. With summer leagues thriving in most cities, the game is now well known, respectable and even vaguely chic" (49). The attempted institutionalization of informal basketball increasingly came to emphasize factors unrelated to the game itself, however, as evidenced by the 1988 suspension of the Annapolis summer league when coaches refused to accede to the mayor's order that all players sign waivers permitting criminal background checks (Riley 1988, B3).

Regardless of the type of play and the skill of the players who use them, basketball courts in an urban park or playground are among the most austere landscapes in all of sports. Hard, flat slabs with painted lines are the norm. If courts at a site are especially popular and are viewed kindly by the public agency responsible for maintenance, those courts might be covered with gritty paint in two colors to highlight the out-of-bounds lines, as is done on tennis courts in more prosperous parts of the city. More often, however, maintenance is so infrequent that lines have faded from sight, and cracks in the pavement make every dribble an adventure.

Playground backboards vary in shape and composition. Metal backboards are most prevalent because of their durability. Whether solid or perforated with holes to cut down on wind damage and to deter graffiti, metal boards offer a springy surface that frequently develops its own special quirks in the form of dents and dead spots that can give court regulars a decided advantage over visitors. Some players have been known to use hammers to give boards "sweet spots" most advantageous to their own styles of play.[42]

Rims invariably are standard steel, although the orange paint that covered them when new may have worn off long ago. Most goals have L-shaped brackets connecting the rim to the backboard with slender rods angling toward the sides of the rim for support, but thicker steel plates that wrap themselves around the back side of the rim have become increasingly popular. Under especially heavy play, especially from players whose abilities to dunk have not reached the point where they can slam the ball through without hanging on the rim, baskets often list at all sorts of odd angles. Many rims eventually are torn off entirely, meaning that roughly one-quarter of the backboards in the average American city are rimless at any given time. Many park authorities and school districts have installed specially designed "double rims" in which two rims are welded together, one on top of the other, with small gaps in between. These rims might not be as authentic, but they are far more functional than the bicycle tire rims and other makeshift rings that may be the only alternative hoops in a neighborhood (Wielgus and Wolff 1980, 103–5). Another response from some maintenance workers has been to mount baskets as much as one foot (30 cm) above their standard height. Players have had mixed reactions to this adjustment in a basic dimension of the game. One player in Alexandria, Virginia, argued, "If you got the strength to push the ball ten feet, a few inches more won't make a difference," but another complained after many unsuccessful attempts to dunk the ball through the higher rim, "I feel like I have a piano on my back. Out here I can't dunk doughnuts, it's a blow to one's ego" (Lait 1989, B1, B5).

Some urban playground baskets have cord nets, although these nylon webs often are taped onto the rims rather than hung from brackets as is done in gymnasiums. Cord nets are rare, however. Two factors account for the urban scarcity of nets that "swish" when a shot is perfect—durability and security. When subjected to constant play, cord nets wear out rapidly, and their lifespan is further diminished because they offer inviting targets to vandals. As a result, chain nets have been substituted on many rims. The links make a rattling clank when the ball drops through, and while chain nets last much longer, these too will wear out or rust away over time. Unauthorized removal of chain nets also is common, although the culprits frequently are a park's most proficient players, who fear the mangling that their hands or teeth might undergo if they are caught in the unyielding net.[43]

The court, the backboard, and the rim are the only essential equipment needed for informal basketball action, and many urban parks offer nothing more. Chain-link fences may separate courts, some benches may provide space for periodic rests, and a drinking fountain may sate players' thirst, although few playground fountains ever seem to be working properly. An accessible restroom may be another necessity for competitors spending entire days at the park, although one or more players invariably live within a block or so, making their households' bathrooms semipublic facilities.

Urban playground courts not only provide a setting for basketball, they shape the way in which it is played. Remote courts at odd hours may be the sites for informal shooting or one-on-one confrontations, but far more frequent are situations when the maximum number of players is using the court. Both baskets on the "best" court often are used for a single full-court game in which the site's premier players compete, with the victorious team permitted to remain on the court against a new challenger as long as it keeps winning. At times when the action is at the far end of the court, a few spectators often dash out beneath the vacated basket to try a few quick shots with extra balls, but they scurry off as soon as the game action returns. Other baskets tend to be used for half-court games. The least desirable courts traditionally are left for smaller children and for females, although the rapidly growing proficiency of many girls and women now enables them to claim more desirable courts and even to play in mixed-gender games. On courts where games have ended and sides are being selected for the next matches, players who have been watching usually move out to shoot baskets. If most players have brought their own balls, as many as a dozen different spheres may pound against the rim in rapid succession. At the other extreme, the presence of only one ball often results in boisterous impromptu competitions in which rebounding is far more important than shooting. At times when all baskets are occupied, waiting players may participate in their own loosely organized dribbling and passing games at courtside or in other parts of the playground.

Because two teams of five players are most common for urban playground games and because other competitions tend to include more rather than fewer players, playing styles take on distinctive traits. Offensive moves that allow a player to weave past as many opponents as possible are most successful, and players constantly work the ball toward the basket in hopes of setting themselves or teammates up for close, easy baskets. Former college player Brian Winters explained, "In parks, you play to win. You can't really shoot from the outside because of the wind and bent rims and all that. You just drive all the time and throw the ball up any old way" (Telander 1973, 56). A standing rule on many courts is that the team scoring a basket gets the ball for another possession, a dictum that encourages players to cultivate their defensive and rebounding skills. Another tradition, which permits players to call fouls only for the most blatant assaults, mandates that players develop physical strength and learn to maintain control under adverse conditions.

The Driveway and Other Suburban Settings

Suburban areas also have parks and playgrounds with basketball courts, and these courts are the preferred locale for games in which three or more players on a team "go at it" against each other using rules closely related to the official game. Suburban playground courts closely resemble their central-city counterparts, but they tend to be fewer in number at any one site, with a pair of baskets at the ends of a single, full-length court the most common arrangement. The diminished visual impact of basketball in these settings is exacerbated by the fact that suburban schoolyards and parks usually are much larger than in central cities, with a large part of the total area covered by grass-covered baseball, football, or soccer fields or simply devoted to open space. General maintenance of suburban recreational facilities tends to be better, although major repairs, such as replacement of shattered backboards or bent rims, may take much longer than in central cities, because basketball generally is given lower priority by suburban agencies than it is in central cities.

Only in densely settled urban areas is basketball best associated with the playground; the prototypical site for suburban play is the driveway. Three major facets of post–World War II American metropolitan expansion—larger families, larger lots, and greater use of the automobile—reached their most tangible collective expression in the backboard facing the driveway by the single-family house. Larger families included more children, whose play tended to be on the lots surrounding their homes to a much greater degree than had been true of earlier generations. Increased use of the automobile encouraged construction of new houses farther from the core of the city where land was cheaper, thereby permitting households to purchase larger lots. The spacing of houses on these lots was too great to economically justify continuation of the alley as a common right-of-way. Garages therefore were attached directly to houses, and driveways were laid to connect garages with the streets. The larger lots also gave children (and adults so inclined) ample room to play, both on grassy lawns and on paved driveways. Under such conditions, backboards readily bloomed on a large share of the new split-levels and ramblers. To illustrate the extent to which the phenomenon could proliferate, backboards were added to ten consecutive houses on one side of a street in a Minneapolis suburb that was settled in the 1950s.

The basketball court on suburban driveways differs greatly in appearance from its analogue on urban playgrounds. Concrete and asphalt are the primary surface materials, but pavement cracks often grow wide and slabs heave substantially, because few parents are willing to maintain a truly level playing surface. On many lots, a sloping driveway makes a horizontal court impractical, forcing players to practice long-range jump shots from spots where their feet are twelve feet (3.6 m) or more below the level of the basket, even though the ground directly beneath the rim is a regulation ten feet (3 m) below the hoop.

Backboards above suburban driveways traditionally were wooden rectangles, but since the 1960s, fan-shaped fiberglass boards have become commonplace. Lighter-weight rims are standard, and a larger share are in good shape than is true in central-city sites, although some display the cockeyed alignment of hoops given heavy use because of intensive play or because older teenagers have unsuccessfully attempted dunks. Cord nets hang from most suburban driveway rims. Chain nets are never seen, and worn-out nets usually are replaced before they disappear. Most nets are white, but a few with blue, white, and red bands hark back to the 1970s when the ABA's tricolored ball was popular with driveway jumpshooters.

The characteristics of the driveway basketball court have shaped the general skills of its players just as surely as have the crowded courts of the city playground. Whether the backboard is perched on the lower edge of a roof above the garage door or is mounted on a steel pole along one edge of the driveway, play is confined to a relatively limited area. When the basket is at the end of a long driveway, for example, a player's range on jumpshots is far longer toward the center of the court than it is toward the sides, and shots from the corners often are impossible because of intervening gutters. Other impediments may also affect play. Former college and pro player Lynn Shackelford's high-arcing shots, for example, reputedly were perfected on his home driveway, where utility wires ran over the center of the court (Wielgus and Wolff 1980, 20).

An equally important facet of driveway basketball is that fewer players can fit on the court. Few lots have a regulation full court; on most, three-on-three half-court games are the penultimate in team competition. As with the Rucker Tournament and its clones in central cities, the three-on-three game, described by Wolff as "basketball's most sociable, symmetrical, and . . . intimate configuration," has become more institutionalized as the sport's popularity has increased.

America's most revered three-on-three competition, the three-day Gus Macker tournament in Lowell, Michigan, has maintained a tongue-in-cheek sense of its real significance as it has grown to cover parts of three streets and adjoining driveways since its start in 1974. The Macker tournament has spawned a horde of imitators, many of which have heavy corporate sponsorship and temporarily close major metropolitan streets (Wolff 1985, 62 ff.; quote on 64).

The density of ballplayers in the suburbs generally is too sparse to support games as advanced as three-on-three, however. Far more common is the classic confrontation of a single player competing only against his or her imagination. Some players used their solitary play to enhance skills like ball handling, as former collegiate and pro star Bill Bradley did by dribbling around folding chairs that represented defenders while he wore cardboard blinkers to improve his peripheral vision (Wielgus and Wolff 1980, 20). For most players, however, solo play invariably means shooting, generally a mix of driving moves toward the basket and jumpshots from more remote locations. Brian Winters observed that playground competition was important, "but there are a lot of times I have to work on my own moves. By myself. In a game, you can't stop and do that." The constant repetition of shots on a suburban driveway may greatly enhance a player's skills, but the quirks of what truly is a home court can inhibit the player elsewhere. "My 25-footer from the driveway is great," confessed Winters. "Too bad I can't take the garage with me to games" (Telander 1973, 56). Similarly, the absence of defenders on the driveway is a situation rarely matched in real games, leading some suburban hoopsters to be characterized as great shooters as long as they're not guarded by anything that moves faster than a garbage can.

The Hayloft and Other Rural Settings

The far sparser settlement patterns of rural areas make informal basketball even more isolated than it is in the suburbs. Playgrounds are nonexistent, and schoolyards are too remote from players' homes to permit play by large numbers of players. The availability of space on farms and ranches permitted placement of backboards and hoops at convenient spots, however, and many future stars honed their skills in rural solitude. NBA sharpshooter Bill Sharman first began playing when his father mounted a backboard against the barn on their property in California, while Hall of Fame player Jerry West developed his skills on the dirt courts at his own and friends' homes in tiny Chelyan, West Virginia (Salzberg 1987, 136, 225). One of the Midwest's premier players in the early 1950s, Carl McNulty, had two baskets on the Indiana farm on which he grew up. One was in the hayloft of the barn, which offered a smooth wooden floor and protection from the weather, but for ten months every year, it was filled with hay. Most play by McNulty, his brothers, and his friends therefore occurred before a basket bolted to the side of the barn on a gravel driveway, where crisp passes were far surer ways to set up shots than were dribbles on the uneven court (Wind 1980, 66).

Rural basketball courts reflect the functional, less-polished demeanor of the farms and other properties where they are found. Just as pastel-colored metal pole barns have slowly modernized the rural landscape, glossy fiberglass backboards have become more common in haylofts and barnyards, but dull-colored wooden boards still predominate. In many locations, the goal is simply bolted to the side of an outbuilding with only a painted outline to approximate a real backboard. Despite the use of discarded soft drink signs from restaurants and splintered plywood sheets left at construction sites for backboards, the importance of basketball often is evident in a court's placement on a farm. Karl Raitz observed that in eastern Kentucky, the only level land on a property will often be cleared and fronted with a backboard atop a pole, while the house trailer is leveled atop stacks of concrete blocks nearby on a sloping site (personal communication, 1989).

The poor quality of many of the surfaces on which rural players compete—often compacted dirt, gravel, or rough wood—retards the development of ball-handling skills. Imaginative players have been able to improvise drills to improve other aspects of their game; NBA star Larry Bird developed his passing techniques and his rapid release of shots by snapping the ball off fences, walls, and whatever else was convenient and moving quickly to grab the ball on the rebound (Wind 1980, 53).

For most players, however, shooting is the primary form of recreation, with peculiar characteristics of the court often making the game more interesting than might be expected. Don Nelson, who was highly regarded as a collegiate and professional player and has been especially successful as an NBA coach, learned not to be long on shots from certain parts of the Iowa farm court on which he played; if he was, Nelson usually had to retrieve the ball from a pile of chicken manure (Wielgus and Wolff 1980, 22). Indiana high school legend Bob Plump, whose winning basket in Milan's cinderella 1954 state championship game victory inspired the late-1980s movie *Hoosiers*, learned the game while playing with friends in a hayloft. The basket was above a door, beneath which was a large manure pile, leading to malodorous consequences for any player who drove too aggressively toward the basket (Newman 1985, 49–50). Another rural player was Jimmy Rayl, one of the Big Ten Conference's all-time leading scorers. Rayl's shooting was perfected in the hayloft of an Indiana barn, where pillars and the roofline forced him to alter his trajectory from different spots on the court. Observers later swore that he continued to use those trajectories even when he was playing in spacious high school and college gyms (Wielgus and Wolff 1980, 20).

The Development of Different Skills in Different Settings

The differences among urban, suburban, and rural courts have long been cited as a reason that different types of basketball players develop different types of skills. Norris Johnson and David Marple tested this notion in a study of professional players active in the NBA and ABA during the 1970–71 season. Comparing performance in six different categories, Johnson and Marple hypothesized that players from different locales had different sets of skills. The first three variables they tested were felt to be measurements of "competitive" skills: the number of rebounds of missed shots, the number of assists (made by passing the ball to a teammate who immediately scored), and the number of free throws attempted (as the player is fouled while trying to score); the other three variables were considered measurements of "solitary" skills: the percentage of free throws attempted that were made, the percentage of three-point baskets attempted that were made, and the number of three-point baskets attempted.

Johnson and Marple predicted that these six measures would all be correlated with the population levels of players' hometowns, with players from larger cities demonstrating greater proficiency in the competitive skills and players from less populous locales being more adept at solitary skills. These relationships were not found to be significant, but minor differences in performance for each of the variables were noted when racial differences were examined. The reasons for higher measures for black players on the "competitive" variables and for higher scores for whites on the "solitary" variables were not, however, clearly evident. Johnson and Marple felt that the average number of players per basket was a critical ratio, and they observed that even in similar types of urban, suburban, or rural settings, the ratio was likely to be larger for blacks than for whites. As a result, they reasoned, the opportunities young players had for different types of practice and play and the emphasis placed on development of different skills by their peers helped shape them into different types of players, with greater or lesser mastery in different facets of the game (1973, 1–12).

Basketball's Settings and the Sources of Professional Players

Not long after basketball was invented, debates began about which places had the best players. Observers noted that different locales nurtured development of different styles of play and different skills. Robert Davies recalled the different regional styles of the 1930s: "In the Midwest, which was considered just outside of New York, it was full-court basketball. In the East, they were bringing the ball up slowly, which made it half-court basketball." Davies helped convert the Seton Hall College team in suburban New Jersey to the up-tempo style and to undefeated seasons. "I think that our style of play made the difference," he reminisced, adding, "Kids outside the city [of New York] were all uninhibited and gung ho. The city kids were very wary and very cautious, and I think that explained their slow style of play" (Salzberg 1987, 47–48).

As intersectional play made confrontations between teams with different styles more common, regional distinctions began to disappear, and *Life* magazine reported in 1945 that sectional styles had been "consolidated into one national pattern" ("Basketball Plays" 1945, 53). Frank Deford, however, felt that regional distinctiveness remained until the 1950s, when the state of North Carolina's four major college teams demonstrated the success not only of adopting different styles of play but also of recruiting players from certain areas to play it. "For years N.C. State . . . was stocked with Hoosier sharpshooters that Coach Everett Case . . . imported from Indiana," reported Deford. "Duke featured Philadelphia players—good ball handling was their trademark— just as [North] Carolina . . . had its Noo Yawkers and Wake Forest had its Southern Baptists and a Methodist ringer or two" (1982, 58 ff.). In a game that many basketball historians felt represented a crucial stage in the game's transformation, North Carolina beat Kansas 54-53 in three overtime periods for the 1957 NCAA championship. While fans from both schools and both states took enormous pride in their team's accomplishments, observers noted that all five of Carolina's starters were from New York, and Kansas star Wilt Chamberlain hailed from the west side of Philadelphia.

Even as colleges began recruiting players from throughout the nation and professional teams ceased to rely as heavily on local talent as

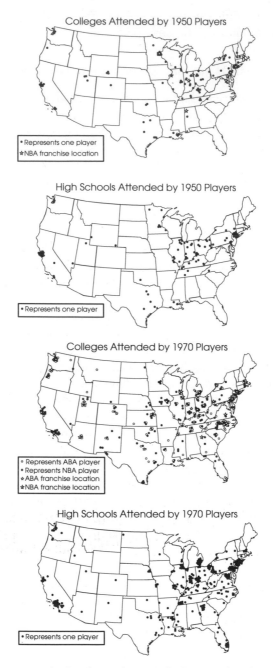

FIG. 6.5. Locations of schools producing all players who played in the NBA and ABA, 1950 and 1970.

they had in their earlier years, arguments raged about which areas were most likely to produce the best basketball players. Thomas Baerwald and Charles Gross (1974) mapped the locations of colleges and high schools attended by all professional basketball players active at the start of the 1950 and 1970 seasons. On both sets of maps, marked changes in geographic distributions reflected significant changes in the locales where basketball was played by men whose mastery of the sport was confirmed by their participation in the top professional leagues.

Two areas were strong high school and collegiate sources of professional players throughout the study period—the Northeast seaboard, especially the New York City area, and the Ohio Valley states, especially Indiana and Kentucky. Few pro players hailed from universities outside those two areas in 1950, but by 1970, the rapid growth of many collegiate programs through broad-scale recruiting was evident. The distribution of locations where 1970 pro players attended high school was also more scattered than it had been in 1950, but the basic reason for this dispersion was demographic. Black players were not permitted on NBA rosters until 1950, when only a handful joined the league, but by 1970, more than 57 percent of the NBA and ABA players were black, a percentage greater than that of any other major sport in the United States (Johnson and Marple 1973, table 1). The rapid increase in the number of blacks playing the sport was clearly evident in the 1970 pattern of players' high schools. Whereas a large share of 1950 pro players had attended high schools in small towns of predominantly white areas in the Midwest, 1970 pro players were far more likely to have played for high schools in larger metropolitan centers like Chicago, Detroit, Indianapolis, Los Angeles, New York, Philadelphia, or Washington. The quality of play in rural parts of the South also improved substantially; nearly a dozen pro players active in 1970 came from predominantly black high schools in northern Louisiana and eastern Texas (fig. 6.5). The 1970 patterns still essentially held two decades later, although a steadily growing influx of international players into the NBA may compel use of a world map to display the colleges and high schools attended by future pro players.

To describe the changing patterns of locales from which professional basketball players have come does not, however, explain why those regions produce a greater relative number of persons especially skilled in the sport. One possible reason suggested to explain why certain places spawn more proficient players is that the children in those locations get an earlier start and therefore have more time to develop their talent. Anecdotes abound regarding early improvisations that some outstanding players used as children, but for every story about a future star shooting a stocking hat stuffed with newspapers through the rungs of a ladder on a fire escape, as Sonny Herzberg did, or tossing a tennis ball into a five-gallon paint can nailed to a telephone pole, as did Robert Davies, there is an equally innovative account of how a child whose future success lay in a much different field first played basketball (Salzberg 1987, 15, 45). Sportswriter Ira Berkow, for example, first tried shooting a rubber ball into a paper bag hung above a hall doorway in a Chicago apartment building, and author Joe Flaherty played in a friend's basement, shooting into a makeshift hoop from which hung a pair of the friend's aunt's bloomers.[44]

The early-start hypothesis also fails to hold up when one considers top-flight players whose introduction to the game came relatively late in their adolescence. Johnny "Red" Kerr, who scored more than ten thousand points and grabbed more than ten thousand rebounds in his professional career, did not play basketball seriously until his senior year in high school (Salzberg 1987, 191–92). More recently, Hakeem Olajuwon grew up in Nigeria playing soccer before his athletic ability and his six-foot, ten-inch (2.08 m) height were directed onto the basketball court. Within five years, he was starting for an NBA team.

If the starting date of a player's introduction to basketball has been a poor predictor of future athletic success, the relative emphasis placed on the sport in the locale where a player grew up provided a surer indicator of how likely a region's players were to excel. Indiana's tradition of basketball excellence was manifest early in the twentieth century in terms of fervent community support for high school teams. Starting players on Muncie High School's 1928 state championship team were given new Ford roadsters, for example, and more than one million spectators still purchase tickets each year to see state high school tournament games (Newman 1985, 41–42). With such strong community interest, one visitor contended, "The best basketball in Indiana is played wherever one happens to be" (Biemiller 1951, 73).

Encouraging Indiana's youngsters to concentrate on basketball to the near exclusion of other sports is so pervasive that an Indiana high school coach stated, "Just about every one of our boys (varsity down to 5th and 6th grade) has some type of basketball goal on his barn, garage, etc. These boys, and especially those in grades 10, 11, and 12, play basketball *every day* of the year. . . . They seem to thrive on playing basketball."[45] A similar phenomenon was noted in Utah, where the predominant Mormon faith placed great emphasis on physical fitness and embraced basketball as an especially effective sport for self-improvement and for evangelism by the church's members (Blanchard 1974, 474). As a result, one resident of Panguitch, a small town in the southern part of the state, related in 1963, "Basketball is really *it* in this town. Look around you at all the nets and goals in the backyards. There's as many backboards as there are TV antennas. In some places there was a basketball goal before there was indoor plumbing. Some of them still don't have indoor plumbing" (Underwood 1963, 60; italics in original).

The landscape of New York City is a far cry from that of Indiana or southern Utah, but the status of basketball among many of its residents is equally high. Barry Tarshis declared, "In Harlem, as much as in most black communities in America, basketball is more religious rite than sport. Kids are at the playground as long as ten hours a day, actually playing as many as six. . . . In a single summer typical ghetto ballplayers will wear out four or five pairs of sneakers" (1972, 14). In justifying his assertion that basketball was a city game rather than the sport of blacks, Rick Telander noted that in Queens and other white neighborhoods, "basketball is still the game for boys; where you are not a total outcast if you spend hour after hour at the playground—at the age of 21" (1973, 55).

The history of basketball as the sport played most seriously by residents of poorer neighborhoods in large American cities is almost as long as the sport itself; "it was the sport of the ghettos long before the ghettos were black," according to David Wolf (1972, 30). Leonard Koppett elaborated: "Excelling in a sport provides an escape route from the ghetto, through college scholarships and professional earnings. This is a classic path in American history, followed by one immigrant group after another—Irish, German, Jewish, Italian, and so forth. When the group moves upward on the economic scale, . . . more and more of its individuals find other opportunities open, and not as many individuals choose to devote time and effort to perfecting sports skills which may exist in latent form" (1973, 33).

Economic improvement may be one factor encouraging children, teenagers, and even some adults in poor neighborhoods to play basketball for hours on end, but another is the lack of any alternative activity. Rick Telander stated, "Outright crime or idleness aside, there is not much else a boy can do." Boys from a variety of Brooklyn neighborhoods invariably answered questions about their early years with one of two alternatives, he reported: " 'I ran with the wrong dudes,' or 'I played basketball' " (1976, 17). David Wolf asserted that famed playground and professional star Connie Hawkins turned to basketball by process of elimination during his twelfth summer: "The apartment was unbearably stuffy during the day. He didn't own a glove, so softball was a hassle. Older boys usually dominated the stickball game in the street. That left basketball" (1972, 33). By contrast, children in more prosperous neighborhoods have a range of sporting alternatives, some of which, such as golf, require too much space and are too expensive to be viable alternatives in older, more densely settled areas.

Whether played on the playground, on a driveway, or in a hayloft, and whether played because of an early and lasting personal love of the game, as a means of bettering their status, or because of peer pressure or community encouragement, basketball players have also been influenced by the fact that their sport often was far better suited to the environments they occupied than were any other sports. Basketball's minimal needs are a ball and a hoop. Proper shoes help, but they are not mandatory. Other players are necessary to enjoy many forms of the game, but as William Otto commented in 1947, "A lonesome kid can develop considerable proficiency at it by himself—behind the barn or in a city alley" (20). "Baseball and football cry out for grass and space," argued Curry Kirkpatrick, "basketball asks only for concrete. Just a little bit of concrete" (1968, 21). One of the joyous ironies of modern recreation is that a sport with the most minimal requirements for facilities has become a means for some of the most varied forms of play.

The Future Realms of Basketball

If basketball's popularity continues to grow as it has throughout the sport's first century, the number of players and spectators will increase to a level that will make it one of the world's foremost athletic activities. While such straightforward extrapolation of statistical trends is dangerous, prospects of basketball nonetheless look particularly bright. Public attention given annually to the collegiate and professional championships in the United States has been paralleled by increasing interest in leagues in nations like Italy and Australia, and tickets to basketball games at the Olympics now are among the most prized passes at those quadrennial competitions.

Famed player and coach Nat Holman suggested that one reason for basketball's popularity as a spectator sport was the fact that most fans at a typical match (Holman estimated the proportion at 80 to 85 percent) actually have played the game at one time or another (Bracklen 1942, 21). Because so many spectators have tried and succeeded (to varying degrees) in accomplishing so many of the moves performed on the court, they can more directly identify with the players than they can for most other sports.

But even more significantly, the vicarious possibilities of basketball work both ways. Just as a fan can watch the spectacular plays of Earvin "Magic" Johnson or Cheryl Miller and see glimpses of themselves, the fan can take on the persona of a hero, pick up a ball, and arc it toward the basket while imagining that it is a last-second shot that will win the championship over the lunging arm of Bill Russell or Arvydas Sabonis. Even if the shot fails to go through the hoop, the mind can offer many legitimate reasons for another attempt, with fouls, violations, mistakes by timers, and other judgments continuing until a "winning" shot is made. The imaginative potential of basketball is just as varied as the ways in which the game is played, and that fact alone will probably keep the landscapes in which it is found so wonderfully varied.

CHAPTER SEVEN

FOOTBALL

John F. Rooney, Jr.,
and
Audrey B. Davidson

In Nebraska the real football action is in Lincoln, the home of the University of Nebraska Cornhuskers, where on six or seven autumn Saturdays the town and stadium are colored a bright red. Known locally as the Big Red Sea, the stadium is jam-packed with people wearing red suits, sweaters, and blazers. Many Nebraskans believe that football has put their state on the map and that the coaches are divinely inspired. Football is the element that unites the state's dry and windswept west with the lush green country around Omaha and Lincoln. It is perhaps the only thing that a Nebraskan can talk about with a Californian, a New Yorker, or an Illinoisan, and feel a real sense of superiority.

On football Saturdays, over seventy-six thousand Cornhusker faithful descend upon Lincoln. Traffic jams around the stadium are monumental as people wind their way through town and campus (fig. 7.1). After the game, the flow east to Omaha and west on Interstate 80 is as thick as it ever gets in this sparsely populated country. Fortunately, there are many watering holes along the way where people can gather for celebrations. Most Nebraskans would like to repeat the experience more than six or seven times a year.

Football Landscape Elements

The football landscape that Nebraska fans enjoy so much has much in common with other college campus game sites, and comprises an elaborate ensemble of a playing field and its surroundings. The size, architectural design, and stadium building materials provide part of the landscape's context. The shape and form of the field, its surface and markings, and the stadium decor add detail. But football's landscape also includes the people who are participating in what anthropologists often refer to as a cultural fest or festival. Thus, a game's ensemble encompasses many elements traditionally associated with celebration. Contemporary football is color, a myriad of symbols, music, mascots, special clothing and uniforms, and even vehicles that identify their owner's bond with a particular football school.

Football's cultural fest is a series of events associated with the traditional rites of autumn—the clean, crisp air, the falling leaves, and the sounds of drums and horns that together elicit an almost primeval exhilaration. These events comprise considerably more than the game itself, and they are, in the words of the late Gregory Stone, the display element of sport (1971, 1–16). The elements are predictable, often spectacular, and, perhaps most importantly, great fun. If the college football weekend is the epitome of the cultural fest, the acme is the "big game" or homecoming. In the words of Edwin H. Cady, "the big game did long ago become a part of American Popular Culture." In collegiate football and basketball, which are embedded in American culture, "the big game [is] a fest, a communal and ritual party, a blow out at which you are authorized to take a moral holiday from work, worry, and responsibility" (Cady 1978, 62). Since only a few young athletes are talented enough to play at the college level, those without talent are trained to be spectators and are indoctrinated by those more experienced in expected festival behaviors during football weekends, including the moral departures Cady describes.

Almost any college homecoming landscape exemplifies the cultural fest. Sororities and fraternities elaborately decorate their houses in school colors as a way to stimulate the celebratory spirit in students and alumni. Frequently the Thursday and Friday nights prior to the game are set aside for walks around the Greek houses and dorms to view the decorations and to select favorites. The decorations provide a context for student shows, eating, and drinking, all of which add to the ambiance and extend the affair well beyond the weekend. Game morning is usually dedicated to a parade of floats, bands, local dignitaries,

FIG. 7.1. Nebraska Memorial Stadium. Five or six times annually the stadium has the third largest population in the state. Known by loyal Cornhuskers as "The Big Red Sea," Memorial Stadium surpassed 200 consecutive sellouts during the 1994 season.

and assorted vehicles which wind their way through the university environs. The parade's theme, actualized in float design and decoration, is almost always concerned with beating the stuffing out of this year's homecoming opponent. Whether the intended victims are Tigers or Lions, Cowboys or Cornhuskers, the message is abundantly clear.

The parade is followed by pregame lunches and parties for visiting alumni. The homecoming game itself contains most of the display elements associated with all big games: marching bands, cheerleaders, pom pom girls, and mascots, all appropriately attired in the team colors. Fans too will be dressed in blazers, sweaters, and hats that identify them with their team. Many spectators will "tailgate." They arrive early enough so they can park their cars, vans, and motor homes near the stadium or at prearranged campus locations. Trunks and tailgates open to disgorge elaborate picnics to be shared with friends and adjoining partyers. Some bring grills to cook on the spot; others did their sophisticated meal preparation in advance and simply unpack their coolers. Specially designated tailgate parking places are frequently reserved a season in advance. People return, with the instinct of migrating fowl, to the same site each year where they rejoin tailgate friends from years past. This ceremonial ritual becomes a pregame, halftime, and postgame fest, and an integral element of the football landscape ensemble. When the fans finally take their seats, they segregate themselves into sections, many exclusive and paid for by generous "donations" (tax-exempt, of course) to the athletic department arm of the university foundation. Those wishing to see the game but unwilling or financially unable to pay the price of exclusivity are relegated to the cheap seats high above the field or in the end zones.

Costume is an important ingredient in the festival of the game, and it involves more than clothing. Ardent fans may paint and decorate their bodies, homes, yards, and vehicles to show support for their team. University of Arkansas "Pig Suey" vans are a common site in Fayetteville and in Little Rock.. Red Cornhusker vans can be found in Lincoln or wherever the University of Nebraska is playing. In fact, vans and campers painted in school colors are a ubiquitous element of the college game. The football costume also includes a wide range of memorabilia—from the traditional pennant, sweatshirt, and jacket to lamps, coasters, bed linens, towels, and even toilet seats. These items function to bond fan to school and perhaps trigger fond memories of football festivals past.

Making a Place for the Game

American football landscapes, and the celebration that is now associated with the game, are an outcome of an evolutionary process that began long ago in England. American football has its roots in the English sport of town ball, a part of pre-Lenten celebrations that date to 1175. It and other forms of early football had no standard playing field. The game did, however, involve the conquering of territory and had the ultimate objective of scoring or crossing a defined goal area. On some occasions the goal was the town square, and the field was a roughly bounded expanse between two towns. Gradually players organized the game and gave it its own place, a rectangular field with goals at either end. They divided the field into two equal halves and placed the goals in standardized locations at both ends. These early fields had no set dimensions and tended to vary greatly in size from place to place (Cady 1978, 17–40; Camp 1974, 3–21).

The American football field gradually emerged from soccer and rugby. Both sports came to America from England as part of British immigrants' cultural cargo. Soccer players, then as now, moved the ball solely by kicking. Rugby allowed participants to run with the ball and throw it either laterally or to trailing players.

Organized competition in the United States has been traced to a number of high schools, particularly in the Boston area, that sponsored teams and established what would now be called an interscholastic conference or league. The high school competition eventually led to the first intercollegiate game (1869) between Princeton and Rutgers at New Brunswick, New Jersey.

The first intercollegiate football game had little in common with the modern version. Twenty-five men played on each side, and the game resembled present-day soccer. By 1872, Columbia, Harvard, and Yale had joined Princeton and Rutgers in intercollegiate competition. Harvard favored a carrying game, similar to that played by the British Rugby Union. It was Harvard's persistence that led to the first rules convention in 1873. Three years later, officials adopted Rugby Union rules, and the carrying game took over at the expense of soccer. Between 1876 and 1883, two innovations placed football on a path which was to change it drastically from rugby. Possession of the ball and a line of scrimmage were legalized, and a team was given three downs to move five yards forward. A standardized field measuring 100 yards by $53\frac{1}{3}$ yards was adopted. The era of power football, in which strategy was based upon player size or mass, had begun (fig. 7.2).

For the next thirty years, the key to moving the football was bulk, power, and momentum. The game utilized only a small portion of the field at any one time, and the flying wedge and the V trick were the most effective plays. Both relied upon forward movement of an inter-locked group surrounding the ball carrier, a strategy that proved deadly. In 1905, the *Chicago Tribune* reported eighteen deaths and 159 serious football injuries. Something had to be done to make the game safer, spread the players, and utilize more of the broad playing field.

President Theodore Roosevelt invited delegates from a number of universities to discuss the game's deterioration. The presidential con-ference produced a number of significant changes, perhaps the most important of which was the introduction of the forward pass. Another required a ten-yard advance for a first down. Both changes opened up the game, and the old power plays lost out to end runs, slants, and downfield passing. The focus shifted from power to a combination of power and speed.

By 1913, football had matured into a game that today's fan would recognize. Changes since then have been minor, basically involving an

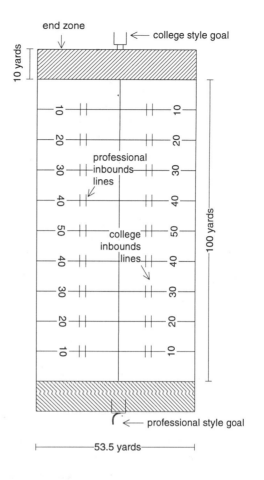

FIG. 7.2. The standardized football field.

increased emphasis on speed, size, strength, and deception. Field dimensions have not changed, but field markings have become more numerous and sophisticated, reflecting greater use of the entire field. For example, when the ball goes out of bounds, it is only brought in seventeen yards, to a near-side hash mark, not to the center of the field. A rule change has moved the goalposts ten yards back from the goal line to the end zone lines at the back of each end zone. In this way the entire field is demarcated and utilized as play space. The field's cross-sectional shape has also changed. It is no longer flat but is raised along the middle with elevations down the center exceeding those at the edges by a foot or more; the slope provides for quick drainage to improve playing conditions in rainy weather.

The most significant change in the field has been in the playing surface material. Modern turf grasses are the product of refined and sophisticated selection, breeding, and testing. Many fields no longer use grass but substitute artificial surfaces such as Astroturf or All-Pro Turf. A faster running surface than grass, artificial turf adds greatly to player speed and maneuverability.

The modern football stadium has evolved to accommodate the increasing numbers of people wanting to watch the action. Early football was sport for sport's sake, viewed by a few spectators standing along the sidelines. With increasing popularity came the need to accommodate additional viewers. The initial solution was to construct wooden bleachers on one or both sides of the playing field. Out of this separation of seating along the rectangular field came the tradition at early college games of placing fans of the home team on one side and those of the opposition on the other. Hence the home side bleachers usually sat many more people than the visiting side. This is still the case at high schools across the United States. Many still have wooden bleachers and home stands that seat substantially more people than the visiting side stands.

As football's popularity grew during the last quarter of the nineteenth century, the demand for seating capacity increased, as did spectator demand for greater comfort and better viewing angles. For example, Yale and Princeton played the first of the annual Thanksgiving Day games in 1876 before a crowd of one thousand. Five years later they met in New York City in front of ten thousand fans, and by 1887, Harvard and Yale played in New York before twenty-three thousand.

In the early 1900s, even a stadium capacity of twenty thousand seats, a number far in excess of the typical student body, faculty, and college town population combined, was often inadequate. By then, football was attracting the general public at rapidly increasing rates, and colleges moved quickly to satisfy the seemingly unquenchable demand for the game. Permanent stadiums appeared during the 1920s. Harvard and Yale, citadels of the Ivy League, built concrete facilities with capacities of thirty-eight thousand and sixty-seven thousand, respectively. Other colleges opted for large wooden stadiums such as the forty-six-thousand-seat facility at Ann Arbor, home of the University of Michigan. These 1920s-era stadiums were indicative of more than just fan accommodation. The large investments by colleges and universities in huge stadiums marked the beginning of an irreversible trend in which institutions of higher learning became entertainment business brokers. Changes in the place where football was played, center stage in the game's landscape ensemble, were brought about not only to refine play but also to polish an academic image and to collect handsome admission fees in the process.

The Stadium-building Era

The 1920s were a time of explosive growth for college football. Stadiums proliferated, and the enormity of the structure, usually the largest building on campus or even in town, was symbolic of the place the game was to occupy in the minds of the sport's growing constituency. Yale built the first big-time stadium, a seventy-thousand-seat structure called the Yale Bowl. In sheer volume, it could easily enclose Rome's Colosseum. Construction of the Yale Bowl and other large stadiums across the country indicated that football had developed into much more than a game between college-age men (fig. 7.3).

By 1922, outsized facilities had also been built at Ohio State in Columbus, at Vanderbilt in Nashville, and at a great number of smaller colleges. Ohio State's horseshoe-shaped stadium had a capacity comparable to the Yale Bowl (roughly 64,025, with temporary seats boosting

FIG. 7.3. The Yale Bowl. Built during the 1920s, it is one of the oldest mammoth stadiums in the United States.

capacity to 70,675). In contrast, the Roman Colosseum's seating capacity was only 45,000, with standing room for another 5,000. The Colosseum's 615-foot length and 510-foot width were dwarfed by the Yale Bowl's 983-foot by 744-foot dimensions. Universities were not alone in the stadium construction boom of the 1920s, as several cities joined in the rush to serve the demand for sports entertainment. Los Angeles boosters built a facility that they hoped would enable them to host the 1932 Olympics—the Los Angeles Coliseum—which had a seating capacity of at least 75,000 and a playing area 345 by 680 feet, contained within a running track. The Coliseum could accommodate several sports, including football, baseball, and soccer. Lights were added to facilitate night games. Chicago fostered a plan for a huge 125,000-seat stadium, which was also intended to improve the city's appearance. The result was Soldier Field, built near the Lake Michigan shore at a scaled-down 100,000 seats. Soldier Field is now the home of the Chicago Bears.

In the interest of selling the maximum number of tickets in these early bowl-shaped stadiums (the Rose Bowl, Cotton Bowl, and Soldier Field, for example), seat quantity became more important than seat quality. Comfort and view were sacrificed to packing them in, as new economic priorities came to the fore. In some cases, such as Soldier Field, over thirty-five thousand seats were found to be too far from the action, or obscured by posts or columns, so recent modifications removed many poor seats, reducing capacity to sixty-five thousand.

Though every college football stadium is unique, as a group stadiums share a similar developmental history that is tied to the game's popularity. At the national level, football interest peaked during the 1920s, but at that time the game was most popular in the Northeast and Midwest. The Ivy League and the Big Ten were the premier conferences of the period, and they were the first to build large permanent facilities. As the game's popularity spread to the South and West, larger stadiums followed. The distribution of large college-owned stadiums is synonymous with the distribution of NCAA Division 1A football teams.

Whatever the time that a college or city built its first substantial facility—from the 1920s through the 1960s—the final product was almost always the result of successive construction stages. Generally, the first stadium seated between fifteen thousand and forty thousand spectators. Most major football schools have added capacity a minimum of three times. Some colleges have moved the field to a new place, abandoning the original site if it would not permit stadium expansion to the scale desired. Other colleges have moved old stadiums to new locations. Other additions such as new decks, end zone seating to fill in the horseshoe, VIP sections where people pay for privacy and luxury, new press boxes, artificial surfaces, lights, and connecting weight training and indoor practice facilities have all added to the complexity of football's landscape.

The following case studies are indicative of the expansion stages through which most collegiate football stadiums progressed. They reflect the game's spread, and the power that fan and alumni emotional attachment has upon the structure of the college campus and the role of football at institutions of higher learning. It is not unfair to say that the size, appearance, and condition of college stadiums are also products of local and state pride.

University of Michigan and Michigan Stadium

Michigan Stadium, home to the University of Michigan Wolverines, is the largest campus stadium and second overall (to the Rose Bowl) in the United States. Constructed in 1927 with a then-enormous seating capacity of 72,000, it has been expanded to hold 101,701. The stadium is touted as the largest college-owned structure designed for a single sport, football (Murry 1989, 27). Through the 1990 season, the Wolverines attracted crowds in excess of 100,000 for ninety-seven consecutive games, and the team has captured the nation's top ranking in game attendance for the years 1973 through 1990 (fig. 7.4). Since construction, Michigan Stadium has attracted a phenomenal 28,000,000 fans to the 388 Wolverine games played through 1990. In addition to being the consistent national attendance leader, stadium and NCAA attendance records were set on November 17, 1979, when the Wolverines played archrival Ohio State before 106,255 fans. The team set an NCAA season record of 731,281 in 1987, and an NCAA season average record of 105,588 per game in 1985.

The Michigan Wolverines first took the field on May 30, 1879, when they played Racine in Chicago. The stadium's first permanent expansion came in 1949 when steel bleachers replaced temporary wooden bleachers and capacity increased from 84,401 to 97,239. A second construction phase came in 1956, expanding capacity to 101,001. The final addition was completed in 1973, bringing the total seating capacity to the current 101,701, a minor increment over the 1956 size. The grass playing field was replaced by 88,285 square feet of Tartan Turf in 1969. It was recovered in 1975 and again in 1982, this time with All-Pro Turf. In the spring of 1988, the university began construction of the $12 mil-

FIG. 7.4. The Michigan Wolverine Stadium. Standing-room-only crowds of 105,000 have made this the nation's most inhabited football place for two decades. Like several other stadiums, capacity was expanded by excavating the playing field and removing the encircling running tracks.

lion Center of Champions' football complex. The center houses medical and training facilities, locker rooms, equipment rooms, a weight room, meeting rooms, staff offices, and a History of Michigan Athletics museum.

Penn State and Beaver Stadium

Beaver Stadium, home of the Penn State Nittany Lions since 1960, is the sixth largest campus stadium as well as the ninth largest overall in the United States. The Nittany Lions have always played on the Penn State campus; the first game in 1887 was on the lawn of Old Main (Thalman 1989, 280). Beaver Field, which then accommodated a crowd of five hundred, was completed in 1893. In 1909, New Beaver Field, which also housed facilities for baseball, lacrosse, soccer, and track, was the team's home until Beaver Stadium was built across campus in 1960.

New Beaver Field had a capacity of 30,000 when it was dismantled,

FIG. 7.5. Beaver Stadium. Its almost 94,000 seating capacity makes it probably the largest structure in central Pennsylvania's Nittany Valley. Few college stadiums have been built all at once but have been enlarged and altered through the years. Close examination of Beaver Stadium will reveal several "seams" where additions have been made.

moved, and combined with an additional 16,000 seats to create Beaver Stadium. Since 1960 Beaver Stadium, originally a horseshoe configuration with a capacity of 46,284, has evolved into a closed structure (with seating in each end zone), nearly twice its original size. The first expansion in 1969 added 2,000 seats. More than 9,000 were installed in 1974, boosting capacity to over 57,000. Two years later the bleachers in the south end zone were expanded, bringing seating to 60,203. Then, in a 1978 construction sprint that spanned the winter, spring, and summer months, Beaver Stadium was sectioned and raised to allow insertion of precast concrete seating forms where a running track had been. Capacity jumped by an additional 16,000 seats, bringing the total to more than 76,600 (fig. 7.5).

Expansion continued with another major addition in 1981 when seating capacity was increased to 83,770. A lighting system was installed in 1984, and the corners of the stadium sported new entry ramps in 1985. Some seats at the top of the end zones were eliminated in favor of walkways. This construction phase left Beaver Stadium with 110 rows on the east side, 100 on the west, 60 rows in the end zones, and a total capacity of 83,370. Recently, the stadium was enlarged again and now accommodates almost 94,000. By 1990, more than 10 million fans had attended Penn State games in Beaver Stadium. Prior to the most recent expansion, the largest crowd was on October 22, 1983, when the team played West Virginia before 86,309 fans.

The Nittany Lions also have an indoor practice site in Holuba Hall. This facility, which is the largest pre-engineered metal building ever constructed in the United States, was completed in 1987. The hall houses two adjacent 60-yard football fields (an Astroturf surface of 80 by 120 yards) and a track with four 110-meter sprint lanes. The facility can be used for regulation lacrosse and soccer games and has been used by the university's football, baseball, field hockey, softball, golf, soccer, lacrosse, and track teams.

Clemson Memorial Stadium

Just before Clemson Coach Jess Neely left for Rice University in 1939, he gave university administrators a message. "Don't ever let them talk you into building a big stadium," he said. "Put about 10,000 seats behind the Y.M.C.A. That's all you'll ever need" (Bourret 1989, 121). Instead of following Neely's advice, however, officials decided to build the new stadium in a valley on the western part of campus. The place was wooded and required clearing, but luckily the site had no hedges. On September 19, 1942, Clemson Memorial Stadium opened with the Tiger football team thrashing Presbyterian College, 32-13. Almost like seeds, those twenty thousand seats installed for opening day would soon grow, and grow.

When the original stadium was built in the early 1940s, much of the work was done by scholarship athletes, including many football players. The first survey stakes were driven by two football team members, A. N. Cameron and Hugh Webb. Webb returned to Clemson years later to be an architecture professor, and Cameron moved on to be a civil engineer in Louisiana.

Part of the attraction of a campus stadium on game day is the body of legend and myth that grows up about past events. During construction, for example, one story holds that Coach Frank Howard put a chew of tobacco in each corner of the stadium as the concrete was being poured. Some claim the tobacco is still there. Or the story about how the sod was laid: "About forty people and I [Frank Howard] laid the sod on the field. After three weeks, on July 15, we had only gotten halfway through. I told them that it had taken us three weeks to get that far, and I would give them three more weeks' pay for however long it took. I also told them we would have fifty gallons of ice cream when we got through. After that it took them three days to do the rest of the field. Then we sat down in the middle of the field and ate up that whole fifty gallons" (Bourret 1989, 121). Even more colorful—and compelling for devoted fans—is the story about the stadium's vernacular name. Although the stadium's structure may have some little-understood effect on play, the reputation it enjoys as a place that almost guarantees a sure win for the home team has earned it the sobriquet "Death Valley." The name apparently was given by the late Presbyterian College coach, Lonnie McMillian. After bringing his teams to Clemson for years and getting whipped each time, the analogy to the biblical Valley of Death apparently seemed appropriate.

On the day of the first game in the new stadium, "the gates were hung at 1:00 and we played at 2:00" (ibid.). No additional construction was undertaken until 1958, when 18,000 sideline seats were added. To accommodate increasing attendance, 5,658 west end zone seats were added in 1960. Together with the large end zone "Green Grass" section, this expansion increased capacity to about 53,000. Later, two upper decks were added to increase seating to approximately 80,000, making it one of the ten largest on-campus stadiums in the country (fig. 7.6).

Despite the additions and expansions, there is still a greater demand for season tickets than can be met. (College football has become analogous to a freeway: the more lanes one builds, the more traffic one generates.) Officials, however, have no plans to expand seating capacity further. Not only do they want to be sure of sustained demand in an era of $800 per seat construction costs, but they are also aware of the mystique fostered by a sold-out stadium each game. Possessing rare and coveted tickets predisposes one to use them, to plan for the event, to ensure that the tailgate party is perfect. To do otherwise would brand one as foolish. How better to add still another dimension to the landscape ensemble that will curry fan enjoyment? If officials change their minds and decide to push Memorial Stadium capacity closer to 100,000, there is still room for more seats over the west stands, enclosing that end like a horseshoe. Luckily, the stadium wasn't built behind the Y. These three examples suffice to illustrate the stadium enlargement process, but dozens (Nebraska and Louisiana State University, among them) mirror the pattern outlined here.

A final point can be made about the effect that stadium building and expansion has upon the fan's sport landscape. The older stadiums

FIG. 7.6. The Clemson University Stadium. Known as "Death Valley," it is the dominant structure in the community. Orange tiger paws painted on downtown streets point the way to campus and the stadium, which is large enough to accommodate over three times the town's population.

were essentially a product of the immediate needs of players and fans: a place to play and a place to watch. The sport place so produced was real or organic in the sense that the experience of player and fan was not anticipated or contrived. The experience of watching a game in such a place was genuine. And the stadium is simply a backdrop for the action on the field. As the old structure, with all of its odd seating quirks, sight angle nuances, and unassuming context within the college campus, is altered by very expensive new seating and additional facilities into an entertainment machine intended to generate profit, the stadium is no longer a product of the game. The stadium becomes the centerpiece of numerous tangential activities. The sport played there is staged, the context for "fun" more subject to external manipulation and less spontaneous.

In the early years, the game was played for the sport of it, and player and fan enjoyment was based on understanding how the game was and should be played, an appreciation of player skill and training and of coaching strategy. As college officials respond to the demand for seating and the stadium is altered and enlarged, it is the game that is in danger of becoming the background against which numerous other activities are played out. Many people have very little understanding of the game—the playbook for modern college football contains dozens of plays, each with options for several players depending on field position, score, and time remaining—and they now attend more to experience the ambiance of the landscape ensemble than to employ their detailed understanding and appreciation of the game.

High School Football Facilities

The landscape of American football is not marked by national uniformity. Pronounced regional differences can be found in the importance of the game from place to place, which can be inferred from the number of college players produced in each state (fig. 7.7a,b). In some communities football has been a cultural cornerstone for decades; in others it is relatively new. There are also differences in choice of stadium-building materials and other artifacts, the sport's economic health, and the significance of competing high school sports, particularly basketball.

Regional differences are greatest at the high school level where the relation between game and community varies most. For example, Texas is frequently referred to as the "Holy Land" of high school football. Here, over twelve hundred schools field teams; many of them are a key element in the emotional glue that bonds Texans to their small towns. Fall is football season. Main Street businesses buzz with speculation about the prospects for the season's games and the health of star players. Fall Friday nights are almost sublime. In small communities of two thousand to three thousand people, the school stadium must accommodate twice that many football fans. The smallest communities must struggle to provide adequate seating for the home folks as well as those who come dozens of miles to root for the visiting team.

The high school football stadium is a ubiquitous feature of the Texas town landscape. Many are imposing structures built of reinforced concrete, equipped with elaborate scoreboards and flanked by billboards touting the wares of local merchants. Most have a running track around the field; many have locker rooms and weight-training facilities on the premises. They are often the showcase structure in otherwise drab and ordinary towns.

A second hotbed can be found in Ohio and Pennsylvania, manufac-

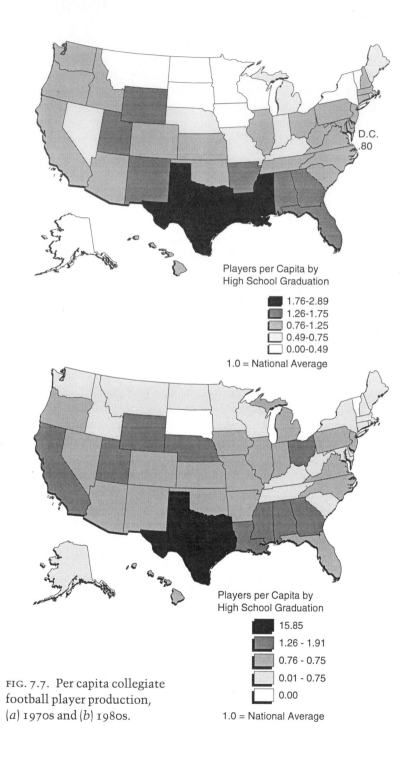

Players per Capita by
High School Graduation

■ 1.76-2.89
■ 1.26-1.75
■ 0.76-1.25
□ 0.49-0.75
□ 0.00-0.49

1.0 = National Average

Players per Capita by
High School Graduation

■ 15.85
■ 1.26 - 1.91
■ 0.76 - 0.75
□ 0.01 - 0.75
□ 0.00

1.0 = National Average

FIG. 7.7. Per capita collegiate
football player production,
(a) 1970s and (b) 1980s.

turing belt states with a deeply ingrained high school football tradition. They, like Texas, have constructed monuments to the game in the form of elaborate stadiums. This regional core may center on northeastern Ohio, especially the Canton, Massillon, and Steubenville area, which marks the middle of industrial Ohio. Here the stadiums are exemplary, and high school facilities accommodating fifteen thousand to twenty-five thousand fans are common.

The pattern of high school football facilities is variable. In many places, few people attend high school games. This regional variation in fan support and participation suggests that the role football plays in local culture differs greatly from one area to another. In many states, education officials foster a sport-for-sports'-sake environment. This means that the emphasis is on equal participation by all students, not the favored few. Fundamentals, discipline, exercise, and teamwork are the desired benefits. Though winning may be important, winning for the glory of the town is not valued as it is elsewhere. The result is players on the field with less polish and fewer fans in the stands. Consequently, there is no need for large tax-supported stadiums when bleachers seating between two hundred and two thousand usually suffice. In the smallest towns, even bleachers are a luxury. Grassy mounds along the sidelines or adjacent to the end zones provide places to park cars and pickups. Parents watch the game in the comfort of the front seat or, if weather permits, on the hood.

Though no inventory of high school football facilities exists, field and survey work shows how regional patterns differ. Participation in high school football is highest in the central plains, Texas, and the southeastern states. These are also the regions with the strongest emphasis on winning (as opposed to encouraging all students to participate); consequently, these areas also produce large numbers of highly skilled and trained players in what might be called "breeding programs." In recent years, Florida, for example, has spawned an increasing number of first-rate high school players. Playing to win and player production have increasingly become southern phenomena.

In general, modest-sized high school playing facilities are associated with those areas—the Dakotas, Montana, Minnesota, and the Northeast—where all students are encouraged to participate in football and other sports. Consequently, few highly skilled players are produced to feed the high profile college teams. By comparison, towns in the high production areas of the South, places where community pride is associated with football success, build large stadiums and auxiliary training facilities. In some places, the size of the football stadium is related more to convenience and cost of space than community pride. In many large cities, for example, substantial football stadiums are often shared as home ground by several different schools. And densely packed urban centers like New York City, Baltimore, and Washington, D.C., have few high school football facilities of any kind.

Technology and Football Stadiums

While the size and quality of high school football facilities throughout the United States are largely functions of the perceived role of the sport, the profit motive of pro football has spawned a number of technological innovations. The newest development on football's landscape is the domed stadium. The first covered and enclosed stadium built in America, the Houston Astrodome, opened in 1965 and was based on a plan conceived by Judge Roy Hofheinz, who was inspired by a trip to the Colosseum in Rome. He was not the first to envision a domed facility: the Los Angeles Dodgers had investigated a domed replacement for their ballpark, but believed it was not commercially feasible. The engineering prototype may have actually been built at Expo '70 in Osaka, Japan. Davis-Brody, a New York architectural firm, designed a pumpkin-shaped structure and hired David Geiger of Columbia University as structural engineer. Because of space limitations and lack of funds, the design team had to settle for a cross section. The result was the model for the contemporary dome.

Domes have been built with steel, wood, and, most commonly, fabric roofs. Some designers have experimented with retractable roofs, exemplified by the Toronto SkyDome (the name would seem an oxymoron), completed in 1989, in which huge reinforced concrete panels slide open allowing fans to enjoy the sun while avoiding chilly autumn and springtime winds and rain. Ironically, this retractable dome technology has been sold to Japan, the home of the original covered stadium (Relph 1990, 105).

Fans attending games played in domes notice their shortcomings. For one thing, they are noisy. For another, players have difficulty seeing high punts and kickoffs. Objects may dangle from the roof, distracting the eye. Also, grass will not grow in the domes, creating the need for artificial turf. The turf is laid on a hard base, which eliminates a natural ball bounce and also contributes to significantly more player injuries.

In the United States, many cities are investing in a domed stadium in the hope that such a facility will attract (or retain) a professional team. While officials may claim that the logic behind building a dome and fielding a team is the extra revenue it brings to the city, in reality, the benefits are more likely to be pride and prestige. A domed stadium can be a huge financial drain on a city or state, and the burden is often passed along to taxpayers. A study conducted by economist Robert Baade revealed that seven of nine cities analyzed had a decrease in their share of regional income following construction of a new stadium (Lancaster 1987, 37). For an enclosed stadium to be profitable, it is essential that the facility have multiple uses. The dome must be a generic sports place, simply a large enclosed space whose most important characteristic is adaptability. The need for such flexibility necessitated the development of movable stands, which allow for changes in seating arrangements and capacity to accommodate football, baseball, basketball, hockey, and rodeo as well as nonsports events. Artificial turf can tolerate extensive foot traffic. This built-in durability allows stadium officials to host additional revenue-producing events such as concerts and trade shows without fear of damaging the playing surface.

Adaptability, though, means loss of the unique and distinguishing characteristics each stadium presents to fans and players and which become associated with the sport experience. The size of the dome required for profit margins usually means that many seats are much too far from the field to allow fans to see much more than stick figures and to appreciate much more than the general motion of the game. One could just as well watch the game on TV.

Artificial Turf and Artificial Lighting

When the builders of the Houston Astrodome discovered that grass would not grow in the shade cast by its roof, there was a frantic search for an artificial substitute. The result was Astroturf, which proved a high density, coarse, and rugged playing surface. In play, the turf was a fast, predictable, and low maintenance surface that soon appeared in numerous outdoor stadiums. Natural grass was removed, replaced by concrete or asphalt, and covered with the green carpet. Football fields were humped even more from center to sideline (frequently in excess of three feet), to insure proper drainage. For a running back, a run around end, from the center of the field toward the sidelines, became a real downhill experience. Swift backs got an added boost of acceleration, and the fast became rockets. Artificial turf also quickened the game, and in the process made it more dangerous. But the perceived advantages of the new surface outweighed the added danger to the players, and most institutions and professional franchises opted to make it the playing surface of choice.

In recent years there has been a gradual swing back to natural grass. Turf researchers have developed grass strains better able to recover from hard wear. Since cold fall weather brings grass growth to a halt and may freeze the field, Purdue University pioneered a hot water piping system (the team is called the Boilermakers, remember?) which is laid under the turf and activated during cold playing conditions to keep the grass active and the surface from freezing. Current preference for artificial turf varies from one region to another. Generally, East and West Coast teams prefer grass, while those in the interior favor artificial turf. For example, only three out of fifteen teams in the Ivy League and Atlantic Coast conferences now have artificial turf. By contrast, just two of the eighteen members of the Big Ten and Big Eight have grass fields. The Pacific Ten and Pacific Coast conferences also have a strong preference for grass.

Traditionally, collegiate and professional football games have been played during the daytime, and high school football is a Friday night event in most sections of the nation. With the advent of ABC Television's Monday night football, however, that association no longer applies, and pro teams have had to install lights if they did not share a baseball facility that already had them. And once the NCAA stranglehold on college telecasts was broken, the major networks and ESPN began to agitate for "prime time" games. The predictable result is that many collegiate stadiums are now equipped with lights for night games.

Conclusion

Football's precursors ranged from the pre-Lenten celebrations of the English to the game as a fest. In the 1990s, however, it is a hybrid game played in an alien place. Some changes were dramatic enough to be called turning points—most notably during the 1920s, when colleges and professional teams across the country built large stadiums. In the decades that followed, additional seating boosted some stadiums' capacities beyond eighty thousand. Later, domed stadiums removed the potential threat of the fall rain and cold, substituting instead an artificial environment that severed traditional ties to the sight of autumn foliage against a blue sky, the smell of wood smoke, and the feel of a bright afternoon's sun. The playing surface is no longer nature's creation, but is now the brainchild of plant breeders or plastics engineers. As a result, play lacks the variability that comes with action on a grassy surface, possibly in rain or snow. The playing environment is now as nearly antiseptic as stadium designers and field managers can make it, and the rich experience of watching a game on an old grass field from open bleacher seats has been exchanged for the poverty of standardization.

Change may alter the place and the game but does not preclude finding the perfect place to play. To the college coach, the perfect place must be "fair," favoring neither team. Players must be able to hear signals; the surface should be fast; there should be no blinding sun or gusty winds. Players often prefer natural grass, although coaches and athletic directors may favor artificial turf because it is faster and almost maintenance free. Equally important, the stadium should be on a college campus, integrated with the academic buildings and dormitories. Coaches prefer old renovated stadiums—places with "spirit and tradition"—to new ones. And when asked to produce a list of favorite place ensembles, coaches often agree on the top ten: Notre Dame, Penn State, Wisconsin, Texas, Texas A&M, Michigan, Georgia, Clemson, Yale, and Berkeley. All have tradition, and all exemplify the game's "display" elements. Texas A&M, for example, has the "twelfth man," Notre Dame a "Touchdown Jesus," Clemson is "Death Valley," Wisconsin's tailgating is famous, Georgia's field lies between hedges, and Texas has a "flag extravaganza."

For players and fans, a perfect game begins with the weather, a cool autumn day—temperature between 40° and 65°—sunny, dry, and wind under ten miles per hour. These conditions are ideal for players to maintain body heat and avoid dehydration. Fans, too, can be comfortable if dressed properly. The stadium should be laid out north to south to minimize direct sunlight in the player's range of vision—and will assure that opposing fans will be seated on the east side so they will have to face the afternoon sun. Seating should surround the field in an enclosed bowl with no obstructed seats. The field should be grass— Prescription Athletic Turf (PAT), developed and first installed at Purdue, is ideal. PAT can be kept at optimum moisture content through a sophisticated subsurface drainage system. It will tolerate mowing and helps prevent injury. The stadium grounds should have a broad grassy expanse, dotted with maples and oaks, for parking and tailgating—close enough to the stadium to permit halftime visits. The perfect place for a college football game is perhaps Notre Dame—or maybe Michigan. It could be Kansas, if the fans cared more deeply. In the end, the perfect place is wherever the cultural fest reaches its pinnacle, where nature and culture unite magnificently on an autumn Saturday.

From a mere game of skill, football has become the basis for local, state, and even regional identity and pride, whether played at high school, college, or professional levels. That identity appears symbolically in the wearing of team colors, mascot decorations, and numerous other ways. Thus, football's landscape ensemble has become more elaborate, and the experience far more complex in heritage and meaning, than a simple game that occurs throughout America on weekends in the fall.

CHAPTER EIGHT

GOLF

Robert L. A. Adams

On February 22, 1888, two gentlemen played a game of golf on a three-hole course that was laid out on the spur of the moment in a cow pasture in Yonkers, New York. The promoter of the event was John Reid, a transplanted Scot and the owner of a set of clubs recently imported from his native land. The occasion was a great success, and all in attendance agreed that this Scottish game held considerable promise. A few months later Reid and four other enthusiasts decided to form an organization to promote their new pastime. A club was formed, Reid was elected president, and the name, the St. Andrews Golf Club, was appropriately selected. Thus, John Reid became the father of American golf, and the nation's first permanent golf club was established—the event to which the origin of golf in the United States is generally traced.[1]

Once a foothold had been established, golf exploded upon the American scene. Many cosmopolitan Americans were introduced to golf in Scotland, England, or on the Continent, and upon returning to the United States, they brought with them an enthusiasm for the "new" game. The popularity of golf spread so rapidly that by 1900 there were nearly a thousand courses in existence.[2] Many of these courses were very primitive, often consisting of but a few holes laid out on essentially unaltered terrain. There were some, though, that rivaled the best in the world, even by modern standards. Of particular note were the Shinnecock Hills Golf Club on Long Island, New York, and the Chicago Golf Club in Wheaton, Illinois. By the turn of the century, golf had spread across the country, but the primary concentration was in the metropolitan Northeast, where over 60 percent of all courses were located. Secondary concentrations existed proximate to urban centers elsewhere, particularly in the northern Midwest. The early footholds of golf were established around the urban citadels of wealth and society, reflecting the elitist origins of the game in the United States.

Since the turn of the century, the continued growth of golf has been marked by two decades of explosive development. The first boom occurred during the 1920s—the Golden Age of Sport. Golf caught the imagination of the wealthy, who, electrified by the play of Bobby Jones, embraced the game and financed the construction of over four thousand golf facilities during the decade.[3] Although courses were built across the entire country, development was particularly rapid in the northern Midwest. Golf remained the game of the elite, and they built clubs in their own image. By 1931, nearly 80 percent of all golf facilities were private—open to members only and often very exclusive and expensive.

The second boom in golf course construction occurred during the 1960s. Following World War II, enthusiasm for golf was rekindled by the exploits of Ben Hogan and Sam Snead and by President Dwight D. Eisenhower's love of the game. Then golf was brought into homes across America by expanding television coverage of professional tournaments, highlighting the feats and charisma of Arnold Palmer. Interest in golf burgeoned and, coupled with favorable economic conditions, it resulted in the addition of over forty-five hundred golf facilities to the U.S. inventory.

Underlying and coincidental with this second boom in golf was a revolution of equal importance—the democratization of the game. During the late 1950s and the 1960s, middle-class interest in golf was stimulated by increased affluence and leisure time and by television, which introduced the game to a broader social spectrum. The golf industry responded by constructing thousands of public courses which were open to all for a moderate daily fee. Today, public golf facilities account for over 65 percent of the total inventory, and American golf has become far more egalitarian.

Across the country, however, the public/private mix of golf facilities is very uneven (fig. 8.1). In the North and West, golf facilities are predominantly public. During the '60s and early '70s, course construction there was rapid and coincided with the democratic revolution in golf. The large, increasingly affluent middle-class segment of the population in these regions embraced the game, resulting in a huge buildup of public facilities. On the other hand, in the South, particularly in the Deep South, there is a relative dearth of public facilities. To the extent that they exist, they tend to be concentrated in resort areas, where they were built to serve primarily tourists rather than local residents. Private club dominance in the South has its roots in racial and social discrimination, but more recently this dominance has been reinforced by the development of real estate courses. These courses have been built as cores of newly constructed residential communities, and they often serve the members of those communities exclusively.

There are now over thirteen thousand golf facilities in the United States, containing over 200,000 golf holes. The national distribution of golf holes roughly mirrors that of the population. The distribution also reveals that golf has strong northern ties despite the fact that it is a warm weather game. The largest concentration of golf holes occurs in

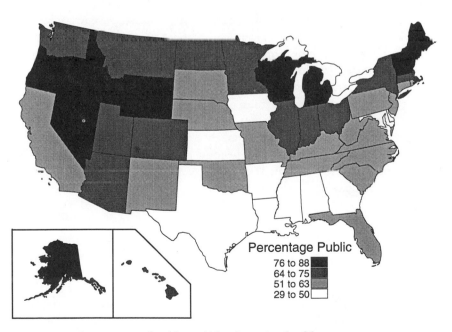

FIG. 8.1. Percentage of public golf facilities in the fifty states, 1989.

the North Central and Northeast regions, which together contain over 50 percent of all courses in the country. Here, golf was established early, and from this early foothold, it has continued to flourish as an important part of the sports fabric of these regions. A second area of high concentration is the South Atlantic region, extending from Virginia to Florida. Although golf has a long tradition here, the principal development has been relatively recent. Increased affluence, mobility, leisure time, and early retirement since the 1950s have fostered a proliferation of courses to serve the growing population of vacationing and retired golfers. Even in the South Atlantic region, then, the northern ties of American golf are evident, for much of the development there has been fueled by tourists and transplants from the North. Throughout the remainder of the country the distribution of golf holes is of a more nodal nature, serving widely scattered concentrations of population. But overall, it can be said that in America where there are people, there is golf.[4]

In the hundred years since the Scottish game crossed the Atlantic, American golf has progressed from a cow pasture in Yonkers to a sport that includes over twenty-four million participants. The theaters of the game today are the country's nearly 13,500 golf facilities, and the centerpieces of these facilities are America's more than 14,500 courses. Course offerings vary greatly among these facilities. Approximately 40 percent of them have only a single nine-hole course, while the remainder offer eighteen or more holes of golf. At the largest facilities, as many as four to seven full eighteen-hole courses may be found. American golf facilities, however, are composed of more than courses. The landscapes of these facilities commonly contain an array of other elements. Some of these elements have been built to serve the direct needs of the golfers, while others have been created to serve a variety of other functions that through time have become associated with the game in this country. In this sense the theaters of American golf are commonly multidimensional landscape ensembles.

The Courses

Golf courses have become nearly ubiquitous features of the American landscape. They have been built in mountains and on plains, in deserts and in swamps, in forests and on grasslands, in cities and in the countryside. They range from the humble nine-hole course built for a few thousand dollars by local residents who donated their time, money, and equipment to the elaborate and sophisticated layout that was professionally designed and constructed for millions of dollars. Some took shape over decades and are as old as golf in this country; others have not seen their first birthday and were constructed in less than a year. Every one of them is unique.

There are few sports where the character of the site of play is so fundamentally important to the game as it is in golf. In golf, the participant is simultaneously engaged in contests against fellow competitors and against the course itself. The course is thus at once a stage and an adversary. In both regards, the nature of the course plays a critical role, confronting the golfer with diverse and changing situations. Holes vary in length, terrain, and configuration, and each is composed of an individualistic assemblage of those elements that constitute the traditional course. The golfer is faced with a different situation on essentially every shot. In large measure, it is from this diversity that the challenge and enjoyment of the game stem.

Despite this diversity, American courses do bear certain similarities of form and character. In part these similarities are related to the Scottish heritage, but they also arise from the differing sets of environmental and human forces that have influenced golf course development in this country and that have provided American courses with their own identities.

The Scottish Heritage

The theaters of most competitive sports are distinguished by their composition and form, and golf is no exception. Golf courses are usually composed of either nine or eighteen holes. Each hole begins at a tee and ends at a green. On long holes, the tee and green are connected by a fairway that is often bordered by rough. Scattered around the course, but particularly bordering greens, are sand traps. Wherever one goes, the same elements and the same general configurations of elements appear. But, unlike with most competitive sports, this commonality has little to do with regulation.

In the *Rules of Golf,* a lengthy and complex document, it is stated that "the Game of Golf consists in playing a ball from the teeing ground into the hole by a stroke or successive strokes in accordance with the Rules." The "teeing ground" is defined as "a rectangular area two club-lengths in depth, the front and the sides of which are defined by the outside limits of two tee-markers." The "hole" is required to be "4¼ inches in diameter and at least 4 inches deep."[5] The teeing ground and the hole are the only prescribed components of the golf course. There are no regulations regarding the number of holes, their length and configuration, the size and character of the tees and greens, the nature and condition of the playing surfaces, or the type and location of hazards. In view of the absence of specifications, it is remarkable that golf courses have such common identities. That they do is a matter of tradition, with roots extending back to the evolution of the game on the linkslands of Scotland.

Golf is an ancient game, but the exact time and place of origin remain mysterious. The game may have been invented independently in Scotland or elsewhere. Or it may have evolved from any of a number of stick and ball games that were played on the European continent during the Middle Ages. Although some of these ancient games had attributes that were similar to golf, no conclusive evidence exists to establish the connection between them and the latter game.[6] The origin of golf remains a matter of dispute, speculation, and conjecture. It may never be solved, or perhaps the trail will lead to the earliest form of *Homo erectus* who, two million years ago, swung a stick at a stone and was excited by the outcome.

Although the origin of golf remains a mystery, there is general agreement on the "home of golf"—that home is Scotland. Golf has been played there for over five centuries, and it was there that both the golf course and the modern game evolved. No records exist to document the first date of play. But it is clear that the game must have enjoyed widespread popularity during the early fifteenth century, for in 1457, it was banned by the Scottish Parliament of King James II which issued a decree that "Futeball and Golfe be utterly cryit doune and nocht usit" (Wind 1948, 18).

The early sites of play were the links or linkslands; thus, courses that evolved in these settings later became known as golf links.[7] Linksland occurs in scattered locations along the coast of Scotland and consists of a narrow zone of marine sands that the wind has shaped into an undulating surface marked by dunes and depressions. The environment was ideal for the early game. The undulating surface and dunes provided variety and challenge; drainage was good; and the vegetation consisted mainly of grasses. Furthermore, linkslands were often held in public ownership—open to all and used for a variety of purposes, including the grazing of animals which provided the close-cropped grass necessary for golf. Geoffrey Cornish and Ronald Whitten, in *The Golf Course*, provide a detailed description of the earliest form of the golf course:

The earliest Scottish links were designed entirely by nature. A typical links consisted of high, windswept sand dunes and of hollows where grass grew if the soil was reasonably substantial. The grass was predominantly bentgrass with a little fescue interspersed. Its stiff, erect blades, characteristic of turf growing in close proximity to salt water, were sufficient to support the leather-bound, feather-stuffed golf ball.

The terrain of a linksland usually dictated the route a player would follow. Golfers who batted their "featheries" about a links naturally aimed theirs shots for the playable sward. The dunes were to be avoided, for the only vegetation that grew there with any regularity was the dreaded whin, a prickly scrub also known as gorse or furze.

There were no trees or ponds on these ancient links, but there were numerous natural hazards. Certain areas of grass would be grazed bare by livestock. Sheep seeking shelter in hollows or behind hillocks would wear down the turf. The nests and holes of small game would collapse into pits. Wind and water would then erode the topsoil from these areas, revealing the sandy base beneath. Such sandy wastelands, sand and pot bunkers dotted the landscape of a links and menaced many a golf shot.

There were no tees or fairways, as such, nor even putting greens. The putting areas were of the same bristly grass that grew everywhere else. It is speculated that the earliest golfers made rabbit holes their putting cups; and if this is the case, perhaps the putting areas were nibbled a little closer by rabbits. But since it was customary to tee one's ball within a club length of the previous cup, a well-manicured putting surface was not known on an early links.

Man had little to do with maintaining the early courses. Bird droppings and periodic showers from the sea kept the turf healthy. The sandy base beneath the soil provided excellent drainage. Grazing sheep and wild game kept the grass clipped, and if it became too lush, the golfer simply abstained from playing. The sandy wastelands and bunkers went unraked, except when smoothed by random gusts of strong wind.[8]

It was in this linksland setting that both the game and the golf course evolved coincidentally over a period of centuries. And the character of that environment left an indelible imprint upon both. The

FIG. 8.2. Golf in a linksland setting.

strategies, equipment, and rules of this cross-country game all developed in response to the situations and problems posed by the linkslands. And from the natural features of the linksland arose the basic elements of the golf course. The "playable swards" became "fairways." Bordering areas of high grass, heather, or gorse became known as "rough." Holes were located in relatively level areas with good grass covers that were to evolve into "greens." And scars that exposed the underlying sand were later to be termed "sand traps or bunkers." The golf course thus evolved as an adaptation to the linksland environment (fig. 8.2). During the first three centuries of play, they were solely the creations of nature, but beginning in the mid-eighteenth century, improvements upon the offerings of nature began. Despite centuries of human modification, however, the modern golf course still reflects the imprint of its linksland origin.

On the early links, there was no standard number of holes. At first, target holes were located in impromptu fashion so that the number varied from place to place and, probably, from day to day at a single place. Later, as the links became more established, the number of holes at each site became set. But that number varied greatly—for example, five on the early links at Leith to twenty-five at Montrose. The eighteen-hole standard did not evolve until the latter part of the eighteenth century, by which time the Old Course at St. Andrews had achieved a preeminent position among the early courses in Scotland. In 1764, the course at St. Andrews was consolidated so that a round consisted of playing eighteen holes (Cornish and Whitten 1981, 16–22). That this was later to become the worldwide standard is further evidence of the importance of the Scottish heritage. And to accommodate this standard, golf courses have subsequently been built in multiples of nine holes, with a standard round at a nine-hole facility being achieved by playing the course twice.

That golf in Scotland was played for centuries prior to the establishment of the eighteen-hole standard also had an important impact upon the game itself. As the number of holes varied from course to course, the total number of strokes taken in a round had little meaning and such scores were therefore not recorded. Rather, a competition was scored based upon the number of holes won or lost—a format that would later become known as "match play" (Cousins 1975, 5–6). Despite the establishment of the standard eighteen-hole round during the latter half of the eighteenth century, the tradition of match play continued. Today it is a common format of amateur play at local clubs throughout the world.

Golf thus developed as a cross-country game with strong environmental ties. Both the game and the course evolved over centuries on the linksland of Scotland, and the character of those linkslands became integrally entwined with each. When golf diffused from these hearths, the linksland heritage was part of the baggage. The baggage was not mandated; it was carried out of tradition, and it became the foundation of golf course architecture worldwide. In varying degrees, the composition of every golf course in America reflects this heritage. The fundamental elements of these courses—the eighteen-hole standard, the tees, fairways, greens, sand bunkers, mounds, and rough—all evolved on the linkslands of Scotland. And from the configurations of these elements on the Scottish links came the principles and subtleties of course design that have guided golf course construction in the United States and throughout the world.

American Identities

While all American courses reflect their Scottish heritage, they also have identities of their own. In part these identities have arisen from environmental constraints, but they are also related to differing sets of human forces that, through time, have influenced course construction in this country. In varying degrees, all American golf courses are human constructs. They are features of the cultural landscape, and, as such, they reflect the attitudes, capabilities, and goals of their creators.

ENVIRONMENTAL CONSTRAINTS

Golf came to America in mature form—a game to be played on courses that had been defined by the linksland tradition. But in America there are few linksland environments, and, as the demand for golf spread rapidly across the country, courses were built in all manner of natural settings—with the obvious result that very few courses replicate the overall appearance of the Scottish links. The impact of the environment, however, goes deeper than this.

Nearly all of the courses in this country have been built in environments that were not only dissimilar to linkslands but were also highly unsuitable for golf in their unaltered natural states. In order to accommodate the game and the golf course, the settings had to be modified. Initially, the most advantageous sites were selected—those with favorable terrain and vegetation that could easily be modified by hand- and horsepower, and where the climate and the natural fertility of the soil could be relied upon to support the course. As the demand for golf spread and as the availability of land in populated areas shrank, golf courses were forced into progressively more marginal situations requiring extensive alteration of the terrain, climate, vegetation, and soils. Over the last thirty years, the situation has become extreme, with many instances of golf courses being relegated to virtual wastelands.

From the time the game landed on American shores, golf course construction has been supported by a growing body of architectural expertise. Prior to the turn of the century, Scottish and English golf professionals were being enticed to this country to advise on the design and construction of courses. Leading the way was Willie Dunn, who was hired to design Shinnecock Hills in 1891. Following Dunn were a host of Old World professionals who brought with them the fundamentals of course design. These early emigrants, including Donald Ross, Tom Bendelow, H. S. Holt, and Alister Mackenzie, guided course construction in the United States through the 1930s.

But America was not solely dependent upon imported expertise. In 1895, Charles Blaire Macdonald, a Canadian by birth who grew up in Chicago, designed this country's first eighteen-hole course—the Chicago Golf Club. Later, in 1909, he created one of America's landmark courses—the National Golf Links on Long Island, New York. Following Macdonald was a cadre of American designers, including A. W. Tillinghast, William S. Flynn, and Hugh Wilson, among many others. Through these men, American design achieved a maturity and status in its own right, as evidenced by the publication in 1927 of George C. Thomas's *Golf Architecture in America*. By World War II, the foundations of golf course design and construction in the United States were well established. Since then, they have been advanced and refined by hundreds of architects who in thousands of instances have faced the challenge of molding the varied, and often highly incompatible, American environments so as to accommodate the golf course as defined by the linksland tradition.

Through time, the designers of American courses have been supported by a wealth of research and innovation in allied fields that has made the creation of courses in the diverse environments of this country possible. Early Scottish and English professionals brought with them the fruits of research by British seed companies on superior grasses, as well as a developing body of knowledge regarding the construction and maintenance of courses in non-linksland settings—knowledge gained largely from the construction of inland courses in England. But golf soon became the recipient of and the catalyst for scientific and technological advances in this country. American turf research began shortly after the turn of the century, leading to the publication of C. V. Piper and R. A. Oakley's *Turf for Golf Courses* in 1917. The 1920s and 1930s witnessed expanded research at a number of universities on turf grasses and turf management, the creation of a "green section" by the United States Golf Association to advise clubs on turf problems and course construction, the founding of the National Greenkeepers Association, and the inception of schools for greenkeepers.[9]

The most dramatic advances, however, followed World War II, particularly during the 1950s and 1960s. A wealth of research by industry and universities generated a huge array of technological advances, among which were new strains of grass attuned to a wide variety of climatic conditions and capable of withstanding heavy traffic; improved fertilizers and a vast array of chemicals to enhance turf growth; modern techniques of turf management supported by sophisticated innovations in maintenance equipment; new techniques in the construction of greens; automatic irrigation systems capable of watering the entire course; and the development of heavy equipment for use in course construction. These innovations have made it possible to build golf courses in every type of American environment except those with temperatures too low to support turf (these temperatures occur only at high elevations or in portions of Alaska).

In recent years, some of the construction feats have been truly remarkable as golf courses have been fabricated out of spent gravel pits, abandoned strip mine sites, closed landfills, Florida swamps, and the rugged granite mountains of Maine. In terms of scope and rapidity of accomplishment, the Stadium Course at PGA West is an outstanding example. Two million cubic yards of earth were moved in order to transform a piece of California desert into a golf course with an undulating terrain reminiscent of the Scottish links (Hoffman 1987, 104). It is a totally human construct—with fabricated terrain, vegetation, and climate. It was opened for play in 1986, only twelve months after work began.

The golf course evolved as an adjustment to a particular physical environment, but in America, the environments had to be adjusted to accommodate the course. Thus arise the contrasts. The Scottish links were, and remain, relatively natural entities—often referred to as God's creations. American courses, on the other hand, are largely artifacts—fabricated from disparate and often unsuitable environments that have had to be molded to accommodate the Scottish game. That over fourteen thousand courses have been built and that the best give the appearance of having been created by nature are due to architectural genius, innovation in allied fields, and American affluence.

No discussion of environmental impacts upon American courses would be complete without mention of surface water bodies. Although on Scottish links water is usually either absent or occurs only occasionally in the form of rivulets, it is a nearly ubiquitous feature of American courses. It exists in the form of streams, rivers, ponds, lakes, and embayments of the ocean. It borders fairways, crosses fairways, fronts and even surrounds greens. It commonly must be played over and around, and on many holes, it delimits and dictates the path of play.

The abundance of water on American courses is related, in part, to the facts that many courses were built on sites that were replete with natural surface water, that other sites were plagued by drainage problems which were solved by the construction of ditches and ponds, and that extensive irrigation systems in the United States often require impoundments for water supply. But more importantly, American golfers and those that design courses for them are captivated by water. Where naturally occurring surface water exists, great care is taken to incorporate it into course design; in its absence, great expense is incurred to provide it—even in the arid Southwest, courses commonly abound in water despite its critical shortage and high cost. In all instances water is not an incidental part of the course; rather, it is a strategic part of the design, carefully incorporated to challenge the

FIG. 8.3. Seventeenth green at the Tournament Players Club at Sawgrass, Ponte Vedra, Florida.

golfer. Many of the most famous holes in American golf involve flirtations with water: among them are the thirteenth at Augusta National (Augusta, Georgia), the sixteenth of Cypress Point (Pebble Beach, California), and the eighteenth at Pebble Beach (Pebble Beach, California). The seventeenth at the Tournament Players Club at Sawgrass (Ponte Vedre Beach, Florida) perhaps epitomizes the American golfer's love affair with water (fig. 8.3). It is one of the most famous, or infamous, par threes in golf, involving a shot of 132 yards over water to an island green. There is no margin for error—the ball finds either the island or a watery grave. The outcome has a resounding finality—either elation or despair. Throughout the United States, water hazards have become critical, almost required, elements of course design—features employed to define the strategies of play, to entice the golfer to gamble, and to heighten the element of risk.

GOLF AS A SCIENCE

It is often said that golf on the links of Scotland is an art, but that in America it has become a science. The playing surfaces in Scotland are usually much harder than those in America, requiring the golfer to bounce and roll the ball to planned destinations. The nature of the terrain and the condition of the playing surface must be considered in

FIG. 8.4. Muirfield Village Golf Club, Dublin, Ohio.

executing a shot. In Scotland, the former is usually moderately to severely undulating and the latter is often irregular and varies greatly on daily and seasonal bases in association with changing weather. The golfer is thus constantly faced with varied and challenging situations, requiring imaginative and artful execution. But even the most artful shot can be spoiled by bad luck resulting from irregularities in the nature and condition of the playing surface.

By contrast, Americans tend to view golf as a science. They are obsessed with the mechanics of the swing and with the belief that the outcome of a shot should be purely a function of technique. Ideally chance should play no role, particularly if it involves bad luck. As settings for this science, the courses have become laboratory-like so that proper execution will yield repeatable and predictable results. American courses, particularly those considered to be the best, tend to have fabricated and highly manicured playing surfaces that provide ideal conditions for the execution of shots and that shots will respond to in a controlled manner (fig. 8.4). The greens and fairways are exactingly designed and constructed and then seeded with special strains of grass. The turf is nurtured with huge applications of fertilizers, herbicides, fungicides, and pesticides and by the construction of elaborate irrigation systems. The grass is mowed with sophisticated machinery so that the height will conform to prescribed standards. The results are soft playing surfaces covered with lush, uniform carpets of grass. Shots can be played to and across these surfaces with little risk that they will be spoiled by bad luck in the form of wild bounces or errant rolls.

Golf in these settings is akin to a cross-country dart game—it is known as "target golf," where well-executed shots can be stuck into soft, receptive greens and target areas on fairways with relative certainty as to the outcomes. It is an aerial game, played over rather than across the surface. The varied, irregular, and changeable playing conditions so characteristic of the Scottish links have been smoothed. In the pursuit of fairness, they have been replaced with artificial, homogenized surfaces that bear closer resemblance to turf farms than they do to the settings in which the game evolved. This is not to say that these courses lack rigor or fail to challenge the golfer. Indeed, they are extremely demanding tests of power and skill. They merely differ from the Scottish links because they have been fabricated to accommodate a different game—target golf (Adams 1987, 29–35).

Since the 1950s, the highly manicured conditions associated with target golf have provided the standard by which American golfers judge courses. Due to the very high costs of construction and maintenance, many courses—particularly the more humble, local public facilities—have not been able to meet these standards. These divergences, however, are a matter of insufficient money rather than ideals. It is safe to say that, given unlimited funds, all American courses would provide the perfectly manicured conditions conducive to the pursuit of golf as a science. To compensate for the lack of such conditions, clubs frequently institute a local rule allowing "preferred lies"—permitting the golfer to move the ball in the fairway so as to achieve a perfect lie (an unthinkable subterfuge to the Scot).

INNOVATIONS IN GOLF EQUIPMENT

Golf equipment has improved for centuries since the game was first played with the "feathery," a leather covered ball stuffed with feathers, and primitive wood clubs. In America, it is the innovations since the 1950s that have had the greatest impact upon the course. Among these innovations have been the use of lightweight steel, graphite, and titanium in club shafts, the development of metal heads for "woods," the perimeter weighting of club heads, the introduction of square grooves on irons, and improvements in both the design and the construction of golf balls. Taken together, these advances have enabled the golfer to hit the ball farther and with greater control.

These changes have influenced the design of new courses and have precipitated the redesign and renovation of many older ones. Courses have been lengthened to conform to modern "power golf"—traditional lengths of fifty-eight hundred to sixty-six hundred yards have been stretched so that many courses now play in excess of seven thousand yards from the back tees. Previous notions regarding the appropriate locations of hazards have been revised in order to preserve the strategic value of these elements. For example, the fairway sand traps on many older courses are now in obsolete locations; they no longer come into play or serve the purpose for which they were designed as the result of the golfer's ability to hit the ball farther. Greens have been enlarged both to accommodate the longer approach shots resulting from course lengthening and also to provide varied and difficult cup positions to test more exactly the shotmaking skills of today's golfers. These changes reflect the continued and coincidental evolution of the game and the course.

The motorized golf cart may not be commonly regarded as a piece of golf equipment, but it is defined as such in the *Rules of Golf*, and millions of American golfers regard it as important to their participation in the game as the golf ball itself. It is also one of the most dramatic and pervasive innovations in golf during this century, having become widely accepted in the United States by the late 1950s. Today it is as much a part of the American landscape of golf as the tees, fairways, and greens. At nearly every course one finds a fleet of carts—some privately owned, some for rent.

The reasons for the popularity of the motorized cart are many. It both caused and benefited from the demise of the caddy. Except in association with professional golf and at a few prestigious clubs, the caddy has virtually disappeared from the American scene. So for those who do not wish to carry their clubs or use a pull cart, the motorized cart provides the only alternative. The cart tends to speed play, thus allowing a course to handle more golfers; therefore, on crowded courses their use is often required. They permit the elderly and physically handicapped to play when otherwise they would be precluded from the game. And over much of the country, but particularly in the South, summer temperatures and humidity are frequently so high as to make play very uncomfortable, or even impossible for some, without use of a cart.

But the most important factors underlying the omnipresence of the golf cart in this country are related to economics and the traits of the American golfer. Revenues from cart rentals are now an important and necessary component of the operating budgets of most clubs, required to offset today's high costs of course construction and maintenance. And these revenues can be huge. For example, the Pinehurst Country Club (Pinehurst, N.C.), with seven courses, maintains a fleet of over five hundred carts. Two golfers renting one of these carts for an eighteen-hole round would pay a fee of $24–$38, depending on their status at the club. Although Pinehurst is an extreme case, it is little wonder that rental carts are available at nearly every course in this country.

In the final analysis, however, the popularity of golf carts is attributable to the fact that American golfers want to use them. Most of the twenty-four million golfers in the United States use electric or gas carts for some or all of their play. Like the majority of middle- and upper-class Americans, golfers are typically out of shape, in a hurry, accustomed to creature comforts, and affluent—traits for which the golf cart is tailor-made.

In replacing walking as a means of getting around the course, the motorized cart has had a significant impact upon the game. To the detriment of most of its users, it has greatly reduced the physical exercise to be gained from the experience. It has also weakened the bonds between the course and the game. In walking, a course gradually unfolds before the golfer in a continuous fashion, allowing one to savor the pleasant surroundings and to appreciate the subtleties and challenges of the course design. Walking reinforces the environmental contexts of the game. Golfing with a cart is a more detached experience. Emphasis is placed upon hurrying from one shot to the next, often on paved and peripheral paths. The environment, rather than providing an integral context for the game, becomes something to be traveled through as quickly as possible. Appreciation for the environmental context of the game is thus diminished in favor of expediency and comfort.

The cart is also reflected in the design and appearance of the modern course. In their designs, architects must insure that carts have access to the entire course, while at the same time insuring that cart traffic does not interfere with play—constraints that can be important determinants of the layout of the course. Further, heavy cart traffic has a detrimental impact upon turf. Thus, carts are often routed away from playing surfaces, but routed concentration of traffic soon results in severe degradation of the paths. To solve this latter problem, cart paths are typically paved. These asphalt ribbons are now common features on courses throughout the country—ugly but necessary consequences of the cart. The motorized cart has, however, provided at least one benefit to course designers; it has released them from the constraint of having to minimize the distance between a green and the succeeding tee. On courses where the use of carts is mandatory, that distance is of little significance, thus allowing architects to disperse holes and often utilize more advantageous terrain.

THE TOUR

In America, the history of professional tournament golf is nearly as long as that of the game (Barkow 1989). During the first two decades of this century, it was poorly organized with only a handful of professionals competing. In the 1920s, professional golf gained greatly in stature as the likes of Walter Hagen, Gene Sarazen, and Bobby Jones ushered in the age of modern tournament golf. But the most dramatic expansion followed World War II, highlighted during the 1940s and 1950s by the feats of Ben Hogan and Sam Snead and later by those of Arnold Palmer and Jack Nicklaus. Today the main professional tournament circuit in the United States is called the Tour. More specifically, it is composed of three tours: the Professional Golfers' Association (PGA) Tour for men, the Senior PGA Tour for men over age fifty, and the LPGA Tour for women. Presently there are over 120 annual events on these tours, with total prize money exceeding 100 million dollars.

The venues for professional golf tournaments are known as "championship courses." There is no strict definition of such courses, and there are no rigid specifications for their design. They do, however, have some generally common identities. They were designed to rigorously test the skills of the world's best golfers. They are long and difficult courses that place a premium on both distance and accuracy. The elements and the configurations of elements do not differ greatly from those on other courses, with the exception of the greens. These tend to be huge, often with multiple tiers and severely undulating surfaces. The size and contours of these greens, in conjunction with an abundance of proximate hazards, offer multiple pin placements that vary greatly in difficulty. The location of the cups can therefore be changed daily throughout a tournament, generally becoming more demanding as the tournament progresses.

Perhaps the most important requirement of championship courses played on the Tour is that they be "fair"—in part due to the format of play and the money at stake. On the American Tour, the almost exclusive format has long been "stroke or medal play," where scoring is based upon the total number of strokes taken in a tournament. It is preferred over "match play" because it is regarded as being a truer and more rigorous test of skill. It also allows more golfers to play in a tournament, and it is better suited to television coverage.[10] In stroke play, the golfer is not involved in a head-to-head match against a fellow competitor; rather, the objective is to beat the field by shooting the lowest score over the total number of holes played. In the quest to shoot the lowest score in medal play, the golfer is in direct competition against the course. The course, therefore, becomes the immediate opponent and, as such, is required to be fair in terms of both design and condition. Poorly executed shots may be penalized, but good shots should be rewarded in a consistent and predictable manner—not spoiled by chance eventualities resulting from irregular or poorly conditioned playing surfaces. On a fair course, the role of chance is minimized, and this has come to be regarded as an essential aspect of the courses played on the Tour. The fate of huge purses should not be determined by luck. Championship courses are thus prime examples of the highly manicured, laboratory-like arenas demanded for the pursuit of golf as a science.

In the proliferation of championship courses, the Tour has had an impact far beyond itself. Over the years, millions of American golfers have played at Tour sites and millions more have been spectators at professional tournaments or have watched on television. They have become very familiar with and intrigued by the championship course, with the result that it has become the model for the construction and renovation of thousands of private and public courses across the country. Most have never achieved true championship caliber due to site deficiencies and lack of financing; nevertheless, they bear at least some of the traits of their prototypes.

Throngs of spectators have attended professional tournaments since the 1920s, but an explosion of spectator interest, which was associated with the booming popularity of golf and expanded television coverage of tournaments, began in the '60s. But increased spectator interest brought with it a new set of problems. Viewing a golf tournament poses difficulties because the action occurs over such a large area. The strategies are to either follow the play around the course or to station oneself at a point of heightened interest and watch as the play proceeds through one's location. The traditional golf course, however, was not designed to handle upwards of 100,000 spectators roaming the course or concentrated around tees and greens. With rising spectator interest in the game, it became obvious that tournament sites would have to be designed to accommodate the spectator, as well as to challenge the golfer. Spectator concerns were incorporated into the designs of some early courses, such as at Augusta National (1932), where some of the greens were located to take advantage of the spectator capacity of

neighboring hillsides and where several mounds were created to enhance the views at critical locations. But courses designed with the
spectator in mind have been predominantly phenomena of the 1960s
and later.

The trend toward spectator facilities is epitomized by the Tournament Players Clubs built by the PGA. The first was constructed at
Sawgrass in Florida in 1980; ten more have since been built at other
locations, and several others have been targeted for future construction.
They are being built specifically to host professional tournaments and
to provide for all the needs that such events generate, including parking
lots, restrooms, concession stands, areas for corporate tents, and provisions for televising the events. The centerpieces of these clubs, however, are their "stadium courses," which are designed with nearly equal
consideration given to the player and the spectator. Massive amounts of
earth are moved to create tiered grass amphitheaters partially surrounding many tees and greens and to build huge spectator mounds at other
strategic locations. The results are part golf course, part theater—offspring of the Tour and a dramatic reflection of its impact upon the
American course.

Since the 1950s, television coverage of professional tournaments
has introduced the game and the beauty of the course to millions of
Americans and has been a major stimulus to the rapid growth of golf
and to the success of the Tour. In addition, through the showcase of
television, many of these tournaments have become classic events of
sport—the U.S. Open, the PGA Championship, the Memorial Tournament, the Crosby Pro-Am (now jarringly renamed the AT&T Pebble
Beach National Pro-Am), and the Heritage Classic, among others. And
the courses on which these tournaments are, or have been, played have
become landmarks of the game, including such names as Pebble Beach,
Harbour Town, Muirfield Village, Butler National, Oakmont, Merion,
Winged Foot, and Shinnecock Hills. One tournament, however, stands
alone—the Masters. It is a true phenomenon of sport, with worldwide
recognition. Among golfers, this event and the Augusta National Golf
Club, where it is played, have taken on legendary, almost mystical,
proportions. For American devotees of the game, watching the Masters,
in person or on television, is regarded as a rite of spring.

AESTHETIC CONCERNS

One characteristic of American golf courses is common to those
the world over—their beauty. The magnificence of many is attributable,
in part, to the outstanding natural beauty of the areas in which they are

located. Cypress Point is surrounded by the spectacular scenery of the Monterey Peninsula; its fifteenth, sixteenth, and seventeenth holes, bordered by the pounding Pacific, are some of the most photographed in golf. The Upper Cascades Course at the Homestead in Virginia is enveloped by the scenic Allegheny Mountains. The lush greenery of La Quinta in California is strikingly backdropped by the contrasting stark beauty of rugged desert mountains. At Mauna Kea in Hawaii, the course stands out like a green jewel set in a black lava field, adorned by breathtaking views of the Pacific. The list could go on and on.

But the attractiveness of golf courses is not dependent upon that of the areas in which they are located. They have their own innate beauty. The fairways appear as verdant ribbons, dotted with glistening sand traps. Each is punctuated by a putting surface of velvety grass, geometrically patterned by mowers. All is clothed in brilliant hues of green. And complementing the beauty of the playing surfaces are the settings in which they are laid out. Some courses are surrounded by essentially unaltered natural environments, providing scenes of strikingly beautiful contrasts. At Desert Highlands, the lush tees, fairways, and greens appear as verdant islands in the brown, sparsely vegetated Arizona desert. Another superb example is Pine Valley, a world-famous course laid out in the Pine Barrens of New Jersey. Here the immaculately manicured playing surfaces stand in stark contrast to the surrounding wilderness of sand, brush, and pine forest. The unaltered natural surroundings enhance the aesthetic appeal of the course by adding a wild beauty of their own and by providing contrasts for the smooth, lush, fabricated playing surfaces. Although the elements differ, the scene is not unlike that of the Scottish links where the beauty of the course is enhanced by the natural and contrasting beauty of the surrounding linksland.

But Americans have a proclivity for taming, ordering, and adorning the settings of their courses—a desire to improve upon nature. At the Medinah Country Club, near Chicago, the manicured grounds, ponds, and stately trees provide an exquisite parkland setting for its three courses, surrounding them with a genteel natural beauty. Sentry World in Wisconsin is nearly equal parts flower garden and golf course—eighty thousand flowers are planted around the sixteenth green alone. And the landscaped beauty of Augusta National is world renowned. On every hole there are plantings of ornamental shrubs and trees which lend their names to each of the eighteen holes. When the dogwood, peach, cherry, magnolia, azalea, and other ornamentals are in bloom, Augusta is a blaze of colors in a sea of green.

American golf courses have been built in all manner of settings, ranging from highly natural to manicured and adorned. In most cases, the combination of the course and its setting results in a landscape of extraordinary beauty—where the colors, hues, and textures change with every weather condition and with each passing hour. One of the abiding precepts of golf course architecture is to design courses within the contexts of their surroundings so that the outcomes will be aesthetically pleasing. Given the diversity of the American environment, this precept has provided one of the major challenges facing the profession. The success of these designers is measured by the beauty of their creations. The beauty is evident to everyone, but for the golfer, it is an integral part of the sport—an important factor leading to participation in the game and providing a constant source of gratification. To counter Mark Twain's declaration that golf is "a good walk spoiled" (quoted in Brussell 1970, 235), there is not a golfer, past or present, who has not endured those all-too-frequent days when the beauty of the course was the only redeeming feature of an otherwise futile and frustrating experience.

ECONOMIC CONSTRAINTS

Over the past three decades, the costs of creating and maintaining golf courses in the United States have escalated dramatically and have placed increasing constraints upon their development. Golf courses require large sites, generally a minimum of 100–120 acres for an eighteen-hole regulation course. But in metropolitan and amenity areas, where the demand has been the greatest, land costs have risen so rapidly that it has been difficult for golf to compete with more lucrative types of land use. Added to the purchase price of land are the costs of construction and maintenance, which today can be huge. Building a first-rate, championship course now commonly costs $4 to $5 million and, if it is open year-round, the annual maintenance costs can range from $450,000 to $550,000 (McElyea and Krekorian 1988, 14). These spiraling costs have severely constrained new course construction since the late 1970s. During the 1960s, approximately four hundred new golf facilities were opened per year; from 1978 to 1989, that average dropped to sixty-three.

Economic constraints have generated new strategies to make golf course construction more economically feasible. One is a retreat from the long championship course designed by high-priced architects to challenge the best golfers. Currently there is a trend toward building courses for average golfers—people who value a well-maintained facility but who often do not have the skills or awareness to appreciate the more sophisticated subtleties of course design. These new courses are designed to minimize the costs of construction and maintenance and are more modest in every respect compared with their championship counterparts. Generally, they are shorter, have smaller greens, and have fewer and less elaborately constructed hazards. Given a suitable site, they can be constructed for approximately one-quarter the cost of a championship course and are proving to be popular alternatives to the latter (National Golf Foundation 1989, 22).

Par-3 and executive courses are known as "short courses," being shorter and more compact versions of the regulation course. Regulation courses exceed fifty-two hundred yards in length, with an eighteen-hole par of 66 or more. An executive course ranges in length from four thousand to fifty-two hundred yards, with an eighteen-hole par of 58–66; a par-3 course has a total length of under four thousand yards, with an eighteen-hole par of 54 (National Golf Foundation 1993, 48). The cost of creating and maintaining these courses is obviously far less than for regulation courses, but they also offer other advantages. They are less strenuous to play and thus are popular with many of the elderly. They require less time to play and thus are often frequented by those with time constraints; and being shorter and less rigorous than the regulation course, they are better sites upon which beginners can learn the game. At present, there are over 700 par-3 courses and over 800 executive courses in the United States, and they provide economical alternatives to the regulation course.

The golf industry in America is facing a difficult challenge. The demand for golf has outstripped the supply of courses, in particular of moderately priced, public golf facilities in metropolitan areas (Adams 1986). At the same time, escalating costs of land and construction in metropolitan areas have greatly reduced the rate of course development. Many of the metropolitan courses that have come into existence since the late '70s require huge budgets to offset the high costs of construction and maintenance. These new courses, therefore, have been built predominantly at private clubs with wealthy memberships or at public golf facilities that can charge very high green fees (usually in resort areas that cater to the more affluent vacationing public). If the rising demand for affordable golf is to be met, it will require a restructuring of the approaches and attitudes that have guided course construction since the early 1960s.

The decades ahead will probably witness substantial change in the American course: more conservative designs of regulation courses and greater reliance upon "short courses" in areas plagued by the shortage and high cost of both land and water for irrigation. The increasing deficit of courses may also promote acceptance of innovations in the game itself, such as "short-ball golf"—an experimental form of the game, played with a ball that travels a much shorter distance than the regulation ball. Short-ball courses can be built on one-quarter to one-third of the land required for a regulation course. At present it is not a well-accepted form of the game, but with technological improvement, it may become so in locations with severe land constraints.

SUMMARY

The golf courses of the United States are hybrids—the offspring of both American and Scottish parentage. They have exploded upon the landscape as human constructs—having been built in a wide range of environments, mostly unsuitable for golf in their natural states, which American affluence and technology could mold to accommodate the game. But the molds were also shaped by a variety of other cultural forces that have left their imprints upon the arenas of the game in this country. Despite a century of evolution, however, American golf courses still bear inherent similarities to their Scottish antecedents. Differences exist, but they are more in the form of refinements than re-definitions. The environmental contexts of the game have been largely preserved. Golf remains a cross-country game to be played on courses defined by the linksland tradition, and the fundamental elements and form of every American course reflect that tradition.

In Search of Perfection

The perfect facility may exist for some sports, but golf is not one of them. First, golf courses are built in disparate environments. Indeed, every site is unique, and the course must be built to accommodate its peculiar advantages and constraints. Each course is inseparable from its singular environmental setting; therefore, the concept of generic perfection is particularly alien to golf courses. Second, golfers differ greatly in their abilities and attitudes toward the course and the game. Evaluation of courses is thus highly subjective. What might provide an exciting challenge to a highly skilled player could be a laborious, frustrating experience for the high handicapper. Third, designing golf courses is very much an art, constrained by few regulations. As in the fine arts, there are certain techniques and principles, but how the architect applies these is quite individualistic, resulting in unique compositions but often recognizable architectural styles. Aficionados of the arts have their favorite compositions and artists; golfers have their favorite courses and architects. But the perfect opera has never been written, and the perfect picture will never be painted, and so, the perfect golf course has never been, and never will be, created.

Excellence, however, does exist, and as in the fine arts, golf has its masterpieces. In American golf, these are perhaps best identified by *Golf Digest*, which publishes a biennial ranking of the top one hundred courses in the United States. It is a very comprehensive evaluation, based upon established criteria. The 1991/1992 ranking represented the work of a national panel of 420 golf course evaluators who rated courses based upon the following criteria:

1. Shot Values: How well do the collection of holes present various risks and rewards? How well does the course test accuracy, length and finesse without overemphasizing any one skill above the other two?
2. Resistance to Scoring: How difficult, while still being fair, is the golf course for the scratch player from the back tees?
3. Design Balance: How varied is the golf course in terms of differing lengths, configurations (including straight holes, doglegs right and left, uphill and downhill shots), hazard placements and green shapes and contours?
4. Memorability: How well do the design features (including tees, greens, fairways, hazards, terrain and vegetation) provide both individuality to each hole and a collective continuity from first tee to last green?
5. Esthetics: How well do the scenic values of the course (including those of its surroundings and backdrops) add to the pleasure of a round?
6. Conditioning: How would you rate the playable areas (tees, fairways and greens) on the date you last played the course? (Whitten 1991, 88)

Any course included on the list of *Golf's Digest's* "America's 100 Greatest Golf Courses" must be truly outstanding, but the very best of the latest ranking are:

1. Pine Valley Golf Course, Pine Valley, New Jersey
2. Augusta National Golf Course, Augusta, Georgia
3. Cypress Point Club, Pebble Beach, California
4. Shinnecock Hills Golf Course, Southampton, New York
5. Pebble Beach Golf Links, Pebble Beach, California
6. Winged Foot Golf Course (West), Mamaroneck, New York

7. Oakmont Country Club, Oakmont, Pennsylvania
8. Merion Golf Course (East), Ardmore, Pennsylvania
9. Muirfield Village Golf Course, Dublin, Ohio
10. Olympic Club (Lake), San Francisco, California. (Ibid., 82)

Every one of these courses is a gem, acclaimed throughout the world of golf. And they have stood the test of time, for all but Muirfield Village were built prior to 1934. In search of the perfect course, one might do well to start with this list, and with considerable justification, might select Pine Valley. It has received the highest score on every ranking since they were initiated by *Golf Digest* in 1966.

For the expert golfer in search of a very demanding test of skill, Pine Valley may indeed approach perfection. It has been described as stern, intimidating, penal, unforgiving, and the world's toughest course. It is a truly magnificent course, but the perfectly manicured playing surfaces stand like islands in the wilderness, surrounded or bordered by sandy wastes, scrub, and forest. Balls missing the targeted playing surfaces are often difficult or impossible to extricate, if indeed they are ever found. It is not a course that is equally playable by all levels of golfers (a criterion that is not used by *Golf Digest*). For golfers at the lower end of the skill scale, Pine Valley could be a nightmare, as it would be difficult for them merely to keep the ball in play.

Pine Valley is a masterpiece, but it is not perfect and neither is any other course in the top 100. The perfect course does not exist, and it never will. And that is as it should be. Every course among "America's 100 Greatest Golf Courses" is a jewel, but each is different and in this diversity lies much of the appeal and challenge of the game.

The Ensembles

American golf facilities contain many features in addition to courses. Typically they are ensembles, composed of collections of elements that have been created to serve a variety of functions. In its simplest form the ensemble is composed merely of a course and a small clubhouse that is built to serve the immediate needs of the golfer. But golf facilities also reflect the integration of the sport into broader American lifestyles. In this regard, the ensembles are often multidimensional in form—loci of a variety of activities which have become associated with the game in this country but which are ancillary to participation. Perhaps most notable of the types of ensembles that compose the theaters of American golf are the private country club, the local public golf facility, the golf resort, and the real estate golf facility.

The Private Country Club

The private country club is distinguished in a number of ways from its counterpart, the public golf facility. First, by definition, it is exclusive—providing access to members only. During the early decades of this century, these clubs were bastions of racial and social discrimination. Although vestiges of this discrimination still exist in some clubs, exclusivity is now more a function of economics. In general, the cost of joining a private club far exceeds that of golf at a public course—with initiation fees, required bonds, and annual dues ranging from $10,000 to $100,000 at the more expensive clubs. Second, the facilities at private clubs reflect the wealth of their memberships. The courses are commonly better designed, more elaborately constructed, and better maintained. And, in addition to golf, country clubs usually offer a variety of other recreational and social pursuits.

If 1888 marks the inception of golf in the United States, then the country club slightly predated it. The Country Club in Brookline, Massachusetts, founded in 1882, is generally regarded as the first of its genre (Curtiss 1932). But once established, the subsequent evolutions of both were so entwined as to be inseparable. The country club became the bastion of "society," and golf became its heart.

There were a number of impetuses for the country club in nineteenth-century America. The nation was undergoing rapid urbanization, and the quality of life in cities was diminishing as a result of increased crowding, crime, and pollution. In response, the urban upper class embraced a "back to nature" movement. In their return to nature, wealthy city dwellers wanted to be neither farmers nor frontiersmen; rather, they were in search of nature with genteel comforts (Schmitt 1969). One of the manifestations of this movement was the rise of the country club. For their members, these clubs provided a combination of country life and city culture. Here "urbanites found a purified and predictable nature both accessible and exclusive" (12).

At the same time, industrialization was producing an increasingly mobile society bent on the accumulation of material wealth. "Greater mobility fractured larger kinship groups, corroded links between generations, destroyed close identity with a special place, and encouraged impersonal and abstract relationships among people" (Rader 1983, 29–30). To counter the impersonality of an increasingly fragmented society, middle- and upper-class Americans flocked to voluntary associations such as clubs. These associations brought together people with common interests, providing them with a sense of community. Country clubs were the associations of the elite. They fostered interaction among the aristocracy and were a means of preserving and enhancing social status (50–68).

Country clubs offered an array of facilities to accommodate and nurture the social values of their members. Among those usually present were ballrooms and dining rooms for formal dances and dinners, accommodations for overnight lodging or vacation use, rooms set aside for games and reading, and lounges for drink and lively conversation. The social calendars of these early country clubs were filled with fashionable activities befitting the elite status of the American gentry (Kobbé 1901, 253–66).

The role of sport in the early country clubs varied. Some clubs were sport-centered, founded to promote participation in one or a number of sports. In others, sport was ancillary to the social function. But in all cases it was present and usually centered around the horse. Many early clubs were founded as destinations for rides or drives from the city. Most included other pursuits for the horseman, including polo, riding to the hounds, the steeplechase, and racing.[11] The dominance of the horse in the country club sports scene, however, was short-lived. Very quickly clubs expanded their offerings to include a wide variety of sports, including tennis, lawn games, baseball, trapshooting, and skating. But of all sports, golf was to have the most profound impact. "While golf did not furnish the initial impetus for the formation of the first country clubs, it was the most potent of all sports in encouraging the spread of clubs throughout the country" (Rader 1983, 66).

Golf was a natural for the country club scene. It was a fashionable game that was being embraced by the wealthy elite. It was an outdoor sport played in orderly natural settings and thus was an ideal outlet for urbanites in search of refreshing contact with civilized nature. Wealthy members provided capital for course construction. And finally, existing clubs often owned enough land to develop a course. In the decades surrounding the turn of the century, golf flourished in country club settings. Existing clubs added golf to their sports menus and golf courses became the foci of newly founded clubs. The following article by Gustav Kobbé appeared in the June 1, 1901, issue of *The Outlook*:

> A magazine article on country clubs written only seven years ago barely mentioned golf, and, if I remember it correctly, does not refer to a single golf club. It is devoted to a few hunt and polo clubs. . . . "The cornerstone of the country club is the Horse," says the writer of the article in question. Were he

writing now he would say that not only the corner-stone, but the cellar, the ground floor, the bel-étage, the attic, the roof, and the chimney-pots of the country club was golf. (266)

By 1920, golf had become the centerpiece of country clubs across the nation. But the real boom was yet to come. The twenties were the heyday of the American country club. As the automobile opened up the countryside, thousands of clubs were built, and many were of truly Gatsbian proportions. But perhaps the grandest of all was Olympia Fields, completed in 1925 near Chicago. For its members it offered not only seventy-two holes of golf but also a clubhouse "with a dining room seating eight hundred, a cafe seating six hundred, only one outdoor dancing pavilion but five hundred feet of veranda. The club operated its own ice-making plant and its own hospital. One hundred families owned cottages in the dell's of the club's 692 acres. Through some oversight Olympia Fields never made provision for its own college and a major league baseball team, but it was possible to live out your life there if your wants were not exotic" (Wind 1948, 236).

Despite having all of the trappings of a country club, Olympia Fields billed itself not as such, but rather as "the world's largest private golf club." During the first three decades of this century, golf became so popular and so dominated the country club scene that the title of private golf club often supplanted that of country club. To this day, however, both terms are used interchangeably, connoting a club open to members only, where the emphasis is upon golf but where other recreational and social facilities are usually available.

With the boom of the country club (private golf club) during the 1920s, golf became more than a sport in America. By this time there were over five thousand golf facilities in the United States, approximately 80 percent of which were private. Golf was still the game of the established social elite, but added to their ranks was a rapidly expanding business and professional class with newfound wealth. For the latter, membership in an exclusive country club was a status-enhancing badge of distinction. At the country club one made the right contacts and socialized with the right people. As Herbert Wind wrote, "at the clubhouse you lived with the people you wanted to associate with, played your bridge, drank your gin-and-tonic, ate your guinea hen, danced your foxtrot, traded your tips on stocks and gave your daughter away in marriage. Home was where you brought your dirty laundry" (234).

Today, golf has shed much of its elitist image and has become far more egalitarian. But the country club and the private golf club are still important components of the American golf fabric. As of 1993, there were approximately forty-five hundred private golf facilities in the United States, constituting a third of the total. Some are as old as golf in this country; others have yet to see their first birthday. Some are grand in scale; others contain only nine holes and a small clubhouse. Some remain highly exclusive and cost tens of thousands of dollars to join; others can be joined by anyone willing to pay a few hundred dollars in annual dues. But regardless of their stature, they embody a common trait—in varying degrees, they serve as the focal point for the leisure and social lives of their members. And the landscapes of these clubs reflect this multipurpose function. In addition to one or more golf courses, one commonly finds other types of recreational facilities, from swimming pools and tennis courts to stables, beach clubs, and skeet ranges at the more expansive clubs. The clubhouse may contain any or all of the following: accommodations for lodging, facilities for serving food and drink (ranging from casual lounges to formal dining rooms), function rooms to serve a full social calendar, handball and squash courts, card rooms, indoor swimming pools, exercise rooms, saunas, and locker rooms. These clubs, whether they are located in a wealthy metropolitan area and have most of the above extra-golf amenities or are situated in a small Great Plains farm community and have but a few, are multidimensional ensembles around which the social and leisure activities of their members revolve.[12] But the heart of the country club remains golf.

The Local Public Golf Facility

These facilities primarily serve local residents and are open to anyone willing to pay a moderate daily fee. Built by private interests or municipalities, most have come into existence since 1950, in association with the second boom in American golf and the attendant democratization of the game. Today they are nearly ubiquitous features of the American golf landscape, but are particularly prevalent in the North and West (see fig. 8.1). They are the alternative to the expensive private club and are the bastions of middle-class golf. Compared with their private club counterparts, they are frequented by golfers who tend to be younger, to have lower incomes, and not to have graduated from college (table 8.1).

Although there are many exceptions, local public courses tend to be more humble than those found at private clubs. Lacking hefty membership fees, they are often designed so as to minimize the costs

TABLE 8.1. Selected Demographic Characteristics of Public vs. Private
Golfers

	Public Golfers	Private Golfers
Average age	37	42
% 50 years & older	22	34
% with household income < $40,000	51	40
% with household income $75,000 & >	9	17
% college graduates	38	50

Data from National Golf Foundation, *Golf Participation in the United States—1989*.
Public (private) golfers play the majority of their golf at public (private) facilities.

of construction and maintenance. Both the courses and the settings, therefore, tend to be more spartan than those found at private clubs. And, as they are frequently the sites of very heavy play, they are commonly constructed to speed the pace of play—being more open, with fewer hazards and obstacles. The combination of heavy play and lack of funds also means that public courses are often less well maintained. Interestingly, the resulting imperfect and irregular nature of the playing surfaces is more akin to the links of Scotland than are the highly manicured surfaces for target golf, which dominate the private club scene.

The landscape ensemble of the majority of these facilities is the simplest of all. In addition to the course, the only other element in the ensemble may be a modest clubhouse, built to serve the immediate needs of the golfer or to house golf-related functions. These facilities are merely arenas for participation in the game—they provide "no frills" golf at a moderate price.

The relatively simple, humble nature of the local public golf facility, however, belies its popularity. It is the most common type of golf facility in America, and for the majority of American golfers, local public courses are the primary sites of play. They are the backbone of American golf, but they are also in critically short supply, particularly in metropolitan areas where private clubs have long waiting lists for membership and are beyond the financial reach of all but the wealthy (Adams and Rooney 1989).

The Golf Resort

In America, resort golf is nearly as old as the game itself. By the turn of the century, golf courses had been added to fashionable resorts from the White Mountains of New Hampshire southward to Florida and westward to California. As written at that time by a chronicler of golf, "No hotel man would think of building a winter or a summer house unless he first considered its location with regard to the golf links, or would think of undertaking a new resort without having links laid out before opening his house" (Kobbé 1901, 264). Although the statement is a bit of an exaggeration, it nevertheless illustrates that golf has long been an established part of the resort scene in this country.

Today golf clubs are part of the travel baggage of a growing segment of the American population. The National Golf Foundation estimates that in 1988 over seven million Americans played golf on trips away from home. During the warm months, traveling golfers frequent resorts across the entire country. During the cool months, the Sunbelt is the destination of hordes of northern golfers seeking to escape winter's blast and retune their dormant games.

Although most American golf facilities have been built to serve local residential populations, there are thousands that are oriented toward vacationing golfers. These resort golf facilities may be connected with a particular resort establishment or they may be public facilities that serve anyone vacationing in a particular resort area. In either case, these facilities are part of the larger landscapes of leisure.

Golf resorts in the United States come in a variety of forms and sizes. At some, golf is the focal attraction. The Lodge at Pebble Beach (California) and the Pinehurst Hotel and Country Club (North Carolina) are such resorts. Both offer first-class lodging and dining facilities, and both are frequented by nongolfers. But in each case the main drawing card is golf, and it permeates the atmosphere. Guests at these resorts have access to a variety of superb courses, but each has a crown jewel—the Pebble Beach Golf Links and Pinehurst Number 2. They are among the finest and most famous courses in existence, drawing golf enthusiasts from around the world. These resorts are truly golf meccas.

More commonly the golf resort is eclectic in form, with golf being but one of many attractions. The Homestead provides a good illustration. It is an old, distinguished resort located in the mountains at Hot Springs, Virginia. It has three golf courses, but golf is by no means the singular attraction. In addition to elegant accommodations and exquisite food, the Homestead offers an array of social and recreational facilities broad enough to cater to the leisure interests of almost anyone. Golf here is part of a multidimensional leisure ensemble that serves a vacationing public with diverse interests. In amenity areas throughout the country, golf is found in similar resort contexts, although few are as elegant and expansive as the Homestead.

In many locations, the concentration of courses oriented toward the vacationing golfer has become so great that the golf resort has become a phenomenon of regional proportions—the golf resort area. Vacationing golfers commonly refer to their destinations as Phoenix, Arizona, or Myrtle Beach, South Carolina, rather than a specific resort. In these golf resort areas, the course offerings abound. They come in the form of general public courses, resort-owned courses, and private facilities that can be played with luck and the proper introduction. The range of choice is huge and varied in terms of both price and character. In many instances, a vacationing golfer could, if he or she desired, play a different course every day for weeks. And the extra-golf amenities are equally numerous—with accommodations, restaurants, shops, and leisure facilities to suit every pocketbook and taste. In a sense, the golf resort area is akin to a Homestead expanded to regional proportions. The scale of the ensemble is merely much larger, and it is composed of a greater number and variety of elements.

Although golf resort areas are found throughout the country, they are most concentrated in the Sunbelt, where golf is a year-round proposition. Here they attract millions of northern golfers, particularly during the cool months. Perhaps the epitome of a golf resort area is Pinehurst, North Carolina. Originating in 1895 as a health spa and winter resort, Pinehurst gained its first golf course in 1898. Today the small village is a golf mecca. The central attractions are the seven eighteen-hole courses of the Pinehurst Country Club, including the world-famous Pinehurst Number 2. But these are only the beginning, for there are now over thirty eighteen-hole courses surrounding Pinehurst—on a nice spring day, these would be played by over five thousand golfers. To complement golf, Pinehurst offers a variety of accommodations and restaurants, highlighted by the elegant, 310-room Pinehurst Hotel, and a full selection of other activities, including tennis, lawn games, horseback riding, swimming, and fishing. But golf is the feature attraction, and Pinehurst is truly a golfer's paradise.

While Pinehurst may epitomize golf resort areas, it does not stand alone. There are many others from which the vacationing golfer can choose. For example, at Hilton Head, a forty-two-square-mile residential/resort complex in South Carolina, the golfer is presented with an array of twenty-two courses, sixteen of them public. The Grand Strand, a sixty-mile stretch of Carolina coast focused upon Myrtle Beach, exemplifies the coincidental development of golf and tourism in this country (Janiskee 1989). Since the mid-1960s, it has grown to become one of the nation's leading resort areas, in 1994 offering over thirty-five thousand rental units and over seven thousand campsites to visiting tourists. Golf has played an instrumental role in this development. In 1964, there were only seven golf courses in the region; thirty years later, there were over eighty, with others in various stages of completion. In 1988, two and a quarter million rounds of golf were played on these courses, 77 percent of them by tourists (Cronin 1990, 12). The emphasis upon golf in the Grand Strand has earned it the reputation, among some, as "the Seaside Golf Capital of the World." But the list of golf resort areas is not confined to rural oases of high golf course concentration: many metropolitan areas in the Sunbelt have become the foci of vacation golf. For instance, the metropolitan areas of Phoenix, Arizona, and West Palm Beach, Florida, with over twenty-two hundred and twenty-five hundred golf holes, respectively, while serving many other functions, are prime golf resort areas in their own right.

Golf is an important aspect of the travel plans of millions of Americans—a fact that has not gone unnoticed by the resort industry. The travel literature is replete with references to the availability of golf.[13] In some resort areas, it is the prime attraction; in others, it is one component in a multileisure resort ensemble. But everywhere in America, the theaters of the game are important elements of resort landscapes.

The Real Estate Golf Facility

Golf courses are beautiful places and, as such, have long been held in high esteem as residential locations. By the turn of the century, cottages for weekend or vacation use began to appear on the grounds of country clubs. Later, with the rise of the automobile, permanent residences became common elements of the suburban golf club scene. Today there are thousands of examples where the attractiveness of golf courses has promoted sequent residential development on their borders.

In the above instances, it was the golf course that provided the impetus for the construction of vacation or permanent residences. They were added to landscapes that were previously developed for the purpose of golf. Recent decades have witnessed the proliferation of a reverse phenomenon—the real estate course, where real estate development has provided the impetus for golf course construction. Developers have capitalized upon the facts that golf courses provide attractive living environments and that, since the early 1960s, there has been an explosion in the popularity of golf in this country. The offspring has been the real estate golf facility, where house lots are developed around and focused upon newly constructed courses. Although these courses provide golfing opportunities, they are primarily created to enhance the attractiveness, value, and salability of the real estate that surrounds them. In this regard, they have been very successful. For an investment of 3 to 5 million dollars, a first-rate golf course can be built that may escalate the value of the remaining real estate tenfold or more. For example, when the Stadium Course at PGA West in La Quinta, California, was built in 1986, the per acre cost of house lots jumped from $15,000 to $140,000 (Stevenson 1989, 37). And since these projects can contain hundreds of building lots, it is little wonder that golf courses have become popular tools of the developer.

The real estate golf facility also offers many attractions to the potential homebuyer. The course provides doorway access to golf, but it is also a manicured park that becomes part of nearly everyone's yard. In the clubhouse, there are restaurants, lounges, and function rooms for social activities. And, on the grounds of the development, one typically finds provisions for a variety of other sports. In addition, the potential buyer is reasonably assured of being surrounded by people with similar tastes and interests by virtue of the facts that they were attracted to the same setting and were able to afford it. And finally, as access to these communities is often controlled, their members are provided a measure of privacy and security.

The popularity of the real estate golf facility is evidenced by the fact that there are over fourteen hundred of them in the United States today. They occur in every state, with the exception of Alaska. The heaviest concentrations are found in the Sunbelt, where Florida leads all states. In the last three decades, most of the Sunbelt has experienced rapid population growth, accompanied by an expanding resort sector. These factors, coupled with the booming popularity of golf, fueled the demand for golf-related housing in the form of both permanent residences and second homes—making the region a natural for the real estate golf facility.

The golf courses of these facilities reflect their intended function. Traditionally golf courses have been laid out in a rather compact fashion such as at the South Course of the Firestone Country Club, in Ohio (fig. 8.5). These compact designs minimize acreage requirements and thus reduce development costs. Real estate courses, on the other hand, tend to be sprawling affairs—laid out so as to maximize the number of building lots bordering tees, fairways, and greens. A good example is the Tournament Players Course at The Woodlands, in Texas (fig. 8.6). The dispersed layout provides for an abundance of house sites around and in the interior of the course. The Woodlands is a planned, fully inte-

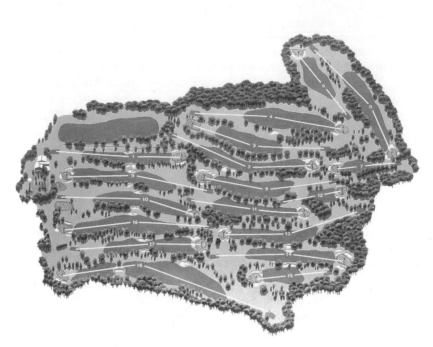

FIG. 8.5. Firestone Country Club (South Course), Akron, Ohio.

FIG. 8.6. The Woodlands, near Houston, Texas.

grated community being developed on twenty-five thousand acres near Houston and is now home to over thirty-six thousand people. It currently contains four real estate courses. Ultimately, as many as five to seven courses are planned, all of which will be the foci of residential development.

While the real estate course may be a boon for the developer, it can have certain detractions for the golfer. The sprawling layouts may involve great distances between successive holes so these courses are often unwalkable; carts are then required, which means added expense and little physical exercise. In some instances, visiting golfers are even provided with a map of the housing development and course so they will not become lost. In addition, for those accustomed to playing golf in more or less natural surroundings, the real estate course can be a jarring experience. It could be termed "back-yard golf," for the game is figuratively, and sometimes literally, played in the backyards of the housing units that line the fairways. In the extreme, when fairway housing is dense and includes high-rises, it can give the golfer the impression of playing through "condo canyon" (Adams and Rooney 1984, 65–75).

There is great variety in these residential golf communities. The size of the development can range from a few hundred acres with one course to thousands of acres with multiple courses. The golf facilities may be public or private. If the development is a retirement community or a residential suburb in a metropolitan area, the dwelling units may be predominantly, or exclusively, permanent residences. In a resort area, such as Hilton Head, the real estate golf facility is usually composed of a mix of permanent residences, second homes, and time-share units (all of which may be periodically rented to visiting tourists). Residences can take the form of single-family homes, villas, townhouses, or apartments. Residential ownership ranges from outright ownership to condominium arrangements and time-share plans. And the price tags are equally varied, ranging from less than $100,000 for apartment condos to millions for the most elegant private homes.

The real estate golf facility is a residential community with a golf heart. Golf permeates the daily lives of its members. It is golf and the golf course that attract residents to the community, and it is the golf that defines the circle of friends with whom members live, play the game, and socialize. In purchasing a home in one of these communities, the buyer also purchases a lifestyle—a lifestyle that revolves around golf.

Conclusion

Golf is an ancient game that has been played in Scotland for over five centuries. It was on the linkslands there that both the modern game and golf course evolved, and the character of those linkslands left an indelible imprint upon both. A little over a century ago, golf spread to America, where it was first embraced by the wealthy elite and later by a broad economic and social spectrum of the population. Today it is a sport of major proportions in the United States, boasting over twenty-four million enthusiasts.

The theaters of the game in America are the over thirteen thousand golf facilities, and they, like all features of the cultural landscape, reflect the desires and attitudes of their creators. The courses have been molded to accommodate the Scottish heritage, as well as various American environmental and cultural constraints. But American golf facilities are commonly more than just arenas for the game. They are often multidimensional landscape ensembles that reflect the fact that, for millions of Americans, golf has become more than a sport—it has become an integral part of their larger social, leisure, and residential lifestyles.

The theaters of the game in the United States have evolved over a century in response to a variety of changing cultural forces. Early development of golf was associated with the private country club—refuge of the rich who were trying to escape the ills of city life, who desired a purifying contact with nature, and who were in search of social ties in an increasingly apersonal urban world. The 1920s witnessed a boom in the popularity of both golf and the country club. The ranks of the established rich were joined by an expanding population with new-found wealth. For these people, membership in an exclusive country club became a badge of distinction. And as the loci of their leisure and social lives, the clubs, while focused upon golf, became multidimensional ensembles.

Increasing use of the automobile moved golf into the suburbs and freed resort golf from the bonds of the railroad. The rise of professional tournament golf cultivated further interest in the game; when coupled with television coverage in the 1950s, it became a major catalyst in the second boom in American golf during the '60s and early '70s. Thousands of courses were built across the country, fueled by American affluence and increased leisure time and assisted by advances in allied fields which essentially freed golf course construction from environmental constraints. Television also awakened broad interest amongst the middle and upper-middle classes. American golf became more egal-itarian, resulting in the proliferation of public courses. Course design began to change in response to the championship courses played on the Tour, innovations in golf equipment, and rising spectator interest in the game. And, since the 1950s, inexpensive air travel and the propensity toward early retirement—coupled with increased affluence and leisure time—have promoted the rapid expansion of resort golf and the residential golf community.

The American theaters of golf reflect the varied cultural forces that have shaped them, but the changes that these forces have wrought have more to do with the ancillary surroundings of the game than with the game itself. Despite a century of evolution, the modern game and the American courses upon which it is played bear remarkable similarities to their Scottish antecedents. Differences exist, but they are more in the form of nuances compared with the evolutionary changes in the arenas of most other competitive sports. Football, baseball, tennis, and track, for instance, have moved from the field to the stadium to artificial surfaces and domed facilities. To the considerable extent that this has occurred, the theaters of these sports have been removed from their original environmental contexts and homogenized, and these changes have altered the nature of the sports themselves—for both participant and spectator. Golf, however, remains a cross-country game with strong and fundamental environmental ties. The environmental contexts and linksland tradition of the sport have largely been preserved—and this is critical to both the game and the courses upon which it is played.

CHAPTER NINE

STOCK CAR RACING

Richard Pillsbury

Richard Petty said good-bye to his fans after a 35-year racing career Sunday. He wasn't victorious in his final race, but there was no doubt he left Atlanta Motor Speedway a winner.
    —*Atlanta Journal/Atlanta Constitution*, November 16, 1992

"Whoever heard of a good ol' boy named Kulwicki?" They will remember him here as the chap who won his points championship (to the 1992 Winston Cup for NASCAR Grand National Racing), then slapped his car into reverse and ran a . . . backwards . . . lap of celebration . . . he calls his Polish victory lap.
    —*Atlanta Journal/Atlanta Constitution*, November 16, 1993

White Lightning, Rednecks, and Blue Ribbon

The Hooters 500 in Atlanta that fall day in 1992 was a pure NASCAR extravaganza. There was hoopla aplenty as 115,000 cheering fans came together to help celebrate Richard Petty, America's most famous southern stock car driver, as he hung up his steering wheel after 1,185 professional races. The race that day, the finale of the Grand National Winston Cup season, came to a classic well-managed NASCAR conclusion. The race itself was just as successful, fulfilling as it did all of its promoter's expectations. Bill Elliott won the race by a mere 7.7 seconds (a matter of feet when traveling almost 200 miles per hour). Alan Kulwicki, a college-educated Yankee from Greenfield, Wisconsin, who further defied current conventional wisdom by building and driving his own automobiles, won the national championship in a massive media blitz. Only 191 points separated the winner (4,078 points) and the sixth-ranking contender for a white-knuckle end to the race for the year's national crown. The crowd left worn out from their endeavors believing that they had attended one of the most important events of their lives. More importantly, they took with them enough material to make lunchroom debates lively for the upcoming winter off-season as they discussed the merits of this upstart Yankee driver, still independent enough to build his own cars; the impact of Ernie Irvin's spinning car on Davey Allison's chances of winning; what it all meant that the King was gone (and why he should have quit years ago); the presence of the third generation of Pettys among the top five finishers in the national crown competition; and how more southerners take their automobile racing seriously than residents of any other region of the United States.[1] Yes, those Yankees up in the Midwest are rabid about their midgets and Indy cars. Yes, stock car races take place in every corner of America. Certainly, other types of cars are also raced in this region. But, only in the South has stock car racing taken on cult proportions to the point that the largest circulation daily newspaper in the region felt it appropriate to expropriate the paper's front page to signal the end of a race car driver's career. Or are these images too a part of NASCAR's masterful creation of a racing empire of mythic importance?

This question is not so naive, nor as simple to answer, as it might first seem. American stock car racing is at once the most highly attended and least watched professional sport in the nation. For example, the Talladega 500 is annually the largest event in Alabama history. Not the largest stock car race, not the largest sporting event, but the largest spectator event of any kind in the history of that state. Yet, even a casual perusal of the grandstands, the infield, or even the parking lots demonstrates that many in this 100,000-plus mass of humanity at any given moment are doing everything but continuously watching the race.

This blatant spectator ambivalence immediately raises questions, especially when it is recognized that the Alabama International Motor

FIG. 9.1. Midget auto racers now include several southern stops in their annual migration from the winter Florida season to the traditional midwestern summer season.

Speedway is far from the nearest population center. Located forty miles out of Birmingham off Interstate 20, the track may be close to an expressway and even has a small general aviation airfield on the track grounds, but it is convenient for almost no one. The track is more than a two-hours' drive from Atlanta, most of an hour from Birmingham, and more than two hours from Montgomery. When this lengthy drive is coupled with the hour or longer wait to get into the facility parking lots for those who arrive less than three hours before the event, one must wonder why so many have traveled so far to watch so little of what they have come to see.

Simultaneously, one finds a very successful small town drag strip almost within earshot of the super speedway. If Alabamians are rabid stock car people, what are they doing with a drag strip for almost every sanctioned stock car track? If southerners are so rabid about stock cars, why does the Nashville Network run live sprint car competition on Sundays? Why does underpowered WTLK-TV of Rome, Georgia, located in the heart of American fox hunting, high school football, and dirt track stock car racing, broadcast both sprint and midget racing (fig. 9.1)? If stock car racing is "the" southern form of motor racing, how did it happen that major midget, sprint, drag, and motor cross drivers call this place their home? The answer to this question is neither self-evident nor easy.

A Short History of Motor Racing

America's first motorcar race took place in the fall of 1893 in Chicago. The *Chicago Times Herald*, under the management of sportsman Charles Bennett, sponsored what has become one of the great, but little known, races in history. Emulating the Paris-to-Bordeaux race, which took place in the summer of that year, the event was scheduled for November 2. Unfortunately, only the American-built Duryea vehicle and the German-built Mueller-Benz of Oscar Mueller were ready. A test event was created for that day between these two automobile builders, with Mueller's car taking the day. The event was rescheduled for three weeks later on Thanksgiving Day. Eleven entrants and six cars actually started the race, but a howling blizzard made the roads virtually impassable. Duryea collapsed from exposure almost within sight of the finish line, and the race judge, who had been riding in the passenger seat, piloted his winning car across the finish line. The first track race was held the following year at the Rhode Island State Fair. More than fifty thousand attended a series of sprint heats held over a four-day period.

Racing in the early days was primarily oriented toward the image of man and machine against the elements. The focus was on endurance runs, such as the famous 1908 "Around the World" race; hill climbs culminating in the famous Pike's Peak run; and speed tests against the clock, first at a convenient site near the car builder, later on hard-packed sand beaches such as Daytona Beach, and finally on the great salt lakes of the Far West. Builders set out to prove their vehicles strong, fast, and reliable.

All races during this period were "stock car" events, at least in a sense. Builders such as Duryea, Winton, and Ford drove their own vehicles as advertising for their fledgling businesses. Formal tracks soon appeared for head-to-head competition, however, and professional drivers quickly took over piloting the period's lumbering behemoths. Tracks began appearing throughout the nation. The most famous, the Indianapolis Motor Speedway, was built in 1908 and paved with 3.2 million bricks in 1909. Racing began immediately, through the track did not gain wide attention until the nation's first 500-mile race was run there, 200 times around the oval track, in 1911. The race was an instant success. A purse of $35,000 attracted a racing field of forty-four cars, and more than seventy-five thousand spectators paid to watch the event.

It soon became clear at Indianapolis, however, that traditional production cars had little place on a high-speed paved oval. "Stock" cars were banned in 1919, and a new breed of racing cars began to evolve. Indy-style racing became popular in the Midwest as the sponsoring American Automobile Association used racing of all kinds as a vehicle to gain national recognition for itself. Smaller versions of the big Indy cars soon appeared, aptly named midgets, and the AAA expanded into a full range of sanctioned racing, primarily concentrated in its home region.

Stock car racing did not die with its ban from Indianapolis, either in the Midwest or elsewhere. Dirt, paved, and high-banked wooden tracks designed for stock car racing soon appeared throughout the nation to host these increasingly popular events. Chicago, New York, Los Angeles, and numerous other large cities became stock car racing centers. Short dirt tracks appeared throughout the smaller communities with the northeastern seaboard, the Corn Belt, the Central Valley of California, and the southern Piedmont from Virginia to Atlanta all hosting important racing activities.

Competitive drag racing began appearing in the 1930s in southern California, though the first dedicated drag strip was not built until 1948 near Santa Barbara. Anything but an instant success, this new form of the sport provided a more pure environment for a classic man-and-machine contest, rather than the jostling stock car events. Long perceived as primarily a California pastime, it probably never was exclusively found there. Organized drag racing quickly spread throughout the nation, especially into the automotive industrial Midwest. Professional and hobby engine builders and sportsmen could concentrate on a single element of the contest with a minimum of extraneous issues to cloud the question of speed and expertise.

European sports cars began appearing in the 1950s around the Northeast, the early bastion of imported cars. European-style road racing soon followed, with the Sports Car Club of America (SCCA) taking on the duties of sponsoring and sanctioning racing events. Not surprisingly, the famous early road racing tracks mirrored the distribution of the activity—Watkins Glen (New York), Lime Rock (Connecticut), Sebring (Florida), and Riverside (California) evoke memories of these open cars and their jaunty drivers. The virtual demise of the traditional sports car in the 1980s brought an end to much of this racing at the professional level. Ultimately, the baby boomers' coming of age marked the rise of "vintage" racing of the earlier cars in their original venues. This is one of the fastest hobby racing growth areas today. The SCCA now sanctions a variety of racing forms, both amateur and professional, but the glory days of the open production sports cars are over, except as nostalgic vintage events.

All of these racing forms were and are found in the American South. Road tracks are found in Atlanta, Savannah, Daytona, and elsewhere, while winter midget racing flourishes in Florida and is making inroads in Alabama. The South hosts its own drag racing association, the International Hot Rod Association, while three of the more well-known National Hot Rod Association events are found in the region. More important are the dozens of drag strips scattered across the region's mountains and plains. These places are not venues for the traveling professional NHRA Winston Cup tour; rather, they are built and maintained to support weekly events, local drivers, and local spectators out to see how their boys are doing. The South is anything but a closed environment for auto racing, and real southerners do eat up other forms of motor racing from motor-cross to vintage Austin Healeys roaring across the rolling Piedmont

The Southern Stock Car Phenomenon

Clearly, stock car racing has never been a regional activity. Active regional circuits have operated throughout the nation in the past and continue to do so today. What distinguishes stock car racing in the South, however, is a competition that verges upon a cult activity. Like basketball in Indiana, tennis in the suburbs, and football in the Pennsylvania coal camps of yore, stock car racing is the ultimate spectator sport for the blue-collar small-town resident in its southern domain. Discussion of races and drivers is a major theme of conversation wherever southern men gather to talk. Bumper stickers, baseball caps, shirts, and other clothing extolling leading drivers are de rigueur among the affected. Racing is as integral to the rhythm of the region's small-town life as Wednesday evening prayer meeting and homecoming on the grounds in the fall.

But if stock car racing is a national sport, why did it become such an

integral part of this region's self-image and mythology? The explanation is as much a reflection of the history of NASCAR racing as it is of
the region's way of life.

Historical Development of the NASCAR Circuit

On February 21, 1948, the National Association for Stock Car Auto
Racing (NASCAR) was incorporated. The new racing association was
intended to be a national organization created "to unite all stock
car racing under one set of rules; to set up a benevolent fund and a
national point standings system whereby only one stock car driver will
be crowned national champion." The association initially created a
three-division system of "strictly stocks," modified stocks, and roadsters. The premier division of "strictly stocks," however, did not hold its
first season of racing until 1949, out of concern for public reaction to
racing (and wrecking) brand-new showroom automobiles during this
period of automobile shortages after World War II.

The optimistically named Charlotte Speedway, a scraggly three-
quarter-mile slightly banked dirt track, was the site of the new association's first race for the "strictly stock" class on June 19, 1949. It was a
success by almost any standard. More than thirteen thousand paying
patrons jammed the wooden grandstand to watch thirty-three stock
cars roar around the track.

Some of the most famous drivers of the day competed, including
Jim Roper, who had read about the event in the "Smilin' Jack" comic
strip while living in Great Bend, Kansas; Sara Christian, the leading
woman stock car driver in the country; and the gaily tattooed Jim
Paschal. Even victory lane helped build the needed mythology of the
new association as Glenn Dunnaway took the checkered flag in his
1947 Ford, only to be disqualified when it was found that he was driving
a "bootlegger" car with illegally modified rear springs that allowed him
to take the turns faster than his fellow competitors. Instead, the prize
went to Roper. The first major NASCAR race thus ended with more
than enough of the stuff from which mythologies are created, including
a lawsuit from the disqualified winner, the beginnings of the boot-
legger-racer myth, a winsome winner, a variety of colorful competitors,
a spectacular wreck (Lee Petty tumbling end over end in the third turn
in his brand-new Buick), and $5,000 in prize money. The stage was set
for the development of big things for the new Association.

The 1950 season was critical in the evolution of the scrappy new
racing association. While great in its own mind, competition was fierce

between NASCAR, the American Automobile Association (the dominant race sanctioning body for almost fifty years), and a variety of
smaller organizations, including the NSCRA (National Stock Car Racing Association), USCRA (United States Car Racing Association), and
ASCRA (American Stock Car Racing Association. NASCAR needed
some spectacular help if it was going to live up to its own press releases.

Help came from a surprising quarter. Harold Brasington, a Darlington, South Carolina, peanut farmer, was so taken with the spectacle of
an Indianapolis 500 race he had attended earlier that year that he
wanted to see a similar race between stock cars in his home region. In
spite of a general lack of enthusiasm from NASCAR, Brasington built a
one-and-one-quarter-mile paved banked track on his Darlington farm
as a venue for his proposed race. It was to be the fastest, longest, and
only paved stock car track on the NASCAR circuit in 1950. He probably
would never have been able to convince the NASCAR officials to
sanction such a race if fate had not intervened in the form of a planned
CSRA 500-mile stock car race scheduled for Atlanta's Lakewood Fairgrounds. Bill France, the moving force behind NASCAR, realized that a
500-mile race was going to take place whether the cars were ready or
not. He quickly changed his position and organized a joint NASCAR/
CSRA-sponsored 500-mile race at the new Darlington track.

All of Bill France's fears about the inability of the cars to race
that distance were realized on that Labor Day Monday in 1950. Only
twenty-eight of the original seventy-five cars were still running when
the checkered flag fell. Bill Mantz won the race, primarily because he
had driven in Indianapolis-type races and knew that traditional tires
would not hold up under racing conditions. He equipped his car with
the same hard compound rubber tires used at Indianapolis to win with a
mere 75.25 miles per hour average speed. His success came at the
misfortune of his competitors, who seemingly spent more time changing tires than racing. The event was a success, however, as more than
twenty-five thousand spectators showed up and the Association received the media attention it sought.

During this early period, NASCAR was as nearly a national association as it would ever become. The shortened 1949 "strictly stock"
season had only eight races: three in North Carolina, two in Pennsylvania, and one each in New York, Virginia, and Florida. The "strictly
stock" class, renamed the Grand National Division in 1950, held
twenty-seven races at thirteen venues. The tracks were widely scattered, with three each in New York and North Carolina, two in Ohio,
and one each in Indiana, Pennsylvania, Virginia, South Carolina, and

Florida. The drivers came from a similarly wide variety of places in 1950. The leading driver was Bill Rexford of Conewango Valley, New York, followed by Fireball Roberts of Daytona Beach and Lee Petty of Level Cross, North Carolina. Four of the top ten drivers in 1950 were from New York, the only state with more than a single top ten driver. The second tier of drivers, however, had strong roots in North Carolina and included Atlanta's three famous Flock brothers.

The changing pattern of NASCAR domination began to become clear by the 1954 season, which featured thirty-seven races at twenty-nine tracks. Three dominant regions of Grand National racing were visible at this time: the southeastern zone concentrating on the Carolinas, the Middle Atlantic zone focusing on New York, New Jersey and Pennsylvania, and the West Coast. While California does not appear significant on the Grand National circuit map, it was critical to NASCAR's larger plans to create a national association. The Association still maintains a strong modified class racing circuit there to this day.

The 1954 season well illustrated the continuing tension between the owners/drivers and the Association, which has hampered NASCAR's push to national dominance from the very beginning. During that year, several of the association's most important drivers either quit racing or joined other associations. These included Tim Flock, who opened a Pure Oil service station after being disqualified from winning the Daytona race; his brother Fonty, who joined SAFE as a driver; Al Keller, who began driving on the IndyCar circuit; and Hershel McGriff, who quit and returned to Oregon. The owners and drivers believed that NASCAR's management was capricious and unfair. The 1954 Grand National spring race at Lakewood was a classic example of their complaints. Thomas, Rathmann, and Baker finished in a virtual dead heat with Thomas taking the checkered flag. As the Rules Committee reviewed the race and listened to protests, they penalized Thomas, Baker, Rathmann, and fifth-place finisher Fonty Flock a lap each for rules infractions. Fourth-place finisher Sosebee was declared the winner. More infractions were brought before the committee, and it was soon discovered that all of the leading drivers had committed major infractions. The claims and counterclaims became so complex and the drivers and owners so angry that the committee ultimately canceled all penalties. Thomas was again declared the winner. In the final analysis, NASCAR's inability to set and maintain a fair set of standards frustrated winners and losers alike. It also furthered the myth.

Two other landmark events of the 1954 season were the running of the first road course race of mixed foreign and domestic sedans, and the first television programs featuring NASCAR racing. The Linden, New Jersey, road race was won by a Jaguar. A Hudson Hornet finished second; an Oldsmobile 88 was third. Television coverage also began with several local television stations developing weekly programs on auto racing, most notably New York City's "Wire Wheels," which featured Daytona Speed Week on its first show.

The familiar pattern of the southern domination of NASCAR stock car racing had begun to emerge by 1959. Forty-four races were run on twenty-four tracks that year. The Carolinas not only dominated the annual schedule but had the best tracks as well. NASCAR continued to sanction modified class races in the Northeast and on the West Coast, but the Grand National series essentially became a southern phenomenon. The '60s and '70s further emphasized these patterns. Grand National races continued to be held in Michigan, the auto manufacturer's backyard; in Pennsylvania, at Pocono; and in Dover, Delaware, to placate the Middle Atlantic hotbed. On the West Coast, they were held at Riverside or Ontario, to help support the strong NASCAR West Coast dirt track program. But somehow, these races always seemed to be less important than their southern counterparts. The South reigned dominant in Grand National racing, and such obscure places as Darlington, Rockingham, Martinsville, Talladega, Concord, and North Wilkesboro became known to all who followed this form of stock car racing.

Grand National drivers also increasingly were drawn from the South. Fourteen of the top twenty drivers were from the Carolinas in the 1964 season, while only two midwesterners and one Californian were found in those exalted ranks. Racing politics, however, may have had as much to do with this shift as regional driving skills. Both NASCAR and the United States Auto Club, the inheritor of the American Automobile Club's activities after they pulled out of major racing promotions because of bad press resulting from too many fatalities, prohibited their drivers from competing in "non-sanctioned" events. Drivers like A. J. Foyt, Dan Guerney, and Cale Yarborough were forced to choose their circuits, rather than openly compete in the biggest race each week as the two largest race sponsoring organizations slugged it out for domination.

Grand National racing as a result became a regional activity while other car types rose to prominence. Glamorous foreign and open wheel racing took over the nation's image of auto racing. Most Americans knew more about the Formula 1 races at Le Mans, Monaco, and the Nürnberg Ring than they did about stock car racing in their own nation. The media simply were not interested in this dirty, ill-organized, middle- and lower-class sport. Dirt track stock car racing did not—and still does not—create the "right" images to gain the attention of the nation's aspiring middle class. Southern racing also had to face the national press's continued anti-Southern bias in the 1960s which hampered NASCAR in gaining positive media attention for its more spectacular Grand National circuit.

Promoters tried everything to gain national attention during this period. NASCAR continued to hold some road track events in the mistaken belief that emulation of sports car racing would bring the coveted national attention that the Association so desired. Mixed "international" events (including a Volkswagen beetle in one race) were occasionally held to demonstrate the abilities and durability of the NASCAR vehicles and their drivers. Race rules are and were constantly modified to make the races more "even." Exciting finishes became standard through careful manipulation of yellow caution flags. Speeds continued to rise, and spectacular "safe" wrecks became common, as safety engineers continued to modify the cars to sustain the most heart-rending crashes while allowing the drivers to walk away.

Today Grand National racing is again at the brink of reaching international attention as a major auto racing series. The 1988 season featured a race in Australia, road races have been revived, a variety of "special" races have been instituted to increase exposure, and seemingly endless exciting finishes and spectacular wrecks have become almost universal. Television coverage on ESPN and the three traditional networks is becoming more common as audience surveys continue to demonstrate an increasingly national following of these events, rather than what the network programmers had long believed was only a regional interest. Today Grand National racing is recognized as a safe weekend television programming investment as the crowd-pleasing crashes continue without the deaths and injuries so common in the '50s and early '60s. Sponsors want action, not blood. Cameras have been mounted in the cars and on drivers' helmets to give the program a sense of immediacy. Endless interviews with drivers and crews, countless camera angles, slow motion sequences, and instant replays have further helped make this essentially dull event appear exciting.

Other kinds of changes are also taking place. The NASCAR racing press is filled with discussions of the changing nature of stock car racing. The traditionalists spend many hours bemoaning the passing of the good old boys and arrival of the businessmen who now dominate the owners' ranks. Drivers don't hang around the bars the night before the race anymore—there's too much money at stake. Indeed, a column in the *Grand National Scene* several years ago predicted that by the turn of the century

the number of tracks would increase from 16 to 32;

the owners would resemble NFL owners—"be real business types";

that television coverage would be prime time;

that the 500-mile race would be replaced by "three-hour" races that fit television schedules;

that European and Japanese manufacturers would be competing;

and that there would be a major "shoot out" between the champions of the two major racing associations at the end of the year—a Super Bowl race of stock car racing.

Stock car racing aficionados are still waiting for these innovations to take place, but it is becoming increasingly clear even to outside observers that this wish list is not quite as bizarre as it seemed when it was published. Essentially the sport is "growing up," in the parlance of the sports promoter. Family racing teams with Bill driving the car on Sundays, brother Ernie acting as engine builder and crew chief, and brother Dan working in the shop and on the crew have all but passed from the scene. More typical today is the Hendrick Motorsports organization, which recently built a fifty-thousand-square foot facility near Charlotte, North Carolina. The Hendrick organization races four or more teams (each with several cars), including three highly competitive Grand National units under different sponsors. The Motorsports operation is just a small part of the Hendricks organization, which includes numerous automobile dealerships and a seemingly endless list of other automobile-related activities. There are not a lot of the traditional southerners left in the new business of stock car racing.

Stock Car Racing and the Southern Ethos

The rise and continuing important role of stock car racing in southern life also has much to do with the region's personality and historic isolation from the mainstream of American cultural life. First, there has been and continues to be a dearth of sports teams based in the South, except for Atlanta. This lack of quality local professional sports entertainment is often solved by local fans following their university football teams. Many southern men do follow their local university basketball and football teams; however, less than 15 percent of NASCAR region southerners have graduated from college and less than 60 percent have graduated from high school. Educational levels in the rural areas, where stock car racing is followed most avidly, are even lower. As a result, it is extremely difficult for fans to get psyched up about the Dawgs or Cocks when they essentially were disenfranchised from this part of regional life at birth.

Car racing, on the other hand, has long been the local spectator sport. Richard Petty, Junior Johnson, and Bill Elliott are local boys with little formal schooling and obvious country origins. They represent the success of the disenfranchised southern man despite the system. These men have it all without a college degree, Ralph Lauren jeans, or Perrier. Fans tell and retell stories of Richard Petty going to a White House dinner in a tow truck. The pressure to get in touch with King Richard has led to the expansion of the Petty racing compound in Level Cross, North Carolina, to house a popular museum and daily tours. Bill El- liott's family team and his use of the popular Ford products made him continually popular, even when his racing fortunes slipped and his family racing team split up to go its respective ways. For example, the Elliotts opened their shops for the first time in 1988, before the breakup of the family team, for a one-day tour. More than ten thousand people found and toured their facilities on that single Sunday afternoon—no mean accomplishment in rural Dawsonville, Georgia.

The typical rural southerner identifies with these drivers. In fact, race fans do not follow the fortunes of Ford or Buick or Chevrolet in these mortal combats; rather, they follow and talk about Elliott and Earnhart and the King (that's Petty, not Presley). The Skoal Bandit, the Coors/Melling team, Kodiak, and many other car and sponsor names may appear on the seemingly endless stream of racing paraphernalia, but it is the driver who is implicitly most important to the fan. Sponsor- ships may come and go, but the drivers are the mythological characters in this fairy tale.

The Theater of Motor Sports

Neither the mythology nor the reality of stock car racing can be totally comprehended outside the actual race setting. While all sports have theatrical aspects, stock car racing gains its primary identity from its stage setting. Tailgate parties and dressing up in the colors of the home team may add to the football fan's enjoyment of the college game—but for many stock car fans these *are* the experience.

In spite of organizational changes, the actual sporting event—the theater of stock car racing—is much the same today as it has always been. Southern stock car racing actually is not a single sport; rather, it is composed of several related events. Each attracts its own unique au- dience with amazingly little crossover. Most fans do not watch "automobile racing" per se; instead, they follow Grand National or some other level of racing. The Grand National circuit may be the beluga caviar of the sport, but caviar is not to everyone's taste. Just as many watch high school football with only a cursory interest in the collegiate or professional game, many race fans avidly follow only short track or even unsanctioned weekly racing with only cursory interest in the Sunday Grand National circuit. Conversely, many of the Grand National circuit fans have neither set foot on a dirt track facility nor would consider attending such lower-class goings on except as a joke or a favor. The result has been the evolution of two almost totally separate racing worlds with great differences in spectator bases and type of spectacles.

Winston Cup Grand National Racing: The Alabama International Speedway

Winston Cup Grand National racing is the epitome of American stock car racing. Many of the races have become household names in the world of sport, even among those who don't follow the sport. Winston Cup racing has largely fallen into two classes: the newer, longer, faster super speedways, such as Atlanta, Talladega, Phoenix, and Daytona, and the shorter, older, slower tracks like Bristol, Martinsville, and Darlington. While each is equal in the race calendar, the larger tracks represent the future and the shorter ones the past. In a sense, the sport is in the same position as was professional football when some teams moved to New York, Chicago, and Philadelphia while others remained in the small mill towns where the NFL originated. The relocated venues became increasingly popular and effective at selling their shows, while the older ones came under criticism because they could not provide the same level of services. Simultaneously, the growing national interest raised questions about franchises being located in those backward, out-of-the-way locations while fans elsewhere in the nation were denied access to live events. The same thing will ultimately happen if Grand National racing is to move into the pantheon of national sporting spectacles. Darlington is historic, interesting, and totally inadequate to meet the needs of a national venue. The future lies in the superspeedways within easy access of the larger cities.

The Alabama International Motor Speedway is the classic super speedway. The track is a 2.66-mile high-speed oval lying almost sunken beneath the red clay of central Alabama. Located a mile south of Interstate 20, the speedway could easily be missed by passing expressway motorists except when a car is hurtling around the track and the sound of that unique exhaust rap of a fully tuned race car rips for miles through the Alabama piney woods.

An impending race becomes evident days before the actual event. Spectators begin arriving on the Thursday before the Sunday race in RV's, pickup campers, and cars to stake out good camping locations for the ensuing weekend. Most early visitors come from out of state, often North or South Carolina, where they regularly arrange their work schedules to take either vacation, sick leave, or extended weekends on these all-important weekends—much like avid deer hunters in Wisconsin and Pennsylvania arranging to become ill on the Friday before opening day.

Most race fans, however, begin the long drive on Sunday morning. Traffic picks up noticeably on the interstates before dawn as fans begin flocking from the farms, small towns, and cities of the region on their way to the track. Heading toward the track, the stream of cars moving east from Birmingham and west from Atlanta soon chokes Interstate 20. Bumper stickers, caps, jackets, and even the cars themselves readily identify the faithful to other members of the faithful. By noon the line of cars waiting to use the Talladega off ramp extends for miles. The avid arrive early and stay late.

The souvenir area, a covey of trailers gathered on a widened pull-off along the approach road, is the first indication that one is nearing the track. About a dozen of these trailers squat in the mud in a spot widened for their use to hawk gladiator trinkets. A large crowd soon forms around the trailers to purchase shirts, jackets, baseball caps, racing newspapers, and every other imaginable item advertising the day's heroes. One trailer is devoted to Elliott; others base their fortunes on several drivers, while others try to cover the field. The breadth of paraphernalia is almost beyond comprehension; the amount of sales amazing.

Once settled in the sea of parked autos and trucks, most spectators do not hurry to their seats. In fact, the parking lot becomes the center of the action for the next several hours. Barbecues are set up next to the tailgate; coolers are opened and the contents consumed. The sweetish smell of marijuana soon hangs heavy over the parking lot as the blue-collar crowd meets old and new friends and the devotees get down to serious beer drinking, eating, and discussion of the ensuing race. Rivalries are dredged up; the technical "equalizer" of the season debated; old stories about previous races discussed.

As race time nears, fans make their way to the stands to drink more beer and ogle the passing "parade" of scantily clad young women roaming back and forth across the front of the stands ostensibly looking for their seats. Crowd response to these young women becomes increasingly pointed as the heat rises and the beer flows. First, wolf calls erupt as the more attractive, less dressed parade down the platform, then rebel yells follow, and finally more explicit comments are shouted out. The drama culminates sometime after the beginning of the race when a young woman accommodates the crowd and parades topless down the front walkway of the stands until the security guards arrive. The ensuing discussion with the security team usually fills the second quarter of the race's tedium.

Oh, yes—the race. At Talladega, the track surface is sunk well below the seat level, and the high speeds attainable on this well-engineered track mean that the race consists of a car whizzing down the front or back straightaway at 220-plus miles per hour past the stands. The cars are identified primarily by the numbers painted on their tops, the only part that one can see from the grandstand. Each auto takes about twelve or thirteen seconds to run the length of the grandstands, and a thirty-car pack makes the trip in about thirty seconds. This goes on, with sufficient yellow caution flags to bunch the pack up when it appears that several cars have too much lead, 188 times or so until the race is over.

This is a facile description of an event, but multiple descriptions are more in order since the Talladega theater has several stages, each with its individual script, actors, and plot lines. The main grandstands have the highest-priced seats and as a result attract the more staid crowd. Sporting a better view of the finish line and a somewhat better view of the entire track because of their height, this stage and its players are more akin to a moderately well-behaved football crowd than the scenes described above. Sideshows are less common, trips to the bathrooms and other facilities are less arduous and interminable, and less abnormal behavior is tolerated by security. The infield stage attracts the most diverse crowd (fig. 9.2). The view from the infield surface is much like watching a road race, restricted to a small section of the track. For those who mount their vehicles and watch from the roofs, however, the infield provides a unique perspective on the entire track. This vantage point also allows watchers to bring vast quantities of whatever they wish in the way of food and beverages, as well as have a big screen TV to watch the race if they desire. This is the perfect place for many of the more technically inclined, excepting the pits, of course. This crowd tends toward the extremes of avid watchers and avid partygoers. The back grandstands, described above, are the least expensive

FIG. 9.2. Talladega International Raceway. Some spectators in Talledaga's giant infield even watch the race from time to time. Note the grandstand in the background.

seats in the entire theater and provide the poorest view. This is the home of the rowdiest fans who come more for the event than the race. Finally, most superspeedways today have the equivalent of box seats with the creation of condominium "sky boxes." This theater is in another world as spectators sit in air-conditioned comfort at the finest vantage point with kitchens, wet bars, comfortable seats, and even beds for the weary. Television coverage, in some tracks feeding directly off the cameras scattered around the track, gives the condominium viewer the total picture in an instant. Most here can not even imagine the event as seen from the back grandstands.

Short Track Racing

The primeval world of stock car racing was the short dirt track, which attracted local amateur and semiprofessional drivers and car builders. In their youth, they were out to make it to the big time; in their later years, they had a good time reliving the past. Short track racing is the purest of all southern racing theaters. Beginning in the 1970s, however, this world began to divide into its own hierarchy.

LANIER RACEWAY—A SHORT PAVED TRACK

Increasing competition and the desire to emulate their more famous Grand National brethren brought a rise in short paved tracks in the South beginning in the 1970s. The idea was that these lower-maintenance, higher-speed venues would provide a more "Grand National" feel to the events and an ability to tap a more affluent spectator pool. They did this, but problems also appeared. The pavement was harder on racing vehicles: tire costs alone inflated drastically. Many underfinanced drivers began drifting away to compete at the remaining dirt tracks in the region. Hobby and older drivers especially were little interested in raising the stakes of competition, especially those who recognized that winning, and thus recouping their costs with the higher purses, was probably out of the question. Too, the skills of driving on dirt did not transfer well onto the pavement. Drivers who were competitive because of their reading of the constantly changing dirt surface lost their edge. The end result was the development of a new racing environment, certainly related to the old one, but one that attracted a somewhat different set of spectators and certainly a different pool of drivers.

Lanier Raceway is not a new track and operated for many years as a typical 3/8-mile dirt track serving a wide variety of people in northeastern Georgia. The expansion of the Atlanta metropolitan area, the growth of nearby Lake Lanier into one of the nation's most intensely utilized freshwater playgrounds, and the development of Road Atlanta across the highway gave the owner an opportunity to attempt to promote this track into one of the region's elite paved short tracks. Once the facility was paved in 1988, it began offering a wider range of racing, including an annual midget race featuring the migrating USAC teams on their way back to the Middle West from the Florida season and a Busch Grand National event.

Paved tracks require larger audiences, and the biggest change was shifting race day from Saturday night to Sunday afternoon. The spectators' demographic profile changed as well. Many of the original spectators seem to have given up this track and probably now watch their racing at Lithonia or Dixie Speedways. Their replacements seem to be more middle class, or at least upper lower class, if one can judge status by their cars, dress, and lifestyle. There is more beer (brought, not bought, as Sunday sales remain illegal), there are more red faces, and more of the behavior common to the super speedways is displayed, although these tracks are too close to home for feminine parades.

The drivers are different as well. The cars have generally been upgraded, although many drivers have raced here in years past. The trailers and stacks of spare tires are more professional, as is the race itself. Most of the serious drivers and fans are still friends, but somehow the mood is more reserved, more middle-class festive.

Speeds are also higher on the paved tracks and accidents more spectacular. One Sunday racing card averaged an accident on every third lap in every race all day long. Even so, the ambulance still was only used once—to hustle a corpulent spectator to the hospital with a severe case of heat stroke—probably brought on by drinking too much beer and eating too much barbecue.

The goal with short paved tracks was to create an atmosphere somewhere between the traditional southerners of the past and the corporate entertainers of the future. Track paving has also raised the stakes, the cars have been improved, the psychological distance between the competitors and the spectators increased, the audience upgraded, and a little more of the traditional South lost. Interestingly, the results of these changes have not been as predictable as they may have seemed initially. Sunday racing was abandoned at Lanier after the first season because response was not as good as anticipated. Indeed, at least one track, the Dixie Speedway in Woodstock, Georgia, installed pavement in the 1980s and subsequently removed it because its spectator pool clearly preferred the dirt environment. Paving of new tracks has virtually come to a halt in the 1990s.

NORTH GEORGIA SPEEDWAY—DIRT TRACK

The bottom rung of stock car racing everywhere, but for many the heart of the sport, is the dirt track (fig. 9.3). These sporting emporiums consist of an embedded, banked dirt track with a wooden, concrete, or steel grandstand along one side. Often the only external sign of these places is the one or two gates along a rural paved road with a simple sign advertising Dixie Speedway or Valley Raceway, and the day and time of racing each week. There seems to be an unspoken assumption that anyone who needs to find one of these establishments already is aware of the essentials of location and season, as both results and racing times are rarely chronicled in the local newspapers. The gulf between these different racing levels is easily seen in the presence of dirt tracks in close proximity to super speedways—interest in small track racing is seemingly unaffected by the larger track's overwhelming presence.

The North Georgia Speedway near nowhere in northwestern Georgia is typical of this lowest rung of dirt tracks. Advertised with a single sign along little-traveled U.S. 441, the facility stands about a half mile down a narrow dirt road in a recently cutover section of rolling land replanted with slash pine. This track is not sanctioned by NASCAR and represents virtually the lowest investment possible. The track surface was scraped out of the red clay with minimal outside and inside (to protect the pits) concrete walls, and a simple concrete stepped grandstand. A chain-link fence mounts the track's outer wall to keep any out-of-control cars on the track and away from spectators. The simple single-color program with a few local advertisements suggests that

FIG. 9.3. The pack coming down the back straightaway at North Georgia Speedway. Dirt track racing always provides intimate and spectacular racing for local fans.

Chattsworth, Dalton, and Cartersville are its service areas, though the license plates and clientele on a typical racing Saturday night suggest that most are not town or city dwellers. Pickup trucks and older American sedans dominate the parking lot, though a few spectators back their pickup campers and RV's up to the fence at the track's corners. The arrival of a Volvo causes a stir. Racing is scheduled every Saturday night; the gates open at 4:30 and racing begins at 7:30. This is the lowest level of racing. The drivers begin arriving soon after the gates open with their pride in tow on dual-wheel trailers.

There are no fulltime professionals among these drivers, although many spend more time preparing their cars than working on their regular jobs. Several classes of cars compete, ranging from essentially street cars with numbers duct-taped on their sides to super modifieds which have no visual relationship with production automobiles.

The track is sprayed with water during the afternoon to keep down the dust. Cars begin warming up to road check their performance and to harden the track surface. The wetting process slickens the track surface to promote long, sliding, high-speed turns, increasing lap speeds. With no mufflers to constrain engine exhaust, the noise is deafening—its not by accident that these tracks are located far from polite society. Racing begins with a minimum of fuss as warm-up laps merge into races. The novice class opens the day's racing. Scant attention is paid to these racers, except by family and friends. Accidents are too frequent to count—the slippery clay track, the mechanically unsound cars (some don't even make it through the warm-up rounds before conking out), and the less experienced drivers all contribute to exciting racing and numerous caution laps. Speeds are low, usually less than eighty miles per hour; the safety equipment is designed for speeds twice that fast.

Dirt track racing is not only the most unsophisticated level of racing, it also attracts a crowd of individuals and families drawn primarily from the lowest, most isolated social and income brackets of the surrounding area. This is largely a family affair, from the drivers, whose wives and girlfriends shout advice from the pits during the race, to the spectators, who bring wife, children, and friends for an evening of entertainment (fig. 9.4).

Most of the audience are regulars who come every week to cheer on their friends and acquaintances. The drivers include old timers who still race for fun; young drivers hoping against hope that they will be noticed by potential sponsors and be able to move up the racing ladder; frustrated men of all ages trying to live out a dream as best they can with their limited resources. The crowd is friendly, the mood a family

FIG. 9.4. The pit/infield at North Georgia Speedway during a race. The typical dirt track pit area is a pretty informal place with lots of free advice.

one, as all are here to have a good time with friends. No one feels the need to put on airs or their Sunday best or act out scenarios. This is the real rural South at its best. The spectators are folks who almost never go to the city, who would feel uncomfortable in shopping malls, who affirm their faith at their fundamentalist church every Sunday morning. They get a bit rowdy on occasion, but these are family events and such goings-on are so rare that they remain topics of conversation for years thereafter.

The short track theater remains amazingly consistent, with change taking place in scale rather than content. Typically the track is lowered three to six feet into the red clay with the excess dirt banked around the sides, especially on the side of the main grandstand. The grandstand is usually concrete with no seats per se. A refreshment stand, track announcers, and officials are located in an office at the top of the stadium which is preferably still at ground level (fig. 9.5). A second grandstand, often wooden, may appear at the opposite side as well. Arrangements are also made for cars to back up to the chain-link fence around the track, outside of the line of sight from the grandstands. Spectators are also, for a somewhat higher fee, allowed to watch the race from the infield, which is typically jammed with cars, mechanics, trailers, and

FIG. 9.5. Lanier Raceway's concrete grandstands and open pit area are of classic design and typical of small tracks throughout the South.

hangers-on of one kind or another. The provender typically is basic barbecue, corn dogs, hot dogs (with or without chili or slaw), boiled and roasted peanuts, soft drinks, and coffee. Alcohol is almost never for sale on the premises, though large quantities are often consumed there. Portable toilets stand at intervals about the track and parking lot.

The modern automobile race is best watched on television from the convenience of one's own living room. Only at the smallest tracks can one see the entire track from the stands, unless one belongs to the handful of spectators who have access to key seats. Most other spectators can see little of the race and may understand even less. Keeping a sense of a major race's ebb and flow from the grandstands is difficult; one must sustain attention through the long periods of tedium to focus on those few interspersed seconds of action. At a recent Daytona 500, for example, nine yellow caution flags controlled the race's outcome. While the yellow flag flies, cars reduce speed and pack behind the lead car. The final two yellows occurred within the last few laps when several lead cars crashed in two spectacular wrecks. Both collisions began when air turbulence reduced car control and one car slid into another, creating a chain reaction of multiple collisions. Exhaust fumes leaking into the driver compartment—stemming from an earlier accident—forced another leader to quit. These events were immediately visible to the television audience through instant replays and multiple camera angles, but largely unknown among those present. Certainly the most sophisticated aficionados could see and interpret these events, but the vast majority could only see the inexplicable aftermath of torn metal and the autos of their favorites being dragged off to the pits.

Why, then, do so many travel so far to see so little? Dale Earnhart and Bill Elliott certainly don't represent the home team. Indeed, many fans are apparently oblivious to the race outcome at all, if the stream of cars out of the parking lots and onto the expressways prior to the end of the race is any indication. Obviously tens of thousands go to the race for reasons other than to see the outcome.

The color, the excitement, the opportunity to mingle with others with similar interests are obvious factors behind most individuals' attendance at professional sporting events generally. For many, it is companionship—an excuse to spend a day with friends or family. Few come by themselves. A break in the normal routine of a humdrum existence is another motivation, though attending a race at Cordele or Asheville verges on being humdrum in its own way. Finally, we must consider the importance of symbolism and identification. Most of the famous Winston Cup drivers appear to be everyday country boys who made good "doing what came naturally." Certainly the dream of driving a machine, much like the one at home in the driveway, flat out against a pack of competitors is a fantasy held by many in the audience.

These races also represent clear linkages with a past rural glory that is quickly fading under the onslaught of city jobs and city living. Southerners are increasingly aware that their way of life is passing. More and more newspaper articles chronicling the past appear each week in the region's newspapers. One must wonder how much of what we see in stock car racing is just a mirror of southern life as a whole.

Winston Cup racing is becoming a national sport, sponsored by national corporations, increasingly driven by drivers named Kulwicki and Unser. Family and individual racing teams are dropping out as the costs of competition skyrocket beyond the resources of all but the very wealthy and well sponsored. Ticket prices of $60 or $80 for the Daytona 500 or Hooters 500 are certainly beyond the reach of many traditional fans. For many, such changes may not be progress.

This is not a conservative plea for the status quo: there is nothing wrong with progress. But for each increment of change, something traditional, something vernacular, is lost. Each year Winston Cup racing is a little less traditional fun and a little more contrived. The competing vehicles are stock in name only. The cars' sheet metal bodies cover specially built tubular steel frames. Mechanics custom-build engines, suspension, handling packages, and steering systems. Only the sheet metal and fiberglass shell retains a resemblance to the car's showroom stock brethren. The sanitizing of the sport "for the good of the breed" brings more sophisticated racing, more money, and more fame, but it also moves the sport from its original—largely rural—regional base into the arena of the new national culture forming in the suburbia of our nation's cities.

How long can traditional, rural southerners support this sport with their presence on Sunday afternoons? How long can the Bill Elliotts and Dale Earnharts maintain their image among the home folks while jetting to races and appearing endlessly in television commercials touting potato chips and laundry soap?

Identification is the basis of support for any sport, and stock car racing is no exception. How does a traditional southern male living in a trailer on a rutted dirt farm road identify with a jet pilot, a television star, and a millionaire?

The mythology that has always bound stock car racing to the rural southerner is clearly in jeopardy, just as the entire southern mythology itself moves toward the brink of absolute change. An extrapolation of current trends in stock car racing clearly brings only one conclusion; the sport's nationalization is eroding its traditional support base. This is not a new phenomenon, and is currently taking place in everything southern from diet to religion. The irony is that the people fostering the changes in racing are themselves affected by how these changes will alter fan allegiance and race attendance. Television sponsorship, for example, is predicated upon large on-site audiences. The televised sport needs spectators to create the crowd atmosphere in which the electronic spectator can vicariously participate—the contemporary sport's equivalent of comedic canned laughter. The sport's increasing televisionication, along with concomitant changes in drivers and management, inevitably increases stress within traditional southern spectators who still haven't adjusted to the other changes taking place around them.

Given these trends, several changes seem inevitable. The traditional races at the more isolated venues—North Wilkesboro, Bristol, and possibly even Darlington—will be none too gently bypassed. The traditional audience attending Winston Cup races will slowly disappear, perhaps to be replaced—television program directors hope—by the newly arriving extraregional migrants who are today filling southern cities.

Will this take place? Possibly not. IMSA exotics and sports car racing, NHRA hot rod events, and vintage car racing have already invaded the larger cities to provide traditional racing for the immigrants. USAC has begun to import midget racing into the region—indeed, at the previously described Lanier Raceway. Some suggest that it is only a matter of time before home-grown sprint cars begin appearing in the region as the rules for stock cars become increasingly distanced from reality. Sanctioned and unsanctioned drag strips abound. The outcome is not as obvious as it might seem.

The traditional southern spectator being shouldered out of the Winston Cup events is also being offered a more reasonably priced surrogate closer to home—racing that retains all those elements which brought them to the sport in the first place. The increasingly common short paved tracks provide racing as it used to be without the high prices, poor seating, and stuffed-shirt city people. But will this rebirth of short track racing bring increased costs of competition, outside sponsorship, outside drivers and cars, and a second disenfranchisement of the traditional southerner?

White lightning, rednecks, and Blue Ribbon beer are images that are disappearing from the southern stock car scene as this regional sport is removing its overalls and becoming nationalized. Whether the sport's mystique was based upon myth or reality, southern stock car racing, like most of traditional southern life, is today at the brink. The long-sought goal of the sport's promoters, sponsors, and media executives to create a national professional sport appears to be nearing reality. All pundits and prognosticators agree that nationalization is in the offing. Less obvious is the impact this process may have upon the those hard-working folk who gave the sport its lore and legend. Will these people be shouldered aside once more by those seeking legitimacy as members of the "New South?" Is it inevitable that the "Skoal Bandit" and other smokeless tobacco-sponsored teams will be replaced by those of detergent and restaurant companies? It seems inevitable that as time passes race crowds will increasingly become more and more akin to those currently attending football and steeplechase events with their catered picnic lunches and beer trailers dispensing the approved sponsoring brew. Nary a cry of "Take it off!" will ring across the back grandstand crowd. These adjustments are not evil, nor to be feared, but they do represent the precursors of change as national culture invades one of the most hallowed traditions of the nation's most regional of landscapes.

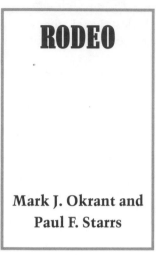

CHAPTER TEN

RODEO

**Mark J. Okrant and
Paul F. Starrs**

Rodeo as Perfect Place; or, "So You Wanna Be a Cowboy?"

No less a writer than the inimitable Bobbie Louise Hawkins, in a savvy little book, *Back to Texas*, perfectly locates the place of rodeo. As Curtis, Bobbie's younger brother, shows off a new pair of boots, he hoists a clad foot into the air. She retaliates: "'Curtis,' I said, 'There isn't a hippy in the world that doesn't want to be a cowboy'" (Hawkins 1977, 111). Devastation is instant. There is, of course, an ongoing and extraordinary connection between the cowboy life of the American West and a vast world public.[1] But what really matters is that so many people, at some fundamental level, have contemplated the primordial relationships with nature that a ranch hand's existence, at least in theory, represents: time outdoors, nature, cows and horses, danger and excitement, fellowship and skill, nurturing and scenery. In the contemporary urban world, marked by overcrowding, dirt, crime, and similar social ills, the American West's open spaces and the sport of rodeo as it successfully evokes them arouse images of an almost perfect place.

Perhaps most of all, there are the moments of glory that come to the cowhand as evanescent prizes amid a much longer life of slow consistency. While caring for cattle, sheep, waters, and rangeland is self-evidently tedious, the work obviously means much to ranching's practitioners. Although the bumper sticker claiming "If you ain't a cowboy, you ain't shit" may be a marvel of indirection, its delightfully subversive effect works well in part because it plays to a universal suspicion that there must be more to life than late-twentieth-century society offers. At a visceral level, we nearly all envy the geography—pristine, populist, parlous, pretechnological—that the cowhand's life, and its public reproduction in rodeo, represents.

Rodeo places animals, wild nature, and bestial wiles inside a bounded arena, adding to the ensemble only a modest human advantage of clever athleticism; the aura of bread and circuses is no accident. However faintly such matters may be spoken of out loud, there are genuine intimations of primitivism in rodeo.[2] The contestants, whether professionals, rank amateurs, college cowboys, duffers, or everyday ranch hands, in their storm and hustle help to suggest some of what western life in the raw might be like. All this makes rodeo what it is: a draw for spectators ranging from the nostalgic and the curious to the obsessed, a supreme attraction for buckle-emblazoned cowgirls and boozed-up ranch hands, and a clarion call for be-zitted boys and wannabe buckaroos. These motley elements are mixed in a crucible of beer cups and dust eddies, with diverse crowds cantilevered against the fences on a cool evening, friends catching up on news, and a community ritually reforming. And it all takes place in a setting that harks back to the West as a clean, ordered place where, if we'd been so lucky, we all might once have been (fig. 10.1).

A popular western maxim, in no way discounted for its obviousness, states that rodeo is a "quintessential part of the American West" (Lawrence 1982, 10). Anthropologist Elizabeth Atwood Lawrence suggests that rodeo, as a direct outgrowth of the cattle industry, preserves the West's pastoral image (10). While there is considerable debate, especially recently, about whether the truest West is found in cities such as Phoenix, Tulsa, Las Vegas, and Denver, or in the region's rural areas, villages, and towns, there is no escaping a widespread public perception that the West is where the people aren't.[3] When Gertrude Stein wrote that "in America there is more space where nobody is than where anybody is; that is what makes America what it is," she tapped a deep vein (1973, 53–54). In this chapter, we examine rodeo's origins, the

FIG. 10.1. Rural rodeo grounds, Alpine, Arizona, 1987. Although the site may be unkempt until just before an event and the facilities modest, rodeo grounds are haven to activities—both professional and amateur—that hark back to the older traditions of range life.

popular image of its performers, and the deeper character of its competitive landscapes, while exploring the geographical distribution of an Old West relic that also symbolizes the New West.

Real to Ritual: Rodeo's Origins

There are obvious links between the development of rodeo and the history of livestock raising in North America. The cattle-raising culture that is today thought of as essentially American is a combination of traits brought to the New World by settlers experienced in livestock handling elsewhere and latter-day adaptations born in the United States.[4] This is a business of many and diverse roots. Even rodeo's contests showcasing a physical mastery of animals are anything but unique to the Americas. Competition, especially in an activity like herding that in many parts of the world is male-dominated, is an expected and cherished part of ritual life.[5] This said, there is no escaping that the sport of rodeo is as American as baseball, football, bowling, or stock car racing. The particular fusion of cultures that made ranching in the American West what it is today also fueled the origins of rodeo.

The herding of livestock, especially cattle, over vast acreages of the public domain (and later private land) is an addition to the American scene spun out from the experiences of different groups of people who were mixing in the Western Hemisphere from the fifteenth century on. Techniques of handling animals were contributed by Spanish and Mexican colonists in what is now the Southwest and California. In Texas after the Civil War, as Terry Jordan and Walter Prescott Webb have pointed out, there began a blending of the practices of black herding cultures of Africa and the Caribbean, Native American riding and hunting techniques, and western European (especially British Isles) livestock management. While the skills prized in rodeo owe most to Hispanic contributions to ranch life, additional events like bulldogging came from the southeastern piney woodland experiences of black and poor white settlers who worked their cattle on foot, with dogs and bullwhips and corrals. Rodeo is a polyglot sport—the name itself taken from Spanish—but among the best rodeo hands variations of race, language, and ethnicity truly match the diversity of the American West's historic and contemporary ranch workers.

As profits from livestock herding spread west from the Appalachians, north from Texas, and east from California, cowhands of noteworthy ability moved with the herds. The cattle drives of the 1860s played an important role in rodeo history. They made open range—and later fenced-range private-land ranching—possible, profitable, and permanent. Cowboys developed and honed skills, disseminating them across the western steppes and grasslands, into the Canadian Prairies, and westward to the Oregon Territory. These areas would become the principal training grounds for performing rodeo cowboys.

The Origin and Development of Rodeo as a Sport

The formal origin of rodeo is clouded. There is a fine line between the time when the activity that we now call rodeo stopped being part of everyday range or ranch work and its attainment of status as a paying sport or a form of entertainment (Hall 1976, 8). The practical abilities of roping, doctoring animals, taming horses, and training horses with skill and verve had high status in the Spanish (and Arab) livestock herding traditions, but they came to be regarded with respect and envy every place cattle grazed. It is important to understand that the basic events of rodeo were nothing unusual on the range: cowhands watched one another, learned, and compared ideas. Special abilities were noted with admiring approval.

Nonetheless, informal competitions were common, and at the once- or twice-yearly roundup—the rodeo—there were frequent tests of everyday skills. The seasonal gathering and sorting of animals was generally not limited to single outfits. Instead, these were large and ritual-rich gatherings of adjoining ranches that celebrated the harvest and apportioned animals to their owners. The rodeo was a community event, including religious observations, much revelry, and dances.

At some Hispanic ranch gatherings, cowboys practiced the *carrera del gallo*. This involved reaching down from the back of a sprinting horse and grabbing the head of a live greased rooster that had been buried up to its neck in sand. Although such events were no doubt entertaining, they were not wholly practical and did not transplant to the modern rodeo arena.[6] Other, more useful skills did enter rodeo as modern events. Roping stampeding mustangs, milking a wild range cow, or throwing a steer by lassoing its head and then sprinting the horse around the animal to yank it down all have immense practical value on the open range, but none of the three is usually seen anymore in rodeos, thanks largely to concern about cruelty.[7] But bull riding, the most brutal (for the rider) of rodeo's spectacles, has never had a whit of modern-day practical value except to allow the greenest of hands a chance to participate in the rodeo—the only equipment needed is a braided fifty-five-dollar bull-riding rope that can usually be borrowed. Just as NASCAR's competitive stock cars bear slim resemblance to any vehicle purchasable at a dealer's showroom, so have the formal rodeo events evolved from practical application to ritual performance.

Much controversy exists about rodeo's place of origin—the range, the ranch, or the town. During the latter portion of the nineteenth century, representatives ("reps") of cattle ranchers were dispatched to gather stray cattle. Although being chosen to go to other ranches as a rep was a vote of confidence, the work was by and large tedious, often leaving cowboys with a good deal of leisure (Fredriksson 1985, 3). As an antidote to boredom, a rep might challenge one or more cowboys to ride some of the unbroken horses—"outlaws" or "broncs"—they had rounded up. Side bets would be made as to whether cowboy or animal would win. Roping skills had a place, too. Although too much roping was hard on cattle, horses, and cowhands alike, impromptu roping contests might be held. On numerous occasions, cowboys from various camps challenged one another to see who was the best saddlebronc rider or steer roper. An instant rodeo resulted. Since there was sparse entertainment to be found on the trail, amusement came in the form of pitting occupational skills against those of another cowboy or outfit.

The practical origins of rodeo's events may well be unique; as Kristine Fredriksson notes, it appears to be the only sport that evolved from an application of work skills for the sole purpose of entertaining

FIG. 10.2. Ranch origins of rodeo traditions: Deep Springs Valley, California/Nevada, 1980. Skills like roping, wrestling calves to the ground, and handling horses with firm cooperation are an essential part of ranch life, evident in activities like the seasonal brandings of this Great Basin ranch. Ranch rodeos are the not-too-distant precursor to modern events, and even a small roundup like this one ends with an impromptu "bull" riding session.

the labor force (cowboys themselves) during slow work periods (4). The rough-and-tumble rangeland pastimes shared by ranch hands were nothing that could be adapted to a craft show, an art gallery, or other avowedly civilized outlets.[8] Range skills were tied to the open spaces where the cowhands practiced their trade; it took time for rodeo to develop into something that could be showcased within the limited confines of an arena (fig. 10.2). Even today, there are hundreds of informal contests in the grasslands and forests of the United States that challenge the same skills that most people see only after paying for a rodeo admission; the practical side of ranch work is as alive as the rodeo rituals. Only as the skills became more commercialized, and as non-cowboy audiences began to cluster to watch these activities, was rodeo transformed from a facet of ranch life into a spectator sport.[9]

Most western historians tap the Prescott, Arizona, rodeo, which began on July 4, 1864, as the sport's oldest formal competition.[10] It is fitting that an Independence Day event captures this distinction, since the Fourth of July is affectionately known as the "Cowboy's Christmas" because of the date's plethora of rodeos—and opportunities to win prize money. On July 4, 1985, twenty-eight professional (sanctioned by the Professional Rodeo Cowboys Association, or PRCA) rodeos were conducted across nineteen states (*Prorodeo Sports News* 1986, 84–87). The Prescott rodeo has a second and more dubious honor: in 1888 it was the first to levy an audience admission charge (Fredriksson 1985, 4).

The "Wild West" Becomes a Show

Rodeo's arrival on the western scene could hardly have been more timely. It came as fencing and ranches were replacing open range, and a different kind of cowhand was needed. Before this, the labor force that had been tapped for trail drives was less than ideal for settling down as ranch hands. Trail cowboys were casual laborers rather than steady wage earners. And since cowboys were reluctant to accept any work that could not be conducted on horseback, this was a period of economic and social difficulty for many of these independent souls.[11] The mobile work force of cowhands traipsing through the West was disposed to take whatever jobs were proffered, and if work added an element of competition and cash dollars, all the better. It was a time for ambition and enterprise to succor the West.

During the early 1880s, editors of several eastern periodicals worried that the cowboy lifestyle was about to fade from the scene. Writers were dispatched to the region in an effort to provide readers with a permanent record of a dying way of life.[12] Ironically, the publishers' premature postmortem breathed new life into all manner of cowboy life, including dude ranching, rodeo, Wild West shows, and a vast industry of pulp westerns, cowboy regalia, and western tourism.[13] Inspired by the stories written about them, a number of cowboys adopted an entrepreneurial spirit that, ultimately, would provide new opportunities to display their skills.

Most famous among these entrepreneurs was a North Platte, Nebraska, native by the name of William F. "Buffalo Bill" Cody. Cody sensed that audiences for cowboy hijinks existed in eastern cities. He held his first "Wild West Show" on July 4, 1882, in his hometown. During the years that followed, Cody introduced curious audiences throughout North America and Europe to his troupe of cowboys, Indians, clowns, ropers, riders, sharpshooters, and assorted western personalities. The demand for Cody's sort of show was so great that, by 1885, better than fifty imitations were touring the United States.[14]

While Wild West shows were an important source of income, they did little to enhance the public's perception of performing cowboys. Throughout their travels, Wild West–show cowboys were derided as "carnival boys" and "wild, loose-figured men," a reputation some amply lived up to. Hoping to establish themselves as legitimate sportsmen in the public mind, a number of hands pushed to develop an organization of rodeo people that would sanction quality competitions (Fredriksson 1985, 11–20). A first effort, the Rodeo Association of America (RAA), formed in January of 1929. The organization standardized rules, coordinated promotion and judging activities, and improved prize money. A sacrifice of independence paid real dividends in cash—rodeo went from being a quaint rural activity to a major western sport. While the term "rodeo" failed to replace "Wild West show" in newspaper and magazine use until the mid-1930s, the development of formal rules and standards did much to establish rodeo's public credibility. Since the '30s, the professional rodeo association has undergone name changes and experienced considerable growth. As the Professional Rodeo Cowboys Association (PRCA), it is the flagship organization of competitive rodeo.[15]

The Cowhand and the Public

For many years, westerners and easterners alike have been curious about the makeup of any individual who would choose to be a cowhand.[16] The travel demands and risk of injury have been great since the earliest cattle drives. More important, there has never been even a basic guarantee of profit: ranch hands are notoriously poorly paid, and there are always some who become rodeo cowhands because they want a shot at big money they could never get at a ranch hand's salary—which, even in the early 1990s, averages less than $1,000 a month, plus room and board. Traditionally, most performing rodeo cowboys have had ranching backgrounds. Anyone who grows up in a ranching environment learns to ride and rope early on. Ranch family members, boys and girls alike, are socialized into a tradition of toughness and independence early in life. Injury comes with the territory, and self-assurance, competence, and common sense are definitely life-prolonging traits. Performing a job without complaint remains a character trait of successful professional cowboys.[17]

Through the years, the cowboy's public image has been enhanced as a consequence of efforts by authors, artists, and the movie industry. Teddy Roosevelt cavorting through the Black Hills of the Dakotas and spending time on dude ranches, helped further the cowboy's image. Owen Wister's 1902 novel *The Virginian* established the cowboy as an American fictional icon. Within a few years, the stories of Zane Grey,

Max Brand, and Will James reinforced a cowboy image that also dates back to the earliest silent films. Since the 1930s, countless stories glorifying the American cowboy's life have appeared in periodicals, from the most august to absolute pulp fiction. And western artists working in bronze, paint, watercolor, silver jewelry, and leather or rawhide have capitalized on a public fancy piqued by the cowhand. It is a great and profitable love affair.

By the end of World War I, movies brought widespread recognition to the cowboy. Urban and suburban youth emulated the style and attire of their favorite movie figures by dressing in a ten-gallon hat, a plaid shirt, Levi or Wrangler jeans with silver buckle, leather chaps, and boots with spurs—an apparel with the added advantage of looking graceful on either men or women (Lawrence 1982, 18). The most daring ran silver conchos down their outside pants seams. The faithful followed the exploits of Tom Mix and Hoot Gibson, just as later generations would be loyal to Randolph Scott, Gene Autry, Roy Rogers, and John Wayne (Gray 1985, 77–79). Inspired by these screen stars, a visit to a dude ranch was the next best thing to heaven for generations of children.[18]

Novels, film serials, magazines, then radio and television brought Westerns into middle-class American living rooms. Roy Rogers and Gene Autry led the way toward a zenith period of television westerns, during the 1950s and 1960s (Savage 1979, 47). Weekly television series appeared, as millions of viewers followed the trials and tribulations of the Cartwrights, Cheyenne, Sugarfoot, Bronco Lane, James West, Rowdy Yates and Rawhide, and other western heroes.

Until recently, rodeos and rodeo performers have not fared as well in the affections of scholars as their range and ranch counterparts. William Savage has observed that the cowboy's heroic status has not been extended wholesale to the rodeo performer (130). Savage disapproved of the cowboy characters created for a number of rodeo films, writing them off as shallow, egocentric, and violent. He also observed that the rodeo cowboy has been a less than satisfactory subject for television.

But as scholars are wary of rodeo's character, advertisers have warmed to rodeo in a big way, notably beer, tobacco, clothing, and transportation interests.[19] In 1985, the PRCA entered into an agreement with cable television's ESPN to provide coverage of competitions, including the Las Vegas National Finals Rodeo and several weekly indoor rodeos broadcast from Mesquite, Texas.[20] Using technologies like slow motion, reverse angles, and instant replays, already familiar from other sports broadcasts, these televised rodeos have introduced urban and nonwestern audiences to the sport's nuances. In just a few hours of watching, a viewer can witness a virtual clinic in rodeo, something that until recently would have required years of exposure to the sport. Offering a view equal to the best seats in the house, televised events helped increase interest in rodeo and rodeo cowboys among nontraditional audiences.

Rodeo's Grounds

On most days of the year, the setting is quiet. Rodeo grounds vary immensely around the United States, Canada, and Mexico, but they are often little more than a small arena a little way out of town, or part of the county fairgrounds, or a place where, for all but a few crucial weeks, cutting horse owners train their animals and jackpot ropers meet after school or on weekends. Many a rodeo grounds grows heavy with range weeds during the weeks that bring spring into summer, and the first job that the rodeo committee must do, right after hoisting the huge "Rodeo Week" sign that billows across the main drag in town, is bring in a Bush Hog to mow the weeds flat, calling on the high school rodeo club to rake away the detritus. Rodeo is everywhere in the West, and the setting is nothing special; it is as casual a part of a western town as a park or the town hall or diagonal parking along Main Street.

Space in a western town is rarely at a premium, and it can take a hundred years for a town to grow out and around the rodeo arena; most communities aren't anywhere near there, yet. The arena at the rodeo grounds can be as simple as a few wood fences, sturdy enough to contain a snot-blowing stomping Brahma bull, but hardly technical in the building. It is the environs that matter most. A few pens contain the rough stock. Most important is a great big area, sufficient for horse trailers to be parked and giving the crowd room to mix with the rodeo contestants. It takes a pretty high-brow and uptown rodeo to rate chain-link fences that start splitting people into different groups; in most rodeo grounds, there is ample space and plenty of time for mingling. The pace of a rodeo, set by the announcer, tends toward the lackadaisical; many of the larger rodeos are several-day affairs, so a hand can take six or eight rides in an attempt to garner the best time or ride. Both the geography and the style of rodeo are unconfining, until the actual arena events themselves are involved.

Rodeo space is vernacular, the product of what is available, what can be paid for, and what the contestants will put up with. A prime

FIG. 10.3. When the rodeo comes to town: Challis, Idaho, 1989. While professional rodeos have a pronounced grandeur, small-town events are favorites for rural residents, who are willing to forgive the modest arena and the less than stellar times the participants turn in, because many of the contestants are family, friends, or at least local talent. This Challis, Idaho, rodeo, with the sky descending into clouds, the grandstands filled with friends catching up on news and gossip, and the rodeo as much a setting as a spectacle, is typical.

rodeo grounds is a public asset—it can earn money from rental fees at other times of the year, and a good arena boss can manage a golden goose. Most important, though, is understanding that there is nothing formal or precise about most rodeo grounds. Like a baseball diamond, they can take virtually any shape, so long as they meet certain basic requirements. The grandstands can be east or west, the chutes at the north or south end, the fences board or steel mesh.

Many rural rodeo grounds are militantly modest, the announcer's booth an unpretentious box dangling above a chute, with access up a ladder through a trapdoor in the bottom of the box (fig. 10.3). While ritzy facilities make for fine television viewing, they mean little in most rodeos. Few sports have such broad conventions for acceptability, in terms of their settings. Since rodeo grounds are community efforts and communal resources, they are only as proud as the locals can make them, which may be barely more than modest. Because the rodeo's social life is so important, a televised rodeo misses an essential aspect when it concentrates on only a part of the whole event. It is as if viewers were seeing a stock car race without the infield, or a baseball game without kids clamoring for player signatures or lines for the concessions or batting practice.

Towns and Spectators

Throughout the United States and the Canadian West, rodeos are staged by professional and amateur organizations. Promoters have taken advantage of diverse outdoor and indoor sports facilities to hold competitions within hundreds of communities ranging in size from small hamlets to the largest cities. Aficionados prefer small town competitions, with their weathered arenas, because these give one a sense of the open, remote ranch country that made rodeo.[21]

During rodeo week, the local main street typically is decorated with banners and posters. These announce not just the rodeo but also the fair, festival, or cultural activity in conjunction with which the rodeo is being held. Ruffles in red-white-and-blue American or red-and-white Canadian colors echo the substantial national pride shared by locals. A parade is held during rodeo week; for some in attendance, this is the major event of the entire rodeo. Rodeo parades within the United States generally are led by performers or western notables dressed in cowboy and cowgirl attire, carrying the Stars and Stripes plus the state flag. Civic leaders, members of fraternal organizations, policemen, and firemen join in the procession (Clayton and Clayton 1988). At the conclusion of the parade, spectators adjourn to the rodeo arena.

The crowd at a rodeo represents a variety of backgrounds and levels of knowledge about the sport. In attendance are ranchers and locals who have spent their entire lives in roping and riding country. These people can identify the competition's rank, the top livestock and the best hands or cowboys, with a quick glance. By contrast, neophytes in the audience—city people, easterners, and foreign visitors—having attended in order to sample a little local color, may have minimal knowledge or interest in the sport's nuances.

Rodeos annually attract millions of spectators.[22] But they start small, and it is community rodeos that remain most alive, if perhaps not most profitable or most sought out by top rodeo hands. Typically, a small town rodeo will lure the majority of its visitors from within a ten- to fifty-mile range.[23] An exception, the Tri-State Rodeo in little Fort Madison, Iowa, through the mid-1970s annually captured in excess of thirty thousand attendees; more than half of these were residents of states other than Iowa, while four-fifths came from outside of the Fort Madison area (*Report of the Iowa Development Commission* 1977).

The Tri-State's draw was especially great because of the event's novelty—perhaps only the great Madison Square Garden rodeo, still held for several days in downtown Manhattan, has been able to compete with the Fort Madison rodeo for locational eccentricity. In many cases, the economic impact of a rodeo is impressive. For the Fort Madison event, local motels were full and retail sales were 23 percent above the norm. Most important, visitors spent better than $300,000 annually in the community while attending the rodeo.

One Wyoming town offers travelers between the Black Hills of South Dakota and Yellowstone National Park more than the usual opportunity to obtain sleep, food, souvenirs, and gasoline. Near the western edge of Cody, attention is unavoidably diverted to a tall, vertical, red-on-white sign spelling RODEO framed by an otherwise pleasant view of the Rocky Mountains.[24] The typical rodeo visitor—clad in designer jeans or Bermuda shorts, souvenir T-shirt, and sunglasses and carrying a camera—will probably see less than championship-level performers, but that is inconsequential. Cody provides visitors with a bona fide western experience. Save for the rodeo sign, the setting at Cody is genuine and generous, and the contestants are proud women and men anxious to perform before large audiences every night during the summer.

A handful of professional rodeos is recognized by cowboys, stock contractors, and officials as being the sport's major annual events. These rodeos—the Cheyenne Frontier Days in Wyoming, Oregon's Pendleton Roundup, the Calgary Stampede in Alberta, Canada, and the Las Vegas, Nevada, National Finals Rodeo—represent the pinnacle of formal competition. These are events for profit; they are run for the rodeo cowhands first and foremost, although with an eye carefully modulated toward fan entertainment. The casual air of the small town rodeo is largely absent. But even some of these behemoth events capture both worlds: no contest better presents a western way of life and the sport of rodeo to a vast audience than Calgary's ten-day competition. J. C. Treacy of NBC Television once proclaimed the Calgary Stampede, baseball's World Series, and the Indianapolis 500 automobile race as "the big three annual [sports] events of the North American continent" (Gray 1985, 114).

The Calgary Stampede was first held in 1886 in conjunction with a large annual agricultural fair known as the Calgary Exposition. While the Exposition succeeded in attracting attention to Canada's western prairies, it clearly needed an added ingredient to boost attendance. The answer was found by Guy Weadick, a transplanted New Yorker with a background in vaudeville and a marvelous capacity as a promoter. Weadick's rodeo, or Stampede, had its first showing in 1912. To insure his show's success, Weadick attracted cowboys and cowgirls from United States, Canadian, Mexican, and Indian rodeos and Wild West shows (ibid., 36). Despite the success of the initial Stampede, it was not until 1923 that the event established a permanent place on the Calgary social calendar.

Numerous traditions are associated with the Calgary Exposition and Stampede, as it is presently known. It is a legendary and continuing practice for a cowboy to ride his horse through a local publican house and out into the street again. This ritual, which has been imitated repeatedly in other locations, is generally presumed to date from July 10, 1923, when a cowboy named Eddie King rode his horse through the Club Cafe in downtown Calgary (ibid., 63).

The year 1923 produced two of the Stampede's other crowd-pleasing rituals. The first of these is the famous chuckwagon races; this most picturesque and dangerous of events has become a Calgary trademark. Interestingly, it was a chuckwagon participant's spur-of-the-moment action that produced the second ritual, the Stampede's flapjack breakfast. The latter was initiated by a contestant who, on a whim, drove his team into downtown Calgary and proceeded to cook breakfast for all comers. The tradition has lasted more than seventy years.

Among the events that add to the Stampede's spirit are a huge square dance held on Calgary's Eighth Avenue, a gambling casino, buffalo rides, an Indian village, a huge stock auction, participation by stars from the worlds of entertainment and sport, and a large open space in which free entertainment is provided for spectators seeking a respite from the day's formal activities (Tidball 1986).

Lest the reader think that rodeo is ignored at the Calgary Exposition and Stampede, the list of events includes all of the traditional rodeo contests, plus several more. Leading rodeo competitors have been attracted to Calgary since the Stampede's inception. In total, attendees are offered a chance to view more than three hundred events. Each year, nearly four million people will come to the Exposition and Stampede grounds, with approximately one-quarter of this number attending the Stampede rodeo. During the first week of July, the city swells with rodeo fans, garbed in white cowboy hats, bellowing the cowboy's cry of "whoopee!" Both are Stampede traditions (Gray 1985, 62). The Exposition and Stampede has brought uncounted millions of dollars in revenue and wages into Calgary. It pays the salaries of 250 permanent employees and supplies hundreds of additional seasonal jobs (184).

Arenas

The typical rodeo arena is an oval (fig. 10.4), but there is plenty of room for local variation. It may be indoors or outdoors, in a small town or big city, permanent or temporary. Generally, there are eight to twelve chutes for the rough stock events centered along one of the oval's long sides. Chutes are small metal or wood-framed pens that confine the animals until their release into the arena. From the tops of these chutes cowboys climb onto the backs of the broncs or bulls below. The rough stock—horses and bulls—are unloaded from vans into fenced-in areas behind the chutes. Next, each animal is herded through a runway into one of the chutes. The chute has a large gate which is swung open, allowing riders and beasts to enter the arena sideways.

At one end of the oval are the entrance gates for the "timed events." These consist of special chutes from which calves or steers are released, as well as a "box" where each contestant, mounted aboard a horse, waits to perform. At the opposite small end of the arena is a penning area where animals from all events are caught following their performances.

The area behind the bucking chutes generally is reserved for contestants, rodeo officials, and special guests. The rodeo announcer and the two judges observe from an elevated vantage point. The announcer is a major element in the operation of a rodeo. He or she provides each performer's name and town of origin, identifies each bronc or bull, and offers other important information about the contestant or stock contractor. The announcer sets the mood during the competition by joking with contestants, reminding people about an injured cowboy, and requesting a round of applause for contestants regardless of the quality of their performance. A catwalk leading to the bleacher seats goes immediately past the pens holding the performing livestock. The opportunity to stand nearly nose-to-nose with a Brahma bull and watch a cowboy preparing for a ride is real and immediate. Having been afforded this opportunity, spectators are generally amply willing to offer each contestant a hearty cheer, whether or not they understand the event's hows, whys, and wherefores.

Newcomers to the sport are generally surprised to learn that no announcement of event winners follows a competition. The victorious contestant is customarily awarded the prize—a trophy belt buckle—in the comparative solitude behind the rough stock chutes (Lawrence 1982, 95). Therefore, casual observers will have no knowledge of the contestants' order of finish unless they maintain a careful record of the

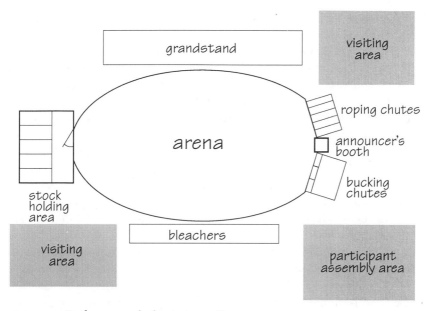

FIG. 10.4. Rodeo grounds: basic ingredients.

competition. Recently, as rodeo has attracted increasing numbers of fans from cities and the country's nonranching regions, the sport has slowly acquiesced to the demands of its neophyte spectators. At indoor arenas within large cities, electronic messages and scores flashed in neon have replaced the announcer's inside jokes and one-liners as the primary source of information.

Rodeo's Events

Rodeos held within the United States begin with a stylish "posting of colors," as American and state flags are brought to the center of the arena by galloping riders.[25] This is traditionally followed by the playing of the Star-Spangled Banner and a recitation of the "Cowboy's Prayer," which requests guidance "in the arena of life" (Hall 1973, 199–200). Next, there is the grand entry parade in which the rodeo stock contractor, pickup riders, clowns, the rodeo queen and her court, and officials straddle their best saddles and ride their flashiest mounts around the arena as they are introduced individually.

Rodeo's competitive events are divided into two categories, the rough stock and the timed events. These are conducted in a set order. Typically, the cattle and horses for the events are provided by stock contractors. PRCA rodeos use animals raised by seventy-eight United States and Canadian stock contractors, each of whom is carefully selected (*Prorodeo Sports News* 1986, 62). The contractors who produce top stock are honored by having the animals placed in the National Finals Rodeo at Las Vegas. The rodeo stock are as much athletes and contestants as the human competitors—anyone who has spent time with the animals sees that the stock, whether Brahma bulls or broncs, are participants of singular ability. Their skill, canniness, and vigor make or break a rodeo rider, so animals that fail to participate vigorously enough do not last. A flank strap, attached over the loins of the bucking animals, provides a signal that it is time to go to work. At small town rodeos, a favorite showpiece for stock contractors before formal events begin is leading little children around the arena while they are seated on the back of the meanest horse in the bucking string. This is implication enough that challenge, not annoyance with a rider, motivates the bucking stock.

The rough stock events pit a rider against a willful horse or bull. The average nonwesterner might be startled to learn that rough stock contestants, like gymnasts, are hardly the physical giants they sometimes seem in media accounts. The average male PRCA rough stock competitor is five feet eight inches and 152 pounds, but these men have broad shoulders and trim waists, and are remarkably resilient under recurrent abuse.[26] Each rough stock contestant attempts to ride an animal for just eight seconds (a six-second ride is required in some junior and women's rodeos). After eight seconds, a buzzer sounds, alerting both the cowboy and the pickup riders or clowns assigned to assist the cowboy that the ride is over.

The winner of a rough stock event is decided by a pair of judges who together assign the ride a total score of 1 to 100 points based upon the quality of performance by both the cowboy and the bronc or bull. Luck of the draw is important. Since an animal's performance is as crucial as the cowboy's, competitors have been known to enter as many as five rodeos on a single day, actually appearing at the rodeo where the stock drawn is most likely to impress the judges (*Prorodeo Sports News* 1986, 110).

In an effort to make a living on the rodeo circuit, a cowboy can travel several thousand miles in a few days, with no guarantee that a payoff awaits. During a year's rodeo season, the top rodeo hand can travel more than 100,000 miles and perform in as many as five rodeos per week, or 150 per season (Fredricksson 1985, 121). A rider must enter a minimum of a hundred rodeos even to hope to qualify for the World

Championship National Finals Rodeo. At the height of the rodeo sea-son, July through August, a cowboy may enter more than one rodeo during a twenty-four-hour period in an effort to accumulate points.

Saddlebronc riding has been described as the cornerstone event of rodeo, for it is a direct descendant of range and ranch activities. During a roundup, outlaw horses were saddled and broken, sometimes with the honor or payroll of an entire ranch on the line (Lawrence 1982, 25). In saddlebronc riding, the rider uses a trimmed-down saddle that lacks a horn. The horse wears a halter to which is attached a rope that is held in one hand. As the bucking chute gate swings open, the saddlebronc rider must have the round-roweled spurs planted well up on the horse's shoulders, which gives the bronc a pronounced advantage through the first several jumps and adds glamour and uncertainty to the ride.

The saddlebronc rider is used as the logo of both the Professional Rodeo Cowboys Association and Wyoming, which is, after all, "the Cowboy State." Saddlebronc riding requires more experience than the other rough stock events, and a fair amount of capital to purchase the special saddle. Strikingly, PRCA bylaws allow local cowboys to enter professional events if the hands work within a fixed distance of the rodeo site, and favorite events for local entries are saddlebronc riding and team roping, which draw most clearly on recognizable ranch skills. Some areas take special pride in the abilities of their local sons—a ranching area within a three hundred-mile radius of South Dakota's northwestern corner, for example, earned a reputation for its great saddlebronc riders. Nearly 50 percent of saddlebronc riders who fin-ished among the top five in the NFR standings between 1929 and 1975 came from hometowns in this region.[27]

Unlike saddlebronc riding, bareback bronc riding has no ranch an-tecedent. It was developed for competitive purposes during the 1950s. The rider uses a "rigging"—a leather strap fitted around the horse's body just behind the withers with an attached suitcase-like handgrip. There is no saddle, nor stirrups, halter, or reins. The cowboy grasps the handle with one gloved hand while the other hand remains free and waving in the air throughout the ride, both as counterbalance and to prove mas-tery of the animal. In both forms of bronc riding, pickup riders help free the cowboy as soon as the go-round is done. The pickup rider rides alongside the bucking animal, allowing the performer to jump onto the pickup horse and then slide to the ground.

Bull riding is the most dangerous of the rough stock events and is immensely popular. Once mounted, a bull will jump and spin with great intensity in an effort to buck the rider off its back. A bull rider has only a rigging rope fastened around the bull's middle to grasp and can use only one hand to hold the bull rope. The greatest danger to bull riders occurs after they are back on the ground. Bulls take an understandable pleasure in continuing their aggressive behavior once the rider has dismounted. If a rider gets hung up in the rigging, joints dislocate and ligaments tear as he is thrown back and forth, dangling by one hand, unable to work free. Or, if the dismount is not smooth, bulls will gore performers or use their hoofs to inflict serious injury. With a bull often topping two thousand pounds, and facing a bovine history of unpredictable behavior, the bull riders are often considered a slightly touched breed apart by other cowboys (Lawrence 1982, 28).

Mounted pickup riders are impractical during the bull-riding competition, since bulls tend to consider attacking horses good sport. Instead, rodeo clowns, or bullfighters, help a cowboy at the termination of the ride. Dressed in clown's wigs, makeup, and loose clothing, they employ a variety of props plus a combination of speed, gymnastics, and bullfighting techniques to distract the bull from the intended target—any dismounted bull rider. The clowns are a favorite among veteran and neophyte spectators alike.

Timed Events

Five timed events appear in professional rodeo—calf roping, steer wrestling, barrel racing, steer roping, and team roping. The first three are standard events, while the last two are common extras. The timed events require precision and cooperation between horse and rider. In most timed events, a mounted cowboy or a team of riders subdues a steer or calf in the shortest time possible. A well-trained saddle horse is an equal partner with the cowboy. While cattle are provided by stock contractors, each contestant in a timed event supplies a horse, complicating travel patterns.[28] Unlike riders who participate in rough stock events, the mobility of participants in timed events is limited by the need to move a horse from rodeo to rodeo. As in rough stock events, overall performance in timed events is influenced by the behavioral tendencies of the cattle a competitor draws. In scheduling appearances, timed event contestants must weigh potential winnings against wear and tear on themselves, their horses, and their vehicles.

An offshoot of ranch work is calf roping. Cowboys traditionally have used trained horses to separate calves from the herd, in an activity mimicked by some formal cutting horse contests, which are separate from rodeo.[29] But branding ties into one of the oldest traditional actions of ranch life, with animals roped and dragged to a central point for branding. In rodeo calf roping, a rider, perched on horseback, casts a loop over the head of a 200- to 350-pound calf, dismounts, throws the animal, then ties three of its legs with a short piece of rope called a "pigging string," which the rider carries in his mouth, much as a hand might do while branding a calf alone on the open range.

Steer wrestling, or bulldogging, is an event invented strictly for rodeo. Steer wrestlers generally are the largest of all rodeo competitors, averaging over six feet tall and 204 pounds (*Prorodeo Sports News* 1986, 36-39). Bulk helps when leaping from a speeding horse to wrestle a steer that may be as heavy as 700 pounds onto its side or back. A top-notch hand can drop a steer in less than seven seconds, with a good ride.

Team roping is an event of great finesse, requiring absolute coordination between two cowhands—a "header" and a "heeler"—and between individuals and horses. The header throws a loop first, catching the steer by the head or horns. Next, with the help of a skillful horse, the header takes quick dallies (turns around the saddle horn) to snub the steer up short, turning it into position so that the heeler can come in behind and lasso both hind legs.[30]

Rodeo's main women's event has long been barrel-racing competition, where performers circumnavigate three large steel barrels, then exit the arena as quickly as possible. Horse training and agility are essentials, and the times can be impressive. But increasingly, women hands enter events that traditionally have been male-dominated (especially roping, which is based on skill, not strength), and for the last decade, women have been doing exceptionally well in many timed events.

Steer roping, also known as "steer tripping" or "steer jerking," has its origins in ranch activity. First, the cowboy ropes the charging steer around the horns. Next, he throws the slack in the rope over the steer's right hip while turning his horse to the left. The result of this action is that the steer is spun around while running at full speed and falls onto the ground. The cowboy's job is complete when the steer's feet are tied. This event is discouraged in many areas since it carries a strong potential for injuring the steer, although it is a staple during the prestigious Cheyenne Frontier Days rodeo.

Other miscellaneous events that are commonly included in rodeos are the wild horse race, the chuckwagon race, and barrel racing. The horses used in the wild horse race are actually wild, untamed, unridden, "outlaw" horses. The chuckwagon race, a fast and dangerous event reminiscent of ancient chariot races, is a principal feature of the Cheyenne and Calgary rodeos. The chuckwagon, pulled by four racing horses with two or three mounted outriders, completes a figure-eight course in the center of the arena, then races around the track surrounding the arena.

For nearly a hundred years, the American Society for Prevention of Cruelty to Animals, the Humane Society, and other organizations opposed to cruel treatment of animals have fretted about the use of flank- or bucking-straps and voiced concern about hot shots, or electric prods, sometimes used to spark animal performances in the rough stock events. Harsh treatment of animals during the timed events is also opposed. Such groups have met with modest success in arousing public sentiment against rodeo within geographical areas far removed from the sport's hotbeds; the living conditions for the rough stock are generally exemplary, and the working career of a top bull, for example, totals considerably less than ten minutes a year. Regional differences in attitudes can be observed among rodeo audiences. Westerners root loudly for the cowboy, while the sympathies of easterners rest somewhat more with the animal (Lawrence 1982, 23).

Rodeo's Geography

A hierarchy has evolved within the rodeo establishment of the United States and Canada. At the pinnacle is the six thousand-member PRCA, the "major league" of professional rodeo.[31] Each year, the PRCA sanctions more than eight hundred rodeos in forty-three states and four Canadian provinces. The competitions offer some $20 million in cash prizes, averaging better than $25,000 per rodeo with Texas, Wyoming, California, Nevada, and Colorado contests contributing the lion's share of prize cash (PRCA Media Guide 1993, 204–5). The winnings at individual PRCA rodeos vary from a few hundred dollars to more than a hundred thousand dollars.[32] The biggest prizes are reserved for the top rodeos, held in such major rodeo towns as Houston, Denver, San Francisco, Salinas, Pendleton, Cheyenne, Calgary, and Phoenix. In 1993, these rodeos offered contestants an average of over $250,000 in total cash prizes (PRCA Media Guide 1993, 204).

The PRCA is not alone in the rodeo competition hierarchy. A second United States–based professional rodeo organization, the International Professional Rodeo Association (IPRA), has an estimated membership of fifteen thousand cowboys. In addition, the Women's Professional Rodeo Association (WPRA) sanctions competition in five events. North of the forty-ninth parallel, professional rodeo competitions are sanctioned both by the PRCA and by the Canadian Professional Rodeo Association (CPRA). The CPRA, formed in 1944, has sixteen hundred members (Gruber 1987, entry 19142).

Below the professional level, collegiate rodeos (the National Intercollegiate Rodeo Association), scholastic rodeos (the National High School Rodeo Association), and community rodeos (Little Britches, American Junior Rodeo, 4-H, plus jackpots and miscellaneous amateur events) are held yearly in many western communities. Competitions are also conducted, in varying frequencies, within other regions.

For rodeo, places matter. At PRCA and other rodeos, much is made of where a hand hails from. Each rider is generally introduced by name and hometown, much as the alma mater of a pro football player is shared during pregame ceremonies (Lawrence 1982, 86). In the mid-1970s, each of the states west of the ninety-eighth meridian produced substantial numbers of PRCA members.[33] But a different picture appeared east of the Great Plains, where only Florida, New Jersey, New York, and Connecticut produced sizable numbers of cowboys. By the end of that decade, a striking pattern was evident: the West was the primary producer of PRCA riders.

But times change, and by the mid-1980s western dominance no longer held. PRCA membership data from 1986 suggested that western states were still big producers of PRCA cowhands, but that several eastern states had captured a respectable spot on the PRCA membership roles. Thirteen states east of the Mississippi[34] and the Canadian province of Alberta also provided rodeo hands in credible numbers. The profits and prestige of professional rodeo are spreading from the West into other regions.

Since the bulk of skills drawn on by rodeo hands are born of experiences that would be most familiar to cattle ranchers, and since many of the extensive livestock ranching operations in the United States are western, rodeo hands traditionally have hailed from small towns.[35] In the mid-1970s, about two-fifths of all PRCA members originated in communities of fewer than 2,500 residents, with another two-fifths coming from places with 2,500 to 50,000 residents. Cities of 100,000 or more people—in which nearly a third of the nations' population resides—produced less than one-tenth of all PRCA members (table 10.1).[36]

The size of places where PRCA-sanctioned competitions were conducted during the '70s and '80s is also interesting.[37] Nearly a quarter of all PRCA rodeos were held in rural areas, with more than 80 percent in places having fewer than 50,000 residents. A tiny percentage of all PRCA rodeos took place in large cities with a half-million or more residents (table 10.2). By contrast, among the four major professional

TABLE 10.1. Hometowns of PRCA Members in 1975

Population	Percentage of PRCA Membership
Less than 2,500	41.5
2,500–49,999	41.1
50,000–99,999	9.3
100,000–499,999	5.9
More than 500,000	2.1

TABLE 10.2. Population Sizes of PRCA Rodeo Sites, 1975 vs. 1986

	Percentage of Total	
Population	1975	1986
Less than 2,500	24.7	18.1
2,500–49,999	56.1	56.8
50,000–99,999	7.1	9.7
100,000–499,999	9.2	12.3
More than 500,000	2.9	3.0

sports, the National Football League's Green Bay Packers were the only major United States sport franchise operating within a small city at the time (Okrant 1977).

By the mid-1980s, the rodeo sponsorship pattern was changing in subtle but important ways. While small urban places predominated among communities holding PRCA rodeos, there was an appreciable decrease in the percentage of rural competitions, accompanied by a slight increase in PRCA rodeos within small and medium-sized cities.[38] This change appears to have marked a gradual upswing in professional rodeo interest within larger sports markets.

High school rodeo, like professional rodeoing, also experienced substantial growth since the mid-1970s. As at the professional level, most activity was in western states, although more high school participation was evident in the southeast and Great Lakes regions. High school competitions are dependent upon generous amounts of local volunteerism. Since high school rodeo is generally not sanctioned by state athletic associations, the sport's success is affected by the level of local interest in providing training, competition space (an arena), stock, prizes (trophy buckles or merchandise), and promotion.[39] Historically, such support was slender outside of the West, but as interest builds, there is a general feeder effect which makes it likely that rodeo will find growing numbers of trained high school athletes moving into the professional and serious amateur ranks. While there may be fewer kids growing up as the children of ranchers, they can learn in school what used to come from the college of hard knocks. The geographical broadening of high school rodeo has to be taken as an indication of mounting grass-roots interest.

Conclusion

Rodeo is an outgrowth of a way of life with origins along the overlapping peripheries of the Anglo-American, Hispanic, and Indian cattle culture areas. Having evolved as a diversion for working cowboys, the sport's geographical distribution reflects the pattern of beef cattle production. Unlike the major team sports, each of which evolved in urban settings, rodeo has been a rural or small town activity practiced within western states and Canadian provinces. With the growth of professional and amateur rodeo organizations, rodeo's popularity as both a participant and a spectator sport has blossomed, but still primarily in the West. East of the Mississippi, opportunities for the day-to-day exposure to ranch and rodeo life that fosters an understanding of the sport's nuances are harder to come by. As a result, rodeo has two faces: one is the United States and Canadian West, northern Mexico, and isolated parts of South America and Australia, whose familiarity with cattle culture sustains considerable interest in rodeo; the other, the remainder of the world, where the sport has been poorly understood and largely unappreciated by the populace as a whole, save for anomalous communities like New Jersey's Cowtown.

The pattern is changing. Rodeo is experiencing substantial growth in the southeastern and Great Lakes regions, as in large urban places within the West. Corporate-funded television broadcasts and advertisements employing rodeo or ranch themes have done much to foster familiarity within nontraditional markets, expediting geographical expansion—the Marlboro mystique is good for rodeo, and cable television has been a godsend. Major corporations have contributed big PRCA prize monies and academic scholarships. Since 1984, the United States Tobacco Company's Copenhagen-Skoal Scholarship program has provided nearly two million dollars in student assistance, and Wrangler has given thousands of dollars in scholarships to Little Britches Rodeo contestants.[40] Such efforts make it possible for more cowboys to compete. Larger prizes and endorsements bring into rodeo young people from a variety of backgrounds—fans and participants who might never have attempted the sport in other circumstances.[41]

North America's ranching economy is changing in a manner that may strongly influence how rodeo is practiced, affecting participants who begin their training in the youth, high school, and collegiate rodeos; these are the sport's training grounds, just as much as the quiet and secluded arenas where cowhands build their loops and practice their hog-tying. While the rodeo community is justly proud of its expansion since 1929, the changes summarized by one authority are noteworthy: "trucks have replaced horses as the primary form of ranch transportation [and] an increasing number of rodeo competitors are non-ranch kids who train to become rodeo cowboys" (Tidball 1986).

As new contestants and competition venues are developed, rodeo will be gradually injected into the mainstream of American sports consciousness, but at what cost to its western traditions? Rodeo remains a tough but charming, and distinctly American, sport, its origins firm in the deepest crevices of ranching culture. That nonranch kids aspire to the glory and cash which have increasingly become part of rodeo life is not entirely surprising—the West is changing also, as city folks retreat to fancied rural idylls, and their children discover that dabbing a loop on a steer from horseback is more fun than lassoing the family dog. The charm of life in the American West will not soon abate, even as the western lifestyle becomes more endangered. In the end, perhaps it might be a consolation to every admirer of the West that there are still those quiet arenas and rodeo grounds scattered near thousands of towns, waiting for new children to fall for the charm of big belt buckles, the insistent hiss of a well-thrown hard-lay nylon rope, and the sweaty smell of an eager horse fidgeting in wait for competition.

CHAPTER ELEVEN

THOROUGH-BRED RACING

Karl B. Raitz

When society depended upon the horse for draft work and transportation, it was commonplace for sporting people to prove the worth of their stock by challenging others to race and betting on the outcome. Horse racing was a popular pastime for the country gentry in seventeenth-century England; and when the American colonies began to develop, the horse was an important part of early sporting activity. Gradually, rules and conventions brought some structure to horse racing, and wealthy breeders sought to improve their winnings by improving the breed. Racecourses and tracks replaced streets and fields as contest venues, and the spectator became a considered part of racing activity. By the mid–twentieth century, horse racing was the most important sport in America, if measured in terms of number of spectators, bigger even than baseball.

Modern racing is not the simple challenge contest of three centuries ago. Today's racetrack brings together a veritable host of participants. The Thoroughbred horse that strides onto one of American's ninety or so racetracks (the number changes frequently) represents the efforts of hundreds of individuals, some of whom may have invested thousands or even millions of dollars in one animal: breeders, horse farm owners, veterinarians, farriers, trainers, grooms, and jockeys. Others manage the track itself: racing secretaries; jockey club directors; track management executives; and maintenance, concessions, and parking attendants. Still other businesses provide record-keeping and publishing functions (*The Daily Racing Form, The Blood Horse, The Thoroughbred Record,* etc.), horse transportation, computerized breeding consulting, and special feed supplies and tack. One company specializes in sewing the racing silks worn by jockeys during each race.

The modern American racetrack also represents another constituency, the tax collector. For several decades, legalized wagering at racetracks has been viewed as a major revenue source by state legislatures. Winnings, of course, are also subject to federal tax. Since the mid-1970s, several states that had not allowed racetrack betting have approved legislation that would encourage track construction to increase tax revenues. Finally, city boosters use horse races to encourage tourism and to foster a positive image, a process that might be called the "commodification of place" (Sack 1988, 642–64). Selling a place through sport has now been carried over into other sports through the construction of large stadiums and the recruitment of professional teams. In racing, this complicated drama is focused on the track, the key element in the complex racing landscape ensemble. This chapter will outline how the place of racing has evolved and how the actors and participants function in their roles to create the complex geography of Thoroughbred horse racing.

The racetrack's importance and the pageantry that attracts spectators might be lost on the person who has never attended a major stakes race at a picturesque track, someone who might only have glimpsed a race like the Kentucky Derby on television on an early May afternoon. For those attending in person, the spectacle of the track landscape ensemble comes to bear, producing a full, if not incomparable, sporting experience. Years of preparation by hundreds of unseen individuals are brought into focus in a two-minute race. No one has captured that experience more eloquently than Irvin S. Cobb, who described the Kentucky Derby of the 1930s:

> If you can imagine a track that's like a bracelet of molten gold
> encircling a green sward that's like a patch of emerald velvet.
> . . . All the pretty girls in the state turning the grandstand into a
> brocaded terrace of beauty and color such as the hanging gardens of Babylon never equaled. . . . All the assembled sports of

the nation going crazy at once down in the paddock . . . and just yonder in the yellow dust, the gallant kings and noble queens of the kingdom, the princesses royal, and their heirs apparent to the throne, fighting it out . . . each a vision of courage and heart and speed . . . each topped as though with some bobbing gay blossoms by a silken-clad jockey. . . . But what's the use? Until you go to Kentucky and with your own eyes behold the Derby, you ain't never been nowhere and you ain't never seen nothin! (Quoted in Chew 1974, 1)

Racing Tradition

America's early racing was based on an English prototype. In seventeenth-century England, the aristocracy controlled the best racing stock, and they laid out racecourses to suit their interests. All races were match races arranged for noblemen's horses. Since the public's interest was of no consequence, racing promoters laid out racecourses not with masses of spectators in mind but simply aligned with random fence lines and property boundaries. Even today, most English tracks are not compact symmetrical enclosed ovals but open, angular turf courses that follow natural topography up hill and down, with the horses in sight for only short distances near the finish line (Herbert 1980, 136). Under the English Stuarts, racing became the Sport of Kings. When the Stuarts' royal noblemen, the Cavaliers, fled Cromwell's influence for the colonies, they helped turn Maryland and Virginia into the "Cavalier Colonies." Here the Cavaliers implanted an aristocratic tradition that would provide America with racing horses and with a passion for turf sports (Hervey 1944, 1:15). From the beginning, riding, horsemanship, and racing were the most popular sports in Virginia. Skill in horsemanship was expected of every gentleman, and even the poorest planters took pride in their horses and their equestrian skills (Lucas and Smith 1978, 18).

The coastal colony settlements stayed where they were in part because the interior was heavily forested and could be cleared only through considerable effort and expense. The great cost of clearing land also prohibited the investment that would have been required to open an area of sufficient size to lay out a large oval racing path. Instead, seventeenth-century racing took place in old tobacco fields, along roads or streets, or on narrow paths hacked through the woods for the purpose. The typical track was a straight course, one-quarter mile in length. It might have been near a church or tavern, or other gathering place. It might have been only ten to twenty feet wide, just enough for two horses to sprint side by side over the irregular ground. An open space at each end of the track was large enough for the rider to wheel the horse around for a return dash to the beginning point (Carson 1965, 108).

The rigid social stratification established by the Tidewater squire-archy was reflected in the structure of racing. The Virginia courts prohibited racing by common laborers, maintaining the sport exclusively for gentlemen (Longrigg 1972, 105). When a match between well-known horses was arranged, large crowds gathered along the race path for a day's entertainment. Entrepreneurs and con men quickly learned that big profits could be made not by betting on the race but by supplying supplementary entertainment. These early race meetings usually consisted of only a race or two, and the cost of attending was substantial, owing to the time required to walk or ride in a carriage to the track. Reluctant to travel for hours simply to watch a quick race and then return home, people made the race into a day-long celebration. Near the starting point, cooks set up booths to sell food and drink. Peddlers hawked their wares. Itinerant healers and magicians entertained, fortunetellers plied their trade, freaks exhibited themselves, and sharps fleeced the innocent in shell and card games. It was like a one-day fair (Hervey 1944, 1:22). Travelers loved the drama of these events, and "quarter racing" became the most animated sport that one could hope to stumble upon (Carson 1965, 108). Quarter racing spread inland to Virginia's Southside, to Tennessee, and across the mountains to Kentucky. Eventually frontier folk carried it south into Arkansas and Texas, where it still survives on the southern plains.

In the North, Richard Nicholls, the first governor of New York after its capture from the Dutch, also personified the Cavalier tradition. He and several other Cavaliers had settled on Manhattan and Long Island, where they established horse racing in a way that would provide a model for contemporary American Thoroughbred racing. Anxious to avoid the inconvenience of racing in the streets, Nicholls "not only began what may be termed organized racing in America; he located it in the precise terrain that ever since has been its chief center and stronghold" (Hervey 1944, 1:6). On Long Island he found a natural prairie, sixteen miles long and two to four miles wide. This open grassland was nearly level and required little construction work. The site of his two-mile turf course was twenty miles from Manhattan in an area that was sparsely populated and difficult to reach. The country track location followed the English preference—it allowed gentlemen to practice their sport in isolation, a situation enforced by the place's inaccessibility to the lower classes.

By the eve of the American Revolution, most eastern cities south of Puritan New England had circular tracks of one mile or more and the older straight courses had largely fallen into disuse. Gambling and racing continued to identify one as gentry. A Virginian, for example, could gain honor and respect only by victories against peers, never by competing against inferiors. For the spectators, who included yeoman whites and slaves, horse racing among the gentry was high social drama. By promoting these popular public displays, the planters helped convince others that gentry culture was something to be esteemed and that therefore the gentry themselves were worthy to control political and economic life in the colonies (Rader 1983, 21).

The 1730s marked a new stage in Virginia racing. The northern mile-long oval track, where a field of horses would compete for a purse, became increasingly popular, while the short quarter-mile match race between two horses was run only infrequently, having moved on to the western frontier. Horses with Arabian blood had been imported into Virginia. This breed was not a sprinter but a distance runner, and heat races of two to four miles became the standard. This more formalized sport was financially supported by Tidewater plantation prosperity (Carson 1965, 118). Between 1730 and 1770, Americans imported about 175 stallions and mares from England, most went to Virginia. These blooded stock filled the paddocks of Tidewater stud farms, which clustered on the Rappahannock watershed, to form American's first race-horse region (Lucas and Smith 1978, 45).

During the early 1800s, the old grass courses were gradually replaced by the prepared track—a surface that had been skinned of sod and proved to be a faster running surface than turf. Americans were becoming more enamored with the phenomena of elapsed time and timed records. Satisfaction no longer lay in simply winning a race; now one hoped for a better time as well. Standardized race distances and fast track surfaces aided record-making performances. Breeders quickly discovered that record-holding colts were in keen demand as studs. The gentry began to lose their exclusive grip on racing as the increased purse awards to winners allowed trainers to recover some of their expenses and, increasingly, common people took up horse racing as a vocation.

To increase financial support for track maintenance and race purses, fences enclosed the new tracks, and owners charged admission for the first time (Adelman 1986, 39). Within the track enclosure, small grandstands, usually about seventy-five feet long and twenty feet deep, stood near the finish line. The roofed-over stand sheltered the women, who could attend at no charge, and their escorts, who were charged a small fee (Holliman 1931, 113). Temporary bleachers stood near the stands. The fashionable set usually avoided the stands, preferring to drive out to the track by coach and view the race from beside the new fence or rail that now enclosed the track. Gentlemen made a ritual of cantering out on their saddle horses to pay their respects to friends in the carriage rows. John Hervey regards this social display as an important reason why people enjoyed attending races. Management recognized this and made efforts to increase feminine attendance by adding conveniences and a social program. Track owners added lavishly decorated clubhouses to the stands, which often included dining rooms and ballrooms for the elite after the races were over (Hervey 1944, 1:248). Booths behind the stands sold sweets and liquor to the lower classes.

Racetrack form evolved during the first century and a half of American racing, responding to changes in land availability and racing stock's increasing prowess. As a sporting attraction that would appeal to spectators, the race was never a pure event. From the beginning, peripheral social activities attracted and entertained as much as the race itself. When the track was enclosed and began to take on its modern form, these activities attracted large numbers of spectators and soon were institutionalized by housing them in a formal structure, or providing an explicit place and opportunity for them to occur.

After 1800, racing continued to be dominated by a social elite, more businesslike but also more controversial. Advocates claimed that racing was a test that improved the breed, and was therefore utilitarian. By the 1820s, a few great runners had emerged, especially Henry and Eclipse, and when these horses were run against local stock, large crowds attended. Race promoters realized that when exceptional horses ran in well-publicized races, the sport would attract visitors who spent money not only at the track but in nearby hotels and restaurants as well (Adelman 1986, 39). Promoters also found that if they were to attract the best horses to their tracks and encourage public attendance, they needed to run more races. The typical meet was a four-mile heat matching two or more horses. After that heat was run, spectators went home. If races were shorter, horses could run more frequently. Experiments with longer race meetings—several races each day for a week or more— were successful at some northern tracks. Though the expense of traveling to the racetracks and paying admission was substantial, attendance grew as the number of races increased. With this new popularity came increasing concern that gambling was attracting a raffish following that had a corrupting influence on local morals. Some localities moved to ban racing for this reason, and during the period before the Civil War many tracks failed.

Despite the claim that racing improved the stock, breeding race-horses was not a systematic or sophisticated process (Hervey 1944, 2:324). Before 1829, the best Thoroughbreds were still being bred to common stock. Gradually, more blooded horses were imported from England; by the depression of 1837, owners were selectively breeding racing stock, asking higher stud fees, and producing colts and fillies that were competitive and exciting racers. Racing's focus continued to be urban in the North, where tracks were established primarily in the larger cities. Small towns and regional capitals became the racing centers in the South. Breeding stables were uncommon in the North, so southern horses from Virginia or Kentucky were frequently brought to northern tracks, especially in New York, where they ran match races against northern stock (Adelman 1986, 45). By the 1840s, racing's national core was centered in the South. Kentucky had become America's Thoroughbred nursery, while the best racing was reputedly found in New Orleans. Georgia had five racecourses, Louisiana and Mississippi each had eight, and Alabama ten. Kentucky had seventeen racecourses, more than Virginia, but the state was rural and poor compared with the South's cotton planters. This meant that Kentucky race purses were small, and the state's horsemen bred horses primarily for sale in other states (Longrigg 1972, 209). Racing in New Orleans was similar to that at many larger southern tracks. The Metarie Jockey Club charged a $2 daily admission, which assured that only the more affluent citizens or astute gamblers could attend. The grandstand segregated fans into three groups; male club members, women, and the public at large, who were seated in a less desirable section. Club members looked on racing as a pastime pursued by gentlemen for the enjoyment of gentlemen (Baker 1982, 178). The racetrack was one of the few places in a city that had more activity, more color and excitement, than the grand hotel. The sport was expensive and exclusive, but the welter of humanity milling about the saddling paddock, the betting ring, and the grandstand became as much an attraction as the races. By the turn of the century, "Racecourses [had come to] mean people—betting, shouting, chewing, spitting, drinking, forgetting, counting their money, cursing their wives. They come from every walk of life" (Herbert 1980, 135).

The Civil War was catastrophic for the South. The plantation system collapsed and with it the wealth that had fostered racing. The breeding areas of Kentucky and other states were pillaged of their foundation stock by marauding cavalries of both Union and Confederate armies. After the war, racing resumed in New York, where it was based on the new system that had been developed at the premier English tracks, Newmarket, Epson, and Ascot (Hervey 1944, 2:340). Southern heat racing had stressed stamina and endurance in horse breeding. The English had adopted shorter races, less than a mile, which demanded speed. Younger horses could manage the short courses, and racing two-year-olds became popular. Track managers in the north found that tracks could be profitable investments if they lowered admission prices and catered to the mass spectator audience. Racing as an exclusive pastime for the rich and well-bred was now on the wane (Baker 1982, 178).

In 1866, the first American bookmaker opened in Philadelphia, making book on cricket, rowing, and racing. This formal betting precedent was followed immediately at the country's racetracks. At first, bookmakers operated free of any regulations or fees. Gradually, track management saw an opportunity to increase profits, so they required the bookmaker to pay a franchise fee to the track for each day of racing. A common fee was $100 at the larger city tracks. If the track had fifty bookmakers, daily revenue would amount to $5,000, even though these professional gamblers might handle $1 million a day. English-style racing and betting opportunities fit together nicely. Short races meant more betting. Track managers conceived ways to increase the number of races and the length of race meetings. The handicap race, which attempted to equalize the competition between horses by requiring the horse with the best winning record to carry greater weight, was widely used. The claiming race, which featured horses that were for sale at a set or claiming price, eventually became the most common type of race at most tracks, and was intended to prevent owners of superior horses from consistently running and winning against slower animals. Regulation or oversight of track operations by local or state officials was often either inadequate or completely lacking. Dishonest trainers and jockeys responded to payoffs from bookmakers to throw races. The profits that accumulated from gate money, concessions, and fraudulent racing made tracks profitable, and investors built new tracks near the larger northern industrial cities to exploit the public. By the 1880s, dozens of tracks surrounded Columbus and Cincinnati, Ohio. Hundreds of tracks appeared across the Middle West from Ohio to Missouri. Competition was cutthroat. Profits attracted gangsters demanding payoffs and political graft (Longrigg 1972, 228–29).

A few wealthy investors who aspired to a clean sport in an attractive setting established tracks. Churchill Downs opened in Louisville in 1875, Washington Park in Chicago in 1884, and Belmont Park on Long Island in 1905. Here men made wealthy by the excesses of the Gilded Age represented a new industrial aristocracy. People like J. P. Morgan, W. V. Whitney, and August Belmont II established racetracks that succeeded in running clean operations while racketeers dominated many others (ibid., 227). Racing, tainted by corruption, spawned an alliance of antibetting and crime control forces in many states that, in turn, led to successful bans on racing. In 1897, there were 314 racetracks in America, but during the early 1900s, state after state banned racing. When New York banned racing in 1908, the total number of tracks across the country fell to twenty-five.[1] The demand for horses plummeted, and the value of blooded stock fell. Breeders tried to find markets for their horses in Canada and England, and many horse owners left the business or migrated abroad where racing continued.

Racing would not be revived until it was brought under strict regulatory control by state racing commissions and jockey clubs. To lift the ban, states would demand clean, fair racing and control of gambling —only then would voters allow a revival. Regulated betting was the key. Kentucky passed a law against bookmaking in 1908. To save the racing venue, Churchill Downs in Louisville instituted a betting system that had been developed in Paris, France. The Paris system prohibited bookmakers and let bettors set the odds by putting all the money bet on a given horse into a common pool. If that horse won, then bettors split the money bet on losing horses held in those pools. This system was called the Paris Mutuel Pool, or the pari-mutuels, and was eventually mechanized by a complex adding machine that recorded all bets and calculated payoffs based on the amounts in the pools. The track manager at Churchill Downs installed some old pari-mutuel machines in 1908. The results were so good that soon afterwards every track in the country adopted the system, and it became the only legal form of betting (Longrigg 1972, 230).

During the Roaring Twenties, racing made a successful comeback as several states repealed repressive legislation. The restoration was to create the racetrack geography that would be maintained into the 1990s. The renewed vigor of racing involved three fundamental processes that reinforced the pattern of track construction: the selective pattern of legislative repeal, the decentralization of urban tracks, and the establishment of tracks at places of opportunity. Southern states in the Bible Belt were loath to approve gambling at racetracks, although there had been a venerable tradition of racing in the region until the

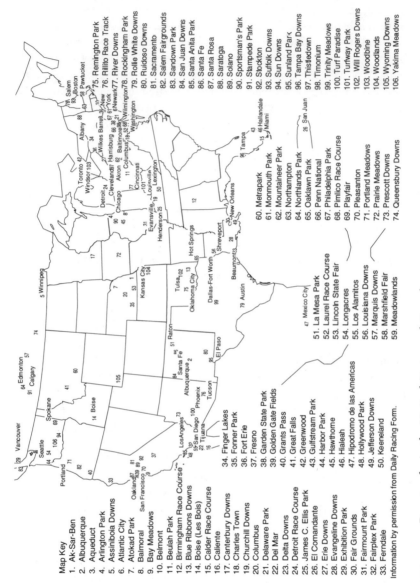

Map Key

1. Ak-Sar-Ben
2. Albuquerque
3. Aqueduct
4. Arlington Park
5. Assiniboia Downs
6. Atlantic City
7. Atokad Park
8. Balmoral
9. Bay Meadows
10. Belmont
11. Beulah Park
12. Birmingham Race Course
13. Blue Ribbons Downs
14. Boise (Les Bois)
15. Calder Race Course
16. Caliente
17. Canterbury Downs
18. Charles Town
19. Churchill Downs
20. Columbus
21. Delaware Park
22. Del Mar
23. Delta Downs
24. Detroit Race Course
25. James C. Ellis Park
26. El Comandante
27. Erie Downs
28. Evangeline Downs
29. Exhibition Park
30. Fair Grounds
31. Fairmount Park
32. Fairplex Park
33. Ferndale
34. Finger Lakes
35. Fonner Park
36. Fort Erie
37. Fresno
38. Garden State Park
39. Golden Gate Fields
40. Grants Pass
41. Great Falls
42. Greenwood
43. Gulfstream Park
44. Harbor Park
45. Hawthorne
46. Hialeah
47. Hipodromo de las Americas
48. Hollywood Park
49. Jefferson Downs
50. Keeneland
51. La Mesa Park
52. Laurel Race Course
53. Lincoln State Fair
54. Longacres
55. Los Alamitos
56. Louisiana Downs
57. Marquis Downs
58. Marshfield Fair
59. Meadowlands
60. Metrapark
61. Monmouth Park
62. Mountaineer Park
63. Northampton
64. Northlands Park
65. Oaklawn Park
66. Penn National
67. Philadelphia Park
68. Pimlico Race Course
69. Playfair
70. Pleasanton
71. Portland Meadows
72. Prairie Meadows
73. Prescott Downs
74. Queensbury Downs
75. Remington Park
76. Rillito Race Track
77. River Downs
78. Rockingham Park
79. Rolie White Downs
80. Ruidoso Downs
81. Sacramento
82. Salem Fairgrounds
83. Sandown Park
84. San Juan Downs
85. Santa Anita Park
86. Santa Fe
87. Santa Rosa
88. Saratoga
89. Solano
90. Sportsman's Park
91. Stampede Park
92. Stockton
93. Suffolk Downs
94. Sun Downs
95. Sunland Park
96. Tampa Bay Downs
97. Thistledown
98. Timonium
99. Trinity Meadows
100. Turf Paradise
101. Turfway Park
102. Will Rogers Downs
103. Woodbine
104. Woodlands
105. Wyoming Downs
106. Yakima Meadows

Information by permission from Daily Racing Form.

FIG. 11.1.1. Racetracks in the United States and Canada, 1993.

Civil War. New England and certain midwestern states also continued to prohibit racing. States with large metropolitan centers saw tax revenue potential; in several cases, investors reestablished racing at new tracks scattered throughout a metropolitan area or in small outlying cities. New York City had four tracks by 1929. Midsummer racing continued upstate at the old Saratoga track that had successfully maintained its aristocratic flavor while other tracks had succumbed to the criminal element and lower-class bettors. Chicago had the old Washington Park track; it added Lincoln Fields in 1926 and the spectacularly beautiful Arlington Park in 1927. In Florida, Hialeah opened in Miami in 1925; within a year, three more tracks had opened elsewhere in the state. Hialeah quickly became a favorite winter racing center for northern trainers and racegoers.

Some states continued to resist approving proracing legislation. This often had the effect of stimulating track construction in an adjoining state to take advantage of a large metropolitan market near a state boundary. This happened in Missouri, where the legislature refused to restore racing. In 1925, investors built an "opportunity track" just across the Mississippi from Saint Louis in East Saint Louis, Illinois. Although the track failed through mismanagement, it demonstrated the possibility of building opportunity tracks near other cities where racing was illegal (Hervey 1937, 65).

The Great Depression had a curious effect on the racing industry. Discretionary spending for recreation was usually the first place expenses could be reduced during a severe economic downturn. Previous panics had meant racetrack failures and a sharply reduced demand for horses. That process was initiated again in the 1930s. Track attendance fell, racing purses went down, and breeders saw the prices of yearlings decline. Yet, the Depression's net impact was positive for a very compelling reason. State governments had discovered that strictly controlled and well-managed racetracks could be taxed to supply desperately needed revenues. Many states repealed their race-prohibiting legislation, created state commissions to supervise racing, and set about mining the pari-mutuels to supplement their budgets (Hervey 1937, 142). By 1933, ten states (California, Michigan, New Hampshire, New Mexico, North Carolina, Ohio, Oregon, Texas, Washington, and West Virginia) had approved racing (Longrigg 1972, 282). With a few exceptions, these states would add to a basic geographic pattern that would hold until the 1980s, when federal payments to state governments were cut back, again motivating governors to look at racing as a potential tax revenue source (fig. 11.1).

Modern Thoroughbred Racing

The Horse

The racetrack's allure now, as in the past, lies in the speed, endurance, and beauty of the horses that run—Thoroughbreds. Consistently reproducing these qualities is a risky and expensive proposition that requires close attention to bloodlines. It is likely that in no other animal, sporting or domestic, has genetic heritage and performance been so closely observed for so long. The bloodlines of all Thoroughbreds running today can be traced back through studbook registrations to the racing stock favored by the royalty of seventeenth-century England. Although there were different strains, many of these racers were small Galloway ponies. During the latter part of the seventeenth century, royal horsemen began to import Arabian stock to cross with the traditional English strains. English breeders imported horses from southwest Asia and North Africa (Arabians and Barbs) and from Turkey, which became the foundation stock for modern Thoroughbreds.

The three founding sires of the line are generally thought to be the Byerley Turk (born about 1680), the Darley Arabian (1700), and the Godolphin Arabian (1724) (Herbert 1980, 13). The *General Stud Book*, the Thoroughbred bloodline record, was first published in 1793. This record is still kept and is a part of the detailed statistics kept on all Thoroughbreds. Breeders consult the *Stud Book* or the *Jockey Club Register* to trace bloodlines as they pursue the ideal combination of sire and dam in the search for the genetic combination that could produce a winning offspring. Owners, trainers, and bettors study the racing records published in the *Daily Racing Form* and the *American Racing Manual* to judge the performance of horses under differing track conditions, race distances, and handicap weights.

While many racing fans may spend a day at the track with only a program to guide their betting choices, the knowledgeable race handicapper will invest hours in studying the *Racing Form* before arriving at trackside. Attention to past performance and bloodlines, then, is part of the fan's "racetrack experience." Those who are essentially oblivious to horse performance history are likely to be satisfied with a racing day marked by good food and drink, the color and pageantry of horses, jockeys, and gaily dressed crowds, and the pleasing vistas of track landscaping. Serious bettors, on the other hand, may never sit in the grandstand but may shuttle from the saddling paddock, where they inspect the horses' condition before the race, to a television monitor, where they watch the action.

The concern for records and statistics continues beyond the horse's retirement from racing. Those horses that were consistent winners during their racing years often become broodmares and breeding stallions. A horse's value is then predicated on the number of stakes races won and total earnings during a racing career. Horses that have won major stakes races like the Kentucky Derby (Churchill Downs), Preakness (Pimlico), or Belmont Stakes (Belmont Park), which together comprise the Triple Crown races, are especially valued because these races are regarded as the premier tests for three-year-olds and so attract the best competition. The conventional wisdom in breeding has usually been that champions produce champions. Horse breeders, then, are keenly interested in mating only the best possible stallions to superior mares. This means that breeding farms focus on the geography of Thoroughbred genes. The best mares are brought to the top stallions. This process is more efficient—that is, transportation and insurance costs are lower—if the stallions and mares are kept in proximity. This need for convenience in the breeding cycle has reinforced horse farm clusters such as the one in central Florida near Ocala, or at Lexington, Kentucky, where one finds the largest concentration of horse farms in the United States.

American horse owners have long sought to improve their Thoroughbred's winning percentage by importing champion racing stock from England and France. In 1925, Claiborne Farm in Bourbon County, Kentucky, imported a French colt, Sir Galahad III, who represented the very best of European racing stock. His success at stud was immediate and sustained. His first crop of offspring included Gallant Fox, Triple Crown winner in 1930. Sir Galahad III went on to lead American's general sire list four times and to rank at the top of the list of broodmare sires for a record twelve years (Hollingsworth 1976, 138).

Each year, more than thirty thousand Thoroughbreds are foaled in the United States. During the late 1970s and early 1980s, rapidly increasing prices for racing and breeding stock encouraged breeders to produce more yearlings. The upshot was a surfeit of horses. Prices declined sharply. The recession that began in the late 1980s had a wrenching effect on breeders because profit often lies not in racing but in breeding. Only a quarter of the foals born in a given year will eventually win enough races to pay for their stud fees, training, transportation, and feed, and only two or three percent will win $100,000 or more. (Keep in mind that the costs of maintaining a racing Thoroughbred will be at least $25,000 per year.) This means that many horses run in claiming races (i.e., horses entered are subject to purchase, or "claimed," for a set price), or at tracks that can offer only small purses, until they are seven to nine years old. Therefore, the majority of Thoroughbred owners lose money on their horses. Some may be satisfied with the glamour of ownership; others can deduct expenses from their taxes. Nevertheless, each year brings a substantial turnover in horse owners. Many Thoroughbreds never make it to the track but are trained for steeplechasing, fox hunting, show jumping, dressage, or polo.

Trainers and Jockeys

Horse racing is a very complex sport: it involves many different historic, economic, cultural, and technical facets that exhibit different yet interrelated geographies. I have briefly examined one geography, the origin and diffusion of racing over time. Another is the seasonal movement of horses, trainers, jockeys, and support personnel from track to track as they follow a circuit prescribed by seasonal change and track racing schedules. A third is the variation in training techniques from place to place, differences that may correspond to tradition, to changes in physical environment, to preferences of horse owners, to track operating schedules, and to many other factors.

In England, horses are trained in three main training areas; New Market, Yorkshire, and the downlands west and south of London. Horses are galloped on grass across rolling hills, on the theory that running on sod uphill will result in better conditioning (Herbert 1980, 62). In America, horses train on dirt racetracks or on specially constructed training tracks where the surface is carefully prepared to imitate the racing track. Many horses train at the larger racetracks such as Belmont (New York), Churchill Downs (Kentucky), and Santa Anita (California). Such tracks may have stall space to house up to two thousand horses at a time. Horses are also broken and trained on farms where they have been foaled and raised, as in the central Kentucky Bluegrass Region around Lexington, or near Ocala, Florida; Middleburg, Virginia; or Aiken, South Carolina. Some farms specialize in training instead of breeding and racing. Successful trainers may own farms that they use as a base of operations. Often these farms are near racetracks or are found scattered across the South to take advantage of warm winter weather in training or rehabilitating horses. Some trainers, for example, may winter in Miami, near the Hialeah track. Others might prefer Aiken.[2]

The rationale for choosing a training site is more complex than warm winters. Private trainers, those who work exclusively for one owner, may receive an annual salary (some may make $250,000 per year, or more), a percentage of the horses' winnings, and living quarters on the owner's farm or at the owner's training facility, which may be associated with a large racetrack (*Louisville Courier-Journal*, December 1, 1985, 20). Public trainers, those who train horses under contract with several owners, receive a percentage of the purses won and are usually free to choose the location of their operations. This group may be attracted to a region where many horse owners live and may build their training facility near a large metropolitan center. Others may not wish to move from one track to another and will choose to train at a track that has a year-round training and racing schedule. Trainers may seek out the very best support facilities and services they can find and establish operations there. This is a major reason why so many trainers have farms near Lexington, Kentucky. Here is the largest number of equine veterinarians in the country. Here also are farriers, bloodstock agents, horse auction agencies, horse insurance firms, boarding farms, feed suppliers, and even businesses that specialize in equine whirlpool hydrotherapy or electronic rehabilitation therapy (*Blood Horse* 1993).

By the mid-1980s, twenty-two states were conducting racing incentive programs. The idea was to enhance tax revenues from racing by trying to break the traditional orientation of breeders and trainers to a few states like Kentucky, California, and Florida. Other states extended their racing dates so that racing was possible all year. These states then offered incentives to breeders and owners to relocate by giving awards to breeders of successful horses bred in the state, awards to owners of successful state-breds, and purses for races restricted to state-breds (Lohman and Kirkpatrick 1984, 168). The state incentive programs also had the effect of attracting trainers who, to comply with the programs, redirected much of their training effort toward racing only in that host state.

Trainers have varied responsibilities. They often help owners decide which horses to buy and may actively participate at auctions. When a trainer takes possession of a horse, the animal's well-being and physical conditioning is his or her responsibility. Grooms and exercise riders must be supervised. Farriers and veterinarians must be summoned at the right time. Above all, the trainer must learn the physical limitations and psychological foibles of each horse and handle each as an individual. Trainers are also healers, having learned early the appropriate techniques for rehabilitating sore horses. A trainer must assess the ability and progress of the stock and make race entry recommendations to the owner. On race day, trainers saddle their horses and direct the jockeys in a race strategy that best fits each horse's disposition and would therefore result in a win.

These varied tasks and responsibilities require knowledge that is taught at no college or technical school. It is learned on the job, often through a long apprenticeship as groom, exercise rider, jockey, or assistant to a trainer. Where, then, do trainers come from? Frequently they are born into the business (Bolus 1984, 101). Parents may have owned or trained horses or may have worked the track circuit. Because of the knowledge and experience required, it is not often that a person can enter this world as a callow outsider and soon become a competitive trainer. Therefore, the geography of trainer origins is likely to be similar to the geography of racetracks and horse farms.

Jockeys, like trainers, must accumulate a considerable body of knowledge and experience with horses before they become competitive on the track. Besides the special physical requirements—exceptional athletic ability and weight of about 100 pounds or less—the jockey must be a student of horse psychology and behavior. Once the young jockey has apprenticed with a trainer, learning the basics of equine management, he or she may hire an agent who will arrange mounts for a percentage of the jockey's income. The agent's fee is usually 10 percent of the winning purse. The typical jockey does not travel a great deal but will remain in one area and ride horses on several tracks within an urban area, such as Los Angeles. The most skilled jockeys are much more mobile because they are in high demand as stakes race riders; they may travel extensively. Their movements closely mirror the schedule of major stakes on the racing calendar, and they may regularly move from one region to another, from coast to coast, or, occasionally, internationally (Herbert 1980, 84).

The Racing Circuit

The racing tradition that grew out of the post–Civil War period involved moving horses from southern tracks in the winter and early spring months to northern tracks in the summer, then back south in the fall in an annual cycle. The expanding national railway system allowed trainers to ship horses hundreds of miles in a few days. Wealthy owners could follow the same circuit, often in their private railroad cars, at their leisure. Race meetings at some tracks were only a few weeks long. Other tracks, especially those near large cities, had longer seasons. Trainers might spend December and January in Louisiana at the Fair Grounds track (New Orleans) or in Florida at Gulfstream Park (Hallan-

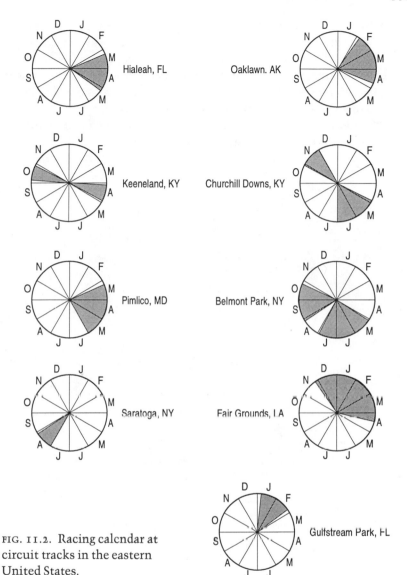

FIG. 11.2. Racing calendar at circuit tracks in the eastern United States.

dale) (fig. 11.2). They might then move on to Hialeah (Miami) for the March and April season there or to Oaklawn Park (Hot Springs, Arkansas), where the season ends in mid-April. From there one might take horses to Keeneland (Lexington), Churchill Downs (Louisville), and Belmont Park (Jamaica, New York), in turn. In August, the equine entourage might repair to Saratoga (New York). Then one could return south by way of Belmont (for the fall season), Pimlico (Baltimore), Keeneland, and Churchill Downs. Each year the circuit is repeated.

As racing seasons became longer, trainers would remain at tracks longer, reducing travel stress on their stock. Many trainers never moved their operations out of state. Some state racing commissions scheduled racing dates almost year-round (figs. 11.3, 11.4). Trainers with mediocre horses could run them in claiming races in California, for example, all year. Since racetracks cannot afford to pay out large sums for frequent

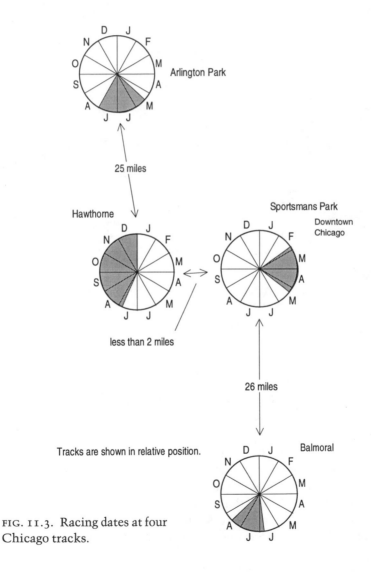

FIG. 11.3. Racing dates at four Chicago tracks.

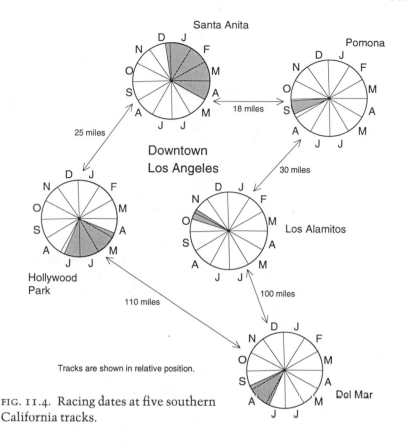

FIG. 11.4. Racing dates at five southern
California tracks.

stakes race purses, most races are for claiming horses. In fact, about 70
percent of all races run in American are claiming races, but they account for only 45 percent of the total purse money. Stakes races, on the
other hand, make up only 3.5 percent of all races but garner 21 percent
of the purse money (Lohman and Kirkpatrick, 1984, 45). A trainer
following such a circuit might start the year at Santa Anita (Arcadia,
California). He or she could then move to Hollywood Park (Inglewood)
some twenty-five miles west. When that season ended in July, the
trainer's string might move to Del Mar, just north of San Diego, then on
to Pomona, and finally, in October, end the season at Los Alamitos.
Except for Del Mar, which is about 110 miles south of Hollywood Park,
these "urban halo" tracks are not much more than twenty to thirty
miles apart. Trainers who favored New York, Baltimore, Philadelphia,
San Francisco, or Chicago could follow a similar circuit.

In northern Illinois, racing is not an appropriate wintertime sport.

Trainers might prefer to winter in the south and then bring their horses into the Chicago halo track circuit in March when the season begins at Sportsmans Park (Cicero) (see fig. 11.3). The circuit would then move some twenty-five miles north to Arlington Park (Arlington Heights), for about forty-five days of midsummer racing. Then trainers could go on to either Balmoral (Crete) or Hawthorne (back to Cicero, a few blocks from Sportsmans Park). It is commonplace for Thoroughbreds following such a circuit to race fifteen or twenty times each year.

The most competitive horses in the nation are prepared for the national stakes race circuit by a small group of highly successful trainers. These horses, only a few dozen out of the thirty thousand that might be racing during a given year, are shipped from one track to another, following the calendar of major stakes that may lead to the Triple Crown series or to the Breeders Cup races, where winning one race could secure a purse of $3 million. The trainers who guide the development of these horses may also have several less-capable horses that will follow a south-to-north circuit or a narrower urban halo circuit. But the trainer will make the requisite trips to the stakes races to accompany the quality horse and direct its training and care.

Breeders and Owners

A diverse group of breeders and owners supplies horses to the racing industry. These labels mask an exceedingly complex interlayering of individuals who comprise the links between racing, business, industry, and farming. Some individuals specialize in breeding horses to be sold on the auction market. Others own racehorses but do not engage in breeding. Some do both. Nationally, horse breeders might be small-scale operators with a farm that produces some type of agricultural commodity. These people might have only a broodmare or two, and they depend on other farm livestock and crops for income. Because their operations tend to be small and self-financed, these breeders usually do not produce horses that are competitive in the major stakes racing circuit. Instead, they supply horses that run on the "minor-league" tracks or, as some term them, the "bush tracks."

At the opposite end of this breeder's spectrum are some of the world's wealthiest individuals who traffic in horses worth millions each. This upper echelon of breeders and owners has a major impact on the landscapes their operations inhabit. During the past century, the elite breeding farm has evolved, complete with signature white plank fences and Palladian-windowed barns; it exudes wealth and success. A proper Thoroughbred is the royalty of farm livestock and must be cared for on a proper farm. Breeding these exquisite animals is an unlikely agricultural pursuit—equiculture would be a better term. The Thoroughbred farm is often an elaborate nursery that is to the commonplace crop and livestock farm what a Georgian mansion is to a log cabin. This scale of Thoroughbred breeding is to be found clustered in only a few favored places: northern Virginia and adjacent counties in Maryland; central Florida near Ocala; and the Kentucky Bluegrass. To be sure, important stud and broodmare farms are found in other states, but they are few and are usually scattered, not concentrated. East Texas and southern California are examples. Some breeding farms are near racetracks that are used for training.

There is a considerable disadvantage in establishing a breeding operation outside an established cluster such as the Kentucky Bluegrass. Stakes-winning stallions are very expensive to purchase, insure, and maintain. Most farms will not own a stallion but will breed their mares to champion stallions housed on stud farms. This means that during the spring breeding season (February through June), as mares come into season they must be quickly transported by van to the stud farm to be bred. The breeding process may take less than an hour, after which the mare is vanned back to her home farm. If a breeding farm lies some distance from the stallion's farm, the inconvenience and expense of transportation can become prohibitive for a large breeding operation. Thus, the breeder's dependence upon the Thoroughbred gene pool encourages farms to cluster together. Other factors also influence breeding farm location. In Virginia and Maryland, farms may lie close enough to large East Coast cities so that wealthy urban owners can visit frequently and follow their stock's progress. Farms in Ocala, Florida, have the advantage of warm winter weather. In Kentucky's Bluegrass the advantages include tradition, salubrious climate, fertile limestone soils under bluegrass pastures, and an elaborate equine support industry that includes expertise in almost every aspect of the horse business. Here horse breeders can call upon horse transport services, including companies that ship horses in elaborately outfitted trucks and companies that specialize in air transport to Europe or Asia.

The typical Bluegrass horse farm is not large. It might have 160 acres, primarily in pasture. Seven full-time employees will care for about thirty horses. The farm is owned by two people in partnership. Each year, the farm boards horses owned by others to help defray expenses and produces about half a dozen Kentucky-bred foals. Expenses for an operation of this size approach $140,000. Labor is the major cost, but this type of farm typically spends $15,600 for feed and bedding, $3,000 for tack and supplies, and $30,000 in stud fees. Additional costs might include some $10,000 for veterinary and blacksmith services (Kentucky Thoroughbred Association 1984, 3). It is difficult to know exactly how many horse farms operate in Kentucky, but the core of active breeding and boarding farms probably numbers no more than three hundred.

Farm owners are a diverse group. Some are third- or fourth-generation farmers whose great-grandparents helped establish the Thoroughbred business in Kentucky during the late 1800s. Their heritage may even extend back to the original land-grant patent holders. Others are the children or grandchildren of successful local business people whose stake comes from whiskey distilling or tobacco marketing. A second group is made up of individuals whose family fortunes were made in industry over the past century: oil, rubber, transportation, mining, real estate, even dog food. A third group has come into the business more recently. Their financial backing may come from Japanese industry, Arab oil, English lotteries, or American business. Money flows from around the globe to buy land and blooded stock in an interlocking international racing industry that links France, England, Ireland, Canada, Australia, and Japan to American breeders.

The farms of the very rich are often much larger than the typical farm described above. These properties may range in size from three hundred acres to over five thousand. Miles of white or black plank fencing enclose the farms, their landscape accentuated by a dozen or more colorful barns, tree-lined lanes, and perhaps a large antebellum home with Greek Revival pediment and columns at the front. Some old farms feature century-old rock fences. Other farms, newly constructed, may employ a team of stonemasons full time to build limestone fences. This aesthetic sense is often carried into the horse barns, which may be oak-paneled and fitted with brass or stainless steel hinges, locks, and other hardware. Million-dollar horses require constant care. Farm employees are aided by fire monitoring and extinguishing systems, and most farms are closed to casual tourists to help reduce insurance rates. None of these fixtures are needed to raise horses, but farm owners seem convinced that the reputation of the farm lies in more than the racing prowess of their horses. It is much easier to sell expensive horses to wealthy owners if the farm is a showplace, other things being equal.

Aesthetically pleasing horse farms have benefits that extend beyond property boundaries. Tourists find the Bluegrass landscape picturesque, if not stunning. Each spring, usually during the Keeneland racing season when the dogwoods and redbuds are in bloom, the country lanes crawl with out-of-state cars as people revel in the scenery. Local hotels, restaurants, and other services all profit, and the tourist dollar turns over within the community. For local residents, the net effect of the horse farm landscape is a salutary one. This extensive green space, threaded by narrow shaded lanes and rock fences and punctuated by wooded pastures and beautiful buildings, is essentially a large park. The residents of Lexington, the city central to the region, recognize that theirs may be the only city in America located in a park. Preservationists agonize over every acre of land lost to subdivisions, malls, and new highways.

Horse owners are often breeders or trainers. Many owners do not own a single acre of farm property. Farm and horse ownership has many forms. The family stable is perhaps the most common type of ownership, and the most prominent on the landscape. Wealthy individuals may establish a private racing stable that includes a farm with a complete complement of facilities, a string of broodmares, perhaps a stallion or two, and horses of various ages in training or following a racing circuit. These owners can afford the best bloodstock and usually are very competitive at stakes races. Television commentators and journalists seek out these owners for interviews or feature stories when they win major stakes races.

The commercial stable is a second ownership form. Again, an individual may establish a farm as a training center (and may include a breeding operation as well) and purchase horses for racing. The commercial stable may attempt to reduce costs by boarding horses for others. The fee for boarding a horse may vary from $5,000 to $7,000 per year or more depending on the type of animal and its dietary and security requirements. The large commercial stable also may include a breeding operation. These stables may house several stallions and dozens or even hundreds of broodmares. Some farms may have ten stallions or more. In Kentucky, for example, twenty-five farms held 87 percent (or 747) of the Thoroughbred stallions recorded in the state during the mid-1980s (Kentucky Thoroughbred Association 1984, 3). Many specialized commercial horse farms house champion stallions, those who have won major stakes races and whose progeny are proving to be winners as well. In the 1960s, such coveted horses began selling for prices that were too high for any but the world's wealthiest to afford.

The solution to the extraordinary cost of breeding stallions was syndication. The procedure had been in use for some time and was used increasingly during the 1940s. In 1949, for example, a Kentucky farm bought the English horse Nasrullah for $340,000. The horse was syndicated into thirty-two shares of ownership, meaning that thirty-two shares at $10,625 each were sold to individuals. In effect, the horse had thirty-two owners. Typically syndicates are closed, meaning that each share owner holds the right to breed one mare to the stallion each year, but no one else can obtain access to the stallion without making special arrangements (Hollingsworth 1976, 143). In 1973, the Horse of the Year, Secretariat, was sold to a syndicate through twenty-eight shares of $190,000 each, totaling $5,320,000 (156).

Through the 1970s and early 1980s, the auction prices for high-quality Thoroughbred stock rose dramatically. Individuals who held breeding shares in the best stallions found a ready market for their breeding seasons. Entrepreneurs started new businesses using computers to match bids by interested breeders to the owners of stallion shares. By 1985, the bids for a breeding season (the term for mating one mare to a stallion) to Northern Dancer had reached $950,000. The Northern Dancer bloodline has produced a consistent record of winning major stakes races and so is highly regarded. Other promising sires commanded astronomical stud fees: Seattle Slew, $750,000; Alydar, $450,000; Nijinsky II, $400,000. The hope of quick profit brought new owners into the Thoroughbred market through limited partnerships, not unlike those designed to buy and hold real estate. Banks and brokerage houses organized horse purchases, usually breeding stock, and sold shares to investors for $10,000 to $50,000 each. The horses were managed by commercial farms, and the partnership managers charged the investors fees for coordinating the horse's activities. This technique gave many investors a part ownership in a Thoroughbred, dispersing, to some extent, the ownership pattern that had been dominated by the very rich. By the late 1980s, the market for Thoroughbreds was saturated. Buyers, reluctant to pay astronomical prices for stud fees or for yearlings, withdrew from the sport. The business went into a deep recession and did not begin to recover until the early 1990s.

Other ownership types have been engaged in the Thoroughbred racing and breeding business for some time. Only a small minority of the horses that race each year are consistent winners and of value as breeding stock. These horses are often owned by trainers looking for the elusive animal that will prove successful. Others are owned by doctors, attorneys, investment bankers, businessmen, or small-scale industrialists whose income is sufficient to afford the price required to board a horse, hire a trainer, and pay all other health, blacksmith, transport, entrance, and jockey fees. The return is often little more than a few small purses. It is the excitement of competition that apparently makes it worthwhile (Collier n.d., 18). Perhaps part of the attraction of owning a racehorse lies in the perception of oneself as part of the elite Thoroughbred culture and chatting about being "in the horse business" at cocktail parties.

The Race Fan

Who are the racetrack patrons? These, after all, are the people whose entrance fees and betting money provide track profits, taxes for state treasuries, and purse money for horse owners. Historically, racing attracted enthusiastic spectators from many social groups, although early racing at formal tracks was often reserved for the wealthy. Today, a trip to any racetrack will turn up a widely varied crowd. Some are serious gamblers who follow the horses from one track to another. Others may visit only one day a year and will spend more in the restaurant or bar than at the betting window. Racetracks are popular with groups who reserve blocks of seats and travel together in chartered buses. Most races are mundane affairs. The large stakes races at major tracks are another matter. It is the stakes race that seems to attract the largest following, perhaps because the fans are swept up by the hyperbole generated by advertising and marketing consultants hired by the track. Whatever the reason, at the stakes race one finds the greatest diversity of social and economic status among the fans. Joe Murray, journalist with the *Los Angeles Times*, describes the scene at the Kentucky Derby, which is run each year on the first Saturday in May:

> Derby Day is like no other day in American sports. For 23 hours and 58 minutes, it is as noisy as a Saturday night in Italy. It is people drinking booze with weeds in it [mint juleps], it is rich men pouring off private planes and poor guys dropping off freights. It is dames who never saw a horse race before in their lives and dames who have lugged the rent money into the track or to the bookie for so many years they have to shoplift to stay even. It is college kids on a beer lark and bankers sipping martinis in the Matt Winn room. It is hot pants and Salvation Army lasses, guys with holes in their shoes and guys who need a tailor to make their clothes and a valet help put them on. It is Gaudy Saturday, as American as Stephen Foster, stud poker, and the girlie show. (Quoted in Peirce 1975, 255)

The Racetrack

Preparing a Thoroughbred for racing competition involves a long chain of processes and many individuals who collectively point the horse toward the objective, the racetrack. The track is one of those special places in society where different social and economic classes come together and interact. The phrase "circle of friends" describes in a cryptic way the kind of social interaction patterns most individuals pursue. A person's social group usually includes family and friends from work, church, or private club. It is unusual for people to socialize regularly with individuals with whom they have little in common. We lead lives that are socially closed to outsiders that we do not know and probably will never meet. Only a few places in our society provide a context for meeting and interacting with people of other social or economic groups. An old-fashioned public market is one. The shopping mall and truck stop may be other examples. The racetrack is such a place. At the track people from across society's spectrum come together. Of course, segregation will separate the elite in the clubhouse from the railside denizens who rode a bus to the track—more on this later. Yet these people will see one another, perhaps exchange pleasantries, and be aware of the other's presence. To this social diversity in the grandstand we may add the professionals who provided and prepared the horses, and the result is a sporting milieu that is diverse and stimulating and an integral part of the racing experience.

Just as there are differences among owners, breeders, and trainers, there are also substantial differences between racetracks. To experience one is not to have experienced them all. Some differences are a matter of management style; others are visual and aesthetic. Many older tracks have attractive grandstands and paddocks with mature trees. The stands at some new tracks suggest postmodern glass cubes. Some tracks are owned by individuals or small groups of investors who run the track as a business. Others, such as Arlington Park in Chicago, are owned by large corporations. Some twenty-seven states now have Thoroughbred racing, and in elections held in the 1980s, referendums on legalized parimutuel betting appeared on the ballot in several other states. In each state, racing and wagering are administered by a state racing commission. It is the commission that assigns racing dates to each track in the state. The southeastern Bible Belt has traditionally shunned racing, but the industrial North has embraced it. Except for Indiana, racetracks operate throughout the manufacturing belt from Illinois east to Massachusetts. Other regions that one does not usually associate with Thoroughbred racing, such as the northern Rocky Mountain states and the Pacific Northwest, have active racing programs.

Building a racetrack is not as simple as finding a large tract of cheap land and hiring a construction company. Track location is contingent

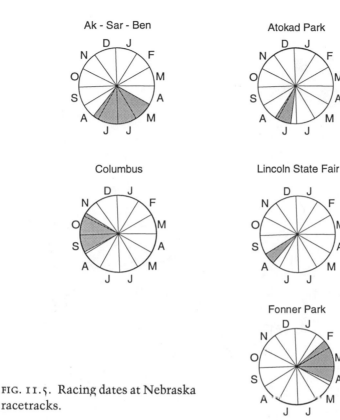

FIG. II.5. Racing dates at Nebraska racetracks.

upon several factors. I have already noted the difference between circuit tracks and urban halo tracks. In part because of state incentive programs, racing circuits have begun to develop within some states. This is also a by-product of state interest in increasing tax revenues from racing. An example is Nebraska (fig. 11.5). The Nebraska state racing commission has allotted racing dates so trainers can take their horses from one track to another without leaving the state. The schedule begins in mid-February at Fonner Park and ends at another track in mid-November (Daily Racing Form 1993, 229–33). Each track is in the eastern part of the state, which is also the most populated half. Further, both Ak-Sar-Ben (Nebraska spelled backward), the track in Omaha, and Atokad Park are near enough to the Nebraska-Iowa border so that patrons might be attracted from the neighboring state and, incidentally, would contribute tax monies to the Nebraska treasury. Nebraska has a 2 percent pari-mutuel betting tax. Other "outtake" monies go for purses (2 percent) and track profit (2 percent). These expenses are withdrawn

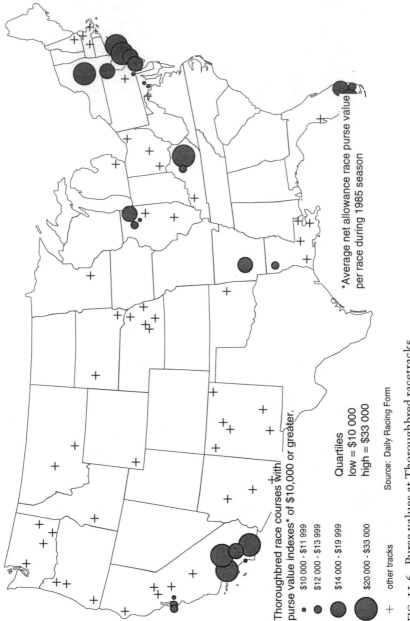

Thoroughbred race courses with
purse value indexes* of $10,000 or greater.

$10 000 - $11 999
$12 000 - $13 999
$14 000 - $19 999
$20 000 - $33 000

+ other tracks

Quartiles
low = $10 000
high = $33 000

Source: Daily Racing Form

*Average net allowance race purse value
per race during 1985 season

FIG. 11.6. Purse values at Thoroughbred racetracks.

from the wagering pool before bettors can collect on their winning tickets (Nelson 1967).

Increasingly, states are looking for additional revenue sources—and often, pari-mutuel betting and racing have been approved with the explicit goal of generating state income. The track geography that results is illuminating. In states with legalized betting, track investors will seek out the largest concentrated urban market and build their track nearby (Totty 1988, 23). Some states may not have a large metropolitan center from which to draw race fans and bettors. Here the idea is to build tracks of opportunity. This type of track is placed close to a population center in an adjoining state in the hope that fans will be willing to cross a state boundary to gamble. This strategy has worked for Nevada casinos for decades. Examples of opportunity tracks can be found in several states (see fig. 11.1). Delta Downs, Louisiana, is between Lake Charles, Louisiana, and Beaumont, Texas, and just over 100 miles from Houston. Fairmont Park, Illinois, is ten miles east of Saint Louis, Missouri. Racetrack wagering was illegal in Texas until 1990. In West Virginia, track owners have taken advantage of the state's two attenuated panhandles to build tracks near urban centers in adjoining states. The Charles Town track is only forty miles from Washington, D.C. In the northern panhandle, Mountaineer Park is forty-three miles from Pittsburgh, Pennsylvania. This track is also only a short drive from Youngstown, Ohio, and about forty miles from Wheeling, West Virginia. These two tracks offer racing almost year-round. Clearly, they do not constitute a circuit within the state but are parasitic to population centers in adjoining states.

Horse people recognize that there is a distinct difference between racetracks. This differentiation is based in part upon the facilities—training tracks, the quality of the track surface, and the quality of stalls and barns. Tracks also can be differentiated according to purse size (Chamblin 1986, 2640). Many tracks do not have the income to pay competitive purses, and, although they may sponsor stakes races, the purse money is not on a par with other tracks (fig. 11.6). The average net allowance race purse value for each racecourse is variable and suggests that the tracks with the lowest purse values would be the least competitive in attracting high quality horses and would more be likely to be part of a local state racing circuit or an opportunity track. In New York, for example, Aqueduct, Belmont, and Saratoga all have purse value indexes of well above ten (meaning that the average purse value for allowance races is $10,000 or more). On the other hand, none of the tracks in Ohio or the western states (outside California) have purse values of ten. It is extremely unlikely that a horse capable of winning a major stakes race would run at these tracks. Instead, these minor league tracks cater to state-bred horses and trainers that either stay at one track year-round or follow a state track circuit.

The Racetrack as Theater

The racetrack is not simply a rude collection of functional buildings. American track design follows certain conventions established over the past century or more, and designers give careful consideration to aesthetics (figs. 11.7, 11.8, 11.9). Most American tracks are oval, unlike English tracks that follow the odd geometries of topography and property boundaries. Some American tracks have both dirt and turf courses, one positioned inside the other. Tracks often have run-in chutes that allow track managers to vary race lengths. At Del Mar, near San Diego, the dirt track is a one-mile oval. A chute extension on the main stretch in front of the grandstand allows one-and-one-quarter-mile races.

Some tracks may have small lakes in the infield, and most are distinctively landscaped. The view from the grandstand is clearly intended

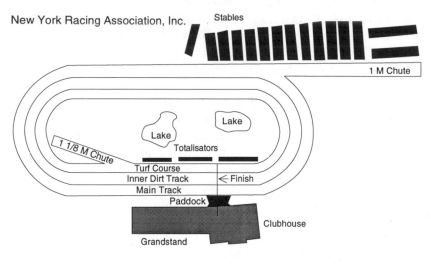

County - Queens. State - New York.
Twelve miles from Manhattan;
　　five miles from Kennedy International Airport;
　　twelve miles from LaGuardia Airport.
Main track - One and one-eigth miles, oval.

FIG. 11.7. Aqueduct.　Inner track - One mile, oval.

Del Mar Thoroughbred Club

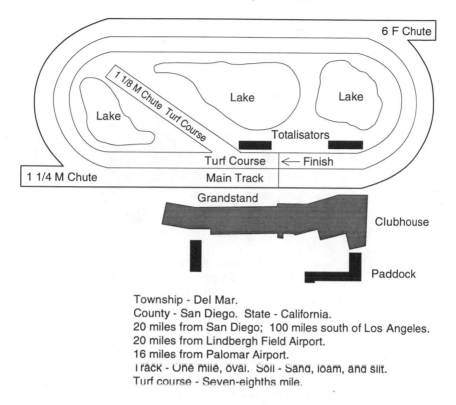

Township - Del Mar.
County - San Diego. State - California.
20 miles from San Diego; 100 miles south of Los Angeles.
20 miles from Lindbergh Field Airport.
16 miles from Palomar Airport.
Track - One mile, oval. Soil - Sand, loam, and silt.
Turf course - Seven-eighths mile.

FIG. 11.8. Del Mar.

to be more than the track surface and the totalizator, or "toteboard," that displays odds, pool amounts, track conditions, and other information for the serious player. At Hialeah, west of Miami, palm trees line the paddock area, a statue of Citation, Triple Crown winner in 1948, stands on a small island in a lily pond, and 450 pink flamingos inhabit the infield lake. At small tracks, the grandstand might be plain bleachers with a roof, but at larger tracks, the stands are often multimillion-dollar structures that provide seating on several levels. The stands often include an exclusive clubhouse where members have special dining, drinking, and seating areas. Older tracks may have distinctive architecture. Keeneland, in Lexington, Kentucky, for example, is finished in distinctive stonework and was recently designated as a national historic monument.

A grassed paddock usually opens the space behind or beside the

Keeneland Association

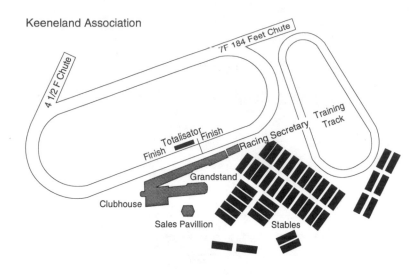

FIG. 11.9. Keeneland.

County - Fayette. State - Kentucky.
Six miles west of Lexington on U.S. 60.
Adjacent to Airport.
Track - One and one-sixteenth miles, oval.

grandstand at most tracks. In the paddock, trainers saddle their horses for the next race, and jockeys and trainers discuss strategy. This place may resemble a golf green with a tanbark path around it and is often awash with race fans who are intent on inspecting their betting choice's physical condition as they attempt to handicap the next race. Some people come to the paddock just to watch other people. Stables stand behind the grandstand or across the track. The curious fan may find time to wander through the area, chat with grooms, and watch the blacksmith shoe a horse. Although most racing fans rarely visit the stables, the sport's true devotees may spend race day morning wandering the area and watching early workouts on the track.

Some racetracks sit amidst rural settings, and the view from the grandstand may encompass distant hills—as at the Downs at Santa Fe, New Mexico. The grandstand at Keeneland looks out over rolling bluegrass pastures and white-fenced horse farms. This spectacular vista helps make this track one of the most visually stunning in America and, many would argue, the perfect place to watch a race (Herbert 1980, 190). Many racetracks were originally built on open land near the edge of a city. As the city grew, subdivisions encroached upon the track and then surrounded it. Today, these are urban tracks. City streets, tiny bungalows, and railroad yards detract from the visual aesthetics that usually accompany the pageantry and pomp that are part of a major stakes race. In the 1920s, when the owners of Churchill Downs in Louisville were finally realizing success in promoting the Kentucky Derby as America's most prestigious horse race, New York columnist Jimmy Cannon said that "Holding this thrilling race in this squalid environment is similar to hanging a Rembrandt in a tenement basement" (quoted in Pearce 1974, 12). Through investment in new buildings and continual repair and painting of the older structures, Churchill Downs has become an attractive venue for racing, although the city around the track has changed little. Recently, track managers have invested $25 million to improve and refurbish the grandstand and supporting facilities. This was done to enhance the track's image, refine its beauty, and maintain its reputation as an appropriate home for America's most important horse race.

To racing fans the Derby is much more than a mere race, and their behavior reveals how important ancillary activities are to the racing experience. For example, the Derby crowd divides itself into social or class groups. College kids and blue-collar workers go to the infield to lie in the sun and drink beer. Since the track provides no bleachers and the crowd is so large, most infielders will get little more than a glimpse of the race. The opposite end of the social gradient is near the top of the grandstand, where, commanding a view of the entire track, is perched Skye Terrace, also known as "Millionaires' Row." The box seats stand between the track and the terrace. For the Derby, box seats start at $900 for a six-seat box near the finish line. These seats are not positioned well enough to rank very far up the social ladder. Seating at the Derby is concomitant with perceived social standing. Some may think it trivial, but as Donald Houghton points out, it is an important benchmark for successful business people and a confirmation of social attainment for those concerned with such matters.

> Practitioners of the Derby Box procurement art, and there are thousands of them in Kentucky, know the seating-chart designations of the Downs as well—or better—than they know their bank balances, for a Kentucky businessman is judged by his Derby box location. To join the game a businessman obviously needs to have a box but to advance in the game a man needs to improve the location of that box. The winners, those who have invested the necessary years, money and sometimes, family influence, are those who hold title year after year to a box in a

prime location. Those are not captains of industry; they are admirals. Equally important is the game for guests. A businessman, like a small schoolboy, is judged by the company he keeps. Give a man a Derby box in one of the track's "better neighborhoods" and surround him with a cross-section of easily recognized celebrities and true Derby devotees claim he may find the hereafter a comedown. (1974, 71)

Keeping the track in acceptable form is not a cheap matter, for structurally, the racetrack is not unlike a small town that will include as many as 100 buildings of different functions tightly grouped at trackside. Roads and walks connect them. Utilities are usually placed underground. Some grandstands are fully enclosed and air conditioned in summer and heated for winter racing. These features make the racetrack a very expensive place to build and maintain (Thomas 1988, 5185). New tracks commonly cost more, if measured on a per-seat basis, than professional sports stadiums because of the space required for boarding horses and for patrons to mill around and wager (table 11.1). The cost of constructing a new racetrack clearly suggests that if a state is counting on such a facility to contribute tax revenue, the location must be very carefully chosen to assure that the potential wagering population is large enough to sustain the track.

Aesthetically, the track can be a very pleasant experience. Track architects are aware that the patron's experience at the races is much more than a series of mechanistic trips to the betting window. The well-

TABLE 11.1. Cost of Selected New Tracks Built or Planned since 1974

Track	Approximate Cost in millions of dollars	Opening Date
Garden State Park (N.J.)	170	1985
Arlington Park (Ill.)	110	1989
Remington Park (Okla.)	90	1988
Birmingham Turf Club (Ala.)	84	1987
Sam Houston Race Park (Tex.)	84	1994
Canterbury Downs (Minn.)	70	1985
The Woodlands (Kans.)	70	1990
Prairie Meadows (Iowa)	51	1989
Louisiana Downs	33	1974
Trinity Meadows (Tex.)	25	1991

Sources: Steve Thomas, "Track Construction," The Blood Horse, September 10, 1988, p. 5185; Jacqueline Duke, "Hurrah for Houston," The Blood Horse, May 7, 1994, p. 2305.

FIG. 11.10. The starting gate at Keeneland Race Course in Lexington, Kentucky circa 1950. Race fans close enough to the rail can feel the ground shake as a dozen thousand-pound Thoroughbreds break from a standing start. Sound, sight, and ambiance are all part of the racing experience.

designed racetrack includes much to be seen, experienced, and enjoyed. One can even enjoy the smells of horses and fresh mown grass; the sight of the jockeys' colorful silks and the owners' and breeders' designer clothes; the afternoon light on flowering trees and shrubs; the crowd's roar and the heavy pounding of hoofs on dirt as the starting gate opens to release the thousand-pound speedsters for a forty-mile-per-hour tour of the course (fig. 11.10). This is part of the racetrack landscape ensemble. It is theater and can be just as important to the racing fan's experience as the order of finish and the payoff on a bet.

Conclusion

Thoroughbred racing in America has a long tradition and an immensely rich character. Racing also has many geographies—but all focus on the track, and the racetrack, as sports places go, is a complex place. It has dozens of individual elements—from the groom mucking out stables on the back stretch to the millionaire owner whispering in the jockey's ear in the paddock—that add to the spectator's experience. The older, traditional tracks tend to be unique, real places that are readily distinguishable from other sports places, or, for that matter, from other racetracks. It is the wealth of place detail in the racetrack's landscape that can provide the fan with a gratifying sporting experience. One need not be a grizzled veteran "railbird" to appreciate the track's stimulus. It begins with the season's air and the light and perhaps some memories to invoke nostalgia, something even a youngster can experience. Imagine the scene as Jack Kerouac recalls the boyhood exuberance of a visit to Rockingham Park, the racetrack in North Andover, New Hampshire, not far from Boston.

> Rockingham was like any other racetrack on a warm drowsy afternoon, but to Mickey it was all gold and magic. In front of the gates there were the cries of hawkers and tipsters selling their tips—"The Kentucky Clocker" or "Lucky Morgan's Green Card"—and there was the flutter and furl of flags atop the grandstand and in the pavilions, the smell of hot dogs and beer in the warm air, hot sunlight on the gravel, and that feeling of lazy excitement which a racetrack evokes when people are entering at the gates and the vast unseen presence of the great track itself awaits them beyond the grandstand with its sudden far-spreading acreage of green infield, its sweeping turns, tote boards, distant barns, and bright striped furlong poles along the rail a mile around. It was the immense, stirring drowsy scene of a day's fate and fortune for all the prancing beautiful horses, and the jockeys, owners, trainers, and bettors gathered in the warm sun there, an epic of men and horses and money that thrilled the little boy's imaginations. (1978, 103)

In fiction or in reality, one cannot separate the sport experience from the sport place.

CHAPTER TWELVE

FOX HUNTING

Karl B. Raitz

Hunting, in its widely varied forms, is one of America's most popular sporting pastimes. Each year, hundreds of thousands of hunters buy licenses, including special permits for hunting ducks, geese, turkey, deer, and other game. State governments have wildlife management programs to monitor game habitat and regulate hunting through restricted licensing. Minnesota, Michigan, and Maine may allow moose hunting but only by persons whose names are drawn in a permit lottery. Montana and Wyoming closely control the annual hunt for white-tailed deer and mule deer in each of several demarcated environmental zones. Beyond the bureaucracies established by states to monitor hunting are a host of commercial businesses whose existence is almost wholly dependent upon the hunter. These include gun, shell, bow, clothing, and accessory manufacturers. L. L. Bean, a large mail order firm, is said to have gotten its start supplying high-quality boots to hunters. In areas of plentiful game, local businesses—motels, restaurants, and even butcher shops—may depend upon the influx of customers during hunting season to enhance annual profit margins.

Several general hunting publications such as *Field and Stream* (circulation 2,000,000), and *Sports Afield* (circulation 535,000) enjoy extensive readership, while specialty magazines serve devotees of specific kinds of hunting. *Full Cry*, for example, is a coon-hunting journal with a circulation of 36,000. While such journals provide a rough measure of hunting popularity, they also illustrate that hunting has its own language and, arguably, its own subculture. Something in the hunting experience is so compelling that it has won a favored place in the national psyche. Its influence is often brought to bear in the perennial debate over gun control, where the argument for restrictive law is consistently beaten back by an extremely effective coalition of gun owners who argue that guns are primarily for hunting or target practice (to hone hunting skills), and that hunting is not only an honorable activity but a right.

Devotion to hunting comes from wellsprings deep in the national psyche. The American appetite for hunting was fostered in Europe, where game has been pursued for food and sport since the Roman era or earlier. This chapter will examine fox hunting, which retains some of its European heritage in ritual and record, and so provides an excellent example of how a hunting tradition originates and spreads from place to place; how it is subject to alteration or modification as social, economic, or political milieus change; and how participation and enjoyment are closely linked to the place and environmental context in which hunting is practiced.

Antecedents

In northwest Europe, after the Roman Empire's passing, a hunting tradition developed in which by law, hunting large game animals like deer and boar was royalty's right and privilege (Longrigg 1975, 17). In medieval England, hunting was formalized into three main types, each of which restricted those who could hunt and where hunting was allowed. Forest hunting was most important and was reserved for royalty. Foresters and woodwards planted and maintained forests and looked after the deer and boars that resided there. Royalty banned dogs from their forests, and trespass by poachers was punishable by fine or even death. A second hunting type took place in the chase, that is, a small section of forested land often enclosed as a park to which an individual had been granted hunting rights. A third type was the warren (open countryside) that estate holders restricted for their own hunting (McLean 1983, 37–38). Vermin, especially wolves and foxes, could be hunted almost anywhere. Royalty issued permits to hunters who would rid the royal forest, the chase, or the warren of the undesirable creatures that preyed upon deer, ground nesting birds, and domestic fowl. Hunters often worked together, each supplying their hound to a pack that would range after vermin and flush them from cover (50).

The hound was to become the most important element in the hunt (excepting the fox), but as late as the 1700s, the dogs used in fox hunting were often an odd mixture of sizes, colors, and dispositions. Gentry and yeomen kept their hounds, one to three couple (two hounds are always called a couple; three are one-and-one-half couple). The hounds would be brought together on selected hunt days. Because individual owners fed and cared for their hounds, the dogs were called "trencher-fed." Hounds may have resembled small beagles, harriers, or large mastiffs. Not trained to work together as a pack, the hounds required considerable guidance and control. Long whips became the essential controlling tool, and a person known as the whipper-in became the valued assistant to the huntsman in directing the hounds and a fixture of the fox-hunting entourage (Blaine 1852, 382). (Today the term "whip" describes a political party officer in Congress who maintains party discipline: the tradition originated with the hunt's whipper-in.)

The seventeenth-century English squirearchy is responsible for modern fox-hunting's form, ritual, and pageantry. These people determined to eliminate vermin from their hunting lands and to have fun doing it. Their hunts began early in the morning, preferably by four A M Since the fox is a nocturnal hunter, an early morning pursuit would catch it before it had time to digest its meal, before it could run. Hunting, then, was slow, often afoot, and usually in dense woodland (Blow 1983, 10). About mid–eighteenth century, the son of a wealthy Derbyshire squire, Hugo Meynell, brought scientific methodology to the hunt. Meynell apparently realized that if one waited until daylight to hunt, the fox could be a speedy and crafty runner. The mixed-blood hounds proved too slow and inept for the daylight hunt, so a faster hound with a good nose and endurance for extended pursuit had to be bred. This represents a basic theme in hunting—that the history of working dogs is closely linked to the differing environments that hunters choose. Through close selection of desired qualities, dogs can be bred to meet environmental requirements in a few generations.

This period in English hunting marks a major turning point in purposeful dog breeding for hunting in new environments. It would happen again as hunters encountered new hunting country. Since hunters now required horses to follow the open country daylight hunt, horses with speed and strength sufficient to jump field obstacles had to be bred and trained. In casting about for a place where this new hunting technique could be practiced to advantage, Meynell moved to the fast grass country in Leicestershire in the 1750s. He purchased the Quorndon estate and established himself at Quorn Hall (ibid., 10–11). In his forty-seven years as Hunt Master in Leicestershire, his innovations caught the attention of fashionable society. Wealthy city folk thought country squires who rode to hounds a bit rustic, but Meynell brought color and excitement to the hunt, and he invented the winter hunt for them. Soon young gentlemen who were setting off on the Grand Tour of Continental spas were also becoming avid fox hunters. The fashion set's involvement in hunting also led to an increased concern for the aesthetic possibilities, and the hunt soon became a venue for fashion exhibition and elaborate ceremony.

Eighteenth-century hunters' dress was informal and far from standardized. In the grander hunts, men wore boots and breeches, stiff long-skirted coats, and three-cornered French hats. They did not favor distinctive colors until a Tory squire made a point of wearing red, the Tory color (the Whig color was blue), when hunting. The association of scarlet with fox hunters' riding habits has long been part of the hunt's aesthetic pageantry, yet was established through historical coincidence (Longrigg 1975, 72).

The Leicestershire hunt's popularity attracted growing numbers of devotees into the 1780s. Enthusiasts believed that this was the beau ideal, the perfect place for fox hunting. Nature, they thought, was in league with the hunters in providing a country of large rolling grassed enclosures where hounds, horses, and hunters could extend themselves, and a soil that seemed to retain fox scent better than almost any other (Blaine 1852, 483). Central to Leicestershire, the little village of Melton Mowbray attracted new residents, hunters who wished to live in the midst of England's best hunt country. Though houses were few and modest, Melton became fox hunting's Mecca, and was to hunting what New Market was to racing (Longrigg 1975, 72). Articulate and literary hunters wrote of the glorious assemblage of rank, fashion, and beauty found at Melton and its surroundings. Many "hunters" came not to follow hounds but to satisfy their passion for riding and displaying their horses and themselves (Blaine 1852, 483).

As fox hunting changed from a practical method for farmers to preserve their poultry to a pastime of exclusivity, conspicuous consumption, and reeve's ritual, critics ridiculed the activity as pointless. To Oscar Wilde, the sport was little more than "the inedible pursued by the unspeakable." Stung by penetrating criticism, hunt advocates explained that hunting was really useful and productive activity. They argued that trainers improved equine bloodstock in seeking faster and more durable animals. Then, since many regular hunters kept as many as six or eight horses at the hunt stables, they suggested that if needed in wartime, these horses could be incorporated into Her Majesty's cavalry. Further, hunters thought that the outdoor experience, especially on bleak winter days, would produce hardy, openhearted liberal-mindedness. Finally, fox hunting was worthy because neighborhood tenants tended horses or followed the hunt on foot or mule, thus bringing the classes together (ibid., 445).

Across the Atlantic, America was still English, and despite irritation with tax and trade policies and growing interest in independence, many Americans, especially the wealthy, were avid Anglophiles. The question was not whether fox hunting would be brought to the New World by people eager to mimic the English, but whether the social and environmental conditions in the raw new land would allow a direct transplantation. Might the hunt require adjustments that would so alter the sport that it would become unrecognizable?

Fox Hunting Comes to America

Early settlers brought hunting to the Atlantic colonies. Old records describe Tidewater Virginians hunting raccoons, opossums, and foxes at night and on foot with "curr" dogs in plantation cornfields or in the woodland and creek bottoms (Harrison 1929, 256). Most hunters did not possess specially bred and trained hounds for hunting, although Robert Brooke brought a pack of foxhounds to Mount Victoria, Maryland, from Whitchurch in Hampshire, England, in the 1650s (Chronicle of the Horse 1986, 40). Mounted Virginia hunters chased wolves, especially on the Piedmont, and seventeenth-century Virginia statutes encouraged wolf hunting to preserve farm livestock. By the early 1700s, hunting pressure had almost eliminated wolves from Tidewater and Piedmont uplands. Fairfax Harrison contends that the experience of an exhilarating chase on horseback for wolves developed into the practice of chasing the fox, the next best available quarry. Hunters sought open country, not the heavy woodlands and unfordable creeks that marked the Tidewater country, so fox hunting came first to the Piedmont. By the 1730s, mounted upland hunters were using hounds to pursue foxes (1979, 156–57). In the 1740s, Dr. Thomas Walker imported English foxhounds to his Castle Hill estate in Albemarle County (Charlottesville). This was apparently a rare event, because most planters did not keep special hounds for fox but used the same hunting dogs for all game. The Virginia-bred hounds apparently fared well in their pursuit of native foxes (Carson 1965, 141).

The Virginia and Maryland fox was gray and behaved very differently from the English red fox. The gray fox gave off less scent, was slower afoot, and tended to run in small circles of four to eight miles, whereas the red fox might run ten to twenty miles or more. The gray took refuge in trees; the red would run until it either outsmarted its pursuers or found a den hole and "ran to ground." A red fox was native to Canada and the northern states but gradually spread south, apparently as farming opened the woodland to produce a more favored habitat. Virginia hunters also imported red foxes from England (Verney 1921, 172). Hunts after gray foxes were often on foot in heavy cover. The hound pack was a composite, each hunter bringing one or two couple of trencher-fed hounds (Carson 1965, 141).

Near Philadelphia, hunters formed a formal hound pack by subscription; in 1766, members formed America's first organized hunt, which became known as the Gloucester Fox-Hunting Club. Eight years later, members adopted a uniform consisting of a brown coat with white buttons, buff waistcoat and breeches, and a black cap (Longrigg 1975, 171). In West Chester, and also on Long Island, New York, huntsmen caught foxes that they released for hunting, but before the Revolution, this type of hunt attracted few enthusiasts (Holliman 1931, 39).

Although the Revolutionary War temporarily interrupted fox hunting, it soon revived, and from 1783 to 1861, people in Maryland and Virginia frequently rode in pursuit of both gray and red foxes. For many, the hunt continued almost as a folk activity with little formal organization. Country squires and ordinary farmers followed trencher-fed hounds on early morning hunts during the late fall and winter season. Boys rode mules; elderly members of the hunting party followed in buggies; and almost everyone participate in the hunt breakfast and social activities that were part of the hunt experience (Gaines 1953, 23). Virginia-bred hounds continued in common use until after the Civil War, although hunters debated their prowess in the field compared to English-bred hounds (Carson 1965, 14). On the larger Piedmont and Tidewater estates, hound packs were kenneled and trained to hunt together but the number of kennels did not increase rapidly until after the Civil War. Before the Civil War, fox hunting was the landed gentry's principal field sport, more popular than shooting and racing, and a sport that extended from Maryland's Eastern Shore to Kentucky's Bluegrass

Region and from southeastern Pennsylvania south to Georgia (Mackay-Smith 1968, 1).

The Yeoman's Fox Hunt

Covering the news like a red fox covering the County with a Walker fox hound on his trail.
—Motto, *Garrard County News*, a weekly newspaper published in Lancaster, Kentucky, 1994

Riding behind a pack of hounds across fields and pastures in an English-style daytime hunt is a pretty picture. But it was seen primarily in the Tidewater and the rolling Piedmont uplands of Maryland and Virginia, and in proximity to Philadelphia and New York. In the back country, the rougher land of the Ridge and Valley, the Appalachian Plateau, the Carolina uplands, and the hill lands of Tennessee and Kentucky, people of common heritage, tradespeople and yeoman farmers, practiced a different type of fox hunting (Fox 1885, 625). In some areas, such as Kentucky's Bluegrass country, this kind of hunting is still popular today. The yeoman's hunt—perhaps American fox hunting is a better term—takes place at night, not in the daytime. The hunt's focus is not on the ride and the ritual, but on the vicarious chase and the hounds' "music." Hunters bring their hounds to a place they think foxes might frequent. They select a hilltop, ridge, or saddle between hills, build a fire, and then release the hounds who set out, unaccompanied by hunters, to locate a fox. The hunters settle in around the fire to tell stories, eat, and drink. When the hounds find a fox they bark, or "give voice," and the chase is on. Through training and hunting experience, hunters recognize their hounds' distinctive voices. They have chosen a hilltop site in part because the sounds of hunting hounds can be heard over longer distances. Unlike the English-style pack hounds, which were carefully trained to hunt together in a tight group for aesthetic purposes, the yeoman's hounds hunt as individuals with the object of using superior speed and scenting ability to get ahead of rival hounds and lead the chase (Mackay-Smith 1968, 4). One enjoys the hunt vicariously by listening to the music of the hounds' voices and following their progress in the imagination. Friends argue about whose hound is leading. The hunter whose hound led the chase earns respect and prestige, for that hound's performance is directly attributed to the owner's knowledge of bloodlines and his skill at breeding a superior competitor.

In part because yeoman fox hunting places primary importance upon the hound's singular performance, and running at speed in rough country night after night demands strength and fitness, hunters are extremely active in seeking breeding stock that will improve performance. Hounds that leave the hunt and return to the fire are an embarrassment to their owners, and most do not live to return to the kennel. If young hounds in training lack speed, scenting ability, or other desired qualities, they are quickly "drafted" (eliminated), either by sale to someone else or by death. Hunters who did not go beyond grade school make bloodlines a scholarship and can often recite their hound's heritage back four generations or more.

In frontier days, hounds were bred from Irish-Maryland, English, and Old Virginia strains. These hounds, especially the Virginia hound, were long-eared, rat-tailed, deep-toned, and black and tan; they were bred for gray fox hunting (Mackay-Smith 1968, 4). The red fox multiplied in the east during the eighteenth century and then moved south to Georgia by 1840, but this hound was too heavy and too slow to pursue it. In the 1850s, the red fox moved west, across the Appalachians toward central Kentucky.

A pair of hunting events during that decade had a spectacular impact on fox hunting and became the stuff of legend. The first event had a major impact on hound breeding that carries through to today. Not only did it result in the appearance of a breed foundation sire, it also nicely illustrates how hunters adapted foxhounds' genetic makeup to enhance their effectiveness within a new environment.

As chronicled by Bob Lee Maddux, the first event took place in 1852, when a stock drover was returning to Madison County, Kentucky, after driving a herd to Tennessee (1961, 20). Hearing barking dogs ahead, he found himself in the midst of a deer hunt. When the first hound appeared from the woods, the drover captured it and took it on to Madison County. There the dog came into the possession of George Washington Maupin, the best-known fox hunter in the state. Maupin named the hound Tennessee Lead (fig. 12.1). This hound proved to be a superior fox hunter, and sired pup litters for neighboring hunters.

The decade's second important event was the red fox's arrival in 1853. Although local hounds had been running fox that they could not catch for a year or two, no one had seen a red fox until a winter day when Washington Maupin and Tennessee Lead jumped a red fox in snow and ran it all day to a den in adjoining Estill County. The chase created a

2C   8

"TENNESSEE LEAD"

Near here in November, 1852, a black & tan hound was stolen out of a deer chase by a horse trader, taken to Madison County, Kentucky, sold to George Washington Maupin. There, as Tennessee Lead, he became the foundation sire of all Walker, Trigg and Goodman fox hounds.

FIG. 12.1. Historic plaque in Tennessee commemorating the foundation sire of the Walker strain foxhound.

sensation, not only because it was the first red fox seen in the state, but because Lead was fast enough and sufficiently clever to puzzle out the fox's trail and "run it to ground" (Mackay-Smith 1968, 32). Lead's successful chase alerted hunters that the hounds that had pursued the gray fox for a generation could not contend with the faster, farther-ranging red. Washington Maupin sent to England for a few hounds in 1857 and crossed them with his Tennessee Lead bloodline. His friend, John W. Walker, shared Maupin's interest in fox hunting and bred hounds with him (fig. 12.2). Their hounds became known as the Maupin-Walker hound—superior in its self-reliance, scenting ability, refusal to run in a pack, and clever hunting habits. These qualities made the hound ideal for yeoman-style high ground hunting, but antithetical for the English-style hunt (Longrigg 1975, 178). The Walker family of Garrard County, Kentucky, and other avid hunters became very active in refining the characteristics of the hound that was to carry their name, and they did it by selective breeding and hunting experience. Within a few decades, the Walker hound was the premier foxhound strain among yeoman hunters, and by 1910, the Walkers bred and sold hounds under their own kennel name (Mackay-Smith 1968, 87).

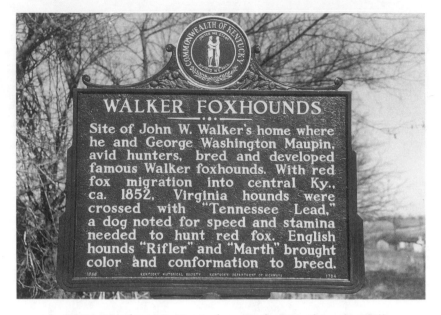

FIG. 12.2. Historic plaque in Kentucky near the site where the Walker foxhound was bred.

Fox Hunting after the Civil War

Among yeomen fox hunters, especially those in Kentucky, Civil War disruptions and the poverty and social disorganization that followed did not eliminate hunting. Many Kentucky hunters still had horses and enough income to maintain their hounds. This was not so for the Virginia and Maryland English-style hunters. Army troops plundered many Piedmont and Tidewater estates; others requisitioned horses for military use. The upshot was that stables were empty, hound packs were dispersed, and fox hunting was in abeyance (Gaines 1953, 23). Those estate owners who still had a few hounds often adopted yeoman-style night hunting that required no organization, no kennels or servants, and little expense. Even the first families of Fairfax and Fauquier counties, the core of the English-style hunt country in Virginia, began fox hunting informally at night after the war (Longrigg 1975, 181).

English-style hunting was eventually revived, thanks largely to the migration of several English farmers into the Virginia hunt country in the 1870s and 1880s. The newcomers were sons of rural English gentry who were attracted by Virginia's immigration program. They settled on the Piedmont and, being accustomed to fox hunting in England, brought their horses and hounds with them to their new farms (Gaines 1953, 23). The new English settlers apparently were not concerned to introduce or practice the high ritual and elaborate hunting customs customary in Great Britain. Perhaps the adoption of formal hunting procedures had to await proper adjustment to the American environment. Although these imported English hounds did well enough with the red fox in the East Midlands countryside, they were no match for demanding American conditions. The immigrants found hunting environments in the two countries entirely different. In England, the cover or coverts were small. Foxes were artificially introduced and encouraged to live in the coverts. The huntsman and whipper-in intensively managed the hounds, and during a hunt they worked hard at encouraging and correcting them. In Virginia, coverts were very large—often woodlands so dense it was impossible to gallop horses in them. Farmers had not cleared the woods of brush and limbs to create parkland nor had hunters stocked the land with foxes. The ride was so difficult that the hounds often left the hunters trailing far behind. Without human direction, the successful hound needed a superb scenting ability and a clever hunting sense. Breeding to American hound strains was required (Brock 1937, 501).

Virginia hunting was also affected by a second group that began to arrive after the Civil War. Many northern business people profited hugely from the war, and as industrialization proceeded in the postwar years, a new group of wealthy industrialists emerged. Some practiced fox hunting in Massachusetts, others in New York or near Philadelphia. But the northern hunts were hampered by severe winter weather. Wire fencing around Massachusetts farmland reduced most hunts there to following a drag—either an aniseed bag or a fox skin dragged on a rope behind a horse along a route selected to avoid private property or wire fences that could entangle jumping horses (Gaines 1953, 23). Unfortunately, this kind of hunting often resembled a steeplechase, not a cleverly worked-out hunt. Wild foxes could be hunted in the South on mild winter days not far from Washington, D.C.

During the 1880s and 1890s, northern entrepreneurs—and some recovering Virginia estate owners—established formal English-style hunt clubs to provide an appropriate venue for their sport. The irony here is that the English-style formal hunt was not fostered by English immigrants but by wealthy Americans who were either Anglophiles and admired this hunting style or found the hunt's trappings—the blooded horses, the trained hound packs, the stables and kennels, the scarlet habit, the huntsman and hunt servants—an irresistible way to display their wealth and imagined social standing. The hunt club often included bedrooms for guests, dining and drinking facilities, and other diversions. It also was exclusive, reserved for members only; thus, it maintained another British hunt tradition, enforced social separation. One example was E. H. Harriman, the New Yorker who owned the Illinois Central Railroad. He arrived in Virginia aboard his private train with hounds, horses, scarlet-coated staff, family, and friends (Longrigg 1975, 181).

Northerners founded some hunt clubs; Virginians founded others. Northerners reconstituted some venerable old hunts established before the Civil War (Wecter 1937, 445). By 1912, Virginia had nineteen formal hunt clubs and almost fifty privately owned foxhound packs (Gaines 1953, 20). Interest in formal fox hunting continued to increase during this decade, bringing prosperity to those parts of rural Virginia near the clubs. Outsiders bought farmland and began improving it by erecting new buildings, stables, and kennels; clearing woodland for pasture; and building better roads. They hired locals to do the work. By 1928, the Masters of Foxhounds Association published a map of northern Virginia hunting land that stretched over ninety miles from Charlottesville north to the Maryland border (Mackay-Smith 1968, facing p. 176).

American hunts attracted visitors from Great Britain and Ireland anxious to assess hunting quality and compare it to that in the Isles. What they found was unlike British or Irish hunting in some ways, illustrating for introspective critics that when cultural practices are moved from one environment to another, adjustments might be required to make the practice work. Yet the tradition may continue to serve the same kinds of individuals and similar purposes. Thus, when Irish traveler Edith Somerville visited the New York hunt country in the 1920s, she not only portrayed the hunting milieu but evaluated how it differed from the hunts she knew. She seemed unimpressed with the quality of hounds and horses and the social pomp on display, but the hunting environment struck her as formidable.

> We saw something of the country the hounds hunt over, and what we beheld filled us with respect, even with awe. They hunt wild foxes, and the coverts are set among great grass fields that are divided by [obstacles] of a size and ferocity that are . . . rarely equalled. Barricades of heavy timber of from 4 to 5 feet high, that pose as the humble and comparatively fragile post and rail, calculated to turn over any horse that "leaves an iron"

on them, and to turn also any save the stoutest heart to water. It is also a common weakness that strange countries, with few exceptions, look to the anxious visitor, unrideable, but it seems to me that the biggest "double" in Meath or the tallest wall in Galway would be less alarming to most Irish riders than the average Long Island "timber." (Somerville 1930, 17)

Contemporary English-Style Hunting

Fox hunt clubs must register with the Masters of Fox Hounds Association to be officially recognized as an organized hunt. This registration continues while the hunt remains active. Some hunts have disbanded over the years because of declining membership or because they lost their hunting country to subdivision development. New hunts have organized, and currently over 250 are recognized across Canada and the United States. As we have seen, enthusiasts organized the first hunts on farmland near large East Coast cities (fig. 12.3). Two of the oldest hunts that have maintained official status are Canadian. The Montreal Hunt began in 1826, the Toronto and New York Hunt in 1843. In Virginia, the oldest hunt in continuing operation is the Piedmont Fox Hounds at Upperville (1840). The Rose Tree Foxhunting Club was established in the Philadelphia suburbs in 1859 but has become inactive, in part because of a loss of hunt country. By the turn of the century, seventeen hunts had been organized.

The oldest Canadian hunts were founded just outside the largest cities in Ontario and Quebec. In the states, the oldest hunts were based a few miles outside the largest seaboard cities in an area that was to become what John Fraser Hart has called the Gentleman Farm Belt (1975, 183–85). The Belt is really a discontinuous zone that lies west of New York, Philadelphia, Baltimore, and Washington D.C., beyond the leading edge of new subdivisions. Here wealthy city folk bought farm land and built country estates with large, luxurious homes and extensive pastures for blooded cattle and horses (Somerville 1930, 68). Some estates are viable farming operations specializing in breeding standardbred or thoroughbred horses or purebred cattle. Many others are beautiful country retreats. A hunt club might obtain permission to hunt on estate land not owned by a hunt member. Often a hunt could arrange a lease or permission to use an area twenty miles or more across and that might include thousands of acres.

From 1900 to the Depression, over fifty new hunts were founded, many of them in the Gentleman Farm Belt, others near major northern

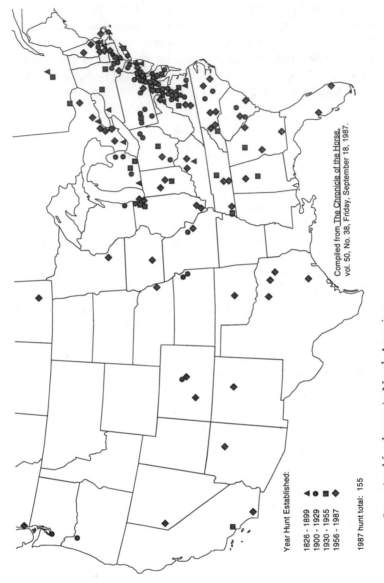

Year Hunt Established:

▲ 1826 - 1899
● 1900 - 1929
▦ 1930 - 1955
◆ 1956 - 1987

1987 hunt total: 155

Compiled from *The Chronicle of the Horse*, vol. 50, No. 38, Friday, September 18, 1987.

FIG. 12.3. Organized fox hunts in North America.

industrial cities where wealthy sports people adopted hunting. By 1929, hunt clubs had been formed in the suburbs of Pittsburgh, Cleveland, Detroit, Chicago, and Milwaukee, although these areas lacked benign winter weather for the traditional October to March hunt season. Hunts were even established in the West—for example, near Denver, Portland, and Seattle. Landscapes there do not resemble the gentrified country of Virginia's Piedmont or southeastern Pennsylvania, and hunters pursue coyotes in lieu of red foxes. In some places (Aiken, South Carolina, for example), hunt clubs had to create desired landscape features that were not part of the existing farm landscape. The Piney Woods had few hedges or rail fences, which were so common around fields in England and Virginia and which provided jumps for mounted hunters. The innovative Aiken hunters designed a jump made of horizontal poles and vertical brush, now called the Aiken jump. They also covered short sections of wire fence with wooden panels, some four to five feet high and twelve feet long. The resulting creation was called a "chicken coop" or simply "coop," and it resembled the roof of a little buried house. As farmers string more wire fences, Aiken jumps and coops have become common, and the extent of hunt country can often be delimited by their presence.

The Depression and World War II eras were not conducive to fox hunt expansion for obvious reasons, although twenty-six hunts were officially recognized during the period (see fig. 12.3). Some additional hunts were established in the Gentleman Farm Belt; others appeared near southern cities—Atlanta, Birmingham, and Memphis—and a few were created near medium-sized northern cities, including Indianapolis and Columbus, Ohio.

The largest increase in organized hunts came after World War II. Between 1956 and the early 1990s, some fifty-eight hunts were formed. Several new hunts now lie within the "Golden Horseshoe," the urbanized west shore of Lake Ontario, which stretches from Saint Catharine, near the Niagara River, west through Hamilton and north to Toronto. This suburban locational theme, repeated near several large cities elsewhere in Canada and the United States, has been augmented by hunts established in areas noted more for open country or recreational opportunity than is the fringe of metropolitan areas. These include the Connecticut Valley, New Hampshire, North Carolina's Piedmont and Blue Ridge, and southern Georgia. Several new hunts have stretched the traditional hunt landscape and environmental associations. Scarlet-clad hunters now ride to hounds near Iowa cornfields, on Oklahoma and Colorado prairies, on Texas scrub oak plains, and on

California coastal ranges. Some new hunts use open farmland with few wire fences. These hunts may pursue wild foxes or coyotes in the desired tradition, but many others must use a drag to control the route their riders follow. Fourteen hunts in New Hampshire, Massachusetts, Connecticut, New York, and Pennsylvania are exclusively drag hunts.

Contemporary Yeoman Fox Hunting

When Edith Somerville visited American fox hunt country in the 1920s, she was perplexed by the yeoman hunters who worked their farms by day and by night cast their hounds after fox. She wrote:

> Then I heard that it was the custom of the hill men of these forest regions [Hickory Nut Gap in Western North Carolina] to meet at some place high up in the mountains . . . and then loose their hounds upon the night while they make a fire, and sit around it, and gossip, and drink (very appropriately) "moonshine" and listen luxuriously to the striving hounds in the forest depths below and around them. This way of hunting is, no doubt, very good fun for the hounds, but for the hunters, it misses the pleasure that there is in following a trencher-fed pack of "Kerry Beagles" in the Kerry Mountains, seeing the tall, light-limbed hounds searching the heather and the clumps of bracken, spreading and clustering, feathering on the line, snatching the pride of place from each other, flinging themselves into the chase with but one wild soul among them—I cannot think that gossip and "moonshine" can make up for the loss of these (1930, 68).

Though Somerville made her visits to a Blue Ridge fox hunt over seventy years ago, the contemporary yeoman fox hunter stereotype is not far removed from the men she saw sitting around the fire. Updated, the image might include a redneck good ol' boy who chews tobacco, drives a pickup with a gun rack, listens to country music, and probably does not hold a regular job. The stereotype is not valid. The yeoman hunters who operate hound kennels must register their kennels with the *International Fox Hunter's Stud Book* (not unlike the registration required of the English-style hunt clubs) if they wish to participate in organized hunting events and to sell hounds for lucrative prices. In the late 1980s, over six hundred hunters registered their kennels. A survey of more than a hundred hunters revealed a wide diversity of social characteristics (Raitz 1988, 5). For example, the typical hunter and kennel owner was fifty-five years old (although the ages ranged from nineteen to eighty-one), had hunted for forty years (with a range from four to seventy), and had owned a kennel for about twenty-seven years (a range from one to sixty years). About three-fourths held jobs. Almost two-thirds of those not working were retired, and one-third (or about 6 percent of the entire group) were unemployed. The hunters worked at a wide range of occupations. Less than a tenth were day laborers, garbage collectors, or in other service professions. About a quarter were farmers, mechanics, plumbers, or in related occupations. White-collar workers, those with office jobs or businesses, made up almost one-third, whereas white-collar professionals, those whose jobs required specialized training and education, constituted another tenth. This last group included engineers, lawyers, doctors, and judges. The remainder were retired or unemployed. Although fox hunting is a rural sport, fewer than one-tenth of the hunters were farmers.

Unlike English-style hunting, which takes place during the late fall and winter months (usually October to March), this group hunts all year long. During the warm months of late spring and summer, the majority of the yeoman hunters hunt each month. The colorful autumn season is most popular, especially October when most hunters are active. Most states do not have a season that limits running foxes with hounds. Many fox hunters limit their activity during trapping and gun seasons to protect their hounds, because they frequently get caught in leg-hold traps or shot by other hunters.

For kennel owners, organized bench trials and hunting competitions are a vital part of hunting. Not only do competitions provide a venue for meeting old friends and socializing, but the value of hounds and the increased stud fees that can be charged are enhanced for those kennels whose hounds win events. The competition usually has two parts. After hounds are officially entered, a bench competition is held in which dogs in different age and sex categories are judged for conformation and desirable hunting qualities (fig. 12.4). The second competition is actual field hunting. A captive fox may be released or a drag might be used. All hounds entering the trial are cast together as a pack—there are often a hundred or more. Judges stand at key observation points or follow the hounds on horseback. Each hound has large block numbers painted on its side that allow judges to record performance in hunting, trailing, speed and driving, and endurance categories. Because these hounds—Walker, Trigg, Goodman, July, and other strains—are bred and

FIG. 12.4. Foxhound bench competition.

trained to be fast individual hunters, they are judged as individual performers. This would be an unfair competition for hounds trained to English-style hunting, where the premier hunting quality is allegiance to the pack. After several hours, officials stop the hunt, total the scores, and announce the winners.

More than a hundred hunt competitions are held each year at national, state, and local levels. The serious competitor travels to several organized events each year. To train and condition hounds for extended competitions, the hunter may take his hounds into the field frequently. This exercise not only keeps the hound's interest at peak levels but it allows the owner to cull out poor-quality animals before they become an embarrassment at an organized hunt in the presence of judges and friends. Because a hunter's reputation derives largely from his hounds' performance, regular hunting and training help assure maximum performance at hunt competitions. Organized hunting has its roots in the traditional hilltop night hunts, where fellowship and the music of the hounds were the reward for a night on the ground. The attraction of high fees for stud services and high prices for puppies from competition winners has helped change a folk sport into a formal, commercial pastime.

Changing Yeoman Hunting Patterns

Foxhound kennels sponsored by English-style hunts are scattered across the countryside outside large cities: Boston, Philadelphia, Cincinnati, Louisville, and Houston (Raitz 1988, 3) (fig. 12.5). Other kennel clusters are distinctly rural: eastern Tennessee, eastern Virginia, the Carolina coastal plain, the southeastern Georgia swamplands, the western Florida panhandle, and especially northern and southern Mississippi and adjacent Louisiana parishes. These areas all have a long tradition of yeoman fox hunting. Kennels clustered in adjacent counties suggest the increased importance of pen hunting. Rural kennel clusters are also the product of a "demonstration effect," which occurs when neighbors try to emulate a successful dog breeder whose hounds command stud fees of $100 or more and who can sell puppies for hundreds, perhaps thousands of dollars each.

Hunting pens are wire fences that enclose between a hundred and a thousand acres. The fence's wire mesh is small enough so that foxes released into the enclosure cannot escape. Although expensive to build, the pens are popular for several reasons. Foxes (or in some places coyotes or wolves) will always be present for the hounds and hunter, a prospect that is not usually the case in the wild. The fence also contains the hounds' hunting range. The dogs are thus protected from the sport's hazards; highway traffic, barbed wire fences, leg-hold traps, and irate landowners with guns. Not only are expensive hounds safer, but they never get lost and are easily called back to the starting point. Hounds following a fox across open land may run for miles, become scattered, or get lost. Pens are especially popular with two different types of hunters. Men with city jobs have limited time to search for lost dogs, and they do not like to waste time on unproductive hunts. Those hunters who are retirees or in poor health also may prefer pens because they do not have to traverse rough ground on foot looking for their hounds.

Pens often include a clubhouse of sorts where hunters can sit and listen to the hounds, cook a meal, and talk or sleep while enjoying shelter from rain or insects. While shelter might be welcome on cold nights, a major trade-off of pen hunting is the loss of environmental awareness and variability. All hunts are in the same place, across the same ground. The environment varies only with the season. The hunt's environmental context is an important aspect of fox hunting. As the hunt landscape in the pen becomes predictable, it is less interesting and less stimulating. Other parts of the hunting experience must be enhanced to main-

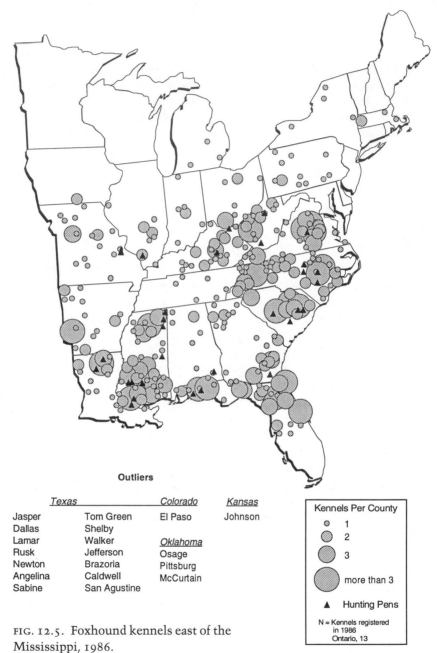

Outliers

Texas		_Colorado_	_Kansas_
Jasper	Tom Green	El Paso	Johnson
Dallas	Shelby		
Lamar	Walker	_Oklahoma_	
Rusk	Jefferson	Osage	
Newton	Brazoria	Pittsburg	
Angelina	Caldwell	McCurtain	
Sabine	San Agustine		

FIG. 12.5. Foxhound kennels east of the
Mississippi, 1986.

Kennels Per County
○ 1
● 2
● 3
● more than 3
▲ Hunting Pens

N = Kennels registered
in 1986
Ontario, 13

tain interest and enthusiasm. The clubhouse, initially a concession to extremes of weather, is an important part of that enrichment.

Unlike fox hunt kennels, hunting pens are not registered and information about them is scanty. The best sources are advertisements and letters to the editor published in the two major journals of American-style fox hunting, *The Chase* and *Hunter's Horn*. Kennels and pens are often found in the same general areas, albeit with some notable exceptions (see fig. 12.5). The largest contiguous area with no pens is southern Appalachia, though there are many kennels in northern Georgia, the western Carolinas, eastern Tennessee, and western Virginia. Much of this land is hilly or mountainous; open farmland is confined to valley bottoms, and large woodland expanses offer few hazards for uninterrupted hunting. A pen in this country might not offer any significant advantage for a predominantly rural hunting population and would unnecessarily restrict the hunting environment.

The character of the hunting place is a key element in the hunting experience. Gray-white fog curls along a valley bottom in early morning; hillsides blaze with autumn color in the afternoon; a nut-cutting squirrel chatters in a hickory overhead. These and a thousand more scenes become a part of the hunt repertoire, augmented by many other sensory experiences: the smell of hounds on a damp morning; the excitement of waiting for the hounds to intersect a scent trail; the first, almost explosive, voice of the hounds as they find scent and fly to the chase; the reflection of orange-red light on friends' faces as they tell stories around a night fire. These events are elements of the hunt experience ensemble.

For some hunters the ensemble may be very comprehensive, while others perceive and appreciate a much narrower collection of experiences. Whatever their degree of perceptual acuity, for most hunters, the place and experience ensemble is central to enjoying a hunt. One might argue that for many types of hunting, or fishing, the taking of game for consumption or as a trophy is the primary source of enjoyment. Is it that simple? Do hunters seek only the "thrill of the kill"? This motivation is not present in fox hunting, for the fox is rarely killed. Hunters want the fox to survive to run another day. It cannot even be argued that the thrill of the chase is central to the yeoman's fox hunt because the chase is done entirely by hounds; hunters are passive observers. There are other reasons why hunting is a pleasing pastime. When asked to describe the best conditions for a hunt, a central Kentucky fox hunter summarized the preferences of many of his colleagues. The memorable hunt day, he said, was one with a "crisp, cool fall morning, particularly after a rain, when the mist and fog is heavy at dawn. [Temperatures are] in the 40's or low 50's, warming as the day blooms." When hunters gather to exchange stories about successful past hunts, they describe the most memorable hunts in terms of the environment where they took place.

Environmental Context in English-Style Hunting

If the place and environmental ensemble are important to the enjoyment of yeoman fox hunters, they occupy center stage in the English hunt. David Brock describes an experience on a day in the English downlands of Kent in southeastern England when the search for foxes had not gone well:

> And even on those days when sport is not of the highest order, there is the feeling that the scene today is just as it was nine, or even nineteen hundred years ago; the same shadows of the same white clouds racing over the long waving grasses; the same larks in the same blue sky—blue sky which here looks so temptingly near; sheep, shepherd, and sheepdog, all unchanged; the same feeling of fresh cleanness in the wind and maybe the same peep of blue seas and white cliffs beyond the yellow gorse. (1937, 248)

Americans who practice English-style hunting exhibit similar appreciation of the setting in which their pursuit of Reynard takes place. Alexander Mackay-Smith published the following account from the records of Virginia's Piedmont Hunt for 1916–1917:

> December 13th gave the greatest day's sport ever known in the Piedmont Country—four clean-cut beautiful runs through delightful riding country lying between Francis Hill and Clifton Mill. Four foxes viewed away, four foxes run to earth—about twenty-five miles of galloping behind the pack—the shortest run no less than three to four miles, the longest twelve to fourteen. A bit of snow on the ground. The most marvelous sky effects and views of the Blue Ridge Mountains in distant sunshine occasionally cut off by snow squalls. (1968, 170–71)

For Mason Houghland, hunting in Virginia or elsewhere requires the appropriate acreage. A club that hunts twice a week needs at least eighty square miles of land, so that during the season, they will hunt the same land only five or six times. Adequate acreage relieves pressure on a small hunt country and also varies the hunting scene so hunters can enjoy the "unfailing charm [of a] country that is a little strange" (1949, 130). For the hunter, there is good hunt country and there is bad. Good country is any place the average hunter can stay with the hounds most of the day. This country should be gently rolling; it should have large enclosed pastures and small, isolated covers or coverts. Many landscape features mar a country for hunting, including large wooded hills; unfordable rivers, creeks or cliff-forming small streams; extensive woodlands, marshlands, or other unridable territory; unjumpable fences; and highways (131).

The seasoned hunter understands the quarry's habitat and will seek access land that supports foxes but also allows clean, aggressive riding. As important for many hunters is the country's aesthetic qualities, which will make some areas favorites over others. Proper habitat, ridable land, and beautiful landscape combine to underwrite the perfect place for fox hunting. Houghland provides a description:

> if we are in search of better country we want grass—bluegrass. This to me is the "sine qua non" of hunting; first because it is beautiful, second because a firm old bluegrass sod is so marvelous to gallop over and third because bluegrass holds scent so well. . . . Climate must be given serious thought, if we are in search of a hunting Elysium. The best hunting climate is that of Middle Tennessee. . . . However, perhaps there is no hunting country on this earth that can compare, despite its colder climate, with extensive areas in the bluegrass regions of Kentucky, that lay back from the river or the bordering hills. (132)

Red foxes are crafty beasts, and as they become familiar with their country they seem to invent new tactics to elude the hounds. Hunters fret at the prospect of losing their fox and terminating the chase early in the day. They study the hunting landscape so they can better understand the fox's behavior and extend the hunt. David Brock presents an example of how a huntsman and his whipper-in "read" the landscape at a check or point where the fox succeeds in confusing the hounds, and the hunt stops until the scent can be found again (fig. 12.6). The hounds are running north toward some dairy cattle grazing in a pasture. The wind is from the west, or left. Often foxes will run among cattle or sheep to confuse the scent trail and put off the hounds. Here, though, the hounds pick up the trail a short distance beyond the cows but are

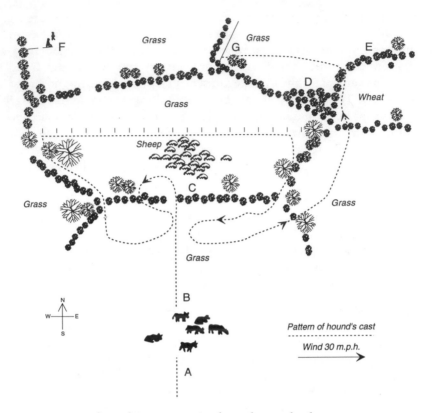

FIG. 12.6. David Brock's map: casting hounds at a check.

checked near a flock of sheep. The question now is, do you give up and go back to the clubhouse after only fifteen minutes of hunting, do you draft (allow the hounds to search) for another fox, or do you study the landscape before you and puzzle out what route the fox has taken so that the hunt may continue? The elements the huntsman must consider are the pattern of fences and hedgerows that provide cover, the small grove of trees and brush at D that often harbors a fox, the underground fox den at E that is supposed to be filled in, the men in the field at F laying drain tile, and the search pattern the hounds are following to raise the fox. To assure that the fox could not have backtracked, the huntsman casts the hounds in a loop into the wind almost back to the initial line of scent, then along fence and hedgerow in a large circle to the right. The men laying drain tile make no acknowledgment that they have seen a fox. The hounds continue back almost to the initial line, where they again pick up the scent and follow it to G, where the hunt resumes following the fence (1937, 234–35). The hunter who can work the check's puzzle and appreciate the role that each landscape element might play in the fox's efforts to escape will enjoy a richer sporting day.

Conclusion

Whether or not the fox cooperates, the hunt's environmental context can have aesthetic qualities that contribute to an enjoyable hunt experience. The physical environment is for fox hunting as it is for mountain climbing, cross-country skiing, and many other outdoor sports, the theater of activity. To hunt well is to know the quarry's physical qualities, the relationship of quarry to habitat, and the vagaries of that habitat as daily weather or passing seasons bring change. The hunter must develop an understanding, an awareness of subtlety in the quarry's physical environment to appreciate its behavior. Knowing this can only increase enjoyment of the experience. Without it, the hunt is only a mind- and bottom-numbing scramble across farmland that might just as well be a steeplechase. Some critics of drag hunts base their views on precisely this point. If there is no fox for the hounds to outwit, they argue—if there is no appreciation of the kinds of coverts that lie ahead and the possible routes the fox might take to reach them, then chasing a drag is merely a ride, and its only merit the exercise it provides for rider and horse. Given this chapter's thesis, however, such criticism ignores the aesthetic value such a ride might have, especially for the perceptive participant.

CHAPTER THIRTEEN

CLIMBING

Robert L. Janiskee

Human beings simply aren't built to live on a ninety-degree world. Nevertheless, given a monolith that is taller than a man— whether it's made of granite, limestone, ice, or cement—twentieth-century humans will come and struggle to the very death with it.
— Jeff Long, *Ascent*

The sport of climbing is blossoming in our society, which is so conscious of recreation and adventure. America's recreational climbing population apparently soared beyond the 250,000 mark in 1994 and was growing at an annual rate of at least 25,000.[1] In Europe, where media coverage of rock climbing and mountaineering events is common, top climbers like François Legrand and Hans Florine are highly paid media stars. Many believe that the sport will eventually attain that status in America too.

Rock climbing, mountaineering, and other forms of climbing are practiced in "the vertical world," which functions as both a physical landscape for the fight against gravity and a mental arena for the fight against fear and doubt. For most people who do not climb, the vertical world is fearsome terra incognita, a realm of perilous and demanding hard work.[2] Climbers, on the other hand, know the vertical world intimately and revel in it. For them, climbing is not a job to be done, it is a game to be played.

Climbing takes place in many different areas, some of which are so good that they can be called "perfect places." Since all climbers have their own preferences, there are thousands of places that are perfect for some people at least some of the time. This chapter describes seven places that by consensus are perfect: Chamonix, Mount McKinley, Ouray, Yosemite, Joshua Tree, Hueco Tanks, and City Rock. Each illustrates a different domain in the climber's vertical world. The Chamonix area of France offers rock climbing in the classic alpine style. Mount McKinley, North America's highest summit, is a storm-swept wilderness peak that beckons mountaineers. Ouray, Colorado, is an ice climber's paradise. Yosemite Valley offers superb "big wall" climbing. Joshua Tree National Park in southern California has become a mecca for "sport climbing," and Hueco Tanks State Historical Park in Texas offers world-class "bouldering." City Rock is a rock gym, one of the new type of indoor climbing facilities springing up all over America.

These are tumultuous times for climbing. As the climbing population has burgeoned, factors such as technological innovation, changing ethics, and environmental protection laws have combined to produce dramatic changes in where and how climbers do what they do. In a sense, climbers are reinventing their sport, mostly to suit a new generation that wants climbing to be more dynamic, convenient, sociable, and competitive. The popularity of sport climbing with fixed anchor protection has attracted hordes of new climbers and a wealth of new climbing opportunities, including facilities for indoor climbing and programs for the blind and other populations with special needs. At the same time, climbing opportunities have been restricted or eliminated in many public and private areas. The federal courts and land management agencies have long recognized rock climbing and mountaineering as legitimate recreational activities.[3] Public land managers, however, are under great pressure to regulate climbing because it threatens environmental resources and entails search and rescue costs that sometimes exceed $100,000 for a single operation (Waterman 1992). Private land is often inaccessible, primarily because of landowner concerns about accident liability. In the global context, policies designed to redress long-term human abuses of mountain environments and their indigenous peoples are certain to yield more restrictions.

Motivation and Risk Management

Like skydiving, caving, and other adventure sports, climbing is a "deep play" activity whose stakes are so high that participation appears irrational (MacAloon and Csikszentmihalyi 1977, 75). The character of the recreational experiences associated with these risky activities is influenced by the participant's awareness that death is a possible result. Roughly ten thousand Americans die each year in accidents attributable to avocational planned risk for fun or adventure, and about two dozen are climbers.[4]

Recreationists place themselves in stressful situations for many reasons. For mountain climbers, the primary motives appear to be values related to personal testing, competitiveness, aesthetics, and travel.[5] It is widely held that stressful situations with total involvement and uncertain outcomes are needed to stimulate optimal performances and the intense physical and spiritual satisfactions that result. For many climbers, the essence of their sport's appeal is captured in the title of the popular book *Mountaineering: The Freedom of the Hills* (Graydon 1992) or in Reinhold Messner's "soothing white loneliness of the big walls" (Bernstein 1979, 49).

Climbing is very competitive, and sometimes even heroic or epic in nature. Many rock jocks inspect the update sections of climbing magazines like baseball players obsessed with box scores. Climbers traditionally have earned public acclaim and peer respect by making difficult climbs, especially initial ascents of peaks or routes. In the past many climbers have wanted to be the first to conquer a mountain, plant a national flag atop it, and bask in the glory of the achievement. The most conspicuous examples of this occurred during the 1930s, when Hitler urged German climbers to conquer seemingly impossible peaks and symbolically claim them for Nazi Germany. Dozens of Germans lost their lives in what were often virtually suicidal climbs (Mitchell 1983, 59–61). Today, most competition entails establishing new routes and repeating older climbs in better style. The elite climbers of the 1990s are making solo, unroped, or very speedy climbs, free climbing pitches that once required direct aid, climbing at very high altitudes without auxiliary oxygen, and making spectacular parapenting (paragliding) or snowboarding descents.[6]

Throughout the sport's history, there have been highly publicized "great problems" such as the Matterhorn, Mount Everest, and Yosemite's El Capitan. Among the better known "peak bagging" goals are all seventy of America's "fourteeners" (14,000+ feet), all fourteen of the world's "eight-thousanders" (8,000+ meters), and the Seven Summits (the highest peak on each continent).

Few believe that even the most elegant theory could ever fully explain why climbers should want to do something that is so risky and unnecessary. When British mountaineer George Leigh Mallory was asked why he wanted to climb Mount Everest (where he vanished in 1924), he allegedly replied, "Because it is there."[7] Leading American sport climber Jim Karn has said, "In the end, nothing about climbing means anything. It's all just a game" (Gadd 1992, 34).

Climbers are not suicidal, so they and other adventure sports enthusiasts strive to keep their risks within manageable limits. There are two general approaches to accepting recreational risk. One entails placing your life in the hands of adventure recreation providers. Given the high level of competence that prevails in the industry, these carefully supervised excursions into the realm of danger involve risks that are more perceived than real. In fact, the risk of serious injury or death during supervised bungee jumping, whitewater rafting, or hot-air ballooning is appreciably less than from driving an automobile.[8] This is also true of indoor climbing and first-day instructional rock climbing, which are heavily protected.

The other major way to handle risk is to accept more exposure to danger and to make a greater personal commitment to acquiring special knowledge and skills. Even with professional supervision, most adventure sports compel participants to assume a great deal of responsibility for their own safety. Climbers like to point out that everyday life is replete with hazards, some entailing greater risk than climbing.

Climbing offers a wide range of recreational opportunity and risk management options. Guidebooks, climbing magazines, and similar publications provide rating information and related advice that climbers can use to select certain routes and steer clear of others. A system developed by the Sierra Club uses five main levels of difficulty for free climbing—that is, climbing that can be done without using artificial aid for progress or rest (Roper and Steck 1979, 306–7). Class 1 climbing is simple hiking, and Class 2 entails rough, off-trail hiking where hands may be needed for balance. A Class 3 climb is a scramble requiring handholds and footholds, and could result in injuries like a broken leg. At the Class 4 level, the terrain is steep and high enough to produce a fatal fall, so most climbers will carry and occasionally use a rope. Class 5 is the level of technical climbing—that is, high-angle travel where the rock, ice, or snow is extremely steep, unprotected falls are likely to be fatal, and skillful rope management and belaying (fall arresting) are essential.

Nearly everyone uses protection at the Class 5 level, usually in the form of a harness connected to a forty-five to sixty-meter kernmantel (core-and-sheath) rope that stretches under tension and safely stops them if they fall (fig. 13.1). Climbers are usually roped together in pairs, with one leading the ascent while the second belays from a secure position. As leaders make their way up the rock, they normally install intermediate anchors to which the rope is attached with D-shaped spring-loaded or locking metal links called carabiners (biners). Quickdraws, short loops of webbing with biners at both ends, are especially convenient for this purpose. Ropes may also be secured with anchored loops of flat nylon webbing called slings, tapes, or runners.

Different adjectival and numerical systems are used in various parts of the world to assess the degree of difficulty encountered in technical climbing.[9] The prevalent scheme in America, the Yosemite

FIG. 13.1. Rock climbing on a top-rope. Heavily protected and carefully supervised rock climbing is a low-risk activity, even for beginners.

Decimal System, subdivides Class 5 climbing (5.0, 5.1, . . . 5.14) on the basis of increasing difficulty for a particular pitch (section between two belaying positions). Thus, for example, a 5.1 pitch is easy, a 5.12 is severely difficult, and a 5.14d is something that only the very best climbers can handle.[10] A route's rating reflects the most difficult technical problems encountered, regardless of extent.

Class 6 climbing is aid climbing, which makes it possible to climb on holdless and overhanging rock. Whereas free climbers ascend with natural holds and high-friction shoes, using anchored ropes only to save them if they fall, aid climbers use mechanical devices for upward progress and rest. This includes tactics such as standing on pitons[11] or in anchored webbing, ascending ropes with Jumars or prusik loops,[12] and using rope ladders to negotiate overhangs. Aid climbing is rated (A0, A1, . . . A5), with the highest ratings indicating high risk associated with difficult, insecure placements of pitons, chocks, slings, or other protection (Roper and Steck 1979, 306). Using aid on pitches that can be free climbed is considered unethical by many climbers, and although it may be illegal and dangerous, some climbers will chop (behead) bolts, flatten hangers, or remove pitons they consider unnecessary.

Climbing routes are also graded (I, II, . . . VII) on the extensiveness of the technical difficulties encountered.[13] Rock climbing routes graded I or II should take only a few hours; those graded III or IV should take most of a day; and those graded V or higher are "big wall" climbs normally requiring several days. Ice climbs are also graded, although rapidly changing conditions make these ratings less reliable.

When Things Go Wrong

A certain unavoidable amount of deadly risk remains the unifying theme of climbing and mountaineering. As if this were not enough, some "adrenaline junkies"—often with the encouragement of corporate sponsors—habitually dispense with normal precautions and take their lives right to the edge. Enchainment, an innovation pioneered in the Alps, involves the nonstop speed-climbing of neighboring peaks linked by parapenting from the summit of one to the base of the next. Some rock climbers make unroped climbs on terrifying cliffs or risk avalanche-vulnerable bivouacs that are virtually suicidal. Some mountaineers make unusually lightweight and risky "super-alpine" solo ascents of Himalayan peaks, even climbing at night (when avalanche risk is lower) or in the dead of winter. Reflecting on the "hi & lite" trend, Steve Howe concluded that "Fatalities will abound, for alpinists view these ascents in overtones of heroic myth, like ice axes driven Excalibur fashion into solid Himalayan ice, to be pulled out only by the next king" (1993, 25).

Climbers at all skill levels tend to take on a bit more risk than they can easily handle. Unlucky or careless climbers can be seriously hurt or killed in falls, or can suffer a variety of traumatic injuries from falling rocks, shifting boulders, tangled ropes, and other hazards (Lentz, Macdonald, and Carline 1985). Mountaineers can fall victim to a wide variety of objective dangers arising from the condition of the mountain and subjective dangers attributable to the shortcomings and mistakes of the climber. Often these dangers are so great that even small mistakes can be fatal. Mountaineers can fall off a rock face or get blown off an arête by hurricane-velocity winds. A collapsing snowbridge can dump them into a crevasse. They can be swept away by an avalanche, smothered by a crumbling snow cornice, crushed by a toppling ice block, or smashed by a rockfall.

Environmental factors such as high altitude and extreme cold can combine with exertion to yield many discomforting and potentially dangerous ailments. Altitude sickness is a syndrome encompassing headache, dizziness, and other minor problems that can grow synergistically to dangerous levels.[14] Frostbite can claim a climber's fingers or other extremities. Oxygen deficiency (hypoxia), fatigue, severe dehydration, retinal hemorrhaging, or snow blindness can leave climbers fatally error-prone or helpless. They can die of hypothermia, high-altitude pulmonary edema (HAPE) or cerebral edema (HACE), extreme exhaustion, stress-induced cardiac arrhythmia, or a stroke. Some have even succumbed to carbon monoxide poisoning from cooking in poorly ventilated shelters. The death rate in Himalayan climbing has been nearly 9 percent, and attempting an eight-thousander can be likened to "playing Russian roulette with a ten-chamber revolver."[15]

Access to Opportunity

Since natural processes have left much of the earth's surface in rugged condition, opportunities to climb natural surfaces of one sort or another are widely available. To this natural bounty humans have added a cultural landscape that includes tall buildings, freeway overpasses, and, more recently, artificial climbing walls with an endless variety of artificial holds. The vertical world can now be anywhere and everywhere (fig. 13.2).

Climbers have traditionally sought natural places, and mountain-

FIG. 13.2. This portable wall was set up at a university athletic field for a climbing competition that attracted competitors at all skill levels.

eers have sought true wilderness—the more remote and unvisited, the better. To explore and document what the natural world has to offer in the way of vertical tests, hordes of mountaineers, technical rock climbers, ice climbers, boulderers, and others have fanned out across the globe. Thousands of climbing books, reports, and guidebooks have been written, and thousands of articles have made their way into climbing magazines and journals.[16] Debating the merits and drawbacks of various climbing areas and routes is a time-honored pastime. This pathfinding process emphasizes excellent climbing, significant achievement, aesthetic appearance, and historical context. Climbers also look for uncomplicated accessibility, good guide services, and reasonable costs.

These observations aside, the best way to identify the perfect places is to note where climbers and mountaineers tend to concentrate.

The Cradle

Traditional rock climbers have a keenly developed feel for their sport's history, which compels many of them to seek out and personally test the renowned climbs. That is a main reason why the Chamonix Valley, in the Haute-Savoie of France, is a perfect place for climbing. It is where, in the mid-1800s, mountain climbing became a sport—that is, a competitive activity with a framework of rules, conventions, standards, and historical context. Mountains had been climbed before then, of course. Notable examples include the scaling of Mount Ventoux by Italian Francesco Petrarca in 1336 and the 1492 ascent of Mont Augille (near Grenoble) by Antoine de Ville, Seigneur de Dompjulien et de Beaupre (Neustadtl 1992). Two of Cortez' soldiers also climbed to the summit crater of Mexico's Popocatepetl volcano to get sulfur for making gunpowder. Nevertheless, Europeans regarded mountains as fearsome wilderness until the latter half of the eighteenth century.

In 1786, at the instigation of Swiss aristocrat Horace-Benedict De Saussure, Michel-Gabriel Paccard and Jacques Balmat assembled a large party of helpers and climbed to the top of Mont Blanc, the highest mountain (15,771 feet) in the Chamonix area and in all of Europe (Brown and de Beer 1957). For the next half century, 90 percent of the climbs in the Alps were ascents and reascents of Mont Blanc. Finally, in the mid-1850s, British climbers operating in the Mont Blanc Massif vicinity ushered in the "Golden Age" of mountaineering by converting alpine climbing from a ponderously slow, expeditionary feat for the wealthy few into a streamlined, dynamic new sport for the middle class.[17] Today, to climb "alpine-style" means to climb without fixed ropes or camps while carrying everything you need on your own back.

Opportunities for first ascents were plentiful in the Golden Age, and peak after peak was climbed. The Golden Age was brought to a close in 1865 when Edward Whymper scaled the "unclimbable" Matterhorn, which is located near Zermatt on the Swiss-Italian border. By 1881, A. F. Mummery had ushered in the modern era of mountain climbing with a very difficult technical climb of the Grepon, one of the near-vertical granite *aiguilles* (needles) in the Chamonix vicinity.[18]

Chamonix is renowned for the excellent quality of its climbing and the splendid way it caters to climbers. The Syndicat des Guides de Chamonix provides the world's most carefully selected and best-trained guides, and the rescue service is superb. During July and August, several thousand climbers board the area's excellent *telepherique* (aerial tramway) system each morning to ride up into the aiguilles and spend the day climbing in the footsteps of the sport's legendary pioneers. Climbing is on solid granite that offers good traction and other desirable features; there are numerous classic routes ranging from fairly easy to extremely difficult; and retreat is usually possible if the weather takes a sudden turn for the worse. Descending to the valley at the end of the day, the climbers find not only comfort and security but many other things that they appreciate—such as the night life and other climbers eager to share information about routes, weather, avalanche conditions, and other matters of vital interest to rock climbers (Mitchell 1983, 72–74). It matters that Chamonix is a hospitable place for people who are young, itinerant, and on tight budgets.

In a typical two-month climbing season, hundreds of climbers are injured and some are killed by rockfalls, hypothermia, lightning, and plunges off the rock or into crevasses. Another sad toll is the price that tourism is exacting on the ambience of Chamonix and other alpine communities. The Alps are being smothered under an avalanche of tourists who spend billions each year on lift tickets, lodging, food, and related items (Denniston 1992, 36). In 1965, highway engineers pierced Mont Blanc with a seven-mile tunnel connecting Chamonix with Courmayeur (its Italian counterpart), and Chamonix is now a landscape of heavy traffic, swarming tourists, new hotels, and pervasive smog.[19]

Icy Peaks

Mountaineering, which mixes climbing and high-altitude survival skills, takes place on snowcapped peaks throughout the world (fig. 13.3). The most famous example of mountaineering is the 1953 expedition that used ponderous, siegelike tactics (now obsolete) to place Sir Edmund Hillary and Sherpa Tenzing Norgay atop Mount Everest, the world's tallest mountain (29,028 feet). Mount Everest is one of the elite eight-thousanders, the fourteen peaks that top 8,000 meters.[20] Because the difficulties and dangers of mountaineering escalate rapidly at such altitudes, scaling any eight-thousander is an impressive achievement. K2, the world's second-highest mountain (28,250 feet), is widely recognized as the most dangerous high peak on earth.

The eight-thousanders and their neighbors are seeing a lot more traffic these days, primarily because commercial expeditions are more numerous, and many accept relatively unseasoned climbers who can

FIG. 13.3. A mountaineering party climbing Hayden Peak in Wrangell–Saint Elias National Park and Preserve, Alaska. Saint Elias is the highest coastal mountain in the world.

pay the steep fees.[21] In 1993, for example, an astonishing forty individuals made their way to Everest's summit on the same day (Hawley 1993b, 34). Long-held notions about the limits of high-altitude mountaineering are being swept away, too. Professional climber Reinhold Messner, the world's foremost alpinist, had climbed all fourteen eight-thousanders by 1986. In that same year Messner also soloed Everest's north face without bottled oxygen or support. In 1988, Christophe Profit climbed Everest in a single day, and Jean-Marc Boivin parapented off the summit. Often instigated by corporate sponsors, audacious climbs of dangerous peaks and rock faces around the world have now become commonplace. One climber was moved to lament: "There are so many people who go to Everest these days it's hard to get [corporate sponsors] excited. Sometimes I think, What do I have to do, climb it backward and naked?" ("Ed Who?" 1993).

Denali offers proof that a peak need not be an eight-thousander to offer mountaineers all the trouble they can handle. It is a perfect place for mountaineering, and several of the established routes are world-class climbs. Denali, Athapaskan for "the High One," is what Alaskans and most mountaineers call Mount McKinley, North America's tallest peak (20,320 feet). Capping the rugged Alaska Range and providing the centerpiece of Denali National Park, Denali is surprisingly accessible and affordable. Most climbing parties check in at the ranger station at Talkeetna,[22] about 115 miles north of Anchorage, and then make the short flight by chartered plane or air taxi to a staging area on the Southeast Fork of the Kahiltna Glacier.[23] Climbers have established at least twenty-seven routes to the summit since the initial ascent in 1913.[24] Most parties attack the mountain's formidable defenses via one of the less difficult "trade routes" like the West Buttress or the Pioneer Ridge. Some take on tougher assignments like the West Rib or the classic Cassin Ridge route, a world-class challenge that follows a buttress on Denali's south face.[25] Whichever route they select, most climbers are members of guided expeditions. The expedition is a time-consuming but conservative strategy in which a climbing party takes several weeks (commonly 16–22 days or more) to wait out storms, become altitude-acclimated, install thousands of feet of fixed ropes, and create a series of progressively higher camps. Some opt for speedy, but very risky alpine-style climbs during the brief interludes when Denali's weather becomes noticeably less miserable.

Denali attracted 1,070 climbers in 1992, or about ten times as many as twenty-five years before.[26] Typically, about 30 to 40 percent of those who attempt Denali are from outside the United States (Sherwonit 1993, 32). Mountaineers everywhere know that getting a place on an eight-thousander expedition not only is very expensive but also usually requires a high-altitude curriculum vitae that includes either Denali or Argentina's Cerro Aconcagua (South America's highest mountain, at 22,834 feet). Denali is a qualifying climb because it is a very high mountain, and because it has what may be the most persistently dangerous weather of any major peak. It is like climbing at 23,000 feet or higher in the Himalayas. Because of its high latitude (62 degrees) and coastal exposure, temperatures during the climbing season may be as low as minus 40 degrees Fahrenheit, with winds of 80–100 miles per hour lasting for days on end.[27] Ferocious winds, heavy snow, and self-doubt turn back half the climbers who get as far as the staging area.

Denali has a reputation as a killer peak, which makes it all the more appealing to climbers bent on impressive accomplishment. Seventy-five climbers died on Denali between 1937 and 1992, including a record eleven in the single month of May 1992.[28] Some came to grief on a deceptively benign-looking chute where at least a dozen people have tumbled to their deaths, including so many South Koreans and Japanese that it has acquired the macabre name Orient Express.[29] One who died on Denali that month was Mugs Stump, one of America's best mountaineers. Stump had climbed hundreds of difficult routes in the United States, Canada, and Antarctica, and his many first ascents included some of the boldest, most talked-about alpine climbs in North America.[30] He knew Denali so well that he had recently soloed the Cassin Route from bottom to top in fifteen hours (Krakauer 1992, 60). Nevertheless, while descending Denali with two clients, Stump fell into a crevasse and was crushed by cascading ice and snow (Kennedy 1993, 79).

Ice Climbing

Mountaineers have always had to cope with mixed climbing challenges, including steeply inclined ice and snow. Today, ice climbing has become rock climbing's "cold weather cousin," an enjoyable pursuit in its own right. It is a pleasant diversion for rock climbers during the winter ("ice is nice and will suffice"), a practice ground for mountaineers, and the first choice of many climbers. To the amazement of many nonclimbers, ice climbers thrive on steep, vertical, or even overhanging ice—especially frozen waterfalls, giant ice pillars and curtains, steep ice-filled gullies, and solidified seeps or drips.

The basic technique for climbing steeply inclined or vertical ice and snow is the two-ax method (fig. 13.4), which was popularized in the 1970s.[31] The ice climber wears boots with front-pointed crampons, wields a sharp-pointed ice ax in each hand, and walks up the holdless icy surface in exaggerated stair-step fashion. Roped protection is made possible with the use of ice screws (anchors that literally screw into the ice) or ice pitons. Even novices can safely negotiate low-angle ice or toprope vertical routes.

The ice climber's domain is very peculiar. Over the course of a climbing season, temperature swings may cause a popular route to form, disappear, and rematerialize several times. Unusual weather may prevent some routes from forming at all or may yield routes that no one has seen before. This accounts for much of the inherent fascination and danger of ice climbing. Rapidly changing conditions present the climber with new first-ascent opportunities or on-sight (unrehearsed) challenges. In addition to the routine hazards of climbing vertical ice, there is the ominous possibility that the climber may not recognize unstable, cracked, or rotten ice that can easily shatter or come loose.

FIG. 13.4. Ice climber using the two-axe method on the Kennecott Glacier in Wrangell–Saint Elias National Park and Preserve.

Glacial and high altitude ice is very abundant, but it is generally found in wilderness areas accessible only to mountaineers. Most ice climbing is done by day-trippers, weekenders, and vacationers who look for climbable ice in less exotic locations. Good places to climb ice in North America include New Hampshire, the Adirondacks and Cat-skills, western Montana, coastal Alaska (especially near Valdez), Que-bec, the Canadian Rockies (especially along the Icefields Parkway), the Colorado Rockies, and various other locales.

One perfect place to climb ice is near the little town of Ouray (population 750) in the San Juan Mountains of southwestern Colorado.

Ice climbers from far and wide converge on Ouray each winter because of the quality of the climbing, the ambience of the town, and the availability of excellent instructional and guide services (French 1993a).

Because of the area's high altitude, rugged terrain, and numerous springs and seeps, Ouray has one of the best concentrations of readily accessible, high-quality ice routes in America. Ouray's elevation is nearly eight thousand feet, which guarantees very cold winters. The San Juan Mountains are so rugged and alplike that the Ouray region, which includes the mining town-cum-ski resort of Telluride, has been promoted as the "Switzerland of the Rockies" for more than a century. It is also billed as the Rockies' "Ice Climbing Capital." Steep ice abounds, and there are over a dozen areas for climbing—some with five-hundred-foot routes. The renowned and sometimes crowded Box Canyon offers ice routes for climbers of all levels. The longer, world-class routes in the higher peaks are best climbed in December before the arrival of heavy snowfall, questionable road conditions, and frequent avalanches.[32] Unfortunately, some of the best routes in the Ouray-Telluride vicinity are inaccessible because they are on land whose owners have strict no-climbing policies. In 1993, negotiations were under way to reinstate access to Bridalveil Falls and Ingram Falls, near Telluride (*Climbing* 1993, 72). Bridalveil, certainly one of the finest ice climbs in America, had been off limits for more than a decade.

Ouray itself is highly appealing to climbers. The backdrop of mountains and cliffs makes for a very dramatic setting. The town is also friendly, uncrowded, and much more affordable than its ski resort neighbors. Locals brag that "Ouray is like Telluride used to be." The opportunity to soak in the historic Hot Springs Pool after a day of strenuous climbing is regarded as one of the town's most endearing charms.

The International Alpine School is one of the important reasons that Ouray is a magnet for ice climbers. The IAS, which is headquartered in Eldorado Springs (near Boulder), provides world-class guide and instructional services for cragging, bouldering, big wall climbs, mountaineering, and ice climbing. Since 1972 the IAS has been offering its popular "Ice Experience" courses for professional guides, Outward Bound instructors, and others who want to learn state-of-the-art ice climbing skills.

Big Walls

Many climbers are fascinated by massive vertical walls, the grade V challenges that soar hundreds or even thousands of feet (fig. 13.5). The

FIG. 13.5. Peter Croft on a Mount Watkins big wall. Massive vertical walls can pose challenges far beyond those of routine climbing.

physical and mental preparation, gear, techniques, and other aspects of big wall climbing differ substantially from those of cragging or bouldering. Big wall climbs entail problems related to fatigue and thirst, untrustworthy belays, heavy haul bags, portaledge bivouacs, sudden storms, and complicated rescue situations.

The world's mountainous areas contain hundreds of big walls, although they are very unevenly distributed. In North America, they are nearly absent in the east but abundant in the mountains and canyonlands of the west. Among the most impressive big wall challenges in the Canadian Rockies and British Columbia Coastal Ranges are classic climbs like Bugaboo Spire, the Devil's Thumb, and Mount Waddington. In the Northwest Territories, the Lotus Flower Tower and some big walls on Baffin Island are also in this class. The Alaska Range features the Moose's Tooth. Among the more popular big walls of the coterminous states are those of the Grand Teton and Devil's Tower in Wyoming, the Black Canyon of the Gunnison in Colorado, Red Rock Canyon in Nevada, and the Canyonlands in Utah. There are few places, however, that can challenge Yosemite for offering a nearly ideal combination of superb climbing, gorgeous scenery, benign weather, tradition, and support amenities.

By any reasonable measure, Yosemite Valley in the California Sierra Nevada is one of the world's premier big wall climbing areas. When glaciers carved into the giant batholith comprising the Sierra core, they left a long, narrow, very deep trough with near-vertical sides of smooth, high-quality granite. In 1890, this gorgeous valley and much of the surrounding area were preserved as Yosemite National Park. With the assistance of its major concessioner, the Park Service added to the seven-square-mile valley floor a small city, complete with hotels, restaurants, shopping centers, and photochemical smog. Climbers are welcome to take advantage of this amenity-rich environment and to use, with certain restrictions, any of the more than three thousand climbing routes that had been established by the early 1990s. These include a marvelous variety of big wall routes in the valley and a nice selection of routes in the nearby Tuolumne Meadows climbing area. The climbing season extends from about mid-April to early October, and the summer usually offers benign weather for climbing—something that cannot be said for many other places with monster granite walls. A concessioner, the Yosemite Mountaineering School, offers a variety of lessons, guided climbs, and related services.

Yosemite's big walls include many fine climbs like Lost Arrow Spire, Middle Cathedral Rock, Sentinel Rock, the Royal Arches, and the Nabisco Wall. The two star attractions, however, are Half Dome and El Capitan, two of North America's biggest, most aesthetically pleasing, and most widely recognized granite monoliths. Like many other difficult climbs, the eighteen-hundred-foot vertical face of Half Dome was once considered "impossible." The initial ascent of the Northwest Face route in 1957 took five days and required the placement of nearly two hundred direct-aid pitons. Down and across the valley is the three-thousand-foot dead-vertical face of El Capitan, one of the world's largest exposed granitic masses. The initial ascent of "El Cap" occurred in 1958 via the Nose Route. This epic struggle, widely reported in the media, took forty-five days of hard labor (spread over two seasons) and entailed the placement of 700 pitons and 125 bolts.[33]

Yosemite's "Golden Age" lasted through the 1960s, but by the 1970s big wall climbing was dominated by younger, better, faster climbers who set higher standards by pushing routes in greater style. Since 1979, some rock jocks have been climbing Yosemite's big walls without rope protection. Half Dome was first climbed "clean" (without pitons or bolts) in 1972 and is now a classic climb for hundreds of talented weekend climbers. In 1986, a pair of climbers teamed up to scale both El Capitan and Half Dome in a single day. By 1992, El Cap had been scaled by a paraplegic, and its Nose Route had been climbed in only four hours and twenty-two minutes. In 1993, Lynn Hill became the first to free climb the Nose Route without artificial aid.

Like many other climbing areas, Yosemite has been the scene of chronic conflict between traditional rock climbers and "sport climbers." Sport climbing was pioneered by Alan Watts at Oregon's Smith Rock State Park in the early 1980s.[34] It evolved out of the belief that traditional climbing is an unnecessarily grim endeavor, and that its objectives, ethics, tactics, and gear are behind the times. Accordingly, sport climbing makes extremely liberal provision for the bolt-protected, comparatively low-risk climbing of crags, boulders, big walls, artificial walls, buildings, and anything else that offers fun. When climbing's popularity boomed in the late 1980s and early 1990s, most of the excitement generated could be traced to the mass appeal of sport climbing's emphasis on safety, gymnastic style, conviviality, and organized competition. Perhaps its most alluring aspect was the incorporation of previously unacceptable techniques, methods, and strategies that could be used to establish thousands of new routes, including many on terrain formerly considered unclimbable.

Typical sport climbers have focused on widely available challenges like pocketed limestone crags and overhangs, boulders, miniature rhyolite walls, and artificial walls or bouldering problems. Many, however, headed for classic climbing locales like Yosemite, where climbing had evolved with strict ethical guidelines. There they crowded the trade routes and left behind eroded trails, damaged vegetation, unburied human waste, chalked-up handholds, shoe-scuffed rock, shiny bolts, and dozens of back-off slings (used for retrieving rappel ropes). Some of them doctored holds with glue or chisels and used power drills to install fixed anchors (practices now banned in national parks), played loud music on boom boxes, and otherwise profoundly altered the aesthetics of the climbing scene.

While climbers of the traditionalist school exercised self-restraint, with most making the switch to clean methods that do not rely on pitons or bolts,[35] sport climbers used bolts and other fixed anchors in great profusion in order to make climbing easier, faster, and safer. Popular routes in sport climbing areas tend to be heavily bolted. Climbers work these routes from bolt to bolt, clipping a quickdraw into each hanger in turn. This fixed protection not only arrests falls but also facilitates "hangdogging." Hangdogging, the practice of resting on the ropes or gear installed for protection, relieves muscle strain and permits a more leisurely approach to searching for holds and thinking through the next series of moves. Traditionalists criticize it as a fundamental breach of ethics, but hangdogging is an integral part of sport climbing.

By the mid-1980s, some sport climbers in North America began rap-bolting, a hotly debated technique that employs rappelling as a prelude to climbing. When rap-bolting, a climber rappels down a rock face to inspect it, install fixed protection, remove loose rock and unwanted vegetation, and rehearse moves.[36] Traditionalists tend to disdain rap-bolters and other sport climbers, claiming that they are gadget freaks who prefer to solve climbing problems in the sporting goods store. They accuse them of trashing mountains, defacing classic routes, cheapening the worth of initial ascents, and generally tainting the sport of climbing. By the early 1990s, the traditionalist/sport climber conflict had become one of the major issues in climbing. Irate traditionalists in some areas were chopping bolts, flattening hangers, chiseling away glue-reinforced or artificial holds, and threatening physical violence.

The Park Service's response to widespread problems like these was to order the preparation of a Climbing Management Plan (CMP) for each "climbing park" and to begin drafting a set of general regulations for managing recreational rock climbing throughout the park system.[37] In 1993, the Forest Service also began drafting climbing regulations applying to fixed anchor use in wilderness areas (Davidson 1993b). Some state parks and other natural areas have climbing plans or memorandums of agreement with local climbing organizations, which also assist in cleanup activities, climber education, and the enforcing of bolting policies and related regulations. In Colorado, for example, the Action Committee for Eldorado (ACE) created a Fixed Hardware Review Committee and devised a system for limited development of new routes based on the local climbing community's preferences (Martin 1993).

Recognizing that the loss of climbing access is the number one problem confronting climbers, the American Alpine Club created the Access Fund in 1989. It became an independent national nonprofit organization with more than six thousand members by 1994. The Access Fund is dedicated to supporting climbers' interests and preserving climbing resources. It not only uses political muscle to fight overly restrictive government regulations, real estate developers, and liability-shy landowners but also helps in developing and supervising Climbing Management Plans, organizing site cleanups, and implementing other worthy projects.

A Place to Dance on the Rock

One of the most illuminating facts about rock climbing today is that most of its practitioners are sport climbers. The rise of sport climbing in recent years did not simply expand the ranks of climbing enthusiasts, it also profoundly altered the way the typical climber thinks about and behaves in the vertical world. When fixed anchors, rap-bolting, and other techniques or methods remove much of the fear from climbing, the vertical world becomes a more user-friendly environment in which climbers can let their athletic, creative, and competitive instincts run wild. Sport climbing is not about flirting with death. It is about donning your neon tanktop, Lycra tights, high-friction technical footwear, climbing harness, and chalk bag, and then joining your friends for "a dance on the rock."

Like surfing, rock climbing reflects local conditions and evolves to accord with the necessities of its place. There are more than five hundred climbing areas in the United States (Access Fund 1992, promo literature), most of them on western lands managed by the Forest Service and the Park Service. High-quality rock climbing opportunities are comparatively scarce in the eastern part of the nation, although challenging routes exist in the White Mountains, the Shawangunks, the New River Gorge, and several other locales. The highest, best, and most abundant climbing routes are in the mountain and desert west, which is loaded with pinnacles, crags, gorges, and other excellent climbing terrain. Colorado has more than three hundred peaks of at least thirteen thousand feet, and the Sierras have at least 246 peaks deemed worthy of climbing (Mitchell 1983, 85). Among the western climbing meccas are Eldorado Canyon State Park near Boulder, Colorado, Smith Rock State Park in Oregon, Red Rock Canyon near Las Vegas, and Joshua Tree National Park in southern California.

Joshua Tree National Park is situated in the Mojave and Colorado deserts about a three-hour drive east of Los Angeles. This popular park has become a premier sport climbing area, and it is also internationally renowned as one of the best "winter retreat" rock climbing areas anywhere. Within this 875-square-mile tract is a strikingly beautiful and very complex mosaic of rugged mountains and seemingly countless granite boulders and outcroppings. These provide sport climbers with a smorgasbord of opportunities to climb on premium quality crystalline quartz monzonite with a very high friction factor, sharp edges, plenty of cracks, about five thousand bolts, and numerous top-rope routes well suited for beginners. There are over four thousand established climbing routes in Joshua Tree.[38] Most of them are only one to three pitches in length, but this tally is still hard to beat in terms of quantity, quality, and variety.

It is highly germane that three-fourths of the Park is designated wilderness, because Joshua Tree's Climbing Management Plan, the first CMP ever implemented in the national park system (in 1993), bans the placement of new bolts or replacement of old bolts in designated wilderness. Climbers must bring their own food, water, and firewood and must comply with numerous regulations (Access Fund n.d.). They cannot climb within fifty feet of Native American rock art and must stay out of areas that have been permanently or temporarily closed to climbing because of the presence of private inholdings, sensitive historical sites, peregrine falcon nesting sites, or abandoned mine shafts. They must park their cars only in designated areas and can ride bicycles only on the roads. Where bolting is still permitted, they must not use motorized drills or leave uncamouflaged bolt hangers or retreat/rappel slings in conspicuous locations. The Access Fund is working closely with park managers to help preserve climber access to Joshua Tree, the long-term availability of which will depend on climbers behaving in ecologically and socially responsible ways.

Bouldering

Sport climbing has made bouldering one of the most dynamic and exciting domains in the vertical world. Bouldering, which was virtually invented by John Gill in the 1960s, is climbing boiled down to its essence.[39] It entails climbing on detached rock formations that are comparatively small, low, and easily accessible. Because of generally nonlethal heights and liberal bolting, enthusiasts can expect to suffer nothing worse than bloody knuckles, sore muscles, and tendinitis.

Some climbers prefer bouldering, although many do it only when they lack the time or opportunity to rock climb. Whatever the motivation, bouldering forces climbers to grapple with problems requiring strength, balance, flexibility, versatility, and creativity.

The western states abound in places offering bouldering opportunities. Some of the best, such as Horsetooth Reservoir near Fort Collins, Colorado, are located within easy day-tripping range of metro centers. Bouldering is extremely popular in southern California, which is blessed with a wonderful array of bouldering problems and routes—and a correspondingly huge number of guidebooks, climbing schools, gear shops, and other climbing-related phenomena. Many crowd-shy climbers try to find their own secret places, but publicity-hungry climbers are just as intent on finding those places and putting up new routes.

The best collection of bouldering problems in America is probably the one at Hueco Tanks State Historical Park, an 860-acre preserve located in the Chihuahuan Desert about thirty-two miles east of El Paso, Texas. About thirty-four million years ago, magma intruded into an overlying layer of softer rock at this site and hardened into syenite porphyry, a type of granite. When the softer rock weathered away, it left three jumbled rock masses and countless natural rock basins (huecos) in which rainwater collected. Native Americans decorated the boulders with about five thousand rock paintings (pictographs), some dating back six thousand years. Sport climbers discovered that Hueco's syenite porphyry rock masses offer not only hundreds of lead climb (roped) routes but at least nine hundred bouldering problems.[40] There are also twenty multi-use campsites, a nearby inexpensive restaurant, and other amenities important to a climbing population that includes many young, cash-strapped "climbing bums." Since Hueco offers comfortable climbing weather only from late October to early April, it is essentially a winter climbing area.

By convention, bouldering problems are rated B1, B2, B3 for difficulty. Hueco, however, is the cradle of the unconventional but fairly popular V (for Vermin) rating system, an open-ended scale beginning at V0 and extending to at least V12.[41] The individuals who put up new problems or routes get to name them. Thus, a climber at Hueco may choose a V1 warmup called "Duodenum," a V5 known as "Dragonfly," or a V10 named "Nobody's Ugly after 2:00 A.M." (Ryan 1992).

Hueco, like many other public climbing areas, has been the site of much conflict over access. Litter and spray-painted graffiti, Hueco's two biggest problems, are not caused by climbers. There are many climbing-related issues, however, such as unauthorized bolting, possible threats to the ancient rock art, and land claims on Hueco Tanks by Tigua Indians (Sherman 1992b, 34). Guidelines for climbing at Hueco are spelled out in a Memorandum of Understanding worked out between the El Paso Climbing Club and the Texas Parks and Wildlife Department. Park managers striving to balance the interests of climbers with the interests of other recreationists and the need for resource preservation have employed a variety of strategies and tactics. By 1993, these included registration and liability release forms, stringent enforcement of visitor rules and regulations, the closing of some climbing areas, a lengthy application process for installing fixed hardware on new routes, a requirement that climbers must have individual back country permits, and a mandatory conservation passport fee.[42]

Rock Gyms

The convergence of social, economic, and technological factors that gave birth to sport climbing made it inevitable that the popular core of the climbing sports would move in from the peaks and crags, through the gym door, and onto walls adorned with fixed anchors and artificial holds (fig. 13.6). It was also inevitable that sport climbing would become a carefully packaged commercial product and a flashy professional sport. Indeed, by the 1990s sport climbing was well on the way to becoming a predominantly urban activity and an integral component of the mass culture scene.

This trend may have welcome environmental consequences, since it will take some pressure off outdoor resources. Some sport climbers seem to have little interest in the Great Outdoors. For these people, and for many outdoor enthusiasts driven indoors by bad weather, climbing means pumping plastic on a climbing wall or a bouldering problem.[43] In a general sense, the arrival of user-oriented opportunity has made climbing a sport like tennis or racquetball; people can climb in the evenings, on the weekends, or maybe even during their lunch hour, and their motives may include fitness, weight control, or simply general health.

Artificial holds and other climbing wall paraphernalia are manufactured in amazing variety and marketed at affordable prices. Thousands of ardent climbers have used this technology to construct their own climbing walls and bouldering problems in basements, lofts, stairwells, and spare rooms, and on or in garages and barns. Portable climbing walls are available for purchase, lease, or rental in some areas.

FIG. 13.6. Youngster on a top-rope at a rock gym. Note the attentive belayer and the large, conveniently spaced holds on this beginner's route.

Climbing walls have been built at some colleges, in some city parks or recreation centers, and by quasi-public organizations such as the YMCA.

Since some people like to climb *on* the city as well as in it, urban climbing (a.k.a. buildering or concrete climbing) has a long and colorful history.[44] Human flies were making news in America and Europe more than seventy-five years ago. In the 1930s, Oxford undergraduates often climbed campus belfries and clock towers, and they even wrote a how-to-do-it guidebook. More recently, urban climbers have scaled thousands of other structures, including the World Trade Center, Chicago's 110-story Sears Tower, and even Buckingham Palace. While it is almost universally illegal, climbers have glued holds on many buildings, freeway overpasses, bridge abutments, and other structures throughout America's cities.

For most sport climbers, the place to climb in the city is an indoor climbing gym, or "rock gym." A rock gym is akin to a fitness center or health club, in that it normally has features such as a weight training room, full-body exercise equipment, locker rooms, showers, and air conditioning. It is distinguished, however, by thousands of square feet of top-roped and liberally bolted climbing walls built to resemble rock faces, and by devices such as fingerboards and Metolius trainers that climbers use for conditioning/strengthening exercises. Walls in the 18- to 40-foot height range are commonplace. Higher ones are also in use, including at least one former elevator shaft and a 110-foot grain silo with twenty-five thousand square feet of climbing walls. Some walls are made with actual textured rock, but most are constructed of plywood or other synthetic materials. Nearly all are equipped with movable holds of various shapes and sizes, which can be arrayed to create a countless number of routes and problems of different degrees of difficulty. A better-quality rock gym will have lead-climb, international competition–quality walls with a variety of realistic features and challenges such as corners, overhangs, and finger-jam cracks. Most gyms have bouldering walls or caves, and some have rappel towers, ice climbing walls, or high-tech simulators like vertical treadmills with holds.

Whatever its accouterments, a rock gym is a place where the curious can try climbing to see if they like it, and thereafter climb as often as they like. Since indoor climbing does not expose climbers to the objective dangers associated with the sport as it is traditionally practiced, it is relatively undemanding and cannot develop many of the decision-making skills vital to survival in the outdoors. Nevertheless, climbers can practice their moves and hone their skills, watch and learn from more experienced climbers, receive professional instruction, stay in shape in the off-season, compete with other climbers, and, of course, see and be seen. Since most climbers are young, it matters that a rock gym provides opportunities to "hotdog" in front of an appreciative crowd, and it can be a great place to meet friends.

The rock gym concept was imported to America from Europe. Climbing walls were first built in France during the fifteenth century to teach soldiers castle-storming techniques. The British revived the climbing wall concept and developed it for recreational use in the 1960s and 1970s; by the late 1980s, there were at least 250 climbing walls in the United Kingdom (Barry and Sheperd 1988). Leadership in wall climbing subsequently passed to the French, who embraced the rock gym concept and made indoor competitive climbing a high-visibility sport in Europe.

During the late 1980s, the rock gym diffused from Europe to the United States, Canada, Japan, and other countries. America's first indoor climbing gym, the Vertical Club, opened its doors in Seattle in 1987.[45] By 1994, more than one hundred rock gyms had been built in metro areas throughout the nation, with the densest concentration probably occurring in the area between Fort Collins and Denver in Colorado.[46]

Since California has over a third of the U.S. climbing population, it is not surprising that it has many fine rock gyms (Woolf and Woolf 1993). One of the best is City Rock, a state-of-the-art climbing gym at Emeryville in the San Francisco Bay area between Oakland and Berkeley. City Rock's focal component is six thousand square feet of variegated climbing terrain that rises to forty feet and conforms to international competition standards (City Rock 1992). Also on the premises are an outdoor speed competition wall, an Olympic-class weight room, aerobic machinery, a well-stocked pro shop, showers, and locker rooms. Shoes, harnesses, and related climbing equipment are available for rent. The gym offers professional instruction at the beginning level and for various special skills, as well as basic skills classes for schools and special groups, summer youth comprehensive training programs, weekend classes for children, and even birthday parties. Climbing competitions are regularly scheduled, and featured events attract top professionals from throughout North America and the world. For example, the 1992 American Sport Climbing Federation (ASCF) National Climbing Competition was held at City Rock. Like most other rock gyms and fitness centers, City Rock offers individual, group, and corporate membership rates as well as daily fee rates for walk-ins.

A Commercially Driven Sport

As an editor of *Climbing* magazine noted, "at some point every growing sport becomes commercially driven: sponsorship increases, the media records the action, endorsements arrive" (Osius 192b, 8). So it is with sport climbing, which is now a large and profitable industry whose endorsements and other subsidies help support professional climbers. A Colorado-focused sport climbing series, the Tour de Pump, has offered competitions for climbers at every ability level since its beginning in 1992. The corporate sponsors of America's 1994 ASCF National Climbing Competition included more than a dozen vendors of climbing sportswear, shoes, rope, walls and holds, training devices, power snacks, and related products. America's four widely circulated climbing magazines (*Climbing, Rock & Ice, Sport Climbing,* and *Summit*) feature glossy ads promoting a wide assortment of goods and services to an audience that is an ad agency's dream. Leading American sport climbers like Jim Karn, Doug Englekirk, Robyn Erbesfield, and Alison Osius have attracted considerable media attention as well as corporate sponsorship. American female "rockstar" Lynn Hill, who won more than twenty World Cup events before her retirement from fulltime international competition in 1993, has appeared on popular television shows and has been featured in articles in *Time, Life, Newsweek,* and the *New York Times Magazine.* Sport climbing's popularity is much greater in Europe, where youth climbing programs are highly developed, prizes and endorsements are more lucrative, and top competitors are revered athletes. The 1992 World Cup Championship at Nuremburg drew five thousand spectators.

Competitive climbing is truly an international sport. The 1993 UIAA World Cup calendar included two events in Germany, two in France, and one each in Switzerland, Norway, Great Britain, Bulgaria, Japan, and Austria (the World Championships). Russia staged its first World Cup competition in 1994. Segments of the World Cup competitions are televised internationally, with some airing on ESPN in the United States. When climbing becomes an Olympic sport, which most experts predict, the additional media coverage will provide a major boost.

The Malleable Perfect Place

Climbing's evolution to its present status as a commercially driven, mass culture phenomenon has yielded some remarkable changes in the technology, aesthetics, and standards of the sport. Were they alive today, Whymper and Mummery would be perplexed by sport climbing ethics, but they would also be delighted by the graceful athleticism of the "dance on the rock" and amazed to see how easily climbers now handle routes that would have been impossible in the Golden Age. Nothing would be more impressive, however, than the sheer diversity of today's vertical world—many more kinds of climbing and many more kinds of perfect places. Perhaps more than anything else, it is this wonderful abundance of choice that sets apart the modern sport and accounts for its burgeoning popularity.

Climbing has its revered traditions, but it has also adapted to the times and offered a niche for everybody. Indeed, few other sports have proven more malleable or accommodating. When heightened environmental awareness sent people streaming into the back country in the 1970s and 1980s, climbing and mountaineering offered perfect places and appropriate means to get in touch with the natural world and the spirit of outdoor adventure. Sport climbing methods made climbing safer and more enjoyable, opening the door to mass participation and the development of many more perfect places and routes. As health and fitness became a national obsession, rock gyms emerged to provide perfect places for stimulating workouts. The rise of commercially driven competitive climbing is simply an extension of the vertical world into one more kind of perfect place, the stadium or arena.

NOTES

CHAPTER ONE. **The Theater of Sport**

1. Mruzak 1983, 121. Compare this perspective with that of Pierre Bourdieu (1990, 159)
2. The symbolism of war or conflict may not be as far-fetched as it initially sounds. The word *yacht*, after all, derives from the middle German word *jacht*, which means hunting ship, a ship used to pursue pirates.
3. The word *trespass* is derived from a Middle English term, found in the 1455 Forest Laws of Scotland, which means passing across; transgression of an order or law.
4. Code of Virginia 1930, 316, 18 2 132. See also Carson 1963, 134 33.
5. Code of Alabama 1975, 209, 9-11-242.
6. *Minnesota Statutes Annotated* 1977, 175, 100.273.

CHAPTER TWO. **Baseball**

1. The "superstadiums" were built in Atlanta, Cincinnati, Houston, New York, Oakland, Philadelphia, Pittsburgh, San Diego, Saint Louis, and Washington.
2. Factual information about the major league ballparks came from two indispensable and encyclopedic sources. Reidenbaugh 1983 and Lowry 1986. The most useful source of speculative connections was James 1986.

CHAPTER THREE. **Cricket**

A version of this essay was read at the annual meeting of the Association of American Geographers in Phoenix, Arizona, April 1988. I am very grateful for the helpful comments made on an earlier draft by Rex Walford (Cambridge University, U.K.); Allen Guttmann (Amherst College, U.S.A.); Henning Eichberg (Idraetsforsk, Gerlev Idraetshøjskole, Denmark); and David Jenkins (Willows Publishing, U.K.), who also very generously allowed me access to his private cricket archives.

1. These three concepts are to be found in Sack 1986, Relph 1976, and Relph 1981, respectively. It should be stressed that Sack interprets territoriality as an expression of human attempts to affect and control geographical space.
2. The terms *elements* and *ensembles* are found in Raitz 1987a, 4–19; the discussion of scientific humanism appears in Relph 1981.
3. A good discussion of the character of folk games is found in Dunning and Sheard 1979. See also Guttmann 1978.
4. The pattern presented here is confirmed in Bowen 1970, 49, and in Brailsford 1987, 41–46.
5. Lennon 1987. Of the 388 players engaged with the seventeen first-class county clubs in 1987, 30, or 7.7 percent, were not qualified to play for England. This is probably an underestimate of foreign players in English cricket, since some will have become eligible to play for England as a result of a residential qualification (data from *Wisden Cricket Monthly* 8, no. 12 [1987]: 26–27).
6. The place of cricket in West Indian life is described in what is perhaps the best cricket book ever written: James 1965.
7. Cricket art is well dealt with in Simon and Smart 1983. See also Arlott and Cardus 1969 and Arlott 1980.
8. See Heald 1986; Sampson 1981; and Kilburn 1966.
9. I am grateful to Helle Ringgaard for a translation of this paper.

CHAPTER FOUR. Soccer

1. James 1963, 70.
2. Walvin 1975, 9–10; Considine 1982, 247–48; Bale 1982, 22–23; Rasmussen 1937, 76–81, 307–38; Huizinga 1955, 196–97.
3. Walvin 1975, 11; Morgan 1984, 53–54; Bridenbaugh 1968, 116–17.
4. Mason 1980, 9–10; Elias and Dunning 1986a, 180–84; Henshaw 1979, 553–54.
5. Considine 1982, 248; Walvin 1975, 14.
6. Hobsbawm (1969, 308) writes that "the function of football teams was to organize the (male) working-class community, normally around two permanently rival, local poles: most industrial cities developed two leading and competing teams." See also Mason 1989, 173; Inglis 1990, 157; Barwick and Sinstadt 1988; and Mitchell and Leys 1950, 317.
7. Walvin 1975, 12–13, 16.
8. FitzStephen quoted in Stow 1890, 118.
9. Coulton 1963, 242; Gardner 1976, 23; Elias and Dunning 1986a, 175–76.
10. Wheatley 1905, 133; Walvin 1975, 15, 17; Holmes 1964, 38; Mitchell and Leys 1958, 142.
11. Elias and Dunning 1986a, 177–79.
12. Gay quoted in Gardner 1976, 25.
13. Douglas-Irvine 1912, 144; Walvin 1975, 15; Myers 1972, 14–15; Rasmussen 1937, 80.
14. Mitchell and Leys 1958, 67; Edward Hall quoted in Stow 1890, 387–89.
15. Rasmussen 1937, 82–88; Elias and Dunning 1986b, 119.
16. Rasmussen 1937, 76–81, 307–38; Thurston 1974, 10, 108, 114–15.

17. Rasmussen 1937, chaps. 5, 8, 13 (quotations from 307, 319, 322–23, 337). The German idea of the stadion, or sports complex, is discussed later in this chapter, when I consider soccer in Germany, Denmark, Czechoslovakia, and the Soviet Union. England's informal parks and spontaneous soccer stadiums are the double antithesis of the stadion idea.

18. Mandell (1984, 155) argues that the strong archival records of early English football exist because "central authorities and the moralists so continuously, vigorously, and futilely opposed it." See also Mason 1980, 10, citing Malcolmson 1970, 89–91; and Walvin 1975, 17–25.

19. Walvin 1975, 26–27; Allison 1978, 209–10; Strutt 1801, quoted in Bayne-Powell 1938, 173–74; Howitt 1840, 527.

20. Walvin 1975, 19, 27–28; Mason 1980, 10, 14, 22–27.

21. Allison 1978, 211.

22. Mason 1980, 9, 12; Allison 1978, 211–12; Walvin 1975, 29, 36–39.

23. Mason 1980, 11; Considine 1982, 249; Inglis 1987, 46.

24. Mandell 1984, 155–56; Guttmann 1978, 127; Walvin 1975, 34.

25. Walvin 1975, 32–34, 40–41; Mandell 1984, 156; Mason 1980, 17–18.

26. Keeton 1972, 12; Walvin 1975, 40, 44, 47.

27. Gardner 1976, 27–28; Mason 1980, 14, 17–18.

28. Gardner 1976, 28–30; Considine 1982, 249–50; Elias and Dunning 1986c, 197–98. The Harrow Rules, from 1830 on, and the Cambridge University Rules of 1863 specified a field 150 yards by 100 yards maximum (Henshaw 1979, 113–14, 330–31).

29. Allison 1978, 212–13; Walvin 1975, 38, 45; Mason 1980, 14–15, 18.

30. Allison 1978, 214; Mason 1980, 47, and maps on 60–68; Bale 1982, 22–29, particularly maps on 26 and 28.

31. Allison 1978, 206–7, 211; Taylor 1976, 307–25. Walvin (1975, 56) writes that "Liverpool . . . before the turn of the century was to establish itself as *the* footballing centre of England" (italics in original).

32. Inglis 1987, 9.

33. Inglis 1987, 10, 140–42, 221–22.

34. Mason 1980, 141, 164; Inglis 1987, 10, 65, 111, 115–17, 140–41, 192–97, 247, 337, 339, 344, 358–59.

35. Mason 1980, 31, 53; Inglis 1987, 9–10, 62, 76, 232, 281.

36. Mason 1980, 139, Inglis 1987, 95, 98, 100, 129.

37. Inglis 1987, 136, 140, 142, 145, 158, 162, 168, 179, 344.

38. Walvin 1975, 70, 74–75; Brown 1960, 219; Inglis 1987, 138–39; Vamplew 1986, 198, 201, which maps early cup winners by region and period.

39. Considine 1982, 250; Gardner 1976, 28.

40. Inglis 1987, 114.

41. Bale 1989, 170–71; Inglis 1987, 98–99, 184.

42. Hobsbawm and Ranger (1984, 301, 306) write of the "all-English football culture" and "the football culture"; Bale (1982, 32) asks if football is "part of northern culture." Priestley (1929, 3–5) has no doubts at the games of Bruddersford United A.F.C: "A man who had missed the last home match of t'United

had to enter social life on tiptoe in Bruddersford" (alias Huddersfield Town) in the 1920s. See also Mason 1980, 181–82, 186n.

43. Inglis 1987, 11–13, 70–71, 86, 122, 133, 179, 187, 232, 247, 260, 265, 317, 323.

44. Mason 1989, 153; Inglis 1987, 209–12, 363.

45. Mason 1980, 150; Mason 1989, 152–53; Inglis 1987, 9–10; Dunning et al. 1990, 78.

46. Mason 1989, 152–53; Mason 1980, 139–40; Inglis 1987, 16–19, 27, 170, 173, 213–14, 222, 247.

47. Inglis 1987, 10–15.

48. Inglis 1987, 12, 18–19, 214, photos of Leitch grandstands on 17, 116, 192, 235, 293.

49. Inglis (1987, 13–14, 47) writes that "generally, pitches are now much smaller than they were before the First World War. . . . The extra yards were used for expanding terraces."

50. Hobson cited in Allison 1978, 215.

51. Inglis (1987, 23–25) reproduces diagrams and plans from Faulkner-Brown's article in the *Architects Journal* (January 1979). See also diagrams in Bale 1989, 170.

52. Brown 1960, 218.

53. Priestley 1929, 4.

54. Smith 1980, 379; Bale 1982, 29, quoting Mason 1980, 180.

55. Lever 1983, 16.

56. Mason 1989, 168; Bale 1989, 30–31.

57. Elias and Dunning 1986d, 85–87; Bale 1989, 147. McKibben 1989 quotes George Gaskell, social psychologist at the London School of Economics, who characterizes members of the "terrace culture" as "inner-city working-class males passionately committed to their teams, traveling around Britain in packs to follow their heroes from city to city. . . . These young men pack in together behind the goals in a sort of weekly celebration. Football is their focus in life."

58. There was singing at soccer games from the 1890s onward. Morgan (1984, 96n) notes hymn singing in the 1890s; Mason (1980, 159) notes prematch singing in the 1891 F.A. Cup Final and quotes the *Manchester Guardian*: "people could be heard—in a rude way it is true—to be taking parts, a thing quite beyond all South country folk"; Brown (1960, 17) writes of crowds coming to Wembley "with songs on their lips, rosettes on their coats"; and Mason (1989, 168) quotes from Howard Jacobson, *Coming from Behind* (London: Chatto and Windus 1983 [61–62]), "The cheering and the singing and the chanting from a crowd big enough to fill several hundred lecture theaters could not fail to have a profound effect on him. . . . As the stand tumbled and thundered around him his flesh thrilled and the spirit within was elevated and chastened." Marsh et al. (1978, 66–68) explain how chant leaders work.

59. Brown (1960, 17–18) writes that "A leather ball . . . is the centre of a ritual in one of the British religions; goalposts are totem poles and the players demi-gods. There are fierce celebrations of the cult all over the country." On Durkheim, sport, and religion, see Lever 1983, 14–17 n.23; a photograph of the "mass" at Anfield after the Hillsborough disaster appears in McKibben 1989.

60. Dunning et al. 1990, 6–7, 19, 24, 27, 45–78, 154–57, 240–41; Dunning et al.

1986, 246, 254–55; Hazleton 1989, 40–41, 66–69, with a needed counterweight in the Letters to the Editor, particularly the letter of V. B. Unnithan, May 14, 1989. The Home Office Committee of Inquiry into Crowd Safety and Control at Sports Grounds (Interim Report: Cmnd. 9585, 1985, 41) writes that "Most football grounds in England and Wales are now built like medieval fortresses, with pens at each end, with barriers designed to prevent spectators from climbing over, with gates, fences and protective wire to prevent rival fans from bombarding each other; and with the use of what is called a sterile area—a no man's land" (quoted in Mason 1989, 168).

61. Dunning et al. 1990, 6, 8; Dunning et al. 1986, 247, 278–79.

62. Dunning et al. 1990, 5–7; Dunning et al. 1986, 248–49. Marsh (1978, 61–64) recognizes at least four clearly defined territories of social groups, age-based and with different levels of aggro-involvement in even the small "end" at Oxford United.

63. Inglis 1990, 56, 70–73; Hazleton 1989, 68.

64. Inglis 1990, 8; McKibben 1989.

65. Inglis 1990, 7–9.

66. Allison (1978, 224) reminds us that the modern game is a "compromise between ancient emotions and modern industrial and urban society"; Dunning et al. 1990, 45–78.

67. Priestley 1929, 3–5; Brown 1935, 63–64. Hobsbawm (1969, 299) calls the peaceful partisans paid-up members of that "national form of working class life, association football."

68. Dunning et al. 1990, 4. McKibben (1989) writes of "tribalism" on the terraces.

69. Inglis 1990, 10, 23–24, 144; Gardner 1976, 36–39; Elias 1986, 128.

70. Inglis 1990, 69, 110–11, 133–36, 238, 278

71. Inglis 1990, 66–79, 112–14, 133–47, 162–63, 223–28, 233, 236–37, 240–46, 268–73.

72. Inglis 1990, 167–76, 195–229.

73. Inglis 1990, 66–79, 102–28, 133–47.

74. Inglis 1990, 10–57.

75. Inglis 1990, 60–65, 84–97, 100–101, 150–54, 164–66, 230–39, 256–81.

76. Inglis 1990, 185–94; Riordan 1977, 21–26, 112–13, 127–28, 133, 135, 149, 262–63, 313.

77. Inglis 1990, 58 59, 80 82, 84–89, 93–97, 148–50, 161–64, 180–82, 282–86.

78. Lever 1983, 40, 130; Stein 1988, 65; Henshaw 1979, 736.

79. Telephone interview with Jorge Matas, deputy consul general of Argentina in San Francisco, November 1991; Henshaw 1979, 36, 85, 201–2, 355, 589, 601.

80. Henshaw 1979, 35–36, 335, 589, 601; Allison 1978, 218.

81. Kendrew 1942, 285–87, 296, 301, 386–91, 399, 402; Inglis 1990, 202–5; Lever 1972, 139.

82. Lever 1972, 140–41; Henshaw 1979, 290, 571–73, 758; Graham 1968, 122; Shirts 1988, 101.

83. Lever 1972, 142–43; Lever 1988, 89–90.

84. Lever 1988, 87; Shirts 1988, 99–103, quoting Freyre on 99; Flynn 1971, 327–30.

85. Henshaw 1979, 89, 290–92, 758; Lever 1983, 75–80, 150–51.

86. Henshaw 1979, 95, 466–67; Lever 1983, 79, 88, 101–2, 114, photos between 120 and 121; Flynn 1971, 327–28; and on "aesthetics in the stands," see Shirts 1988, 101.
87. Lever 1983, 88–89, 135–36; Henshaw 1979, 91, 99–101, 153, 157–98, 558, 609–10, 643–45.
88. Kendrew 1942, 379–85, 399, 401–2; quotation from Lever 1983, 126.
89. Henshaw 1979, 114–15, 476, 485–86, 568–70, 645, 735–36.
90. Roger Williams (1643), Stansbury Hagar (1895), William Wood (1634), and William Strachey (1849) all cited in Culin 1975, 697–99.
91. Gardner 1976, 164–65; Henshaw 1979, 741–42.
92. Conversations over many years with two semi-professionals who came to work in Whittall's Mills, Worcester, Massachusetts: Joe Taylor of Burnley F.C. and Tommy McMillan of Dunfermline Athletic, head groundsmen at Clark University's Beaver Brook fields, 1965–92; Henshaw 1979, 745–46.
93. Henshaw 1979, 511–12; Considine 1982, 253.
94. Bowden 1990, 2–3, 12, 60–61, 82–91.

CHAPTER FIVE. **Tennis**

For their advice and material contributions to this chapter, I gratefully thank Rudolf Donath, Hugh Macindoe, Dorothy and John Meunier, Carolyn Miller, Sue and Jerry Ransohoff, Ken Rosewall, Marianne Ryan, and Keith Stewart.
1. Arlott 1975, 826–27; Whitman 1932, 22–29.
2. United States Tennis Association 1979, 4 (hereafter USTA).
3. Arlott 1975, 828–29; Brace 1975, 47.
4. Arlott 1975, 605; USTA 1979, 4.
5. Hadfield 1979, 246; Haley 1978, 134.
6. Duncan 1979; Bright 1979.
7. Duncan 1979, 93; Keighley 1979, 53.
8. Wind 1979, 213; Cameron and Salinger 1984, 121.
9. Tingay 1983, 19; Miller 1987.
10. Wind 1979, 17–19; Stern 1986, 188–91.
11. USTA 1979, 7; Whitman 1932, 112–23.

CHAPTER SIX. **Basketball**

1. "Basketball: Attracting 80,000,000" 1936, 37; Rooney 1974, 49.
2. Coe 1987, 138; Henderson 1981, 40, 207–8; Cuddon 1979, 92.
3. Culin 1907, 600, 603; Smith 1972, 354–55.
4. Quotation from Mandell 1984, 188–89; Gutman 1988, 70–81.
5. Naismith 1941, 42–52, 61–63; Menke 1963, 164–65; Arlott 1975, 68–69.
6. Spears and Swanson 1978, 163–64.
7. The atmosphere of creativity at the Springfield YMCA also resulted in the invention of volleyball by William Morgan in 1895, as described in Walters 1963, 994.
8. Mokray 1963, 3; Betts 1974, 130–31.

9. Spears and Swanson 1978, 165; Mokray 1963, 3.

10. Mokray 1963, 5–6; Wind 1980, 56.

11. Betts 1974, 131–32; Cuddon 1979, 92.

12. Spears and Swanson 1978, 165; Mokray 1963, 17.

13. Bauer 1974, 42 ff.; "Hooping It Up" 1977, 85; Spears and Swanson 1978, 297.

14. Van Riper 1967, 63; Koppett 1973, 23–28.

15. Cuddon 1979, 92; Deutsch 1975, 9.

16. Naismith 1941, 73; Mokray 1963, 4.

17. Naismith 1941, 66; Spears and Swanson 1978, 165.

18. Koppett 1973, 97; Mokray 1963, 7.

19. Hollander 1979, 7; Mokray 1963, 4; Koppett 1973, 98–99.

20. Naismith 1941, 93–95; Koppett 1973, 99.

21. Mokray 1963, 8; Cuddon 1979, 92; "Peach-Baskets into Profits" 1935, 32.

22. Naismith 1941, 54, 66–67.

23. Naismith 1941, 67–68; Koppett 1973, 98.

24. Mokray 1963, 2; Menke 1963, 165.

25. Naismith 1941, 71–72; Koppett 1973, 98; Mokray 1963, 7.

26. Koppett 1973, 102; Mokray 1963, 7.

27. Koppett 1973, 100; Mokray 1963, 8.

28. Deutsch 1975, 101; Koppett 1973, 104; Mokray 1963, 8.

29. Koppett 1973, 99–102; Mokray 1963, 8; Arlott 1975, 63.

30. Koppett 1973, 100–101; Mokray 1963, 8.

31. Salzberg 1987, 69; Deutsch 1975, 128.

32. Cuddon 1979, 95; McCallum 1987, 40.

33. Hollander 1979, 576; Newman 1979, 29; Cuddon 1979, 95.

34. Deutsch 1975, 9; Mokray 1963, 9.

35. Van Riper 1967, 36–37; Deutsch 1975, 9.

36. Mokray 1963, 8; Spears and Swanson 1978, 217.

37. Wind 1980, 55, 85; Spears and Swanson 1978, 290.

38. Deutsch 1975, 62; Salzberg 1987, 18.

39. Deutsch 1975, 128; Salzberg 1987, 196.

40. Jares 1968, 16–19; Hollander 1979, 83.

41. Axthelm 1970, 3–5; Kirkpatrick 1968, 20–23.

42. Wielgus and Wolff 1980, 99–101; Telander 1976, 182.

43. Wielgus and Wolff 1980, 107–8, Telander 1973, 58.

44. Berkow 1983, 88; Flaherty 1971, 10.

45. Al Harden, head coach of Fountain Central High School in Veedersburg, Indiana, quoted in Rooney 1974, 165; italics in original.

CHAPTER EIGHT. Golf

1. Marking the inception of golf in the United States with the founding of the St. Andrews Golf Club in 1888 is not without dispute. There is clear evidence that golf was played at various locations earlier and that a number of golf clubs were established prior to St. Andrews. St. Andrews, however, was the first club to be founded that can document an unbroken tenure to the present. It thus lays claim

to being the oldest permanent golf club in the United States. For a discussion of early golf in the United States, see Browning 1955 and Wind 1948.

2. Unless otherwise specified, all data used to describe the number of U.S. golf courses, golf facilities, and golfers were obtained from the National Golf Foundation, Jupiter, Florida. Thanks go to Joseph Beditz of the NGF.

3. A golf facility is a club or complex that contains one or more golf courses.

4. For a more detailed discussion of the evolution and geographic structure of American golf facilities, see Adams and Rooney 1985 and Adams and Rooney 1989.

5. U.S. Golf Association and the Royal and Ancient Golf Club of St. Andrews 1988, 17, 16, 12. The "flagsticks" are also defined in the *Rules of Golf* and might be regarded as a prescribed parts of the course, except that the rules do not state that they are required (although by convention they are always present).

6. For discussions of the origin(s) of golf and similar antecedent games, see Browning 1955 and Stirk 1987.

7. Use of the term *links* has become broadened through time to include courses located in any coastal environment—or indeed, any golf course.

8. Cornish and Whitten 1981, 16. This outstanding book traces the evolution of the golf course and golf course architecture from the early days of the game in Scotland to the present.

9. For a detailed discussion of the evolution of golf course architecture and advances in allied fields, see Cornish and Whitten 1981.

10. In a match play tournament, the field is whittled to two players for the last round, and the tournament ends when one player has a lead in the number of holes won that exceeds the number of holes remaining to be played. In stroke play, the tournament ends on the last hole for the entire field, and with prescribed tee times, the time that the tournament will end is relatively predictable (except when ties send the contest into extra holes); therefore, the stroke play format is better suited to the constraints of television.

11. Whitney 1894, 17–32; Martin 1895, 302–21.

12. For a discussion of the diverse nature of country clubs in the United States, see Boyle 1963.

13. See, for example, Lanier 1989.

CHAPTER NINE. **Stock Car Racing**

1. A sad footnote to this discussion, yet another sign of changing times, marks the deaths of Alan Kulwicki, while being flown in his corporate sponsor's jet to a race in Tennessee, and Davey Allison, while piloting his personal helicopter to watch a friend run test laps in Alabama, during the 1993 season.

CHAPTER TEN. **Rodeo**

1. "Cowhand" is a more accurate and less sexist term than cowboy. But in this chapter, references to cowboys should be taken as militantly ungendered; rodeo announcers, for example, habitually refer to women contestants as "cowboys," and so shall we. Cowboys are, of course, not just an American phenomenon.

There are rodeo clubs complete with letter-perfect cowboy regalia in Germany, France, and England. The styles are borrowed and much aided by effective geographical movement—working "hands" throughout the Americas draw upon the Spanish-Moorish traditions that came in 1492, in addition to the herding traditions of Europe, Africa, and anyplace else where livestock are raised for meat, milk, traction, or hides.

2. Depending upon how such activities are valued, rodeo probably belongs in the same rank as hunting, circuses, bullfighting, prizefighting, and maybe equestrian events like the steeplechase—events that include some element of genuine physical danger from animals, but where human skill can prevail with elegance.

3. Hall 1976, 8. Skepticism about the precise place of the rural West as matched up to the urban is a set piece in the new western history and geography. For a general discussion, see Limerick 1987; for a more current view, read Starrs 1992, 7–15.

4. For details, see Jordan 1993 and Jordan 1981. A remarkable treatment, short and sensible, is Strickon 1965, 229–58. See also Webb 1981.

5. In many places, it is children who tend the animals. Usually, however, boys dominate: Heidi is more exception than rule. In large parts of Africa and through much of Europe, the Middle East, East Asia, and the Americas, animal tending is a male practice.

6. Vaquero practices in California, and along the Spanish borderlands, included nearly all of the modern rodeo sports. But the *carrera del gallo* was a peculiar favorite: see Baur 1988, 26–37, or Westrich 1985, 38–43.

7. The California ranching practices included "tailing" a recalcitrant animal bent on leaving a herd by grabbing its tail, wrapping it around a saddle horn, and spurring a horse to jump forward, throwing the steer or cow tail over head and pointing it back into the herd. Or there was the placing of a bull and a boar together so they would fight (which led Horace Greeley to his "bulls and bears" metaphor for Wall Street). Modern rodeo events seem pallid by comparison.

8. The private activities—rawhide braiding, saddle making, rein making, the construction of spurs or silver bits, chap building, sketching, painting, or writing—have clearly found a vast public outlet as well: look at any "western" gallery in the United States to see where "cowboy" art (which was once vernacular, before it became more precious) finds outlets. Russell and Remington, Will James and Andy Adams, after all, began as real cowhands.

9. Hall 1976, 8. See also Clayton and Clayton 1988 and Stoeltje 1989. The transformation is not especially surprising, and there were many outlets. Wild West shows brought some of the West's more flamboyant practices to eastern audiences. And the many eastern tourists who went West to see the sights, after the 1890s often staying on dude ranches, were quick to admire, adopt, and promote roping skills, bronc riding, and other dude ranch fare. See Borne 1983, 117–18, for a discussion. The relationship between the cowhand and the rodeo cowboy is not dissimilar to that of the ranch hand and the dude wrangler.

10. Fredriksson 1985, 4; Freeman 1988.

11. It is no accident that one of Remington's most famous paintings shows a cowboy on foot, opening a gate. The title—"The Fall of the Cowboy"—is as much a reference to a cowhand having to work on foot as to the looming prevalence of

fences on the formerly open range. At least part of the reason true cowboy boots have three- or even four-inch heels, undershot to a heel cap the size of a quarter, is to prove that the hand rarely has to walk.

12. Or, as Jay Dusard, a well-known photographer, has commented: "The vanishing breed has been busily vanishing for the past three-quarters of a century, but they haven't finished the job yet. Each succeeding generation of grizzled veterans has lamented into the record the passing of the true cowboy. Yet these same crusty-handed waddies have invariably undermined their own stand by passing on to the next group of aspiring cowpunchers the old skills, nuances, and survival tricks" (1983, 19).

13. The definitive treatment of these changes remains Pomeroy 1957, but see also Jakle 1985.

14. Fredriksson 1985, 11. The literature on the Wild West shows is quite respectable. There are at least four books: Blackstone 1986; Bold 1987; Fredriksson 1985; and a particularly acute series of articles in Hassrick et al. 1981.

15. Fredriksson 1985, 6. The variations in professional rodeo associations are many. Some of them involve a variety of women's (cowgirl) associations, as discussed in Allen 1992 and Jordan 1984.

16. Just as women were prominent in western ranching, female cowhands were pivotal players in the early years of rodeo. See LeCompte 1993.

17. Lawrence 1982, 87–88. Women were at least as tough as men, as shown in LeCompte 1989.

18. Fredriksson 1985, 113; Borne 1983.

19. Fredriksson 1985, 183–200. Corporate sponsorships have had a great impact. The most prominent contributor has been the R. J. Reynolds Tobacco Company; others include United States Tobacco, Wrangler Jeans, United Airlines, Coors Beer, Dodge Trucks, Justin Boots, and Resistol Hats.

20. Beyond the broadcasts of ESPN, it is difficult to turn on almost any cable station that boasts a southern or western constituency without seeing rodeo events broadcast in the summer or fall. They make for grand television, and there is even some specialization—instead of showing all the rodeo events, there are "theme" broadcasts showing just bullriding, for example. (Patty Daly, Professional Rodeo Cowboys Association, interview by Mark Okrant, Colorado Springs, Colorado, January 3, 1988.)

21. Ranch rodeos still exist and are a mainstay of rural western life: see Clayton and Clayton 1988 and Lawrence 1982, 21.

22. *USA Today*, February 18, 1987. An estimated 16 million people attended PRCA rodeos during 1986.

23. Survey of selected western Chambers of Commerce by Mark Okrant, August 1988.

24. Small surprise that Cody, Wyoming, is also the home of the Buffalo Bill Historical Museum. Cody is at once a medium-size gateway city to Yellowstone National Park, a center for dude ranching (even today) in western Wyoming, and the town where Buffalo Bill Cody spent considerable time (his hotel—the Irma—burned down just a few years ago). His original house was moved from Nebraska to Cody; the level of obsession is notable.

25. See Gary Snyder's delightful poem "The Grand Entry," with its memorial to the Nevada County rodeo: "The many American flags / Whip around on horseback / Carried by cowgirls" (Snyder 1983, 77).

26. *Prorodeo Sports News*, 62, 20–31; Hall 1976, 24.

27. Hutchins 1977; Okrant 1977.

28. Veteran rodeo hands will often maintain connections with local ranchers or amateur rodeo riders and will make arrangements to borrow horses, if they cannot bring their own. But a skilled horse makes an immense amount of difference—decisive, in many cases.

29. The trained cutting horse is a throwback to the Spanish fine-reined tradition of training, and a well-schooled cutting horse is not only invaluable on the range but also worth a mint. Snaffle-bit futurities (for younger horses), cutting contests, and even the gymkhana events, popular among young riders, are showcases that are allied to the spirit of rodeo, if more in keeping with practical ranch work.

30. "Dally roping," required by the team roping event, is a skill taken directly from the Spanish and Mexican traditions and is exceptionally dangerous—if a digit is caught between the rope and the saddle horn, when the seven-hundred-pound steer hits the end of the rope, fingers can pop off and sometimes do. Nonetheless when dallying (from the Spanish *dar la vuelta*) is artfully done, nothing is prettier.

31. 1986 PRCA membership data.

32. The accounting aspect of rodeo is treated in Hibdon 1989, 237–48.

33. Alaska and Hawaii excepted—although Hawaii has a very pronounced cowboy and rodeo tradition that is becoming evident on the mainland.

34. Iowa, Missouri, Arkansas, and Louisiana; the southeastern states of Florida, Georgia, Alabama, Mississippi, Tennessee, and Kentucky; the Great Lakes states of Wisconsin, Illinois, and Indiana.

35. With more cattle in the United States actually raised east of the Mississippi than west of it, there is no denying that stock farming is not uniquely western. But the crucial style of ranching—raising animals over vast acreages—which has provided the raison d'être of ranching from the nineteenth century to today is predominant in the West.

36. Okrant 1977, and census data from *Rand McNally Road Atlas: 1977*.

37. By definition, PRCA events are the larger ones—the other sanctioning organizations probably fill a niche in smaller towns.

38. 1986 PRCA membership data; *Rand McNally Road Atlas: 1986*.

39. Jim Peterson, South Dakota High School Rodeo Association, interview by Mark Okrant, Mobridge, South Dakota, August 1987. Rodeo can be dangerous indeed. Meyers et al. (1990) discuss injuries among collegiate rodeo athletes and find that 92 percent of the injuries come in the "rough stock" events, and also that 40 percent of collegiate rodeo athletes suffer injuries.

40. *NLBRA Rodeo Committee Guide* 1986, 4: 41–44.

41. Fredriksson 1985, 105. There has been an influx of well-educated contestants. Fredriksson estimates that one-fourth of all PRCA cowboys are college educated.

CHAPTER ELEVEN. **Thoroughbred Racing**

1. Longrigg 1972, 230; Herbert 1980, 127.
2. *Blood Horse* 1978, 3289. See also Zelinsky 1980, 817–24.

CHAPTER THIRTEEN. **Climbing**

1. Personal communication from the Outdoor Recreation Coalition of America, a trade association of outdoor companies. Some industry sources place the number at a half-million in 1994.
2. Mitchell 1983, 227–33. Research shows that nonclimbers tend to think that climbing is either ridiculous, sublime, purposeful, or a natural activity (137–52).
3. Menocal 1992; National Park Service 1993.
4. Meier 1987, 25; Williamson and Miskiw 1992, 64. During the period 1951–91, reported mountaineering accidents resulted in 3,455 injuries and 985 deaths. One striking characteristic of climbing magazines is that each issue (some are quarterly; others publish six issues annually) contains an obituaries section.
5. Allen 1987; Ewert 1985; Gardiner 1990; Helms 1984.
6. Hamilton 1979; Mitchell 1983, 104.
7. Bernstein 1989d, 118–19. It is doubtful that Mallory actually said this.
8. Meier 1987, 25; see also Fair 1992, 38–40.
9. Among the systems in use by the late 1980s were the UIAA (Union Internationale des Associations d'Alpinisme), American (including both the Yosemite Decimal and the National Climbing Classification System schemes), English/Welsh, Extended Saxon, Scottish, Australian, Czechoslovakian, and East German (Barry and Sheperd 1988; Mitchell 1983, 88–89).
10. Subcategories (a, b, c, d) are used at some levels. The scale is open-ended, and standards have been rising rapidly in recent years. Since climbers making initial ascents tend to overstate their difficulty, consensus ratings are more reliable.
11. Pitons, also called pins or pegs, are wedge-shaped spikes driven into cracks for use as anchors. There are various types, including the knife blade–thin RURP (Realized Ultimate Reality Piton), which is the size of a postage stamp.
12. Jumars are mechanical devices that lock on the rope and are used for ascending or descending in stairstep fashion. Prusiks are stirrup-like foot loops attached to the rope with friction knots that slide when unweighted.
13. Roper and Steck 1979, 306–7. The scale is open-ended.
14. Hackett 1978; Lentz, Macdonald, and Carline 1985.
15. Culberson 1993, 159. The death rate includes Sherpas, who have been serving as porters for climbing and trekking expeditions since Nepal began welcoming climbers in 1949 (Carrier 1992).
16. By 1976 there were at least thirty-four hundred English-language climbing books (Neate 1980). The American Alpine Club's library had about fifteen thousand books in 1993.
17. Bernstein 1989b, 52–53; Ullman 1964, 38–43.
18. Bernstein 1989b; Whymper 1871.
19. Bernstein 1989c; Stone 1992.

20. The official Nepalese name for Mount Everest is Sagarmatha, which apparently means "the summit of the skies" in Nepali (Bernstein 1989a, 48). The local name remains Chomolunga, "Goddess Mother of the Earth" (Carrier 1992, 76). The other eight-thousanders are K2 (Godwin Austen), Kangchenjunga, Lhotse, Makalu, Dhaulagiri I, Cho Oyu, Manaslu, Nanga Parbat, Annapurna I, Gasherbrum I (Hidden Peak), Broad Peak, Gasherbrum II, and Gosainthan (Shisha Pangma).

21. In 1993 Nepal increased the Everest permit fee by 500 percent to $50,000 per team of up to five members, plus $10,000 for each additional member to a maximum of seven (Osius 1992a, 34). There is a trash deposit of $4,000 per team (refundable upon removal of climbing detritus), plus Khumbu Icefall route maintenance fees of over $200 per climber (Hawley 1993a, 55).

22. Staffed year-round since 1984, the ranger station at Talkeetna provides assistance and information to climbers before, during, and after climbs in the park. Registration and briefings (offered in six languages) are mandatory (National Park Service 1987, 28–29). Rangers also patrol Denali from a camp at about 14,300 feet on the West Buttress (Krakauer 1992, 55). By 1994, Denali's climbing and rescue program cost $600,000 a year, and the Park Service had proposed to charge each climber a $200 fee beginning in 1995 (Davidson 1994, 50).

23. It was on Denali's flanks in 1932 that a plane made the first glacier landing in support of climbing (Ullman 1964, 112).

24. Everett 1984, 91; Ullman 1964, 100–111.

25. Culberson 1992; Roper and Steck 1979, 19–24.

26. Sherwonit 1992a, D-14; Sherwonit 1993, 32.

27. National Park Service 1987, 4. Gusts of 150+ mph have been observed.

28. Waterman 1991; Krakauer 1992; Sherwonit 1992a. By 1992 there were at least thirty-three unrecovered bodies on the mountain (Sherwonit 1992b).

29. Krakauer 1992, 60. Foreigners account for a disproportionately high percentage of the deaths and rescue situations on Denali. This has led to speculation about possible cultural influences (Sherwonit 1993), and the Park Service recently decided to place more emphasis on foreigners in its climber education presentations.

30. Krakauer 1992, 60; Kennedy 1993, 78–79.

31. Barry 1987; Chouinard 1978.

32. The prime avalanche season is December through March, and climbers in the Ouray area are well advised to carry avalanche beacons. Avalanches have killed at least sixty-five people in Ouray County (French 1993b, 93).

33. Roper and Steck 1979, 254–68. Some of the original pitons from the Nose Route climb sold for more than $300 each at a 1992 auction (Davidson 1992).

34. Stevenson 1993, 16–19; Stuller 1987; Watts 1993.

35. Clean climbing employs wedge nuts, cams, and other ingenious devices designed for insertion into cracks and crevices as temporary, easily removable anchors.

36. Stuller 1987; Vetter 1992, 61. A rappel, abseil, or ropedown is a means of descending a cliff on a looped rope using the friction of the rope around the climber's body, or through a special device, to control the rate of descent. Recreational rappelling has become a sport in itself.

37. Colliver 1993; National Park Service 1993.
38. Access Fund n.d. [1992], 1; Vogel 1992.
39. Ament 1992; Blunk and Achey 1993.
40. Piana 1992; Sherman 1992a.
41. Ryan 1992, 54. "Vermin" is the nickname of the originator, John Sherman. As of 1994, Hueco had at least several "undoctored" V12 boulder problems.
42. Davidson 1993a; HTSHP 1992; Ryan 1993; Sherman 1992b.
43. While some artificial holds are made from real rock, wood, or ceramic clay, most are cast from plastic (polyester resin) to which a natural grout of crushed rock or sand is added for texture (Raleigh 1992).
44. Schultheis 1984, 178; Long 1980, 253–55; Wetzler and Howells 1992, 34, 36.
45. America's first purpose-built artificial climbing wall is thought to be Schurmann Rock (formerly Monitor Rock), which was erected in 1941 in the William G. Long Camp near Seattle (Meldrum and Royle 1970, 30; Neate 1980, 43).
46. Martin 1993. During 1992–93, nearly sixty different commercial rock gyms placed ads in major climbing magazines.

REFERENCES

Access Fund, The. n.d. [1992]. *Climbing Information—Joshua Tree National Monument*. Los Angeles: Access Fund.

Adams, Robert L. A. 1986. "The Crisis in Public Golf Course Development." In *Golf Projections 2000*. Jupiter, Fla.: National Golf Foundation.

———. 1987. "Same Name, Different Game." *Sport Place* 1/2.

Adams, Robert L. A., and John F. Rooney, Jr. 1984. "Condo Canyon: An Examination of Emerging Golf Landscapes in America." *North American Culture* 1.

———. 1985. "Evolution of American Golf Facilities." *Geographical Review* 75.

———. 1989. "American Golf Courses: A Regional Analysis of Supply." *Sport Place* 3.

Adelman, Melvin L. 1986. *A Sporting Time: New York City and the Rise of Modern Athletics, 1920–70*. Urbana: University of Illinois Press.

Allen, Michael. 1992. "The Rise and Decline of the Early Rodeo Cowgirl— The Career of Mable Strickland." *Pacific Northwest Quarterly* 83.

Allen, Stewart D. 1987. "Risk Recreation: A Literature Review and Conceptual Model." In *High Adventure Outdoor Pursuits: Organization and Leadership*, edited by Joel F. Meier, Talmadge W. Morash, and George E. Welton. 2d ed. Columbus, Ohio: Publishing Horizons.

Allison, Lincoln. 1978. "Association Football and the Urban Ethos." In *Manchester and Sao Paolo: Problems of Rapid Urban Growth*, edited by J. D. Wirth and R. L. Jong. Stanford, Calif.: Stanford University Press.

———. 1980. "Batsman and Bowler: The Key Relation of Victorian England." *Journal of Sport History* 7.

———. 1985. "Cricket Is a Comin' In." *New Society* 72.

Ament, Pat. 1992. *Master of Rock: A Lighthearted Walk through the Life and Rock Climbing of John Gill*. Lincoln, Neb.: Adventure's Meaning Press.

Arlott, John. 1955. *The Picture of Cricket*. Harmondsworth: Penguin.

———. 1980. "Art." In *Barclay's World of Cricket*, edited by E. W. Swanton and John Woodcock. London: Collins.

———. 1984. *Arlott on Cricket*. Ed. D. R. Allen. London: Collins.

Arlott, John, and Neville Cardus. 1969. *The Noblest Game*. London: Harrap.

Arlott, John, ed. 1975. *The Oxford Companion to World Sports and Games*. London: Oxford University Press.

August, Marilyn. 1986. "Roland Garros." *World Tennis* 34.

Australian Sports Commission. 1985. *Australian Sport: A Profile*. Canberra: Australian Government Publishing Service.

Axthelm, Peter. 1970. *The City Game: Basketball from the Garden to the Playgrounds*. New York: Harper's Magazine Press, 1982. Reprint, New York: Penguin Books.

———. "The City Game Grows Up." *Newsweek*, August 11.

Baerwald, Thomas J., and Charles F. Gross. 1974. "The Production of Professional Basketball Players." Paper presented at the Annual Meeting of the Association of American Geographers, Seattle.

Bailey, Paul. 1978. *Leisure and Class in Victorian England*. London: Routledge.

Baker, William J. 1982. *Sports in the Western World*. Totowa, N.J.: Rowman and Littlefield.

Bale, John. 1981. "Cricket in Pre-Victorian England." *Area* 13.

———. 1982. *Sport and Place*. London: C. Hurst; Lincoln: University of Nebraska Press.

———. 1986. "Sport and National Identity: A Geographical View." *British Journal of Sports History* 3.

———. 1989. *Sports Geography*. London: Spon.

———. 1994. *Landscapes of Modern Sport*. London: Leicester University Press.

Barkow, Al. 1989. *The History of the PGA Tour*. New York: Doubleday.

Barry, John. 1987. *Snow and Ice Climbing*. Seattle: Clondcap.

Barry, John, and Nigel Sheperd. 1988. *Rock Climbing*. Harrisburg, Pa.: Stackpole Books.

Barwick, Brian, and Gerald Sinstadt. 1988. *Everton v. Liverpool*. London: BBC Books.

"Basketball: Winter Sport Attracting 80,000,000 Spectators Each Season." 1936. *Literary Digest*, December 12.

"Basketball: Favorite of 20,000,000." 1937. *Literary Digest*, January 2.

"Basketball Plays." 1945. *Life*, January 22.

Bauer, Douglas. 1974. "Meet the Bullettes . . . Mediapolis, Iowa's Most Celebrated Export." *Today's Health*, March.

Baur, John E. 1988. "Sporting Life in Early Los Angeles." *Californians* 6.

Bayne-Powell, Rosamund. 1938. *Eighteenth-Century London Life*. New York: Dutton.

Belloc, Hilaire. 1921. "The North Sea." In *Great Hours in Sport*, edited by John Buchan. London: Thomas Nelson.

Berkow, Ira. 1983. "The Game—and Life—Goes On." *New York Times Magazine*, August 21.

Bernstein, Jeremy. 1979. The Endless Climb of Reinhold Messner. *Reader's Digest*, October.

———. 1989a. "Little-Known Facts about the World's Best-Known Mountain." In *Mountain Passages*. Rev. ed., 1st Touchstone ed. New York: Simon and Schuster.

———. 1989b. "Whymper and Mummery." In *Ascent: The Invention of Mountain Climbing and Its Practice*. Rev. ed., 1st Touchstone ed. New York: Simon and Schuster.

———. 1989c. "Une Bonne Ballade." In *Ascent: The Invention of Mountain Climbing and Its Practice*. Rev. ed., 1st Touchstone ed. New York: Simon and Schuster.

———. 1989d. "Some Walk-Going." In *In the Himalayas*. Touchstone edition. New York: Simon and Schuster.

Bess, Philip H. 1987. "Bill Veeck Park." In *The National Pastime*, edited by John Thorn. Garrett Park, Md.: Society for American Baseball Research.

Betts, John R. 1953. "The Technological Revolution and the Rise of Sport, 1850–1900." *Mississippi Valley Historical Review* 40.

———. 1974. *America's Sporting Heritage: 1850–1950*. Reading, Mass.: Addison-Wesley.

Biemiller, Carl L. 1951. "Hoop-Happy Town." *Holiday*, February.

Birkett, Norman. 1957. Foreword to *Village Cricket*, by A. Forrest, London: Hale.

Blackstone, Sarah J. 1986. *Buckskins, Bullets, and Business: A History of Buffalo Bill's Wild West*. Westport, Conn.: Greenwood Press.

Blaine, Delabere P. 1852. *An Encyclopedia of Rural Sports*. 2d ed. London: Longman, Brown, Green, and Longmans.

Blanchard, Kendall. 1974. "Basketball and the Culture-Change Process: The Rimrock Navajo Case." *Council on Anthropology and Education Quarterly* 5. Reprinted in *Play, Games, and Sports in Cultural Context*, edited by Janet C. Harris and Roberta J. Parks. Champaign, Ill.: Human Kinetics, 1983.

Blofeld, Henry. 1978. *The Packer Affair*. London: Collins.

Blood Horse, The. July 24, 1978.

———. 1993. *The Source, 1993–94*. Lexington, Ky.: The Blood Horse.

Blow, Simon. 1983. *Fields Elysian: A Portrait of Hunting Society*. London: J. M. Dent.

Blunk, Scott, and Jeff Achey. 1993. "Bouldering and the Essence of Climbing." *Climbing* 137.

Bold, Christine. 1987. *Selling the Wild West: Popular Western Fiction, 1869–1960*. Bloomington: Indiana University Press.

Bolus, Jim. 1984. "Harvey Vanier: From Lucky Pete to a Fine 'Fellow.' " *Horseman's Journal* 35.

Borne, Lawrence. 1983. *Dude Ranching: A Complete History*. Albuquerque: University of New Mexico Press.

Bourdieu, Pierre. 1990. "Programme for a Sociology of Sport." In *In Other Words: Essays Towards a Reflexive Sociology*, edited by P. Bourdieu, translated by Matthew Adamson. Stanford, Calif.: Stanford University Press.

Bourret, Tim, ed. 1989. *The Clemson Football Guide*. Athletic Department, Clemson University, Clemson, S.C.

Bowden, Martyn J. 1990. *Hamlets: A History and Geography of Sutton Fuller Hamlets Soccer Club, 1969–1989*. Sutton, Mass.: Putnam House.

Bowen, Ezra. 1969. "I Finally Got the Point." *Sports Illustrated*, February 10.

Bowen, Roderick. 1970. *Cricket: A History of Its Growth and Development throughout the World*. London: Eyre and Spottiswode.

Boyle, Robert H. 1963. *Sport—Mirror of American Life*. Boston: Little, Brown.

Brace, Reg. 1975. "Tennis—It's the Real Thing." *Grand Prix Tennis Annual*. London: Commercial Union Grand Prix.

Bracklen, Milton. 1942. "10,000,000 Fans Are Mad about It." *New York Times Magazine*, January 25.

Brailsford, Dennis. 1987. "The Geography of Eighteenth-Century English Spectator Sports." *Sport Place* 1.

Bridenbaugh, Carl. 1968. *Vexed and Troubled Englishmen, 1590 to 1642*. New York: Oxford University Press.

Bright, James L. 1979. *The Tennis Court Book: A Player's Guide to Home Tennis Courts*. Andover, Mass.: Brick House.

Broadribb, Gerald. 1985. *Next Man In: a Survey of Cricket Laws and Customs*. London: Pelham.

Brock, David. 1937. *To Hunt the Fox*. London: Seeley.

Brookes, Christopher. 1978. *English Cricket*. London: Weidenfeld and Nicolson.

Brown, Graham, and Sir Gavin de Beer. 1957. *The First Ascent of Mont Blanc*. London: Oxford University Press.

Brown, Ivor. 1935. *The Heart of England*. London: Batsford.

——. 1960. *London*. London: Newnes.

Browning, Robert. 1955. *A History of Golf*. New York: Dutton.

Brussell, Eugene E. 1970. *A Dictionary of Quotable Definitions*. Englewood Cliffs, N.J.: Prentice-Hall.

Cady, Edwin H. 1978. *The Big Game: College Sports and American Life.* Knoxville: University of Tennessee Press.

Cameron, Robert, and Alistair Cooke. 1980. *Above London.* San Francisco: Cameron.

Cameron, Robert, and Pierre Salinger. 1984. *Above Paris.* San Francisco: Cameron.

Camp, Walter. 1974 [1891]. *American Football.* New York: Harper and Bros.

Cardus, Neville. 1929. *Days in the Sun.* London: Cape.

———. 1930. *Cricket.* London: Longman.

———. 1972. *Cardus on Cricket.* London: Souvenir Press.

Carrier, Jim. 1992. "Gatekeepers of the Himalaya." *National Geographic* 182.

Carson, Jane. 1965. *Colonial Virginians at Play.* Williamsburg, Va.: Colonial Williamsburg.

Castro, Janice, and Timothy Foote. 1976. "Sex and Tennis." *Time* 108.

Chamblin, Keith. 1986. "Alabama Bound for Racing." *Blood Horse,* April 12.

Chew, Peter. 1974. *The Kentucky Derby, The First 100 Years.* Boston: Houghton Mifflin.

Chouinard, Yvon. 1978. *Climbing Ice.* San Francisco: Sierra Club Books.

Chronicle of the Horse, The. 1986. 49.

City Rock. 1992. "City Rock Gym." Emeryville, Calif.: City Rock [advertising brochure].

Clayton, Lawrence, and Sonja Irwin Clayton. 1988. *Ranch Rodeos in West Texas: Abilene, Albany, Anson, and Breckenridge, with a Play Day Benefit in Albany—Ranch Cowboys Team Up to Show How They Do Their Work.* Abilene, Tex.: Hardin-Simmons University Press.

Clerici, Gianni. 1975. *The Ultimate Tennis Book.* Chicago: Follett.

Climbing. 1993. "New Hopes for Telluride Ice." *Climbing* 137.

Code of Alabama. 1975. Charlottesville, Va.

Code of Virginia. 1950. Charlottesville, Va.

Coe, Michael D. 1987. *The Maya.* 4th ed., rev. London: Thames and Hudson.

Cole, K. J. 1982. "The Beginnings of Club Cricket." *Wisden Cricket Monthly* 6.

"College Girls and Basket-Ball." 1902. *Harper's Weekly,* February 22.

Collier, Terence. n.d. "Acquiring a Horse." *Thoroughbred Ownership: A Guide for Potential Owners and Breeders.* Elmont, N.Y.: Thoroughbred Owners and Breeders Association.

Colliver, Gary. 1993. "Personal Freedom and the Management of Climbing." *Climbing* 138.

Conniff, Richard. 1988. "After a While, Nothing Seems Strange in a Stadium with a 'Lid.' " *Smithsonian,* January.

Considine, Tim. 1982. *The Language of Sport*. New York: Facts on File.

Cornish, Geoffrey, and Ronald Whitten. 1981. *The Golf Course*. New York: Rutledge.

Cosgrove, Dennis, and Stephen Daniels. 1988. "Iconography and Landscape." In *The Iconography of Landscape*, edited by Dennis Cosgrove and Stephen Daniels. Cambridge: Cambridge University Press.

Coulton, G. G. 1963. *Chaucer and His England*. London: Methuen.

Cousins, Geoffrey. 1975. *Golf in Britain*. London: Routledge and Kegan Paul.

Cronin, Don. 1990. "Golfer's Paradise." *USA Today*, March 22.

Cuddon, J. A. 1979. *The International Dictionary of Sports and Games*. New York: Schocken Books.

Culberson, Matt. 1992. "In the Eye of the Beholder." *Climbing* 134.

——. 1993. "Sherpa Use and Misuse: The Climber's Responsibility." *Climbing* 136.

Culin, Stewart. [1907] 1975. *Games of the North American Indians*. Paper accompanying the *Twenty-Fourth Annual Report of the Bureau of American Ethnology to the Smithsonian Institution, 1902–1903*. Washington, D.C.: U.S. Government Printing Office. Reprint, New York: Dover Publications.

Curtiss, Frederic. 1932. *The Country Club, 1882–1932*. Brookline, Mass.: Privately printed for the Club.

Daily Racing Form. 1993. *American Racing Manual*. Lexington, Ky.: K-3 Communications.

Davidson, Sam. 1992. "Access: Big Falls, Big Fun." *Climbing* 135.

——. 1993a. "No More Pranks at Hueco Tanks." *Climbing* 136.

——. 1993b. "New Regulations in the Works to Limit Bolt Use." *Climbing* 138.

——. 1994. "Access Alert: Management and Policy." *Climbing* 144.

DeBroke, Willoughby. 1921. "A Crowded Day." In *Great Hours in Sport*, edited by John Buchan. London: Thomas Nelson.

Deford, Frank. 1982. "A Team That Was Blessed." *Sports Illustrated*, March 29. Reprinted in *The World's Tallest Midget: The Best of Frank Deford*. Boston: Little, Brown, 1987.

Denniston, Derek. 1992. "Alpine Slide." *World Watch*, September/October.

Deutsch, Jordan A., text; David S. Neft, Roland T. Johnson, and Richard M. Cohen, comps. 1975. *The Sports Encyclopedia: Pro Basketball*. New York: Grosset and Dunlap.

Dodgson, Charles L. [Lewis Carroll]. 1883. *Lawn Tennis Tournaments—The True Method of Assigning Prizes with a Proof of the Fallacy of the Present Method*. London: Macmillan.

Donleavy, J. P. 1984. *De Alfonce Tennis: The Superlative Game of Eccentric*

Champions: Its History and Accoutrements, Rules, Conduct, and Regimen. New York: Dutton/Lawrence.

Douglas-Irvine, H. 1912. *History of London.* New York: James Pott.

Duncan, S. Blackwell. 1979. *How to Build Your Own Tennis Court.* Blue Ridge Summit, Pa.: Tab Books.

Dunning, Eric, and Kenneth Sheard. 1979. *Barbarians, Gentlemen, and Players.* Oxford: Martin Robertson.

Dunning, Eric, et al. 1986. "Spectator Violence at Football Matches: Towards a Sociological Explanation." In *Quest for Excitement,* edited by N. Elias and E. Dunning. Oxford: Blackwell.

——. 1990. *The Roots of Football Hooliganism: An Historical and Sociological Study.* London: Routledge.

Dusard, Jay. 1983. *The North American Cowboy: A Portrait.* Prescott, Ariz.: Consortium Press.

Earley, Mary-Dawn, ed. 1983. *The Great Australian Annual.* Sydney: Kevin Weldon.

"Ed Who?" 1993. *Outside* 18.

Edwards, John. 1979. "The Home-Field Advantage." *Sports, Games, and Play: Social and Psychological Viewpoints,* edited by Jeffrey H. Goldstein. Hillsdale, N.J.: Erlbaum.

Eichberg, Henning. 1984. "Olympic Sport—Neocolonialism and Alternatives." *International Review for Sociology of Sport* 19.

——. 1985. "De Rette og Krumme Linier." *Centring* 85.

—— 1986. "The Enclosure of the Body—On the Historical Relativity of 'Health,' 'Nature,' and the Environment of Sport." *Journal of Contemporary History* 21.

Elias, Norbert. 1986. "The Genesis of Sport as a Sociological Problem." In *Quest for Excitement,* edited by N. Elias and E. Dunning. Oxford: Blackwell.

Elias, Norbert, and Eric Dunning. 1986a. "Folk Football in Medieval and Early Modern Britain." In *Quest for Excitement.*

——. 1986b. "Leisure in the Spare-time Spectrum." In *Quest for Excitement.*

——. 1986c. "Dynamics of Sport Groups with Special Reference to Football." In *Quest for Excitement.*

——. 1986d. "The Quest for Excitement in Leisure." In *Quest for Excitement.*

Ellul, Jacques. 1965. *The Technological Society.* London: Cape.

Evans, Richard. 1983. "Out of This World—25 Vacation Spots." *World Tennis* 30.

——, ed. 1983. *Tales from the Tennis Court: An Anthology of Tennis Writing.* London: Sidgwick and Jackson.

Everett, Boyd N., Jr. 1984. *The Organization of an Alaskan Expedition.* Pasadena, Calif.: Gorak Books.

Ewert, Alan. 1985. "Why People Climb: The Relationship of Participant Motives and Experience Level to Mountaineering." *Journal of Leisure Research* 17.

Fair, Erik. 1992. "Rock Climbing." In *California Thrill Sports*. San Francisco: Foghorn Press.

Fielden, Greg. 1987–91. *Forty Years of Stock Car Racing*. 4 vols. Ormond Beach, Fla.: Galfield Press.

Flaherty, Joe. 1971. "When Happiness Used to Be a 12-Foot Set Shot." *Life*, April 9.

Flower, Raymond. 1976. *The History of Skiing and Other Winter Sports*. New York: Methuen.

Flynn, Peter. 1971. "Sambas, Soccer, and Nationalism." *New Society*, August 19.

Fox, John, Jr. 1885. "Fox-Hunting in Kentucky." *Century* 50.

Fredriksson, Kristine. 1985. *American Rodeo: From Buffalo Bill to Big Business*. College Station: Texas A&M University Press.

Freeman, Danny. 1988. *World's Oldest Rodeo: 100-Year History, 1888–1988*. Prescott, Ariz.: Prescott Frontier Days.

French, Diane. 1993a. "High Action On and Off the Ice at Ouray Festival." *Climbing* 136.

———. 1993b. "Ouray, Colorado, U.S.A." *Summit* (Spring).

Frith, David. 1987. *Pageant of Cricket*. London: Macmillan.

Furlong, William Barry. 1962. "Where Basketball Is a Ritual." *New York Times Magazine*, March 4.

Furnas, J. C. 1969. *The Americans: A Social History of the United States*. New York: Putnam.

Gadd, Will. 1992. "Karnage: Jim Karn in the 1990s." *Rock & Ice* 50.

Gaines, William H., Jr. 1953. "John Peel in Virginia: Fox Hunting in the Old Dominion, Frolicsome and Fashionable." *Virginia Cavalcade* 3.

Gale, F. 1871. *Echoes of Old Cricket Fields*. London: Simpkin Marshall.

Gallwey, W. Timothy. 1974. *The Inner Game of Tennis*. New York: Random House.

Galtung, Johann. 1984. "Sport and International Understanding: Sport as a Carrier of Deep Culture and Structure." In *Sport and International Understanding*, edited by M. Illmarinen. Berlin: Springer-Verlag.

Gardiner, Steve. 1990. *Why I Climb: Personal Insights of Top Climbers*. Harrisburg, Pa.: Stackpole Books.

Gardner, Paul. 1976. *The Simplest Game*. Boston: Little, Brown.

Gray, James H. 1985. *A Brand of Its Own: The 100-Year History of the Calgary Exhibition and Stampede*. Saskatoon, Sask.: Western Producer Prairie Books.

Graydon, Don, ed. 1992. *Mountaineering: The Freedom of the Hills*. 5th ed. Seattle: Mountaineers.

Gelber, Stephen. 1983. "Working at Playing: The Culture of the Workplace and the Rise of Baseball." *Journal of Social History* 16.

Graham, Richard. 1968. *Britain and the Onset of Modernization in Brazil, 1850–1914.* Cambridge: Cambridge University Press.

Green, Benny. 1987. "Great Bores of Tennis Past and Present." *Punch* 293.

Gruber, Katherine, ed. 1987. *Encyclopedia of Associations,* pt. 2. Detroit: Gale Research.

Gutman, Bill. 1988. *The Pictorial History of Basketball.* New York: Gallery Books.

Guttmann, Allen. 1978. *From Ritual to Record.* New York: Columbia University Press.

Hackett, Peter. 1978. *Mountain Sickness: Prevention, Treatment, and Recognition.* 6th ed. New York: American Alpine Club.

Hadfield, Miles. 1979. *A History of British Gardening.* 3d ed. London: John Murray.

Haley, Bruce. 1978. *The Healthy Body and Victorian Culture.* Cambridge, Mass.: Harvard University Press.

Hall, Douglas Kent. 1973. *Let 'er Buck.* New York: Dutton.

———. 1976. *Rodeo.* New York: Ballantine Books.

Hamilton, Lawrence. 1979. "Modern American Rock Climbing: Some Aspects of Social Change." *Pacific Sociological Review* 22.

Hamlyn, Mary. 1985. "Instant Cricket Storms Lord's." *Observer.* N.d.

Hargreaves, John. 1987. "The Body, Sport, and Power Relations." In *Sport, Leisure and Social Relations,* edited by John Horne et al. Sociological Review Monograph 33. London: Routledge.

Harrison, Fairfax. 1929. "The Genesis of Foxhunting in Virginia." *Virginia Magazine of History and Biography* 37.

Hart, John Fraser. 1975. *The Look of the Land.* Englewood Cliffs, N.J.: Prentice-Hall.

Hassrick, Peter H., Richard Slotkin, Vine Deloria, Jr., Howard R. Lamar, William Judson, and Leslie A. Fiedler. 1981. *Buffalo Bill and the Wild West.* Brooklyn, N.Y.: Brooklyn Museum.

Hawkins, Bobbie Louise. 1977. *Back to Texas.* Berkeley, Calif.: Bear Hug Books.

Hawley, Elizabeth. 1993a. "Slow Season In Nepal's High Mountains." *Climbing* 137.

———. 1993b. "Record Crowds Maul Everest." *Climbing* 139.

Hazleton, Lesley. 1989. "British Soccer: The Deadly Game." *New York Times Magazine,* May 7.

Heald, Tim. 1986. *The Character of Cricket.* London: Faber.

Helms, Michael. 1984. "Factors Affecting Evaluations of Risks and Hazards in Mountaineering." *Journal of Experiential Education* 7. Reprinted in *High Adventure Outdoor Pursuits: Organization and Leadership,* edited by Joel F. Meier, Talmadge W. Morash, and George E. Welton. 2d ed. Columbus, Ohio: Publishing Horizons, 1987.

Henderson, John S. 1981. *The World of the Ancient Maya*. Ithaca, N.Y.: Cornell University Press.

Henshaw, Richard. 1979. *Encyclopedia of World Soccer*. Washington, D.C.: New Republic Books.

Herbert, Ivor, ed. 1980. *Horse Racing: The Complete Guide to the World of the Turf*. New York: St. Martin's Press.

Hervey, John. 1937. *Racing in America, 1922–1936*. New York: Jockey Club, Scribner.

———. 1944. *Racing in America, 1665–1865*. 2 vols. New York: Jockey Club, Scribner.

Hibdon, James E. 1989. "The Economics of Rodeo Cowboys." *Social Science Journal* 26.

Hobsbawm, E. J. 1969. *Industry and Empire*. Harmondsworth: Penguin.

Hobsbawm, E. J., and T. Ranger, eds. 1984. *The Invention of Tradition*. Cambridge: Cambridge University Press.

Hoffman, Davy. 1987. *America's Greatest Golf Courses*. New York: Gallery Books.

Hoggart, Richard. 1958. *The Uses of Literacy*. Harmondsworth: Penguin.

Hollander, Zander, ed. 1979. *The Modern Encyclopedia of Basketball*. 2d rev. ed. Garden City, N.Y.: Doubleday.

Holliman, Jennie. 1931. *American Sports, 1785–1835*. Durham, N.C.: Seeman Press.

Hollingsworth, Kent. 1976. *The Kentucky Thoroughbred*. Lexington: University Press of Kentucky.

Holmes, Urban Tigner, Jr. 1964. *Daily Living in the Twelfth Century*. Madison: University of Wisconsin Press.

"Hooping It Up Big in the Cornbelt." 1977. *Time*, March 28.

Houghland, Mason. 1949. *Gone Away*. Berryville, Va.: Blue Ridge Press.

Houghton, Donald. 1974. "When Cash Registers in the Millions." *Courier-Journal and Times Magazine*, April 28.

Howe, Steve. 1993. "Night-Naked." *Summit* (Spring).

Howitt, William. 1840. *The Rural Life of England*. London: Longmans, Green.

Hueco Tanks State Historical Park. 1992. "Hueco Tanks State Historical Park Regulations." El Paso, Tex.: HTSHP.

Hugill, Peter. 1984. "The Landscape as a Code for Conduct: Reflections on Its Role in Walter Firey's 'Aesthetic-Historical-Genealogical Complex.'" *Geoscience and Man* 24.

Huizinga, Johan. 1970. *Homo Ludens: A Study of the Play Element in Culture*. New York: Harper and Row.

Immen, Wallace. 1990. "Fancy Suites Lack Ball-Game Atmosphere." *Globe and Mail* (Toronto), April 21.

Information Please Almanac, The. 1989. 42d ed. Boston: Houghton Mifflin.

Inglis, Fred. 1977. *The Name of the Game: Sport and Society*. London: Heinemann.

Inglis, Simon. 1987. *The Football Grounds of Great Britain*. London: Collins Willow.

———. 1990. *The Football Grounds of Europe*. London: Willow.

Institut National de la Statistique et des Etudes Economiques (INSEE). 1986. *Annuaire statistique de la France 1986*. 91st ed. Paris: Ministère de l'Economie, des Finances, et de la Privatisation.

Jackson, Peter, and Susan Smith. 1984. *Exploring Social Geography*. London: Allen and Unwin.

Jakle, John. 1985. *The Tourist: Travel in Twentieth-Century North America*. Lincoln: University of Nebraska Press.

James, Bill. 1986. *The Bill James Historical Baseball Abstract*. New York: Villard Books.

James, C.L.R. 1963. *Beyond a Boundary*. London: Stanley Paul.

Janiskee, Robert L. 1989. "The South Carolina Grand Strand Golf Resort Region." Paper presented at the Annual Meeting of the Southeast Division, Association of American Geographers, Charleston, W.Va.

Jares, Joe. 1968. "Dandy in the Dome." *Sports Illustrated*, January 29.

Johnson, Norris, and David Marple. 1973. "The Basis for Acquired Skills." University of Cincinnati, Department of Sociology. Mimeo.

Jordan, Teresa. 1984. *Cowgirls: Women of the American West*. Garden City, N.Y.: Anchor Books/Doubleday.

Jordan, Terry G. 1981. *Trails to Texas: Southern Roots of Western Cattle Ranching*. Lincoln: University of Nebraska Press.

———. 1993. *North American Cattle-Ranching Frontiers: Origins, Diffusion, and Differentiation*. Albuquerque: University of New Mexico Press.

"Kansas Town with Basketball Fever, A." 1958. *Life*, March 3.

Karpf, Anne. 1988. "Match Points." *Listener* 119.

Keating, Frank. 1987. "Only Four Can Play." *Punch* 293.

Keeble, Lewis. 1959. *Principles and Practice of Town and Country Planning*. 2d ed. London: Estates Gazette.

Keeton, George W. 1972. *The Football Revolution*. Newton Abbot, England: David and Charles.

Keighley, Michael J., ed. 1979. *A Guide to Tennis Club Planning, Building, and Financing*. North Miami, Fla.: Industry Publishers.

Kendrew, William G. 1942. *The Climates of the Continents*. New York: Oxford University Press.

Kennedy, Michael. 1993. "The Dream." *Climbing* 136.

Kentucky Thoroughbred Association. 1984. *A Report on the Survey of Kentucky Thoroughbred Breeding Farms.* Lexington, Ky.

Kerouac, Jack. 1978. *The Town and the City.* New York: Harcourt Brace Jovanovich.

Kilburn, J. M. 1980. "County Grounds of England." In *Barclay's World of Cricket,* edited by E. W. Swanton and John Woodcock. London: Collins.

Kircher, Rudolf. 1928. *Fair Play: The Games of Merrie England.* London: Collins.

Kirkpatrick, Curry. 1968. "A Place in the Big-City Sun." *Sports Illustrated,* August 5.

Kobbé, Gustav. 1901. "The Country Club and Its Influence upon American Social Life." *Outlook* 68.

Koppett, Leonard. 1973. *The Essence of the Game Is Deception: Thinking about Basketball.* Boston: Little, Brown. A *Sports Illustrated* Book.

Krakauer, Jon. 1992. "Mean Season on Denali." *Outside* 17.

Kuntz, Paul G. 1973. "The Aesthetics of Sport." In *The Philosophy of Sport,* edited by Robert G. Osterhoudt. Springfield, Ill.: Charles C. Thomas.

Lait, Matt. 1989. "Cities Seek Order on the Court." *Washington Post,* July 29.

Lancaster, Hal. 1987. "Stadium Projects Are Proliferating Amid Debate over Benefit to Cities." *Wall Street Journal,* March 20.

Lanier, Pamela. 1989. *Golf Resorts.* Oakland, Calif.: Lanier.

Lawrence, Elizabeth Atwood. 1982. *Rodeo: An Anthropologist Looks at the Wild and the Tame.* Knoxville: University of Tennessee Press.

LeCompte, Mary Lou. 1989. "Champion Cowgirls of Rodeo's Golden Age." *Journal of the West* 28.

———. 1993. *Cowgirls of the Rodeo: Pioneer Professional Athletes.* Urbana: University of Illinois Press.

Lee, Laurie. 1957. "A Festive Occasion—Letter from Cannes." *Encounter* 9.

Lennon, David. 1987. *Cricket Mercenaries.* London: Pavilion.

Lentz, Martha J., Steven C. Macdonald, and Jan D. Carline. 1985. *Mountaineering First Aid: A Guide to Accident Response and First Aid Care.* 3d ed. Seattle: Mountaineers.

Lester, Ted. 1980. "Time to Divide Field into Zones." *Cricketer International* 61.

Lever, Janet. 1972. "Soccer as a Brazilian Way of Life." In *Games, Sport, and Power,* edited by Gregory P. Stone. New Brunswick, N.J.: Transaction Books.

———. 1983. *Soccer Madness.* Chicago: University of Chicago Press.

———. 1988. "Sport in a Fractured Society: Brazil under Military Rule." In *Sport and Society in Latin America,* edited by Joseph L. Arbena. Westport, Conn.: Greenwood Press.

Lewis, Peirce. 1979. "Axioms for Reading the Landscape." In *The Inter-*

pretation of Ordinary Landscapes, edited by Donald Meinig. New York: Oxford University Press.

Limerick, Patricia Nelson. 1987. *The Legacy of Conquest: The Unbroken Past of the American West.* New York: Norton.

Lohman, Jack, and Arnold Kirkpatrick. 1984. *Successful Thoroughbred Investment in a Changing Market.* Lexington, Ky.: Thoroughbred Publishers.

Long, Jeff. 1980. "In the Constellation of Roosters and Lunatics." In *Ascent: The Mountaineering Experience in Word and Image.* Vol. 3, edited by Allen Steck and Steve Roper. San Francisco: Sierra Club Books.

Longrigg, Roger. 1972. *The History of Horse Racing.* New York: Stein and Day.

——. 1975. *The History of Foxhunting.* New York: Potter.

Louisville Courier-Journal. December 1, 1985.

Lowenthal, David. 1985. *The Past Is a Foreign Country.* Cambridge: Cambridge University Press.

Lowenthal, David, and Hugh Prince. 1965. "English Landscape Tastes." *Geographical Review* 55.

Lowry, Philip. 1986. *Green Cathedrals.* Cleveland: Society for American Baseball Research.

Lucas, John A., and Ronald A. Smith. 1978. *Saga of American Sport.* Philadelphia: Lea and Febiger.

Lukermann, F. 1964. "Geography as a Formal Intellectual Discipline and the Way in Which It Contributes to Human Knowledge." *Canadian Geographer* 8.

MacAloon, John, and Mihaly Csikszentmihalyi. 1977. "Deep Play and the Flow Experience in Rock-Climbing." In *Beyond Boredom and Anxiety,* edited by M. Csikszentmihalyi. San Francisco: Jossey-Bass.

McCallum, Jack. 1987. "The Three-Point Uproar." *Sports Illustrated,* January 5.

McCallum, John D. 1978. *College Basketball, U.S.A.: Since 1892.* New York: Stein and Day.

McCrone, Kathleen E. 1988. *Playing the Game: Sport and the Physical Emancipation of English Women, 1870–1914.* Lexington, Ky.: University Press of Kentucky.

MacDonnell, A. G. 1935. *England Their England.* London: Macmillan.

McElyea, Richard, and Gene Krekorian. 1988. "Changing Economics of Golf." *Golf Market Today* 28.

Macindoe, Hugh G. 1987. "The Tennis Court on the Boulevarde [Sydney, Australia]." Manuscript.

Mackay-Smith, Alexander. 1968. *The American Foxhound, 1747–1967.* Millwood, Va.: American Foxhound Club.

McKibben, Gordon. 1989. "Soccer Deaths Wound English." *Boston Globe,* April 23.

McLean, Teresa. 1983. *The English at Play at the Middle Ages.* Berks, England: Kensal Press.

McPhee, John. 1972. *Wimbledon—A Celebration.* Photographs by Alfred Eisenstaedt. New York: Viking.

Maddux, Bob Lee. 1961. *History of the Walker Hound.* Cookville, Tenn.: privately printed.

Malamud, Bernard. 1952. *The Natural.* New York: Farrar, Straus and Cudahy.

Malcolmson, R. W. 1970. "Popular Recreations in English Society, 1700–1850." Ph.D. diss., University of Warwick.

Mandell, Richard D. 1984. *Sport: A Cultural History.* New York: Columbia University Press.

Mandell, Richard D. 1972. *The Nazi Olympics.* New York: Ballantine.

Marsh, Peter, et al. 1978. *The Rules of Disorder.* London: Routledge and Kegan Paul.

Martin, Claire. 1993. "The Secret to Access." Weekend, *Denver Post,* February 19.

Martin, Edward. 1895. "Country Clubs and Hunt Clubs in America." *Scribner's Magazine* 18.

Martin, H. B. 1936. *Fifty Years of American Golf.* New York: Dodd, Mead.

Martin-Jenkins, Christopher. 1984. *Cricket—a Way of Life.* London: Century.

Mason, Tony. 1980. *Association Football and English Society, 1863–1915.* Brighton: Harvester.

——. 1989. *Sport in Britain: A Social History.* Cambridge: Cambridge University Press.

Meier, Joel F. 1987. "Is the Risk Worth Taking?" In *High Adventure Outdoor Pursuits: Organization and Leadership,* edited by Joel F. Meier, Talmadge W. Morash, and George E. Welton. 2d ed. Columbus, Ohio: Publishing Horizons.

Meldrum, Kim, and Brian Royle. 1970. *Artificial Climbing Walls.* London: Pelham Books.

Menke, Frank G. 1963. "Basketball." *Encyclopedia of Sports.* 3d rev. ed. New York: A. S. Barnes.

Menocal, Armando. 1992. "The 'Legal' Status of Climbing." *Rock & Ice* 47.

Meyers, Michael C., J. R. Elledge, J. C. Sterling, and H. Tolson. 1990. "Injuries in Intercollegiate Rodeo Athletes." *American Journal of Sports Medicine* 18.

Milburn, J. M. 1966. "Australia." In *The World of Cricket,* edited by E. W. Swanton. London: Michael Joseph.

Miller, Carolyn B. 1987. Photographs of tennis club in Kalemegdan Fortress, Beograd, Yugoslavia.

Miller, Glenn. 1991. "Designers Wanted Stadium to Be FAN-tastic." Sec. Spring Training with the Twins, Fort Myers, Fla. *News-Press*, March 7.

"Million Witnesses, A." 1939. *Scholastic*, February 18.

Minnesota Statutes Annotated. 1977. Saint Paul, Minn.

Mitchell, Richard G., Jr. 1983. *Mountain Experience: The Psychology and Sociology of Adventure*. Chicago: University of Chicago Press.

Mitchell, R. J., and M.D.R. Leys. 1950. *A History of the English People*. London: Longmans, Green.

——. 1958. *A History of London Life*. Harmondsworth: Penguin.

Mokray, William G., comp. and ed. 1963. "History of Basketball." In *Roland Encyclopedia of Basketball*. New York: Roland Press.

Morgan, Prys. 1984. "From a Death to a View." In *The Invention of Tradition*, edited by E. Hobsbawm and T. Ranger. Cambridge: Cambridge University Press.

Mruzek, Donald J. 1983. *Sport and American Mentality, 1880–1910*. Knoxville: University of Tennessee Press.

Muirhead, Desmond. 1970. "Building the Golf Course." In *Land: Recreation and Leisure*. Special Report, First Annual Land Use Symposium. Washington, D.C.: Urban Land Institute.

Murry, Mike. ed. 1989. *1989 Michigan Football Media Guide*. Ann Arbor: University of Michigan Athletic Department.

Myers, A. R. 1972. *London in the Age of Chaucer*. Norman: University of Oklahoma Press.

Naismith, James. 1941. *Basketball: Its Origin and Development*. New York: Association Press.

National Golf Foundation. 1989. "Exploring Other Opportunities for Success." *Golf Market Today* 29.

——. 1993. *Golf Facilities in the United States*. Jupiter, Fla.: National Golf Foundation.

National Park Service. 1987. *Mountaineering in Denali National Park and Preserve*. Denali National Park, Alaska: National Park Service.

——. 1993. "[Rock Climbing] Advance Notice of Proposed Rulemaking and Management Statement." *Federal Register*, June 14, pp. 32878–80.

Neate, W. R. 1980. *Mountaineering and Its Literature*. 2d ed. Seattle: Mountaineers.

Neilson, Brian. 1986. "Dialogue with the City: The Evolution of the Baseball Park." *Landscape* 29.

Nelson, Arvid E., Jr. 1967. *The Ak-Sar-Ben Story: A Seventy-Year History of the Knights of Ak-Sar-Ben*. Lincoln, Nebr.: Johnsen Publishing Co.

Neustadtl, Sara. 1992. "Move Over Columbus." *Summit* (Fall).

Newman, Bruce. 1985. "Back Home in Indiana." *Sports Illustrated*, February 18.

Newman, Gerald, ed. 1979. *The Concise Encyclopedia of Sports*. 2d rev. ed. New York: Franklin Watts.

NLBRA Rodeo Committee Guide. 1986. Colorado Springs, Colo.: National Little Britches Rodeo Association.

Okrant, Mark. 1977. "Toward a Geography of Rodeo." Paper presented at the 73d Annual Meeting of the Association of American Geographers, Salt Lake City.

Olivová, Vera. 1985. *Sport and Games in the Ancient World*. New York: St. Martin's Press.

Oriard, Michael V. 1976. "Sport and Space." *Landscape* 21.

Osius, Alison. 1992a. "Looking for a Home: An AAC Update." *Climbing* 135.

———. 1992b. "Questions of Buck$ and Balances." *Climbing* 134.

Otto, William. 1947. "Hoop-Happy Town." *Collier's*, January 11.

Patterson, O. 1969. "The Ritual of Cricket." *Jamaica Journal* 3.

"Peach-Baskets into Profits." 1935. *Literary Digest*, December 28.

Pearce, John Ed. 1974. "The Bluegrass Stakes." *Courier-Journal and Times Magazine*, May 2.

Peirce, Neal R. 1975. *The Border South States*. New York: Norton.

Petit Larousse illustré. 1978. Paris: Librairie Larousse.

Piana, Paul. 1992. *Great Rock Hits of Hueco Tanks*. La Crescenta, Calif.: Mountain 'n' Air Books.

Piper, C. V., and R. A. Oakley. 1917. *Turf for Golf Courses*. New York: Macmillan.

Pomeroy, Earl. 1957. *In Search of the Golden West: The Tourist in Western America*. New York: Knopf.

Priestley, J. B. 1929. *The Good Companions*. London: Harper.

Prorodeo Sports News. 1986. Vol. 34, Championship Edition. Colorado Springs, Colo.: Professional Rodeo Cowboy Association.

Professional Rodeo Cowboy Association Media Guide, 1993 (PRCA Media Guide). 1993. Colorado Springs, Colo.: Professional Rodeo Cowboy Association.

Prunty, Merle, Jr. 1963. "The Woodland Plantation as a Contemporary Occupance Type in the South." *Geographical Review* 53.

Rader, Benjamin G. 1983. *American Sports: From the Age of Folk Games to the Age of Spectators*. Englewood Cliffs, N.J.: Prentice-Hall.

Raitz, Karl B. 1985. "Interpreting America's Leisure Landscape." Paper presented at the Geographical Dimensions of Sports Studies Conference, West London Institute of Higher Education, England.

———. 1987a. "Perception of Sports Landscapes and Gratification in the Sport Experience." *Sport Place* 1.

——. 1987b. "Place, Space, and Environment in America's Leisure Landscapes." *Journal of Cultural Geography* 8.

——. 1988. "American Fox Hunting: Landscape Ensemble and Gratification." *Sport Place* 2.

Raleigh, Duane. 1992. "The Modular Squad: A Real Look at Fake Holds." *Climbing* 135.

Rand McNally Road Atlas: 1977. Chicago: Rand McNally.

Rand McNally Road Atlas: 1986. Chicago: Rand McNally.

Rasmussen, Steen Eiler. 1937. *London: The Unique City.* New York: Macmillan.

Raverat, Gwen. 1953. *Period Piece.* New York: Norton.

Reidenbaugh, Lowell. 1983. *Take Me Out to the Ball Park.* Saint Louis: Sporting News.

Relph, Edward. 1976. *Place and Placelessness.* London: Pion.

——. 1981. *Rational Landscapes and Humanistic Geography.* London: Croom Helm.

——. 1987. *The Modern Urban Landscape.* London: Croom Helm.

——. 1990. *The Toronto Guide.* Toronto: Department of Geography, University of Toronto.

Report of the Iowa Development Commission. 1987. Des Moines, April.

Richards, Gilbert. 1972. *Tennis for Travelers: The International Guide to Hotel, Motel, Resort, Park, and Other Tennis Courts Available to Travelers.* 3d ed. Cincinnati, Ohio: Richards Industries.

Riley, Rochelle. 1988. "Fans Take Time Out to Remember League." *Washington Post*, July 10.

Riordan, James. 1977. *Sport in Soviet Society.* Cambridge: Cambridge University Press.

Rooney, John F., Jr. 1974. *A Geography of American Sport: From Cabin Creek to Anaheim.* Reading, Mass.: Addison-Wesley.

Rooney, John F., Jr., and Richard Pillsbury. 1992. *Atlas of American Sport.* New York: Macmillan.

Roper, Steve, and Allen Steck. 1979. *Fifty Classic Climbs of North America.* San Francisco: Sierra Club Books.

Ross, Alan, ed., 1981. *The Penguin Cricketers' Companion.* Harmondsworth: Penguin.

Ryan, Bruce. 1984. "Activity Clustering in Urban Recreation." *North American Culture* 1.

——. 1986. "Landscape Preference and Leisure Personality." *Urban Resources* 3.

Ryan, Gary. 1992. "Wintering in Hueco." *Sport Climbing* 3.

——. 1993. "Hueco Tanks Update." *Sport Climbing* 3.

Sack, Robert D. 1986. *Human Territoriality: Its Theory and History.* Cambridge: Cambridge University Press.

——. 1988. "The Consumer's World: Place as Context." *Annals of the Association of American Geographers* 78.

Salter, Christopher, and William Lloyd. 1979. *Landscapes in Literature.* Resource Paper in College Geography, no. 76-3. Washington, D.C.: Association of American Geographers.

Salzberg, Charles. 1987. *From Set Shot to Slam Dunk: The Glory Days of Basketball in the Words of Those Who Played It.* New York: Dutton.

Sampson, Aylwin. 1981. *Grounds of Appeal.* London: Hale.

Sandiford, Keith. 1984. "Victorian Cricket Technique and Industrial Technology." *British Journal of Sports History* 1.

Saretsky, Theodor, comp. 1985. *Sex as a Sublimation for Tennis: From the Secret Writings of Freud.* New York: Workman.

Savage, William W. 1979. *The Cowboy Hero: His Image in American History and Culture.* Norman: University of Oklahoma Press.

Scaino, Antonio. 1951. *Trattato dei Givoco della Palla.* . . . First published in Venice, 1555. Translated by W. W. Kershaw under the title *Scaino on Tennis.* London: Strangeways Press.

Schickel, Richard. 1975. *The World of Tennis.* New York: Ridge Press/Random House.

Schlosberg, Jeremy. 1987. "Who Watches Television Sports?" *American Demographics* 9.

Schmitt, Peter J. 1969. *Back to Nature: The Arcadian Myth in Urban America.* New York: Oxford University Press. Reprint 1990, Johns Hopkins University Press.

Schultheis, Rob. 1984. *Bone Games: One Man's Search for the Ultimate Athletic High.* New York: Random House.

Scott, Eugene. 1973. *Tennis: Game of Motion.* New York: Crown/Rutledge.

Seward, A. K. 1986. "An Attempt to Perpetuate a Cultural Identity through Traditional Games in the Face of Influence of Western Sports in Papua New Guinea." In *Sport, Culture, and Society,* edited by J. A. Mangan and R. B. Small. London: Spon.

Sherman, John. 1992a. *Hueco Tanks: Climber's and Boulderer's Guide.* Evergreen, Colo.: Chalkstone Press.

——. 1992b. "The End of an Era." *Climbing* 134.

Sherwonit, Bill. 1992a. "Denali's Deadliest Season." *Anchorage Daily News,* July 12.

——. 1992b. "Denali Climbers' Memorial." *Climbing* 135.

——. 1993. "Foreign Affairs." *Climbing* 137.

Shirts, Mathew. 1988. "Socrates, Corinthians, and Questions of Democracy and Citizenship." In *Sport and Society in Latin America,* edited by Joseph L. Arbena. Westport, Conn.: Greenwood Press.

Simon, Robin, and Alistair Smart. 1983. *Art of Cricket.* London: Secker and Warburg.

Smith, Jerald C. 1972. "The Native American Ball Games." In *Sport in the Socio-Cultural Process*, edited by M. Marie Hart. Dubuque, Iowa: Brown.

Smith, Peter, 1975. *Houses of the Welsh Countryside*. London: Royal Commission on Ancient and Historical Monuments in Wales and Her Majesty's Stationery Office.

Smith, Paul. 1980. "Saturday Afternoon Fever." *Times Literary Supplement* (London), April 4.

Snyder, Gary. 1983. *Axe Handles*. San Francisco: North Point Press.

Somerville, Edith A. 1930. *The States through Irish Eyes*. Boston: Houghton Mifflin.

Spears, Betty, and Richard A. Swanson. 1978. *History of Sport and Physical Activity in the United States*. Dubuque, Iowa: Brown.

Speer, Albert. 1970. *Inside the Third Reich*. New York: Macmillan.

Starrs, Paul F. 1992. "Dilemmas of a New Age—A Half-Millennium of Landscape Change in New Mexico and the Southwest." In *National Rural Studies Committee: Las Vegas, New Mexico, A Proceedings of the Fifth Annual Meeting*, edited by Emery Castle and Barbara Baldwin. Corvallis, Ore.: Oregon State University Press/Western Rural Development Center.

Statistiches Bundesamt Wiesbaden. 1987. *Statistiches Jahrbuch für die Bundesrepublik Deutschland 1987*. Stuttgart: W. Kohlhammer.

Stein, Gertrude. 1973 [1936]. *The Geographical History of America; or, The Relationship of Human Nature to the Human Mind*. New York: Vintage/Random House.

Stein, Steve. 1988. "The Case of Soccer in Early Twentieth-Century Lima." In *Sport and Society in Latin America*, edited by Joseph L. Arbena. Westport, Conn.: Greenwood Press.

Stern, Robert M. 1986. *Pride of Place—Building the American Dream*. Boston: Houghton Mifflin.

Stern, Theodore. 1948. *The Rubber-Ball Games of the Americas*. New York: American Ethnological Society 17.

Stevenson, Bill. 1993. "Smith Rock: Three Generations of American Sport Climbing." *Sport Climbing* 3.

Stevenson, Gary. 1989. "The Marketing of the Game." *Golf Market Today* 29.

Stirk, David. 1987. *Golf: The History of an Obsession*. Oxford: Phaidon Press.

Stoddart, Brian. 1986. *Saturday Afternoon Fever—Sport in the Australian Culture*. Sydney: Angus and Robertson.

Stoeltje, Beverly J. 1989. "Rodeo from Custom to Ritual." *Western Folklore* (Notes and Comments) 48.

Stone, Gregory. 1971. "American Sports: Play and Display." In *The Sociology of Sport*, edited by Eric Dunning. London: Cass.

——, ed. 1971. *Games, Sport, and Power*. New Brunswick, N.J.: Transaction Books.

Stone, Peter B., ed. 1992. *The State of the World's Mountains: A Global Report*. Atlantic Highlands, N.J.: Humanities Press International.

Stow, John. 1890. *A Survey of London*. London: George Routledge.

Strickon, Arnold. 1965. "The Euro-American Ranching Complex." In *Man, Culture, and Animals: The Role of Animals in Human Ecological Adjustments*, edited by Anthony Leeds and Andrew P. Vayda. American Association for the Advancement of Science, no. 78. Washington, D.C.: AAAS.

Strutt, Joseph. 1801. *The Sports and Pastimes of the People of England*. London: T. Tegg.

Stuller, Stu. 1987. "King of the Hangdogs." *Outside* 12.

Sullivan, Robert. 1987. "Requiem for a Pit." *Sports Illustrated*, March 23.

Talady, John M. 1992. "Big Brother Isn't Watching." *Climbing* 132.

Tarshis, Barry. 1972. "The Harlem Boys of Summer." *Saturday Review*, September 30.

Taylor, A.J.P. 1976. "Manchester." In *Essays in English History*. Harmondsworth: Penguin.

Telander, Rick. 1973. "They Always Go Home Again." *Sports Illustrated*, November 12.

——. 1976. *Heaven Is a Playground*. New York: St. Martin's Press.

Thalman, Budd L. 1989. *1989 Penn State Football Yearbook*. State College: Nittany Valley Offset.

Thomas, George C. 1927. *Golf Architecture in America*. Los Angeles: Times-Mirror Press.

Thurston, Hazel. 1974. *Royal Parks for the People*. Newton Abbot: David and Charles.

Tidball, Bill. 1986. Interview by Mark Okrant. Stampede Historical Commission, Calgary, April 25.

Tiffin, H. 1980. "Cricket, Literature, and the Politics of De-colonisation." In *Sport: Money, Morality, and the Media*, edited by R. Cashman and M. McKernan. Kensington: New South Wales University Press.

Tingay, Lance. 1983. *The Guinness Book of Tennis Facts and Feats*. Enfield, Middlesex: Guinness Superlatives.

Tinling, Ted, and Rod Humphries. 1979. *Love and Faults—Personalities Who Have Changed the History of Tennis in My Lifetime*. New York: Crown.

Todd, Terry. 1979. *The Tennis Players: From Pagan Rites to Strawberries and Cream*. Guernsey: Vallency Press.

Totty, Michael. 1988. "DeBartolo Could Be Facing a Long Shot in Bid to Launch a Thoroughbred Track." *Wall Street Journal*, September 30.

Tuan, Yi-Fu. 1974. *Topophilia: A Study of Environmental Perception, Attitudes, and Values*. Englewood Cliffs, N.J.: Prentice-Hall.

Ullman, James R. 1964. *The Age of Mountaineering.* 3d ed. Philadelphia: Lippincott.

Underwood, John. 1963. "The Only Game in Panguitch, Utah." *Sports Illustrated*, March 4.

U.S. Bureau of the Census. 1986. *Statistical Abstract of the United States 1987.* 107th ed. Washington, D.C.: U.S. Department of Commerce.

———. 1987. *Statistical Abstract of the United States 1988.* 108th ed. Washington, D.C.: U.S. Department of Commerce.

———. 1993. *Statistical Abstract of the United States 1993.* 114th ed. Washington, D.C.: U.S. Department of Commerce.

U.S. Golf Association and the Royal and Ancient Golf Club of St. Andrews. 1988. *Rules of Golf 1988.* Far Hills, N.J.: U.S. Golf Association.

U.S. Tennis Association (USTA). 1979. *Official Encyclopedia of Tennis.* New York: Harper and Row.

USA Today. February 18, 1987.

Vamplew, Wray. 1986. "Sport." in *Atlas of Industrializing Britain, 1780–1814.* London: Methuen.

Van Riper, Guernsey, Jr. 1967. *The Game of Basketball.* Champaign, Ill.: Garrard.

Vecsey, George. 1991. "More Odd Ball Parks Needed in Baseball." *New York Times*, 8 March.

Verney, Richard G. 1921. *Hunting the Fox.* Boston: Houghton Mifflin.

Vetter, Craig. 1992. "Limestone Cowboys." *Outside* 17.

Vogel, Max. 1942. "They're Playing Basketball in New York City!" *Recreation*, January.

Vogel, Randy. 1992. *Joshua Tree: Rock Climbing Guide.* 2d ed. Evergreen, Colo.: Chockstone Press.

Walford, Rex. 1983. "The Spread of First-Class Cricket Venues since 1945: A Study in 'Colonial Expansion.' " In *Geographical Perspectives in Sport*, edited by John Bale and Charles Jenkins. University of Birmingham, Department of Physical Education.

Walley, Wayne. 1992. "TVB: Voters Watching Sports." *Electronic Media*, August 31.

Walters, Marshall L. 1963. "Volleyball." In *The Encyclopedia of Sports*, edited by Frank G. Menke. 3d rev. ed. New York: A. S. Barnes.

Walvin, James. 1975. *The People's Game.* London: Allen Lane.

Waterman, Jonathan. 1991. *Surviving Denali: Accidents Study, McKinley 1903–1990.* 2d ed. New York: American Alpine Club.

———. 1992. "The Last Great Problem." *Climbing* 134.

Watts, Alan. 1993. *Climber's Guide to Smith Rock.* Evergreen, Colo.: Chockstone Press.

Webb, Walter Prescott. 1981 [1931]. *The Great Plains.* Lincoln: University of Nebraska Press.

Wecter, Dixon. 1937. *The Saga of American Society: A Record of Social Aspiration, 1607–1937*. New York: Scribner.

Weiss, Paul. *Sport: A Philosophic Inquiry*. Carbondale: Southern Illinois University Press.

Westrich, Lolo. 1985. "The Frontier Chicken." *Californians* 3.

Wetzler, Brad, and Bob Howells. 1992. "Dispatches: 1989." *Outside* 17.

Wheatley, Henry B. 1905. *The Story of London*. London: J. M. Dent.

Whitman, Malcolm D. 1932. *Tennis Origins and Mysteries*. New York: Derrydale Press.

Whitney, Caspar. 1894. "Evolution of the Country Club." *Harpers New Monthly Magazine* 90.

Whitten, Ron. 1991. "Twelve New Members Join the Club." *Golf Digest* 42.

Whymper, Edward. 1871. *Scrambles amongst the Alps in the Years 1860–1869*. Cleveland: Burrows.

Wielgus, Chuck, Jr., and Alexander Wolff. 1980. *The In-Your-Face Basketball Book*. New York: Everest House.

———. 1986. "Warmup." *Sports Illustrated*, November 19.

Wilkinson, Sylvia. 1973. *The Stainless Steel Carrot: An Auto Racing Odyssey*. Boston: Houghton Mifflin.

Williamson, John E., and Orvel Miskiw, eds. 1992. *Accidents in North American Mountaineering* 6, no. 3, issue 45. New York: American Alpine Club.

Wind, Herbert Warren. 1948. *The Story of American Golf*. New York: Farrar Straus.

———. 1979. *Game, Set, and Match: The Tennis Boom of the 1960s and 70s*. New York: Dutton.

———. 1980. "The Heart of Kokomo." *New Yorker*, April 14.

Wolf, David. 1972. *Foul! The Connie Hawkins Story*. New York: Warner Paperback Library.

Wolff, Alexander. 1985. "The Only Game in Town." *Sports Illustrated*, July 8.

Wooler, Wilfred. 1984. "Cricket at Cardiff Arms Park." In *Taff's Acre*, edited by David Parry-Jones. London: Collins.

Woolf, Rob, and Elaine Woolf. 1993. "Sport Climbing Guidebooks and New Products." *Sport Climbing* 3.

World Almanac and Book of Facts 1989; 1988, The. New York: World Almanac.

Yergin, Marc L. 1986. "Who Goes to the Game?" *American Demographics* 8.

Zelinsky, Wilbur. 1980. "Lasting Impact of the Prestigious Gentry." *Geographical Magazine* 52.

CONTRIBUTORS

Robert L. A. Adams is professor emeritus of geography at the University of New Hampshire. His research on sport has appeared in *Geographical Review, North American Culture,* and *Sport Place.*

Thomas J. Baerwald is program director for geography and regional science at the National Science Foundation. He is the former director of the Science Museum of Minnesota. His research has appeared in *Geographical Review, Urban Geography,* and *The Transportation Research Record.* He is coauthor of *Prentice Hall World Geography* for the secondary school level.

John Bale is senior lecturer in geography at the University of Keele, Staffordshire, U.K. He has published articles on sport in *Area* and in the *British Journal of Sports History,* and his books include *The Landscape of Sport* and *Sports Geography.*

Martyn Bowden is professor of geography at Clark University. He has published his research in the *Journal of Historical Geography, Annals of the Association of American Geographers, Economic Geography,* and *GeoJournal.* He has authored *Hamlets* and coauthored *Geographies of the Mind* and *Reconstruction Following Disaster;* he has a chapter on sport in *Place, Power, Situation, and Spectacle: A Geography of Film.*

Audrey B. Davidson is professor of economics at the University of Louisville. She has published in the *Journal of Economic Behavior and Organization, Public Choice,* and the *Review of Social Economy.*

Robert L. Janiskee is professor of geography at the University of South Carolina. He has published in *Annals of Tourism Research,* the *Journal of Cultural Geography, Environmental Review, Urban Concerns,* and the *Southeastern Geographer.*

Brian J. Neilson is professor of Romance languages at the University of California, Berkeley. He has published on baseball parks in *Landscape.*

Mark J. Okrant is professor of geography and coordinator of tourism studies at Plymouth State College, New Hampshire. He serves on the editorial boards of the *Journal of Travel Research* and the *Journal of Travel and Tourism Marketing*. He was the associate editor of *Tourism—A Vital Force for Peace*.

Richard Pillsbury is professor of geography at Georgia State University. He has served as inaugural editor of *Sport Place* and as editor of *North American Culture*. His research has been published in the *Annals of the Association of American Geographers;* he is the author of *From Boarding House to Bistro: The American Restaurant Then and Now* and coauthor of *Atlas of American Sport*.

Karl B. Raitz is professor of geography at the University of Kentucky. He is coauthor of *Rock Fences of the Bluegrass* and *Appalachia: a Regional Perspective*. His articles have appeared in the *Annals of the Association of American Geographers*, the *Geographical Review*, the *Journal of Cultural Geography*, *Landscape*, the *Journal of Geography*, and *Sport Place*.

John F. Rooney, Jr. is professor and head of the department of geography at Oklahoma State University. He is the author of numerous books and articles on the geography of sport, including *A Geography of American Sport* and *The Recruiting Game*. He recently coauthored *Atlas of American Sport*.

Bruce Ryan is professor of geography at the University of Cincinnati. His articles on leisure and recreation have been published in *North American Culture* and *Urban Resources*.

Paul F. Starrs is professor of geography at the University of Nevada. His forthcoming book on the geography of cattle ranching in western North America will be published by Johns Hopkins University Press.

INDEX

ILLUSTRATIONS CREDITS

1.1. Adapted from Prunty 1963, 18; by permission, *Geographical Review*.
1.2. Adapted from Stern 1948, 121; by permission, AES.
1.3. Adapted from Oriard 1976, 39; by permission, *Landscape*.
1.4. Adapted from Martin 1936, facing p. 7.
1.5. Adapted from Raitz 1987a, 17; by permission, *Sport Place*.
1.6. Photo by author.
2.1–2.8. Photos courtesy of the National Baseball Hall of Fame and Museum, Inc., Cooperstown, N.Y.
3.1. Adapted from Brookes 1978.
3.2. Diagram by author.
3.3. Photo by Daniel Eaton.
3.4. Adapted from Raitz 1987a, 17.
4.1. Diagrams by Margaret Pearce, Clark University Cartographic Lab.
4.2. Photos by author.
4.3. Charts by author.
4.4. Diagrams by Margaret Pearce, Clark University Cartographic Lab.
4.5. Diagrams by author.
5.1. Photo courtesy of S. W. Jones, head custodian, Beaumaris Castle.
5.2. Diagram by author.
5.3. Photo courtesy of Sarah McCance, Wimbledon Lawn Tennis Museum.
5.4. Photo courtesy of the United States Tennis Association/Russ Adams.
5.5. Photo courtesy of Blair Gregory, Sea Pines Plantation Company, Inc.
5.6. Cartoon by Jensen; reprinted, by permission, from *Punch*, June 26, 1985.
6.1. Photo courtesy of the Edward J. and Gena G. Hickox Library, Naismith Memorial Basketball Hall of Fame, Springfield, Mass.
6.2. Photo courtesy of the Edward J. and Gena G. Hickox Library, Naismith Memorial Basketball Hall of Fame, Springfield, Mass.
6.3. Diagrams by Georgia State Cartography Lab.
6.4. Photo courtesy of the Edward J. and Gena G. Hickox Library, Naismith Memorial Basketball Hall of Fame, Springfield, Mass.
6.5. Map by Thomas J. Baerwald and Charles F. Cross.
7.1. Photo courtesy of the University of Nebraska Sports Information Office.
7.2. Diagram by author.
7.3. Photo courtesy of the Yale University Sports Information Office.
7.4. Photo courtesy of the University of Michigan Athletic Public Relations Office.
7.5. Photo courtesy of the Pennsylvania State University Sports Information Office.
7.6. Photo courtesy of the Clemson University Sports Information Office.
7.7. Diagram by author.
8.1. Data from National Golf Foundation.
8.2. Photo by author.
8.3. Photo courtesy of Stephen Szurlej.
8.4. Photo courtesy of Larry Petrillo.

8.5. Diagram courtesy of Elizabeth Peper and Harry N. Abrams, Inc.

8.6. Diagram courtesy of Elizabeth Peper and Harry N. Abrams, Inc.

9.1–9.5. Photos by author.

10.1–10.3. Photos by Paul F. Starrs.

10.4. Diagram by Paul F. Starrs.

11.1. Data from *Daily Racing Form*.

11.2–11.6 Data from Daily Racing Form, *American Racing Manual*.

11.7–11.9. Diagrams courtesy of Daily Racing Form, *American Racing Manual*.

11.10. Photo courtesy of the Keeneland Race Course Library.

12.1. Photo by author.

12.2. Photo by author.

12.3. Data from *Chronicle of the Horse*, September 18, 1987.

12.4. Photo courtesy of *The Chase*.

12.5. Data from *International Fox Hunters Stud Book Registrations; The Chase* 57, December 1986/January 1987.

12.6. Adapted from Brock 1937, 235.

13.1. Photo courtesy of Chris Robinson.

13.2. Photo by author.

13.3. Photo courtesy of Chris Robinson.

13.4. Photo courtesy of Chris Robinson.

13.5. Photo by Phil Bard.

13.6. Photo by Phil Bard.

LIBRARY OF CONGRESS CATALOGING-IN-PUBLICATION DATA
The theater of sport / edited by Karl B. Raitz.
    p.   cm.
    Includes bibliographical references and index.
    ISBN 0-8018-4908-X (acid-free paper). —
ISBN 0-8018-4909-8 (pbk. acid-free paper)
    1. Sport facilities—United States—Location.   2. Sports—Social
aspects—United States.   3. Man—Influence of environment—United
States.   I. Raitz, Karl B.
GV429.T44   1995
796'.06'873—dc20   94-37027